Narrative Art in the Mahābhārata: The Ādī Parva

The study analyses the baffling nebulous mass of material with which the epic begins, bringing out the central theme of each of the sub-parvas to provide insights into the Vyasan Vision and the Master's mastery of his epic art. It helps the reader to understand the intricate web of inter-connections of events and characters so that a clear, logical and intelligible picture emerges of the very involved and confused panorama of the Mahabharata. Parallels from comparative mythology and literature enrich the study and there is a continuous concern to highlight the agency of women throughout the epic.

Pradip Bhattacharya, International HRD Fellow (Manchester), retired in 2007 as Additional Chief Secretary (Development and Planning), Government of West Bengal. Chaired the Eastern Zonal Cultural Centre's National Symposium on "The Pancha Kanya of Indian Epics", Dec. 2003; panelist for the 2nd International Conference on Indic Culture and Civilization's panel on "Pancha Kanya" organised by MANUSHI and the ICCR, Dec. 2005; chaired sessions on "the Mahabharata and Media" in the National Manuscript Mission's national seminar, Feb.2007 and on "Narrating the Mahabharata" and "Cultural rooting of Mahabharata" in the IGNCA's international conference, Feb.2011. Now Regional Editor (East) for the Mahabharata Encyclopaedia Project of the Mahabharata Pratishthanam, Bangalore; Member, Board of Governors, IIM Calcutta and of the editorial boards of the *Journal of Human Values* and *MANUSHI.* Edited and authored thirty books and numerous articles on values in management, public administration, ancient history, comparative mythology.

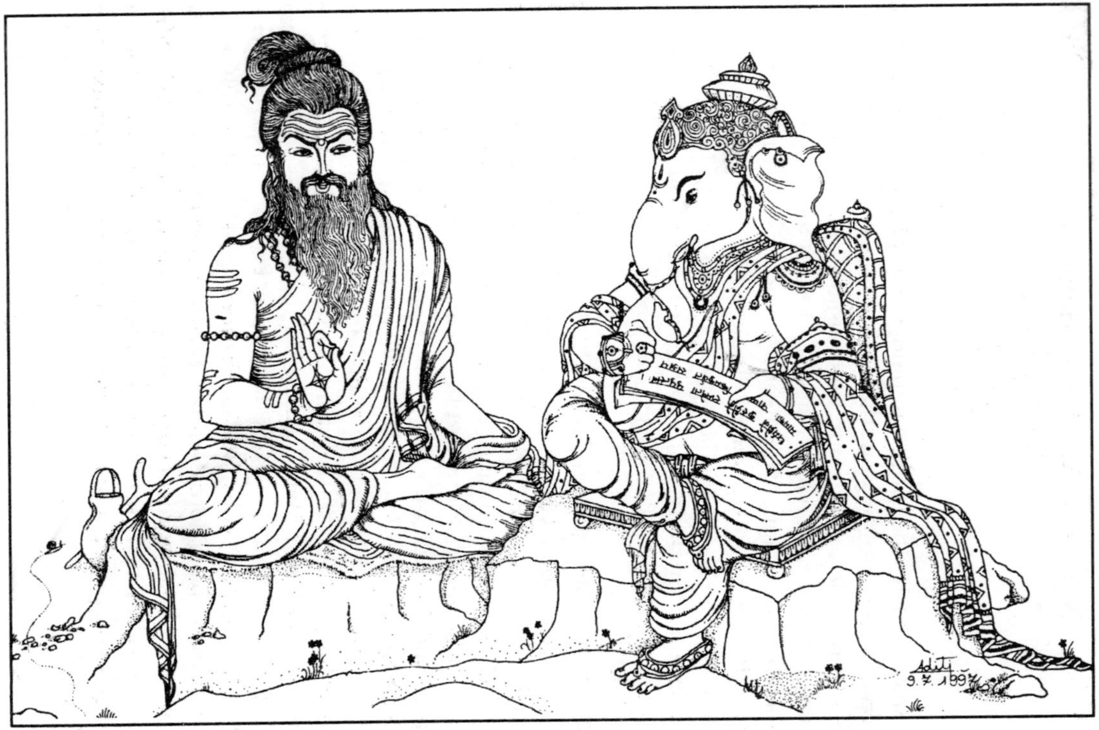

“Vyasa dictating to Ganesha” by Aditi

Narrative Art in the Mahābhārata: The Ādi Parva

Pradip Bhattacharya

DEV PUBLISHERS & DISTRIBUTORS

New Delhi

Published by:
DEV PUBLISHERS & DISTRIBUTORS
2nd Floor, Prakash Deep,
4735/22, Ansari Road,
Darya Ganj,
New Delhi-110002
Phone : 011-43572647, 9810236140
e-mail: devbooks@hotmail.com
website: www.devbooks.co.in

ISBN 978–93-81406-01-4
First published 2012

Printed in India

For my wife, Dr. Nandita Bhattacharya MD, to whom I owe the completion of the doctoral dissertation on which this book is based. But for her relentless and loving persistance it would never have been completed.

A true sahadharmini

Contents

Introduction

Vyāsa, master raconteur, weaves together a bewildering skein of threads to create a many-splendoured web from which there was no escape for the listener of those days and there is none even for the reader of today. The thousands of years that separate us from Vyāsa have not, surprisingly, dimmed the magic of his art that had entranced Janamejaya and Shaunaka. Here is stunning evidence of the power the epic exerts:

> "Shells were exploding over Leningrad. Enemy bombs were falling on the streets stirring up clouds of dust. On one of those spring days during the siege, Sanscrit language was being heard in the building of the Academy of Sciences on the Neva River embankment, in a room overlooking the side that was safer during the artillery strikes. First, in the original, and then in translation, Vladimir Kalyanov, a specialist on India, was reading Mahabharata, a wonderful monument of Indian literature, to his colleagues, who remained in the besieged city. He had started the translation before the war. He translated during the hard winter of 1941, with no light, no fuel and no bread in the city. Two volumes of books—one published in Bombay and the other in Calcutta—were lying on the table in the room. In the dim light of a wick lamp, he was comparing these two editions of Mahabharata, trying to find the best and the most accurate translation of the Sanscrit into Russian.
>
> "When, after the war the first book of Mahābhārata—Ādi Parva was published in Leningrad, Jawaharlal Nehru, Prime Minister of India, noted with great satisfaction that, even during the

hardest times, the translation of the Indian epic into Russian was never interrupted."[1]

What is it in this epic-of-epics, eight times larger than the *Iliad* and the *Odyssey* combined—denounced as "a literary monster" by Winternitz, and as "monstrous chaos" by Oldenberg—that appeals so irresistibly to the modern man in search of his soul, when the audience for which it was composed—the enthroned monarch and the forest-dwelling sage—has long sunk into the dark backward and abysm of time?

Seeking answers to questions such as these, I found a storyteller par excellence laying bare, at times quite pitilessly, the existential predicament of man in the universe. If, later in the epic, Vyāsa shows us what man has made of man, here, in the very first book, he plumbs the depths of the humiliatingly petty pre-occupations of the Creator's noblest creation. Indeed, the dilemmas the characters find themselves enmeshed in cannot even be glorified as 'tragic'. Perhaps, that is why we find the epic so fascinating—for, how many of us are cast in the heroic mould? We do not have to strain the imagination to reach out and identify with Yayāti or Shāntanu. We need no willing suspension of disbelief to understand why the Brahmin Drona should sell his knowledge to the highest bidder, or why Drupada does not protest too much when his daughter is parcelled out among five brothers who had routed him in a skirmish. Passions do, indeed, spin the plot and we are betrayed by what is false within. Then, as now, there is no need to look for a villain manoeuvring without.

If we resonate in empathy with the sense of tears in human things, we also thrill with joy on meeting the indomitable spirit of woman in an epic that many misconceive as celebrating a male chauvinist outlook. Whether it is Shakuntalā proudly asserting her integrity and berating the cowardly Dushyanta in open court; or Devayānī demanding that Kacha return her love and imperiously brushing aside a lust-crazed husband; or Kuntī refusing to pervert herself into a mindless son-producing machine to gratify the twisted desires of a frustrated husband—time and again it is woman standing forth in all the splendour of her spirited autonomy as a complete human being that rivets our attention and evokes our admiration.

I have pursued a method that allows the epic to grow, as it were, upon the reader. Taking the P. Lal transcreation as the peg on which to hang the analysis, I have gone through the *Ādi Parva* chapter by chapter, section by section, bringing out the delicate nuances of meaning, the deft dovetailing of one tale into another, the underlying thematic unity, the incisive and at times relentless exposè of the frailties that the flesh is heir to, that make up the genius of Vyāsa. Begun in 1968 and brought out in monthly fascicules, a completely revised transcreation, each *Parva* contained in a single volume, was published from 2005 correcting all the errors of commission and omission I had noted in my studies. I have followed this revised edition.

Why the P. Lal transcreation? It is the only English version to follow the complete "vulgate" *shloka*-by-*shloka,* eschewing the not very consistent text of the Critical Edition with its numerous excisions in favour of the extant complete redaction. Possibly because of the same reason the Clay Sanskrit Library based its translations on the edition with Nilkantha's commentary, but they are almost all in prose. Further, Prof. Lal's is the only translation that is a transcreation, consciously attempting to provide a sense of the original by effortlessly shifting from verse to prose as Vyāsa's text demands, simultaneously preserving the Sanskrit ethos. We are not brought up short by jarring medieval turns of phrase that are anything but Vyāsa as with J.A.B. van Buitenen's "barons", "chivalry" and the like. *Mahātmā, pranāma, namaskāra, āshrama* and similar words, redolent with the flavour of Bharatavarsha's air and earth and water, abound. The Lal version does not, however, have many passages occurring in the Southern and the Bengal recensions (such as Arjuna's wooing of Subhadra disguised as a hermit, Draupadi's previous births as Nālāyani, Mudgālani and Vedavati, the chariot duel between Krishna and Shishupāla, etc.)

The attempts at translating the longest epic in the world in full began with H. Fauche's French translation (1863-1870). Unfortunately, he died leaving it incomplete. Now L. Ballin continues the work. A new French translation by Guy Vincent and Gilles Schaufelberger has brought out four volumes so far arranged thematically, not following the original chronological schema. In St. Petersburg, the Russian translation was started in 1941 by V. Kalyanov and is nearing the end. In the USA, J.A.B. van Buitenen of Chicago University died after finishing the first five Parvas. Two other American Universities are continuing the work, but do not follow the sequence of the original. The other American project by the Clay Sanskrit Library has run out of sponsors. We have to revert to the 19th century for an almost complete English translation by K.M. Ganguli published by P.C. Roy (1883-1893). A parallel effort was undertaken by the Rector of Serampore College, M.N. Dutt slightly later. Both are vitiated as they either omit or Latinise passages "for obvious reasons" in the prevalent Victorian ambience. In 1968 Professor P. Lal took up the first verse-by-verse transcreation of Vyāsa's monumental composition in English. As of now, 16 and a half of the 18 books have been published before Prof. Lal passed away in November 2010, leaving the moksha-dharma portion of the *Shānti Parva* and the *Anushāsana Parva* in its entirety to be completed.

I have avoided use of diacriticals as they impede the flow of the text, except where necessary to indicate elongaged vowels: "ā" instead of "aa" as in "arm", "ī" instead of "ee" as in "see", "ū" instead of "oo" as in "too".]

PRADIP BHATTACHARYA

25th December, 2010
Kolkata, India

1. http://www.300.years.spb.ru/eng/3.spb 3.html?id=5

Acknowledgements

I am deeply grateful to Padma Shri Professor P. Lal D.Litt., Jawaharlal Nehru Fellow, formerly Professor of English, Calcutta University and Visiting Professor at several American Universities, who supervised the research for my doctoral dissertation despite his many commitments and for making available to me freely his ongoing transcreation of the *Mahābhārata*. His constant encouragement, gentle yet incisive guidance and his penchant for putting intriguing questions that shake one out of complacency have been invaluable. His demise on 3.11.2010 is an irremediable loss to the world of literature and publishing.

To my aunt, the late Parjijat Ghosh, former head of the Higher Secondary section of Gokhale Memorial Girls High School, I am obliged for the gift of her own copy of the 1903 first edition of Kaliprasanna Sinha's Bengali translation of the epic. To my elder sister Dr. (Smt.) Gita Talukder, who unfortunately passed away before she could see this book in print, I am grateful for the loan of her copy of the K.M. Ganguli English translation of the epic. I am deeply indebted to the late Jayantilal Parekh of Sri Aurobindo Ashram, Pondicherry, for sending me an out-of-print copy of M.V. Subramaniam's rare study, *The Mahābhārata Story* and for introducing me to the *Aryashastra* diglot (Sanskrit-Bengali) edition of the *Mahābhārata*.

I am grateful to my Personal Assistant Shri Avijit Basak and to computer expert Shri Himangsu Nandi of the Administrative Training Institute, West Bengal, for their ungrudging help in correcting errors of commission and omission.

I acknowledge with deep gratitude the irrepayable debt I owe to my parents—the late Lt. Col. Gunindra Lal Bhattacharya, BSc (Delhi), MA (Delhi), LlB (Cal) and Smt. Suprobhat

Bhattacharya, BA (Delhi), BT (Punjab), Cert. App. Psy. (Cal), MA (Sagar). To them I owe the abiding interest in our heritage that has so profoundly enriched my life. My father gladly allowed me use of his excellent study of Rabindranath Tagore's treatment of the Kacha-Devayānī story vis-a-vis Vyāsa. My mother, now 92, painstakingly copied out extracts from many works for my reference, unfailingly adding penetrating insights from her lifelong study of psychology and philosophy.

To Dr. Maitreyi Deshpande, Hony. Secy. of the Bhandarkar Oriental Research Institute, I am most obliged for the speed with which she granted permission for using illustrations from the Critical Edition.

Finally, I am much obliged to Shri Pankaj D. Jain who came forward with such alacrity to publish this study so quickly.

PRADIP BHATTACHARYA

25*th December*, 2010
Kolkata, India

1

Anukramanikā
The Genesis and the Vyāsan Vision

Anukramanikā literally means an index, a table of contents, but it is more than that in the *Mahābhārata* and also less. For, it is really an introduction providing not only the genesis of the epic, but also a summary of its main events up to the end of the Kurukshetra holocaust, besides clearly setting forth the moral universe within which Vyāsa places his tragic story of the end of a Yuga, the passing of the era of heroes. It is only by the way that it lists the eighteen major divisions (*parvas*) of the epic, and that too in terms of an organic image: that of a tree, which is repeated yet again in another form to describe the Kauravas and the Pāndavas in moral terms. Indeed, the epic itself is an Yggdrasill upholding the entire ethos of purānik Bhārata in its massive trunk and all-encompassing branches, or like the mystic *ashvattha* tree of the Upanishads with its roots in heaven and its branches interleaving the universe. For, what is not in the *Mahābhārata* is not to be found anywhere.

The *Anukramaṇikā* performs yet two more crucial tasks. One is the recital of the benefits accruing from listening to the epic; and here the secret of the *Mahābhārata* is very clearly stated. It is a *kāvya,* revealing the Truth in a form suitable for "men of small learning" (*shlokas* 72 and 265) who are apt to distort the true meaning of the Vedas. The other is the haunting lament of Dhritarāshtra over the slaughter of his kin—a lament that is not to be found again in the epic *Shalya Parva* 2 has his lament over Dauryodhana with the refrain "What is it but fate)." It is a lament that strikes the keynote of this massive work: the sense of tears in human things—above all in human beauty and strength and valour, all of which pass away in the *Ragnarok* of a fratricidal war, embracing all of Bhārata.

The *Anukramanikā* begins with the arrival of the wandering rhapsode, Ugrashravā ("awesome-voiced") popularly known as Sauti, at the hermitage of Shaunaka in the forest of Naimisha that becomes the common seat for narration of the Puranas too. Here he "bowed courteously" to the sages who, tired with Shaunaka's twelve-year long sacrificial sessions, eagerly welcome this son of Lomaharshana ("he who makes the hair bristle" with his wondrous tale-telling). Vyāsa immediately characterises Sauti as an inveterate teller of tales. The sages enquire of him where he has been and, says Vyāsa,

> "Fluent Sauti needed only this prompting to place before the august and holy assembly a full and dignified account." (*shloka* 8)

Sauti tells them that, after hearing the entire *Mahābhārata* recited at the great snake-sacrifice of Janamejaya (which forms the hub of the first quarter of the *Ādi Parva*), he visited several sacred spots, including Samantapanchaka, the site of the cataclysmic war that he had just heard described. Longing to horripilate his august audience with hair-raising stories, Sauti launches into lyrical praise of the sages, begging them to specify what they wish to hear. The *rishis* cast their vote in favour of "the greatest story ever told" which "sums up the Vedas; other sacred texts are commentaries on it," namely, the *Mahābhārata*

It is interesting that the sages insist (*shloka* 21), "we would like to hear it exactly as it was recited—by sage Vaishampāyana, under the direction of Vyāsa himself." This offers an insight into the great emphasis placed upon accurate oral transmission that was the basis of the *smriti* tradition and offers a tribute to the computer-like memory of Sauti capable of carrying the burden of a hundred thousand *shlokas.* Incidentally, the K.M. Ganguli version of this *shloka* slips in bit of utterly misplaced bucolic heartiness: "as it was *cheerfully* recited." The British "cheer" is hardly the connotation of *tushta,* which means "satisfied, pleased"; the idea being that reciting the epic is always a matter of satisfaction or pleasure to the reciter.

Sauti begins with what would appear to be a conventional invocation of the Supreme Being; but a crucial statement which he makes before launching into an account of the Creation shows that it is not merely a conventional exercise, particularly when read in conjunction with *shloka* 72 and the concluding portion of the *Anukramanikā.* If the *Mahābhārata* is the Word of Brahmā revealed, Sauti certainly needs to invoke the Supreme Being's assistance. Sauti says, "Some poets have already sung this story; some are reciting it now before others; and others will sing it in times to come". Besides indicating why there are so many different recensions of the epic, it also recalls *shlokas* 26-29 in the *Mumuksha khanda,* section 3 of the *Yoga-Vāshishtha Rāmāyana.* Here Vashishtha tells Rāma:

> "There have been ten successive incarnations of this Vyāsa who has done such wondrous acts and is famed for his vast knowledge. Myself and Valmiki have been contemporaries many a time, as also born in different ages and very many times. . . . This Vyāsa will again be born eight times hereafter, and again will write his *Mahābhārata* and the Purāna histories."

The opening verses describing Creation are some of the most majestic and impressive compositions of all time that have been transcreated with biblical reverberations:

> "At first, there was no light,
> no radiance, only darkness;
> then was born the Egg of Brahmā,
> exhaustless and mighty seed of life . . .
> in it shone the true light, Brahmā,
> Eternal, incomparable, inconceivable,
> omnipresent, invisible, and subtle,
> from which flow being and non-being." (*shlokas* 29, 31, the P. Lal transcreation)

The translation here truly becomes a transcreation, a thing

of great beauty and immense significance, catching unforgettable echoes of the *Genesis*:

> "And the earth was without form, and void; and darkness was upon the face of the deep. And the Spirit of God moved upon the face of the waters."

and of *Paradise Lost*, Book I:

> "Thou from the first
> Wast present, and with mighty wings outspred
> Dove-like satest brooding on the vast abyss
> And mad'st it pregnant."

This concept of the universe emerging from the Cosmic Egg runs through nearly all mythologies, particularly the Middle-Eastern and the Puranik, finding detailed treatment in the second section of the *Vishnu Purāna* (*shlokas* 52-59). These narrate how all the different attributes were brought together in the egg-form in order to create an organic, integral, all-comprehensive oneness, animated by the *hiranyagarbha Brahman,* containing mountains, islands, oceans, planets, all the spheres of existence, gods, anti-gods, men and all other creatures. It is a point of historico-cultural significance that this idea does not figure in the "Song of Creation" (*Rigveda* X.129), which puts unanswered questions only:

> "At first there was neither Being nor non-Being,
> no kingdom of air, no sky beyond it.
> Who straddled what, and where? who gave shelter? . . .
> Only one thing, Breath, breathed, breathing without breath,
> nothing else, nothing whatsoever."

It goes on to give a unique picture of Creation:

> "Then rose Desire, primal Desire
> the primal seed, the germ of spirit.
> . . . Being was a manner of non-Being.

And a line cut Being from non-Being transversely:
What was above it, what below it?
Only mighty makers, mighty forces,
action flowing freely and a fund of energy."

It closes with the enigmatic pronouncement

"The Primal Creator, whose eye
controls this world from highest heaven,
Whether he made this world or did not make it,
he surely knows. . . .
Perhaps, he also does not know." – (Lal, 1965)

Vyāsa, however, knows quite clearly what he is about:

"From this egg came grandsire Pitāmaha Brahmā,
lord of all creatures, Prajāpati, greatest of the gods,
Existent till the final dissolution,
the Thinking One,
Creator of the Universe,
The Supreme Lord." (*shloka* 32, my translation)

There is a touch of humour in *shloka* 41, "The number of devas, for example, was thirty three thousand thirty three hundred and thirty three" and Sauti adds, "this is a brief account (*sankshepalakshana*)" hoping, no doubt, that the sages would urge him to recount this in detail and allow him to unleash a blizzard of stories. Thankfully for us, the audience refuses to rise to the bait.

With the beginning of this mathematical jugglery we get, for the first time, an indication of the stupendous reproductive capacities of the Puranik kings:

"Devavrata had one son, Suvrata; Suvrata had three sons . . . each of whom had countless children. Famous Dasajyoti had ten thousand, Satajyoti ten times that; and Sahasrajyoti had ten times the number of Satajyoti's children." (*shlokas* 45-46)

Here is the traditional raconteur's unadulterated delight in leaving his audience agape with the sheer volume of numbers as in the biblical *Numbers*. The only occasion on which we find Sauti generously refraining from exercising this acknowledged privilege is when he is asked to recite the names of all the snake-sons of Kadrū, in the *Āstīka parva.* He merely says, "I am afraid it will bore you, but let me give you just the chief ones", and is content with reeling off the names of some seventy-five snakes.

Sauti now proceeds to recount the problem faced by Vyāsa when he wanted to teach the epic to his pupils and how it was solved. To help him out, Brahmā pays a visit and there is a delightful touch of sly humour as Vyāsa sets about thoroughly convincing the Pitāmaha of the encyclopaedic nature of his work. By the time he has finished, Brahmā hastily declares, "It shall be a poem (*kāvya*) no poet in this world will equal" (*shloka* 73) and vanishes. An extremely significant clue is lost when *kāvya* is rendered as "poem". The word comes from *kavi* which, like the Celtic-Teutonic "vates", means "seer", one who pierces through appearance to the reality, the truth hidden behind. To render this as "poem" deprives Brahmā's statement of its force and ruins the logical correlation with the previous statement (*shloka* 72): "I am aware that you have *revealed* the Word of Brahman in the language of truth." The *Mahābhārata,* therefore, is "revealed truth" and it reveals the Divine Word. "The mystery of the Vedas, and other mysteries, I have explained", says Vyāsa in *Shloka* 62. Towards the end of this *parva,* in *shloka* 265, Sauti states why Vyāsa chose this particular form: "But the Veda fears men of small learning, for they distort it." Hence, Vyāsa couched the innermost secrets of the Veda in the guise of stories in the *Mahābhārata* to be passed on in easily memorable fashion to everyone, even the uninitiated, who could thus gather some of the esoteric spiritual truths hidden in the forgotten symbolic language of the Vedas. This is best exemplified in the story of Uttanka in the *Paushya parva.*[1]

To overcome the problem of teaching the vast epic to his pupils, Vyāsa calls on Ganesha, the remover of obstacles. This Ganesha-Vyāsa encounter is an excellent instance of the delicate wit of the *Mahābhārata* despite its omission in the Critical Edition which doubts its authenticity. Ganesha agrees to act as Vyāsa's amanuensis on one condition: his pen must not stop even for a second. And a very sensible proviso it is, otherwise he could well be stranded with Vyāsa through much of eternity! Vyāsa agrees, but with a stipulation of his own: "Stop wherever you don't understand" (*shloka* 79). To gain breathing space, Vyāsa dictated some profoundly abstruse verses numbering 8800 famed as the *Vyāsa kūta* that puzzle even the all-knowing gods. Several scholars mistakenly cite this as the original length of the composition. Prof. Lal's transcreation of *shloka* 83 in twentieth century idiom scores easily over K.M. Ganguli's translation in conveying the humour through a swiftly conjured-up word-picture:

> "Even the omniscient Ganesha took a moment to consider; while Vyāsa, however, continued to compose other verses in great abundance." (Ganguli)
> "Even the omniscient Ganesa had to scratch his head over them, while Vyāsa went on with his business of prolific composing." (Lal, 1968)

Sauti adds:

> "But to this day no one has been able to plumb the subtle meanings in those tightly knotted Shlokas." (*shloka* 82)

The episode by itself provides ready material for the euhemerist who would interpret it thus: Vyāsa's problem is to communicate the spiritual truths veiled in the Vedas to the general public. In order to find the language and form easily comprehensible by them, he has to take the help of Gana-īsha, "lord of the masses", who renders these esoteric mysteries into language that the uninitiated can follow.

The four verses that follow form a description of the ignorance-dispelling illumination emanating from the *Mahābhārata*. Here Prof. Lal's verse rendering is far superior to any of the translations so far:

"The wisdom of this work, like unto an instrument of applying collyrium, hath opened the eyes of the inquisitive world blinded by the darkness of ignorance." (K.M. Ganguli).

"Like a stick of collyrium,
The wisdom of this poem opens the eyes
Of a world swathed in darkness." (Lal)

Even better is the transcreation of *shloka* 87—terse yet poetically evocative:

"The womb of nature is a house of darkness.
This darkness is scattered by the lamp of history."

Sauti proceeds to describe the contents of the epic in terms of a vivid tree-image which deserves closer reading because of the sections he picks out for mention. Sauti omits much of the *Ādi Parva,* and the *Sauptika* (the murder of the Pāndava progeny and the Pānchālas by Ashvatthāmā), *Anushāsana* (Bhīshma's advice to Yudhishthira about *Dāna-dharma*), *Mahāprasthānika* (the departure of the Pāndavas from the world), and *Svargārohana Parvas* (their state after death). Out of the sprawling *Ādi Parva,* Sauti picks out the *Pauloma* and the *Āstīka* sections, calling them the roots of the Mahābhārata-tree—and very rightly so. The former satisfies Shaunaka's query about the Bhrigu-genealogy while leading on to the snake-sacrifice that constitutes the substance of the latter and is the occasion for the recital of the epic by Vaishampāyana. The third section of the *Ādi Parva* that Sauti mentions is the *Sambhava,* described as the trunk of the epic, for it contains the entire history of the Kuru race starting from Dushyanta, going right up to the return of the Pāndavas to Indraprastha and the amorous exploits of Arjuna during his voluntary exile, thus fairly establishing them as the centre of interest. The *Sabhā* and the *Aranya* (*Vana*) *Parvas* are termed perches for birds in this epic-tree. Then, out of the latter, Sauti perceptively picks out the *Arani* section for particular mention as the "organic knot". In it we have the memorable confrontation of Yudhishthira with Death, where we obtain our only clear view of the inner man and his philosophy of life. Buddhadeb Bose regards this as the key to the entire *Mahābhārata*, which he studies as the search of Yudhishthira for peace, to be at rest with his inner self. Sauti goes on to describe the *Virāta* and the *Udyoga Parvas* as the pith (for the Pāndavas gather their forces in these for the climactic holocaust) and the *Bhīshma* and *Drona Parvas* as the main branch and the leaves. The *Bhīshma Parva,* containing the *Gītā,* undoubtedly deserves the appellative Sauti bestows. What is arresting is his curious description of the *Karna Parva* as the lovely flowers of the tree, which indicates the regard the narrator has for this most tragic of heroes, deprived of birthright, his mother's love and his brothers, compelled to fight them because of his dedication to the honour of his word. However, to call the *Shalya Parva* the fragrance of these flowers seems just a figure of speech. Both the *Strī* and the *Aishīka Parvas,* the cool shade of the tree, provide the catharsis after the holocaust with lamentation *in extenso,* while the *Shānti Parva* brings the closure of "calm of mind, all passion spent." The *Ashvamedha Parva,* containing a re-iteration of the *Gītā*'s tenets as also much from Bhishma's counsel in the *Shānti Parva* and the conquests of the Pāndavas after the war, is the ichor flowing through the tree, while the *Āshramavāsika Parva,* where the old generation passes away in the forest, is the site where the tree grows. That is not just another poetic metaphor just for the sake of extending the tree-image, but hints at the environment in which purānik civilization was cultured, a profound exposition of which is given by Rabindranath Tagore in his "Tapobhumi". The curious description of the *Maushala Parva* as the core of the Vedas is difficult to understand. The Sanskrit is *maushalah shrutisankshepah,* i.e. "the Maushala is the quintessence of the *shruti* (Vedas)". Here one sees the complete destruction of the powerful Yādavas by their own protector, Krishna, together with the passing away of Balarāma and Krishna and the realisation of Arjuna that in their absence he cannot fight even ordinary dacoits wielding clubs. In other words, he realises that without contact with the Divine, man by himself is nothing. And with that realisation, the Pāndavas know it is time to leave the world behind and seek the Divine. Perhaps it is for this philosophic insight that Sauti describes this usually neglected *Parva* as so very important.

Completing this image, Sauti adds a remark that is yet another indication of his profession. This epic, he says, is a source of livelihood to illustrious poets (*shloka* 92). He is referring to wandering rhapsodes like himself who, like the medieval minstrels and troubadours of Europe and the bards of Rajputana, literally lived off such tales of great heroes, gods and nymphs.

By way of relating the major features of the epic, Sauti picks out the glory of the house of Kuru, the virtue of Gāndhārī, the wisdom of Vidura, the constancy of Kuntī, the divinity of Krishna, the rectitude of the Pāndavas and the wickedness of the Dhārtarāshtras. That is how the epic appeared to the narrator and the millennia have not made much change in the audience's perception, except that the efforts of Rabindranath Tagore, Ramdhari Singh Dinkar, Buddhadeb Bose, Shivaji Sawant, Dipak Chandra, P.K. Balakrishnan, Gurudutt and Narendra Kohli have created an exaggerated impression concerning the role of Karna, investing him with a superman-halo which is not justified by the *Mahābhārata* as it stands.

Sauti now tells us a very important fact: originally, the *Mahābhārata* consisted of twenty thousand *shlokas* (twenty four thousand in some versions), leaving aside the fringe episodes, which Vyāsa composed after arranging the Vedas. He added a list of contents running to a hundred and fifty *shlokas* and taught it to his son Shuka and four disciples (Vaishampāyana, Sumanta, Paila, Jaimini) directing each to publish his own rendition. Vaishampāyana's is the only one to be recited in the presence of the composer himself. The other editions are lost but for Jaimini's *Ashvamedha Parva* which is very different from Vyāsa's composition in both matter and form.[2] At the end of the *Mahābhārata* Sauti tells us that its composition took Vyāsa three years; (*Svargārohana Parva,* 48). He brought it before the world only after the deaths of his three sons—Dhritārashtra, Pāndu and Vidura. Thus, we are made aware that Vyāsa is actually presenting before us the biography of his family. Later, Vyāsa composed another version running to six lakh *shlokas* (sixty lakh in some recensions) of which one lakh *shlokas* are known in the mortal world while thirty lakh are in the world of the gods, fifteen lakh in the sphere of the ancestors, fourteen lakh in the abode of Gandharvas—the entire composition running to *shashthim shatasahasrāni,* i.e. sixty lakh verses. K.M. Ganguli left it an unresolved mess as his parts add up to sixty lakh, while he says the whole is of six lakh. Nārada, says Sauti, recites it to the gods, Asita-Devala to the ancestors, Shuka to the Rākshasas and Vaishampāyana to humanity. In other words, the extent of the composition is adjusted depending on the demands of the audience. It can be begun at three different points: from the very first verse; from the story of Āstīka; from Uparichara's tale. At the close of this, we find another delightful touch individualising Sauti, who, after mentioning that Vaishampāyana recited one lakh *shlokas* to the world of men, adds, "I might add that I, Sauti, have also recited one lakh *shlokas*", of which he is quite justifiably proud (*shloka* 107).

The next two *shlokas,* 198 and 199, are crucial because they define Vyāsa's moral perspective. Once again that organic tree image is used. The Dhārtarāshtras and Pāndavas are described in terms of giant trees, one born of passion, the other of Dharma; the root of the one is the weak-minded Dhritarāshtra, that of the other Krishna, Brahmā and Brahmins.

Now, in just twenty eight verses Sauti provides a succinct resume of the Kuru-Pāndava story unrivalled for its brevity followed by the exquisite self-exculpatory lament of Dhritarāshtra with its haunting refrain *tadā na shamse vijayāya Sanjaya,* "I no longer hoped for victory, Sanjaya". The lament consists of a record of the chief achievements of the Pāndavas following their escape from the house-of-lac, but the chronology is garbled, as would be natural in someone whose entire kin has been slaughtered. Thus, instead of beginning with the house-of-lacquer episode, Dhritarāshtra begins with Arjuna's winning of Draupadī, an episode that disturbed him profoundly as is shown when he repeats it after four *shlokas.* After all, it secured for the exiled Pāndavas the alliance of the powerful Pānchālas—traditional rivals of Hastināpura—and immediately led to their being welcomed back by Dhritarāshtra. He mentions two other matrimonial alliances: that of Arjuna with Subhadrā, forging an alliance with the Yādavas, and that of Arjuna's son with Virāta's daughter, thus providing the Pāndavas with yet another major ally in the Matsyas. One would have expected a reference to Bhīma's rakshasan affair with Hidimbā, since Dhritarāshtra gives Ghatotkacha two whole *shlokas.* Another event repeated twice is the slaying of Jayadratha (*shlokas* 191, 196) despite the presence of Drona and other mighty warriors.

Some of the *shlokas* in this lament offer revealing insights into the secret of the Pāndavas' success. The fact that Yudhishthira, bereft of kingdom, continued to receive the support of his brothers and that they faithfully followed him into exile is one of these. It shows what a master-stroke of strategy it was on part of Vyāsa, Krishna and Kuntī to insist, defying social norms, that Draupadī should be the common wife of all five brothers. This forged a nexus of unbreakable unity that their opponents sought in vain to break and which formed the foundation of their ultimate victory. The other factor is that holy men followed the Pāndavas into exile in the forest, thereby ensuring that thirteen years of exile did not result in a regression to brutish instincts but rather led to a refinement of the spirit through this constant association with ascetics. As Buddhadeb Bose points out, Yudhishthira utilises this entire period of forest-exile for a persistent search after the secret of inner peace and the key to prevent destructive conflicts in life. This pointer is reinforced in *shloka* 166 where Dhritarāshtra refers to the questioning of Yudhishthira by the Dharma-*yaksha* over the corpses of his four brothers. Another important insight is offered by *shlokas* 151 (Vidura arranging the escape of the Pāndavas from the lacquer house) and 176 (Krishna and Bhīshma advising the Pāndavas and Drona blessing them), showing the internal weakness of the Dhārtarāshtras with their main pillars of strength, Bhīshma and Drona emotionally ranged with their enemies, culminating in revealing the manner of their deaths to the Pāndavas, besides not killing a single one of the brothers despite slaughtered thousands. *Shloka* 186 reveals the bitterness the blind monarch is that neither Drona nor Bhīshma could kill one of the Pāndavas despite all their prowess. *Shloka* 165 betrays his deep-seated hatred of Bhīma, as he laments that Karna had him in his power and let him escape with a few insults. Another interesting feature is that the only references Dhritarāshtra makes to unjust fighting are the killings of Drona and Duryodhana but not that of Karna, despite the indignation that this particular act of Krishna and Arjuna usually arouses in readers, including Tagore, Dinkar and Sawant. On two occasions, in *shlokas* 198 and 201, Dhritarāshtra bewails the fruitless misdirection of infallible weapons (Karna uses India's *shakti* missile against Ghatotkacha instead of Arjuna and Ashvatthāmā misuses the *Nārāyana* weapon) not because they were misused but because thereby none of the Pāndavas was killed.

It is, indeed, a remarkably self-revealing lament of the blind monarch's true feelings: blinded by love for his sons, hypocritically always trying to appear fair in his treatment of the Pāndavas (*shloka* 142) but all along longing for their annihilation and going on hoping against hope until the bitter end when Ashvatthāmā is cursed by Vyāsa and Krishna for wounding the child in Uttarā's womb.

Dhritarāshtra is quite obviously astonished and not a little piqued that so insignificant a warrior as Nakula should have worsted Ashvatthāmā in battle, making his chariot run around in circles (*shloka* 200), and that the innocuous Yudhishthira should have defeated Duhshāsana, Kritavarmā and Ashvatthāmā and finally slain the redoubtable Shalya (*shlokas* 204-5). There is no expression of horror or even regret over the planned burning-alive of the Pāndavas in the lacquer-house despite the assertion "I made no distinction between my sons and the sons of Pāndu" (*shloka* 142). Rather is he full of sorrow that they escaped because of Vidura, his step-brother and chief advisor.

Only thrice, in *shlokas* 155, 180 and 210, do we find Dhritarāshtra voicing sentiments of horror or sorrow regarding the sufferings of Pāndavas. Of these, the first is the attempted disrobing of menstruating Draupadī husbanded-yet-husbandless (*rajasvalam nāthavatimanāthavat*) in public by Duhshāsana. However, there is a curious twist to it because the next *shloka*, 156, expresses the king's sorrow that Duhshāsana "was foiled in his efforts to strip Draupadī" whereupon "what was there for me to look forward to, Sanjaya?" In other words, Duhshāsana's reprehensible act would have been redeemed in his father's eyes if it had not been a failure! Incidentally, this is the only reference in the epic to the attempted stripping other than in the *Sabhā Parva*, which raises the suspicion that the lament is an interpolation.[3] From these outbursts, it is clear that even after the decimation of his entire progeny, the *prajñā chakshuh*, prophetic-visioned, monarch has not learnt anything. That apart, this remarkable epithet sums up the plight of Draupadī in a unique fashion, which has been explored inimitably by Shaoli Mitra in her riveting one-woman performances, *Nāthavati Anāthavat* and *Kathā Amrita Samān.*

The second voicing of regret is for the killing of Abhimanyu, but it is also qualified by *shloka* 190 where he laments that this led to Arjuna's vow of *saindhava* to kill Dhritarāshtra's son-in-law Jayadratha. The only unqualified expression of sorrow for the Pāndavas occurs in *shloka* 210 concerning the slaughter of the sleeping Pānchālas and the sons of Draupadī, which Dhritarāshtra terms as "horrible" (*vibhatsa*). *Shloka* 211 could also be construed similarly, concerning Ashvatthāmā wounding the child in Uttarā's womb.

All in all, we have here a fascinating and complex picture of a man's turbulent emotions when he has lost all his sons and most of his kin in a war that he might have been able to prevent had he not been blinded by his doting love for his sons.

> "My own sons were impulsive and disliked me for I was old and blind. I endured it, because I loved them, and because my state was miserable. I was a fond old father to a son whose folly grew daily." (*Shloka* 143)

How bitter are his concluding utterances:-

> "And I pity Gāndhārī.
> All her children dead,
> grandchildren, parents, brothers, relatives.
> The Pāndavas have fought
> an excellent war: they have now
> a kingdom without a rival.
> Ten, I am told, in all
> have survived this grief-giving war.
> Three of us Kauravas.
> And seven Pāndavas.

Eighteen akshauhinis of Kshatriyas slaughtered." (*Shlokas* 214-15)

After *shloka* 168 there is a verse found in the Bengal recension, which deserves inclusion:

> "When I heard that Kīchaka and his hundred brothers had been killed by Bhimasena to vindicate the honour of Draupadī, I no longer hoped for victory, O Sanjaya."

The slaying of Kīchaka was a crucial factor contributing to the Pāndava victory. With him alive it would have been extremely difficult for them to enlist the aid of Virāta on their side.

The entire lament of Dhritarāshtra is supremely ironic. The man who has given up all hope of victory is the one who is ultimately the victor. While retiring from this world the Pāndavas appoint Yuyutsut, Dhritarāshtra's sole surviving son, regent of the entire empire, with the boy Parikshit, Arjuna's grandson, as the titular monarch. The wheel has come full circle. By dropping it, the critical edition merely succeeds in depriving us of a splendid instance of narrative art.

This, however, is not the only ironical feature. Dhritarāshtra starts narrating these incidents to Sanjaya in order to show him that "I am indeed a man with prophetic vision". Yet, this blind king who claims to be a Teirisias, having ostensibly given up hope of success as early as the escape of the Pāndavas from the lacquer-house, persists in going on nursing a will-o-wisp right till the end when Ashvatthāmā is cursed by Vyāsa and Krishna for mortally wounding the child in Uttara's womb. Is there a hint that he was hoping that Ashvatthāmā would succeed in slaying the unborn child who was the only hope of the Pāndavas, resulting in the final victory of Dhritarāshtra with the ultimate coronation of his son Yuyutsut as emperor when the Pāndavas left? Unlike another blind king Dyumatsena who lost his kingdom and got it back as his daughter-in-law Sāvitri's boon, it is the burden of Sisyphus that weighs down the blind king, who compulsively goes on hoping for ultimate success, struggling against what he knows to be inevitable: the annihilation of all his dreams.

The lament is important not only for its rich irony and its poetic cadences. It is the only place in the epic where we are given the entire struggle as seen through the blind eyes of the defeated prophetic-visioned king. Hence, it is worthwhile to enumerate the incidents that stand out in Dhritarāshtra's memory as key events in the long drawn struggle for supremacy. Though not chronologically in sequence, the verisimilitude of the narrative art cannot be questioned. The events flash before his inner eye disparately:

> The vows of Duryodhana, Karna, and Shakuni; Duryodhana mocked by the Pāndavas in Indraprastha; the game of dice; Arjuna winning Draupadī and the Pānchālas joining the Pāndavas; Arjuna abducting and marrying Subhadrā; Arjuna gratifying Agni and defeating Indra in the burning of Khāndava forest; the escape from the house of lacquer; Bhīma killing Jarāsandha bare-handed; Rājasūya celebrated by Pāndavas; Duhshāsana outraging Draupadī's modesty in public and failing to disrobe her; Yudhishthira losing his kingdom in the dice game but not abandoned by his brothers; holy men following Yudhishthira into exile; Arjuna obtaining the Pāshupata weapon from Shiva, other weapons from Indra and routing the Kālakeyas and Paulomas; Arjuna visiting Indra's abode and defeating the Asuras; Bhīma leading the Pāndavas unscathed into the forbidden land of Kubera; Arjuna rescuing the sons of Dhritarāshtra from the Gandharvas; Dharma-yaksha questioning Yudhishthira; the Dhārtarāshtras failing to track down the disguised Pāndavas in Virāta's court; Arjuna routing the Kaurava heroes single-handed in Virāta's kingdom; Kīchaka slain by Bhīma; Uttarā's marriage with Abhimanyu; Yudhishthira, though exiled, able to raise seven armies; Krishna seeking the welfare of the Pāndavas; Nārada declaring Krishna and Arjuna to be Nara and Nārāyana of Brahmā's realm; Krishna coming on a peace-mission and returning disappointed; Duryodhana's fruitless conspiracy to imprison Krishna who revealed to them all creation in himself; Kuntī consoled by Krishna; Bhīma, Drona and Krishna advising and blessing the Pāndavas; Karna refusing to fight as long as

Bhīshma remains in the fray; Krishna, Arjuna and the Gāndīva together; Krishna revealing his universal form to Arjuna; Bhīshma not killing a single Pāndava; Bhīshma revealing the manner of his death to the Pāndavas; Arjuna cutting down Bhīshma, using Shikhandi as a shield; Arjuna slaking Bhīshma's thirst; Vāyu, Indra and Srya helping the Pāndavas and wild beasts terrorising the Kauravas; Drona unable to kill the Pāndavas; Arjuna slaying the *samsaptakas*; Abhimanyu's prowess and his slaying; Arjuna's successful implementation of the *saindhava* vow; Krishna watering Arjuna's horses while Arjuna single-handed fought-off all opponents; Sātyaki cutting through Drona's elephant army to join Arjuna and Krishna; Karna releasing Bhīma despite having him at his mercy; Karna using Indra's weapon against Ghatotkacha; the slaying of Drona; Nakula defeating Ashvatthāmā; Ashvatthāmā misusing his weapon and failing to kill the Pāndavas; Bhīma drinking Duhshāsana's blood; Karna slain by Arjuna; Yudhishthira defeating Duhshāsana, Kritavarmā and Ashvatthāmā and killing Shalya; Sahadeva slaying Shakuni; Duryodhana hiding inside the lake and his unjust killing; the slaughtering of the Pānchālas and Draupadī's sons; Ashvatthāmā wounding the child in Uttarā's womb, being cursed for it, and his weapon repulsed by Arjuna.

It is significant that Arjuna is mentioned most often (28 times in the 68 *shlokas* composing the lament), Krishna following close behind (18 times), Yudhishthira (7 times) and Bhīma (5 times). It is Arjuna, not Bhīma, who is seen as the Nemesis by Dhritarāshtra, having acquired celestial weapons and the help of Krishna. On the Kaurava side, Dhritarāshtra mentions Bhīshma the most (8 times) and then Karna (7 times), which reveals which figures dominated the blind monarch's imagination: his own heroes do not even reach double figures in his own estimation!

Sanjaya consoles the frantic king with a list of twenty-four kings who, having obtained great fame and prosperity in life, calmly accepted death. Apparently, these kings were the traditional staple of consolation, because Nārada had previously related their story to Shaivya who was grieving over the loss of his children. Unfortunately, we do not know anything more about this king or how he lost his children. The lesson in resignation is something like the theme of the Old English lyric *Deor's Lament* with its recurring refrain: "That sorrow passed away, so may this." Sanjaya proceeds, on his own, to enumerate some sixty-five kings who, though righteous and noble, had to die. Why should Dhritarāshtra, therefore, grieve for his sons who were "envious, selfish, passionate and vicious" (*shloka* 240)? This long list of names is perplexing because nothing is found about ninety percent of them in them in the Purānas or elsewhere. It recalls the similar catalogue in the oldest of English poems, *Widsith.* These are names which, doubtless, evoked vistas of heroic lore for the poet's contemporaries, but which carry no significance for us, as those tales are no longer extant.

Sanjaya's concluding advice is the conventional observation that Fate and Time are ruthless destroyers, so why should the wise man sorrow? But this trite sentiment is expressed in lovely cadences and looks forward to the awesome apotheosis of Krishna in the *Gītā*:

> "Cosmic Time Kala brings everything.
> Being and non-being,
> Pleasure and pain.
> Kala creates and Kala destroys,
> Kala is the fire and Kala the extinguisher,
> Kaḷa is the god of good and evil.
> Kala cuts us down and Kala creates anew,
> Kala is awake when all things sleep.
> Kala stands straight when all things fall.
> Kala shuts in all and will not be shut.
> Is, was, and shall be are Kala's children.
> O Reason! Be witness! Be stable!" (*Shlokas* 244-248)

The superb transcreation recalls the calm resignation of *The Wanderer,* where the Anglo-Saxon bard muses,

> "Everything is full of hardship in the kingdom of earth; the

decree of fate changes the world under the heavens—So spoke the wise man in his heart and sat apart in thought. Good is he who holds his faith."

The transcreation carries echoes of Shakespeare's *Sonnets* and *The Rape of Lucrece.* Time becomes a *leit-motif* in the epic, reaching its shattering climax in the awesome vision Arjuna is given in the *Gītā.*

Sauti speaks of the benefits obtainable from a devoted perusal of the epic. In a series of exquisite similes he extols its greatness:

"As the full moon opens the waterlily with soft light
So this Purāna expands the mind of man with light of shruti."
(*Shloka* 86)

He stresses what Brahmā told Vyāsa: that in this epic the Supreme Truth has been revealed (*shlokas* 253-57) and that is why to read it with the proper attitude is to be freed from sin. What this attitude should be has been described by Vashishtha to Rāma in the twelfth section of the *Mumuksha Khanda* of the *Yoga-Vāshishtha-Rāmāyana*:

"Be still to attend to knowledge by keeping your mind fixed in yourself and, being freed from pride and passion, incline yourself to pure truth."

Thereby the listener will achieve that mystic and intuitive state in which he is able to grasp the inner significance of the stories he hears in this epic.

From the point of view of cultural history *shlokas* 268-270, which close the *parva,* are significant. Here is the apotheosis of the *Mahābhārata,* which is weighed against all the Vedas by the gods and is found to be greater than the Vedas in substance and seriousness. This, along with the statement that Vyāsa wrote the epic after he had arranged the Vedas into four parts and the invocations to Agni by the *Shārngakas* in the *Khāndavadahana parva* that occur in the *Rig Veda* (X.142), show the break with the Vedic period while indicating that the Rigvedic age extended up to the composition of the epic. With this, the Puranik culture is firmly established and the Vedas become more and more objects of remote veneration, understood by fewer and fewer people, and considered chiefly as texts for performance of sacred rituals. Their hidden depths could be plumbed anew and the inner truth brought to light only by another *rishi*, a seer-poet of our times, Sri Aurobindo.

References

1. P. Bhattacharya, 1984
2. Its first English translation by Shekhar K. Sen, edited by me, has been published by Writers Workshop, Kolkata in 2009.
3. *Annals of the BORI* vol.LXXXVI, 2005 (published 2006) pp.149-52 and in Kalyan Kumar Chakravarty, ed. *Text and Variation in the Mahābhārata* (Delhi : Munshiram Manoharlal, 2009), 89-99

2

Parvasangraha
The Contents

Parvasangraha is possibly the most tedious portion of the epic being, by and large, a catalogue of names—almost a list of contents. It remains, however, a valuable specimen of the mnemonic art and its effects. We come across a number of repetitions and the chronological sequence appears hopelessly muddled. Thus, in *shloka* 56 the story of Sāvitrī is said to follow the rescue of Draupadī from Jayadratha, but *shloka* 63 puts it after Krishna's peace-mission to the Kaurava court, and *shloka* 201 has it after Draupadī's abduction and the *Rāmāyana* recital. Similarly, the removal of Karna's earrings by Indra is placed after the journey of the Pāndavas to Pulastya in *shloka* 197, while in *shloka* 203 it comes after the Draupadī-Jayadratha episode. Undoubtedly, many of these repetitions acted as aids to the rhapsode's memory and their mnemonic value is quite distinct from the literary one.

This *parva*, as Prof. Lal has pointed out in his preface to the 1968 edition, falls into four parts: the genesis of the *samanta-panchaka*; an explanation of the word *akshauhini*; a list of contents; and finally the benefits obtained from studying the epic. Moreover, the listing of the eighteen major *Parvas* and one hundred minor *parvas* is not insignificant. Sauti omits some, stresses others, and merely mentions the rest. Thus, he particularly singles out the short *Strī Parva* in a memorable verse (*shloka* 321):

"To hear it is to be moved, if the heart has feeling;
to read it is to weep, if the eye has tears."

Sauti seeks to convey some idea of the distinctive quality of each *parva* by the use of stock epithets such as "wonderful", "excellent" and the ubiquitous *romaharshana*—that virtually untranslatable epithet meaning "exquisitely horripilatory so as to make the hair stand on end with delight, without any suggestion of horror" which is a favourite of Sauti's. Prof. Lal rightly comments, "The catalogue of parvas may sound monotonous to the English reader, but in the original there is a sound pattern in the *shlokas* that provides a saving melodic grace (which) is impossible to convey in translation, though some idea of it can be given by keeping the original Sanskrit titles of the parvas." *Shloka* 43 is a good example:

purvānukramāni purvam dvitiyah parvasamgrahah /
paushyam paulomāstīkamādivamshāvataranam //

It is significant that Sauti selects for special mention certain sections of the *Sambhava* sub-parva of the *Ādi Parva*, namely: the House-of-lac episode; the Hidimbā incident, the killing of Baka, the confrontation with Chitraratha, the winning of Draupadī, the Vidura-embassy to Drupada, the re-establishment of Pāndavas in a kingdom, and Arjuna's exile. Sauti has not cared to mention the miraculous births of the Pāndavas, the first confrontation between Arjuna and Karna in the weapons-exhibition, or the shameful Ekalavya episode.

Similarly, in the *Sabhā Parva* Sauti particularly picks out the episode of offering *arghya* to Krishna from the Rājasūya sub-parva. In the *Udyoga parva*, Sauti concentrates on the section on Krishna's arrival to pick out the stories of Mātali and Gālava related by Nārada to Duryodhana to convey a lesson; the thrilling call-to-arms by Vidula to her son related by Kuntī to Krishna for conveying a message to her sons; and Krishna's vain effort to make Karna join the Pāndavas. What we fail to find in the main body of the epic is the story of Shveta that Sauti mentions in verse 65—one of the many lost legends of purānik heritage.

From the *Gadā* sub-parva Sauti selects the description of the holy spots and of the river Sarasvatī for special mention. Strangely enough, there is no mention of the gruesome *Sauptika Parva.* Instead, its latter portion, "the dread-inspiring" *Aishīka* where Ashvatthama uses the "final solution" is listed, followed by the funeral obsequies and the lamentation of widows (*Strī Parva*). Gāndhārī's cursing of Krishna is omitted. From the *Shānti Parva* he singles out for mention the killing of Chārvāka, the coronation of Yudhishthira, the allotment of responsibilities of governance and of quarters to the Pāndavas, and then the sections containing Bhīshma's advice to Yudhishthira, along with the questions put by Shuka and Brahmā, the origin of Durvāsā and his confrontation with Maya (missing from the epic). In his list, Sauti leaves out one sub-*parva* after the *Anugitā* that concerns Vaishnava Dharma occurring in the Bengal recension. It is of doubtful authenticity as is the celebration of Shiva's glory in the *Shānti* and the *Anushāsana Parvas.*

Reviewing this list of contents we hardly find any major omissions or inconsistencies on Sauti's part. What appears to be a peculiarly named section in the Lal transcreation of *shloka* 55, "the dilemma of Mārkandeya" is really quite an innocently titled section "Mārkandeya samasyā." The meaning of *samasyā* is basically "putting together, mingling," and only derivatively "problem, knot, dilemma". The correct translation would be "the meeting with Mārkandeya (of the Pāndavas)".

This list very firmly makes the *Khila Harivamsa* an integral part of the epic, specifying that it includes the deeds of the child Krishna, his slaying of Kamsa and finally the *Bhavishya Parva* containing wondrous prophecies. Taking these into account, the epic is supposed to have a hundred *parvas.* Kaliprasanna Sinha, who translated the entire epic into Bengali in 1903, omitted the *Harivamsa* because its style was in no way similar to that of the composer of the *Mahābhārata,* besides being much inferior. It is a pity that all translations of the epic have omitted the *Khila,* which is virtually a smaller and earlier *Bhāgavata Purāna* and completes the glorification of Krishna in another way, more explicitly as the Yādava-leader and the divinity as he is popularly conceived, quite distinct from the Krishna of the *Gītā.*

Having given this outline of the *parvas* and set out the bones, Sauti proceeds to articulate them into a skeleton with some skin stretched over the framework, so that we get to know what "this history full of subtleties, intricate logic and Vedic profundities" (*Shloka* 42) looks like. Arranging the hundred *parvas* into eighteen main sections, Sauti proceeds to give more details, section-wise. *Shlokas* 87-91 are merely a repetition of *shlokas* 43-48 concerning the *Ādi Parva.* But from *shloka* 91 to 102 Sauti adds details about the *Paushya, Pauloma, Āstīka* and *Sambhava parvas,* which were merely names earlier, and proceeds to reiterate, at yet greater length, the incidents from the House-of-lac episode onwards.

This *Parva* is rounded off with a long passage celebrating the glory of the epic as the repository of the entire Hindu ethos. Abounding in conventional eulogy, there are a number of repetitions by Sauti in this portion. Thus, *shlokas* 386 and 387 are transcriptions of *shlokas* 39 and 40 (the body and the servant similes) while *shloka* 339 repeats Brahmā's praise of the epic in *shloka* 73 of the *Anukramanikā.* Occasionally we do come across a genuine poetic touch as in *shloka* 384:

> "The five elements swaddle the three worlds.
> This excellent poem swaddles poets' imaginations."

A remarkably felicitous transcreation this, capturing the precise nuances of the original through that single word 'swaddle'. Compare the ponderous K.M. Ganguli version:

> "As the formation of the three worlds proceedeth from the five elements, so do the inspirations of all poets proceed from this excellent composition."

Van Buitenen's "modern" translation is not much better:

> "From this supreme epic rise the inspirations of the poets as the configurations of the three worlds rise from the five elements."

Shloka 118 describes the story of the five Indras, occasioned by the problem of Draupadī's marriage, as *adbhut*, i.e. "wonderful". The story is marvellous in every sense of the word, being the solitary instance of instant myth-making on Vyāsa's part. To overcome Drupada's misgivings about the polyandrous marriage, Vyāsa produces on the spot an extremely convenient yet unique myth, calculated to amaze and stupefy all listeners, succeeding completely in achieving his purpose. The myth is enlarged in the Southern recension where Draupadi's previous births are as Mudgalāni-Nālāyani-Indrasenā (daughter of Damayanti) and Shaibyā Bhaumāshvi who married five sons of *rājarshi* Nitantu named Sālveya, Shurasena, Shrutasena, Tindusāra and Atisāra.[1]

Sauti proceeds to list the major episodes in the eighteen *parvas* with just two excursions into poetry in *shloka* 140 describing Draupadī "tossing like a boat on the stormy waves of her ocean of sorrows" and *shloka* 322 about the *Strī Parva* (quoted above). That boat metaphor looks forward to the *Sabhā Parva* where Karna compares her to a boat rescuing the Pāndavas from drowning in misfortune, which Krishna repeats in the *Udyoga Parva*. After *shloka* 376, which completes the account of the eighteen *parvas*, there are two *shlokas* in the Bengal recension omitted in the Lal transcreation which state that the *Svargārohana Parva* relates the sojourn of Karna in hell and his release, along with the meeting of Yudhishthira with the other heroes in heaven and their attaining their respective stations in heaven.

Again, after *shloka* 378 the Bengal recension has nine *shlokas* summarising the *Khila* as follows: Vishnu's birth in Vasudeva's clan and his upbringing by Nandagopāla, full of wondrous deeds; the slaying of Kamsa and Jarāsandha; the abduction of Rukmini and the building of Dvārakā; the slaying of Kalinga and Dantavaktra and Satyabhāmā's marriage; the killing of Dhenuka, Narakāsura, Kāliya, Hayagriva, Keshi and Kālanemi; the cutting-off of Bāna's thousand arms to rescue Aniruddha and his bride; the stories of Varāha, Narasimha, Vāmana and Pushkara. All these are related in a thousand chapters, the *Khila* running to twelve thousand *shlokas*.

However, despite the tone of conventional eulogy there is, as Prof. Lal points out in his Preface, no smugness. Sauti exhorts the sages:

"O rishis work!
Let good men throw off sloth." (*Shloka* 390)

That is another way of reminding them of Vashishtha's advice to Rāma on how to listen to the scriptures in order to reap the maximum benefits in the *Yoga-Vāshishtha-Rāmāyana* (*Mumuksha Khanda*, chapter 12). Very much in the manner of the medieval *Everyman,* Sauti points out:

"Dharma is your only friend in the next life.
Who is so clever as to keep
Wealth and women forever with him?
They pass away, they pass away." (*Shloka* 390)

Just as the significance of the *Anukramanikā* had been succinctly stated in *shloka* 267 of that *parva viz.* "I repeat: whoever reads the first section, reads the whole *Bhārata*", similarly in *shloka* 395 of the *Parvasangraha,* with which it ends, Sauti offers the *raison d'etre* for the elaborate, if dull, list of contents, once again using the boat image:

"The wide ocean is crossed by small boats.
The large and excellent epic called the *Bhārata*
is easily grasped with the help of this *parva.*"

This immediately recalls *shloka* 52 of the *Anukramanikā*:

"The sage Vyāsa presented this storehouse of knowledge in detailed as well as condensed forms, because the learned of the world are eager to know it at length and in abridgment."

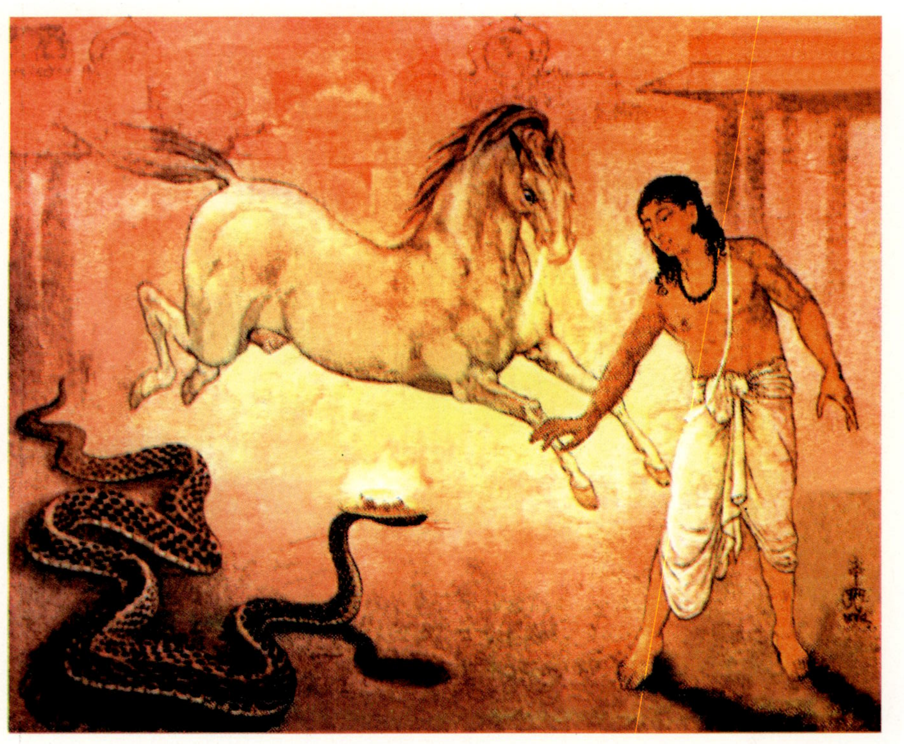

"Uttanka in Nagaloka" courtesy BORI

3

Paushya Parva

The *Raison D'etre* of the Snake Holocaust

Paushya parva is possibly the most 'teasing' portion of the *Ādi Parva.* After the dull *Parvasangraha,* it suddenly sparks our interest and delights with its poetry, at places teasing us out of thought into eternity. And yet, it is the only *parva* that is largely in prose.

Take, for instance, the title itself: Paushya is casually mentioned only midway in the *parva* as having appointed Veda his preceptor, as did Janamejaya (*shloka* 84); and it is Veda's disciple Uttanka who is asked to fetch the ear-rings of Paushya's wife. The *parva* could, as well, have been named after Uttanka, who is the subject of 102 out of the 187 *shlokas* in this section. Paushya is mentioned barely a dozen times.

Then, again, why this peculiar narrative of a dog being beaten up by Janamejaya's brothers, which opens this *parva*? Granted that this happens to be the progeny of the "celestial bitch Saramā" (*shloka* 11), but what is the reason for giving it so much importance?

A little textual analysis reveals that a master storyteller is at work. Sauti has started weaving his incredibly involved web of narrative, where an apparently irrelevant episode turns up hundreds of *shlokas* later as the seed of a crucial event. A canine presence intriguingly dogs the protagonist right from the beginning, reappearing at his ancestor's side at the very end. At times, the intricacy is so great that Sauti himself forgets to link up the loose thread finally. One example of this is this opening section of the *parva.* Saramā's curse makes Janamejaya seek out

Somashravā, born of a snake that drank Shrutashravā's semen, and make him his priest. Somashravā observes a special principle: he will immediately grant whatever a Brahmin asks. Having appointed him *purohita*, Janamejaya leaves on a campaign to annex Taxila, and the narrative abruptly shifts to Āyodah-Dhaumyah and his disciples. The intention appears to have been to link Somashravā to Āstīka (both snake-born). Āstīka would ask for the snake-sacrifice to be stopped and Somashravā, bound by his vow, would have to agree. Unfortunately, by the time Sauti comes to this point in the 56th chapter of the *Āstīka parva*, he has forgotten all about Somashravā—who thus loses his only claim to memorability—and lets Janamejaya be persuaded by all the Brahmins present to give in to Āstīka. And so the first 22 *shlokas* of the *Paushya parva* remain in limbo, unconnected with anything that has gone before or comes afterwards; except for the hound of heaven.

The *yajña* that Janamejaya is engaged in when the *parva* opens is not the great snake-sacrifice but a sacrifice he was conducting at Kurukshetra. He starts thinking of the *sarpasattra* at the end of the *parva* after Uttanka has urged him to avenge his father's assassination by Takshaka. The *Shatapatha Brāhmana* (13.5.41) refers to such a horse-sacrifice by the king and his three brothers.

We now have what appears to be a digression about the virtues of blind and punctilious obedience to the preceptor's orders: the stories of Ārunī, Upamanyu and Uttanka. They were the three disciples of Āyodah Dhaumyah—a teacher who bids fair to surpass Dickens' Mr. Squeers—using Ārunī as a plug for a breach in a canal and driving Upamanyu blind through starvation. Veda, the lucky one, is merely condemned to the existence of a Johannes factotum about the house. Veda, in turn, has a disciple named Uttanka who, robbed by Takshaka, plants in Janamejaya's mind the seed of revenge, leading to the snake holocaust. Thus, we find the cunning artificer at work as Sauti the professional teller-of-tales finally brings Vyāsa's epic to its starting point, answering the unasked question present in the mind of every member of the audience from the beginning: why did the *sarpasattra* take place during which the *Mahābhārata* was recited?

The episodes concerning these three disciples cast fascinating light on the teacher-taught relationship in ancient India in which utter dedication and unquestioning faith in the teacher's commands were required of the pupil. This attitude built up a condition of receptivity in the student and the various experiences he underwent acted as stepping-stones to the achievement of the final goal when the preceptor would declare:

> "Because you followed my bidding so carefully, you shall prosper. All the Vedas will shine in you, all the Dharma Shastras also." (*Shlokas* 34-35)

Ārunī achieves this and, in the process, is metamorphosed into Uddālaka by using not just his finger but his entire body to plug the breach in the dyke. He becomes famous as the originator of the doctrine *tat tvam asi* ("thou art that") in the *Chhāndogya Upanishad*, and as the father of Shvetaketu who laid down the law regarding monogamy for Brahmins (*Ādi Parva* section 121).

His compatriot Upamanyu has a weakness for cow's milk. We meet him again in the *Anushāsana Parva*, section 14, when Krishna seeks guidance from him concerning the glory of Shiva, and learn the cause for this craving. His parents, like Ashvatthāmā's, were too poor to afford a cow; and this craving led to his *tapasyā* for Shiva's *darshana*. Upamanyu's guru relentlessly prevents him from concentrating on his stomach by denying him, in stages, from eating alms, milk and even the froth spat out by suckling calves until, driven by hunger, he chews *arka* (Calotropis gigantea) leaves and goes blind. That is when he turns his sight inwards to invoke a vision of dazzling beauty with numerous Rigvedic echoes, particularly of the Ashvins rescuing Vandana from a pit to the light (*Rig Veda* 10-39) and restoring sight to Rijarashva (1.116):

> "Golden eagles!
> Essences that vanish in the sky!
> Undecaying, free from error!
> Birds with golden beaks
> Justly-wounding, ever-victorious!

Lords of Time!
Poets of the Sun!
Makers of the tapestries of the years,
Black-threaded night and white-threaded day!"

(*Shlokas* 62-63)

The passage is a veritable *Vyāsa kūta* for any translator but the exquisitely poetic transcreation amply succeeds. An equally difficult passage is Uttanka's invocation in *shlokas* 145-148, followed by the startling act of blowing into a horse's anus:

"These girls
Are Nature,
Weaving weaving
Endlessly
A cloth
With black and white
Threads,
Creating
Worlds, millions
Of beings, who live
On these
Worlds.
Thunder-wielder!
World-saviour!
Vritra-slayer!
Namuci-slayer!
O Shining
Black-cloth
Weaver!
Truth and untruth
Revealer!
Rider of the
Nectar-born
Horse
Ocean-churned,
The horse
That is Agni

Different-formed!
Lord of the three worlds,
O Purandara, O Vishnu
O Supreme Being,
I bow to you! Namo-astu!
Black cloth
Weaver!
Truth and untruth
Revealer!"

One would hardly dispute that Prof. Lal has succeeded in his attempt "to convey the sense of swift movement and change in *vartayanti* (repeated thrice in different forms) in the repetition of 'weaving' and the short running lines", as he says in the Preface.

The *Paushya parva* is remarkable for a passage that is possibly unique in Puranik lore: the exchange of curses between Paushya and Uttanka. Uttanka revokes his curse when Paushya admits his mistake, but the king cannot, because,

> "A Brahmin's heart is butter-soft, though his words may be razor-edged. With a Kshatriya it is the opposite: his words are new-churned butter, his heart a cutting tool." (*Shloka* 124)

Now comes the unique portion in *shloka* 126 where Uttanka tells Paushya:

> "You said I would never be a father because I had declared the food unclean when it wasn't. But it *was* unclean. Your curse, therefore, is futile. I'm convinced of this."

Here is the only instance of a curse being declared futile and that too on extremely logical grounds. Durvāsā's victims would surely long for Uttanka-like courage and logical force to overcome his totally irrational and off-the-cuff curses. This incident raises certain basic questions about the very nature of a curse: is it pre-cognition or some type of induced mental-block or enforced emotional impulse?

But to hark back to the theme of teacher-taught, which is one of the major concerns of this *parva,* if not its only theme, the third pupil of the terrifying Āyodah-Dhaumyah is Veda who is exceptionally lucky. Or perhaps it is just his over-all mediocrity that saves him from experiencing the sort of merciless flaying his two colleagues have gone through. He is merely asked to stay with his guru and serve him, but that seems to be no easy task:

> "Like an ox bearing his owner's yoke, he bore heat and cold, hunger and thirst, without complaint. Many years passed before his guru was satisfied." (*Shloka* 79)

Veda, when he himself becomes a guru, remembers those hard days and is never strict with his own pupils. Uttanka, one of them, wins Veda's appreciation by refusing to have intercourse with his guru's wife in his absence, though urged to by her companions as it is her fertile period. Veda, understandably, promptly pats Uttanka on the back and gives him leave to push off. Obviously, he does not relish having pupils around who are approached in this fashion by the women of his household! Uttanka, however, is not to be fobbed off so easily. He seems to belong to Āyodah-Dhaumyah's breed, and, like Vishvamitra's obdurate disciple Gālava, insists on paying tuition-fees before he can call it quits, for:

> "He who gives instruction
>   without getting something,
> and he who takes instruction
>   without giving something—
> bitter hatred grows between them,
>   one of these two dies." (*Shloka* 93)

Veda refers him to his wife—that same lady whom Uttanka had refused to impregnate. She demands the earrings of Paushya's wife, and warns him that if these are not produced on the fourth day, "you know what to expect", as Prof. Lal transcreates in delightfully modern idiom. Showing gratitude to the preceptor, therefore, could be fraught with mortal danger if the teacher's wife had not been appeased! The experience of Gālava with Vishvāmitra (*Udyoga Parva*, section 106) is a similar lesson.

The references to "Dhritarāshtra" (*shloka* 138), a king of the snake-race and in *shloka* 135 to "Airāvata" another snake-king looks forward to section 23 of the *Āstīka parva* where Dhritarāshtra and Airāvata are mentioned as two of the principal snakes in *shlokas* 5 and 13. This sharing of names by the Kauravas and the Nāgas is a narrative technique whereby the fraternal conflict is lifted to supra-mundane levels, as we shall see in the account of Garuda.

The entire story of Uttanka narrated by Sauti is retold by him in a different form as told by Vaishampāyana to Janamejaya in chapters 56-58 of the *Ashvamedhika parva*, along with a fascinating confrontation with Krishna and with Indra disguised as an untouchable (sections 53-55). In this version, Uttanka's preceptor is Gautama who does not give him permission to leave and become a householder although he has grown old serving him, as Veda had with respect to Āyodah-Dhaumyah. Finally, Uttanka, collapsing under a load of firewood, complains to Gautama who restores his youth and marries him to his daughter. On asking Ahalyā, Gautama's wife, when he insists on giving *guru dakshinā*, she wants the earrings of King Saudāsa's wife. Saudāsa is King Kalmāshapāda, turned into a *rākshasa* by Vashishtha's curse (*Ādi Parva,* 175-76). Uttanka obtains the earrings, cleverly escapes being eaten-up, loses them to a snake of Airāvata's family and recovers them with the help of Indra and Agni in horse-shape. Some details about the earrings are given by Queen Madayanti: they produce gold and their wearer is free from the pangs of hunger and thirst and from poison, fire and wild animals. The gold-producing quality links them up with the earrings of Aditi, mother of the Ādityas, that are stolen by Narakāsura and have to be recovered by Krishna (*Harivamsa*). The encounter with Indra and the bull is changed into a separate episode where Indra as a *chandāla* offers the parched Uttanka his urine to drink. Uttanka refuses (as in the *Ādi Parva* he initially rejects the order to eat the bull's dung) and later learns that this was *amrita.*[1]

In the *Vana Parva* we find that this king, like Pāndu later, is cursed to die in intercourse for having killed Vashishtha's son while he was engaged in intercourse. Responding to his plea, Vashishtha, like Vyāsa later with Vichitravīrya's widows. impregnates Madayanti. She suffers an abnormally long pregnancy—replicated, again, in Gāndhāri's case—and terminates it by cutting open her womb with a stone (*ashmaka*). This son is named Ashmaka. We have here the first instance of what has come to known as a Caesarian section which ought to be renamed "Ashmakan section."

Reference

1. Their symbolic purport is discussed in my *Secret of the Mahābhārata*.

4

Pauloma Parva

Weaving in Skilled Unmindfulness

As the *Paushya* sub-*parva* ended, we looked forward eagerly to Janamejaya's response to Uttanka's exhortation against Takshaka:

> "Burn him to ashes! Burn him in the fire of a great snake-sacrifice! Do what is right, mahārājā! Order the sacrifice now!"

However, as we turn to the *Pauloma* sub-*parva,* we find ourselves confronted suddenly with what appears to be an uncalled-for break in the narrative with the insertion of a digression about the history of the Bhrigu race. If it is a digression, it is one well worth having, with some of the finest poetry we have come across so far and the memorable romance of Ruru and Pramadvarā. Take, for instance, the invocations to Agni in *shlokas* 22-25 and 27-29 of section 5, Agni's self-description in *shlokas* 6-11 and Brahmā's appeal to Agni in *shlokas* 19-24 of section 7, about which Prof. Lal writes in his Preface: "I mean more by 'poetic' here than beauty of imagery, memorable expression and high imagination. They enshrine, as the greatest poetry tends to do, moral values":

> "O Agni,
> You who live in the hearts
> Of men, as witness
> Of goodness and wickedness,
> Give me the truth! . . .
> Lord of creatures, Agni,

Destroyer and preserver
of the three worlds, . . .
But as all turns pure
When touched by the Sun,
So will all turn pure
When passed through your flames,
Agni, Supreme Energy,
Self-born god, Agni . . .
Receive for yourself,
And receive for the gods:
Eat impure and pure."

But to return to the problem of the inexplicable break in the narrative, we find that this sub-*parva* brings us back suddenly to the storyteller and his audience, as if beginning the story anew. This could well indicate that this is one of the several beginnings of the composition:

"Lomaharshana's son, Ugrashravā Sauti, learned in the Purānas, stood before the rishis performing the twelve years' sacrifice of Kulapati Shaunaka in the forest of Naimisha."

Sauti, once again, asks the sages what he should recount for their recreation and edification. They ask him to wait till Shaunaka returns from the *yajña* and to relate what he is asked to by the Kulapati. Is there a touch of apprehension or guilt that without waiting for their guru they had urged Sauti, with unbecoming eagerness, to recount the marvellous epic? Hence, the moment they get the chance, they cry a halt and await the pleasure of the head of the clan, who "knows all the marvellous stories dealing with gods and demons . . men, nāgas and gandharvas." As they admit,

"The point is, Sauti, that he is the supervisor of this sacrifice . . . it is proper that we should wait until he arrives." (verses 4, 8)

Shaunaka begins with a somewhat patronising query whether

Sauti is as much a master of the Purānas as his father Lomaharshana was (no doubt that name itself is a tribute to the manner in which his audiences were held spellbound by his literally hair-raising narratives). Sauti, in his reply, firmly announces that he has mastered not just what his father knew but, "What the noble Brahmins previously studied, what was studied and narrated by Vaishampāyana" (54). Thereby he places himself in the great tradition of wandering storytellers who spread the epic tales throughout what was India in those days and bound the multifarious communities within the folds of a common cultural ethos.

Shaunaka, as one would expect, wants to hear the history of his own forefathers: the race of Bhrigu, famed for Chyavana and Parashurāma. Naturally, the reader starts wondering how Sauti will get around to relating the Kuru-Pāndava story that he has already outlined to the other sages in the preceding three parvas. It is here that we find the brilliance of the storyteller's art: the cunning selection of the single thread from the tangled skein of Bhrigu-history which leads him straight to the snake-sacrifice once again, prompting Shaunaka to ask the inevitable "why", launching Sauti fairly into the great ocean of the *Mahābhārata* with no dangers of another untimely call to beach the ship before he reaches his destination.

Sauti simply ignores the great names in the Bhrigu dynasty such as Jamadagni and Parashurāma. Even Chyavana is disposed of quickly with no reference to Sukanyā who restored him to youth by pleasing the divine physicians, the Ashvinikumāras. Sauti is steering clearly with the help of the story of Ruru and Pramadvarā (moving and romantic enough to please his host and thus avoiding any impression that he is treating Shaunaka's request in a cavalier fashion), to the point where Ruru insists on knowing, "Why did Janamejaya decide to destroy the snakes, and how? . . . Why were they rescued by the wise Brahmin Āstīka? I would like to know this." (12.1-2)

Tantalisingly, Sauti ends by telling Shaunaka that Ruru "hurried home and asked his father, and his father told him the story" (12.6). Is Shaunaka left with any option but to repeat Ruru's two questions and thus begin the *Āstīka* sub-*parva*? One suspects that Sauti was not much interested in narrating the pious and rather dull ancestry of Shaunaka. We find him, with great gusto, plunging back into stories calculated to raise-hairs-on-end, much to the unspoken delight of his host's disciples who have been waiting for this since the *Anukramanikā*.

The name of this chapter, like that of the preceding *Paushya parva*, is an enigma. The episode of Pulomā is by no means the central one. The Ruru-Pramadvarā story is equally extensive. Possibly the name was given since the Pulomā affair comes first. Sauti would not have digressed into the story of Pulomā and would probably have launched straight into Ruru's tragedy had it not been for Shaunaka's curiosity about the genesis of Chyavana.

This episode raises some ticklish ethical questions with Agni becoming the symbol of conscience, the inviolable witness to Truth. Bhrigu's wife was originally betrothed to the *rākshasa* Puloma (here is the first instance where male and female are identically named; we will come across this again in the story of Jaratkāru in the *Āstīka* sub-*parva* and much later with the cannibal Hidimb). Subsequently, her father changed his mind and gave her as a gift to Bhrigu. That is why it is her father whom the *rākshasa* describes as "perfidious" in *shloka* 24 of section 5. Puloma, the *rākshasa*, urges Agni to tell him whether the lady belongs to Bhrigu or to him, thereby landing the god in great perplexity for, "He was afraid of speaking an untruth, and afraid that Bhrigu might curse him." (5.30)

Agni refuses to answer the question, and merely states the facts of Pulomā's prior betrothal to the *rākshasa*, followed by her marriage to Bhrigu according to the prescribed rituals. Not receiving a direct reply, the *rākshasa* abducts Pulomā. In the process Chyavana is born, dropping from the womb (his name means 'the dropped one'), reducing the abductor to ashes with his effulgence. Later in the *Sambhava* sub-*parva* we will find Aurva, springing forth from his mother's thigh, similarly striking the murderous Haiheyas blind. The enraged Bhrigu curses Agni to become omnivorous for having confirmed to the *rākshasa* that this woman was the same Pulomā to whom he had been betrothed. Agni's reply carries a touch of delicate humour: he refuses to reciprocate the curse, but by way of punishment subjects Bhrigu to a recital of the sacred fire's virtues and indispensability: "Listen to me, Brahmin—you may know all that I am going to say, but I will repeat it." (7.5)

In *shloka* 27 Agni rejoices not because Brahmā has shown him a way to avoid impurity and sin even while letting the curse come true. It is only Uttanka who can be sure that a curse based on a false premise cannot come true and that too as it was made by a Kshatriya. Even Agni and Brahmā have to accept a Brahmin's curse. We shall meet Agni again in Khāndava forest, having lost his appetite with consuming too much *ghee*, begging Arjuna to arrange a change of diet to flesh and blood!

Scholars beginning with V.S. Sukhthankar, the editor of the Critical Edition, have argued that retelling of the epic to Shaunaka, a Bhārgava, along with other indications in the text show that the original epic was extensively "Bhriguized". This even goes to the extent of Sauti naming the potter in whose house the Pāndavas take up residence in Pānchāla as "Bhārgava" in the *Parvasamgraha.* As far as the *Pauloma* is concerned, the close link between Agni and Bhrigu is an echo of the Vedic tradition. In the *Rig Veda,* the Bhrigus are in a somewhat Promethean role: they carry Agni to mankind and are celebrated for kindling it from wood. Perhaps, Bhrigu was originally a name of Fire itself. The Rigvedic references show that this clan of seers established and diffused the fire-sacrifice among the Aryans. They are said to have found Agni hidden amid the waters and to have taken him thence to the homes of mankind. Another person celebrated for "finding" fire in the wood of a tree is Pururavā the lunar dynast.

Section 8 contains the exquisite love-story of Ruru and Pramadvarā that inspired Sri Aurobindo's *Love and Death,* one of the loveliest short poetic romances in the English language. An extremely significant myth, it is the Indian counterpart of the Orpheus-Eurydice and Admetos-Alcestis myths of Greece. Ruru, like Alcestis, willingly sacrifices part of his life span for his beloved. The difference is that Ruru does this to bring Pramadvarā back to life, whereas Admetos seeks to enhance his life span by persuading someone else to die in his stead. That is why where Vyāsa's tale becomes an unforgettable romance, the

Greek myth remains a celebration of Herakles' divine prowess in conquering Hades and bringing back Alcestis to the world of the living. In that respect, Herakles is more akin to the indomitable Sāvitrī, who by sheer spiritual force makes Death restore her husband to life without giving in an inch—a splendid monument to Kāma's victory over Kritānta.

Sri Aurobindo's *Love and Death* relates the Greek and Hindu worlds in a unique re-telling where Ruru, like Herakles and Orpheus, visits the terrifying nether regions through the depths of the ocean:

> "And like a living thing the huge sea trembled . . . towards him
> Innumerable waters loomed and heaven
> Threatened. Horizon on horizon moved
> Dreadfully swift; then with a prone wide sound
> All Ocean hollowing drew him swiftly in,
> Curving with monstrous menace around him."

In this Hindu Hades, Ruru sees

> ". . . a dais brilliant doubtfully
> With flaming pediment and round it coiled
> Python, Naga monstrous, Joruthcaru,
> Tuxuc and Vasuki himself, immense,
> Magic Carcotaca all flecked with fire . . .
> . . . On the wondrous dais rose a throne,
> And he its pedestal whose lotus hood
> With ominous beauty crowns his horrible
> Sleek folds, great Mahapudma; high displayed
> He bears the throne of Death. There sat supreme
> With those compassionate and lethal eyes,
> Who many names, who many natures holds;
> Yama, the strong pure Hades sad and subtle,
> Dharma, who keeps the laws of old untouched,
> Critanta, who ends all things and at last
> Himself shall end. . . . "

Where Orpheus had charmed Hades with his music to give him back his love, Ruru boldly stakes his claim in the name of

Love:

"But at the name of Love all hell was moved.
Death's throne half faded into twilight;"
He accepts the condition laid down,
"And with a sudden fury gathering
His soul he hurled out of it half its life,
And fell, like lightning prone. Triumphant rose
The Shadow chill and deepened giant night.
Only the dais flickered in the gloom,
And those snake eyes of cruel fire subdued.
But suddenly a bloom, a fragrance. Hell
Shuddered with bliss. Resentful, overborne,
The world-besetting Terror faded back
Like one grown weak by desperate victory."

Ruru was Pramati's son by the celestial nymph Ghritāchī (a rather raucous name for an *apsarā*!), while Pramadvarā, like Shakuntalā earlier, was the abandoned daughter of Menakā. Both *apsarās* will be found recurring later in the epic performing critical functions. Ghritāchī will be responsible for the births of Shuka (from Vyāsa's spilt semen) and Drona (from Bharadvāja's). Both flesh-mortifying sages lost sexual control when they saw Ghritāchī bathing. Menakā, of course, seems to specialise in abandoning her offspring. Pramadvarā dies of snakebite before marriage:

"She lay on the ground, like one asleep, the slim-waisted girl, looking even more compelling in death than in life." (8.21)

A happy choice, that word 'compelling'. The description is hauntingly evocative of two very similar scenes. One is Shakespeare's *Anthony and Cleopatra*:

"She looks like sleep,
As she would catch a second Antony
In her strong toil of grace." (V.2.248)

The other is Sri Aurobindo's *Love and Death*:

"She for a moment stood
Beautiful with her love before she died;
And he laughed towards her . . .
He saw a brilliant flash of coils evade
The sunlight, and with hateful gorgeous hood
Darted into green safety, hissing, death."

Ruru vows to exterminate the serpent race, as did Janamejaya, and his encounter with the sage Sahasrapati, turned into a snake-lizard by a curse, is the occasion for recital of the famous *shloka: ahimsā paramo dharmah sarvaprānabhritam smritah* that formed the core of Gandhiji's philosophy of non-violence. Prof. Lal writes in his Preface:

> "In the context, it is a slippery sentence, spoken by the non-poisonous snake-lizard to the furious Ruru who raises his staff to kill him. Clearly, a creature on the point of being beaten to death will find the gospel of non-violence extremely agreeable."

However, a close reading of the text does not substantiate this. The *dundubha* does not propound the doctrine of *ahimsa* when about to be killed. At that point, it merely tells Ruru that he, knowing right from wrong, should not kill something just because it resembles a serpent, and Ruru desists. It is only after regaining human form that *dundubha*-Sahasrapati reminds Ruru that a Brahmin should never take the life of any creature, though a Kshatriya may since it is his *dharma.* Gandhiji, of course, argued that it was nobody's *dharma.*

As an example of his statement, Sahasrapati mentions āstīka who, at Janamejaya's snake-sacrifice, rescued some terrified snakes. Ruru, eager to learn why this sacrifice was instituted and why the snakes were saved, rushes to his father who tells him the story that forms the *Āstīka* sub-*parva* where we will be introduced to the epic idiom of Vyāsa.

5

The Āstīka Parva-I

The Raconteur's Art

The *Āstīka* has Vyāsa at his best as the weaver of tales: stories spring from within one another in delightful succession till the *parva* becomes a veritable Chinese box of unending surprises. Of course, Vyāsa is completely in the background with Sauti the raconteur weaving the magic web spellbinding his audience. In the *Pauloma* Sauti led up to the snake-sacrifice and stopped short with the cryptic statement that Ruru learnt the story from his father Pramati, leaving Shaunaka dangling. The *Āstīka* opens with the inevitable flurry of queries from Shaunaka, avid for the full narrative in detail. Watch how skilfully Sauti plays the line to reel-in the catch all the more surely: "It's a long story, Āstīka's," Sauti replied. "But I shall give it in full if you will listen" (*shloka* 4). What a masterly transcreation gaining immeasurably over other translations through the use of colloquial idiom!

First we learn from Sauti that the Naimisha forest dwellers heard it first from his father—a recital at which he was present too. Now he will repeat that narration verbatim (13.6-8). So here is a second generation bardic rendition recorded for posterity.

But there is more to come of tantalising art. Sauti, in some 48 *shlokas*, reels off the story of the wandering ascetic Jaratkāru, the birth of āstīka and his stopping of the snake-sacrifice. While narrating this, he deftly slips in a reference to the snakes having been cursed by their mother to be consumed in the sacrifice performed by Janamejaya (15.1), to counteract which Vāsuki marries off his sister to Jaratkāru. Shaunaka now confesses, "Now that you have roused our curiosity, Sauti, we would like to hear from you in detail of the learned and virtuous Āstīka" (16.1).

However, by now Shaunaka has understood that the easiest way to cut short the suspense and have the storyteller satisfy his curiosity is some blandishment. And Prof. Lal's rendering beautifully conveys the nuances of the gentle wheedling:

> "Gentle Sauti, your speech is sweet, rightly accented and delivered. It gives us pleasure. You speak like your father. Your father was always ready to oblige us. Tell us the story as your father told it." (16.2-3)

Thereby, Shaunaka wipes out whatever slight Sauti might have suffered when, at their first encounter, he had voiced implicitly some doubts about his mastery of the Purānas compared to his father (*Pauloma* 5.1-2). Appeased, Sauti proceeds to narrate the full version, running to 33 sections incorporating the Churning of the Ocean, the story of Garuda, Parikshit's incurring the mortal curse, his son Janamejaya's performance of the snake-sacrifice in revenge, Āstīka's birth and his success in saving the snake-race. After all, what could move a raconteur more than an appeal that praised his delivery and equated him with his father, the famous horripilator Lomaharshana, he who made the very hairs of the body stand on end with delight!

Thus motivated, Sauti narrates the birth of Garuda and his snake-cousins in just twenty verses and proceeds to the wager between Vinatā and Kadrū over the divine horse Uchchhaihshravas, the Indian Pegasus, "born from the ocean churned for *amrita*". Here is yet another irresistible bait dangled before Shaunaka, but slipped in with such artful artlessness that the reader passes it by till he is brought up short by Shaunaka's abrupt—and inevitable—interruption:

> "Why and where did the gods churn the ocean for nectar, out of which, as you say, this lithe and lustrous horse was born?" asked Shaunaka. (17.4)

Sauti responds with a long and brilliant account of this pivotal episode of Indian mythology.

After this, Sauti concentrates exclusively on the story of Garuda with only two digressions: the wrath of the Sun-god who wants to destroy all creation and the story of Vibhāvasu and Supratīka, two quarrelling brothers turned into elephant and tortoise, who serve a worthy cause by quenching Garuda's hunger and providing him adequate energy to wrest *amrita* from the gods to free his mother from bondage to her co-wife. Incidentally, we also get to know why snakes have forked tongues.

The *Parvasangraha* describes the *Āstīka* as *lomaharshana*, a word that has no satisfactory equivalent in English ('exquisite', as Prof. Lal renders it, just describes one aspect). Literally, it means the type of story that makes one's hair stand on end with delight-and-horror. This means that the *Āstīka* is not only lyrically exquisite but also highly imaginative, even horripilatory, in parts.

Lyrical it is beyond question: witness the lovely descriptions of Meru, the hymn to the glory of Garuda, the exquisite vignette of the Alamba trees and the Edenesque isle of snakes, to mention only a few. The transcreation of the Meru passage is possibly the finest achievement. Its superiority over other translations in English becomes clear if we compare van Buitenen's version:

Van Buitenen: "There is an all-surpassing mountain that blazes like a pile of fire and casts forth the splendour of the sun with its golden glowing peaks—Mount Meru."

Lal: "There is a mountain called Meru,
a flaming heap
of splendour.
Sunlight falls on it
and scatters
at the summit. . . .
It cannot be measured:
men of adharma
cannot come near it. . . .
Mind cannot
conceive of it." (17.5-6, 8)

What indescribable archetypal memories does it not stir deep within the psyche of the Indian reader! To quote from Prof. Lal's Preface to fascicule 5:

> 'The Buddhist Sumeru, the Greek Olympus, the Hebrew Mount Zion are all Meru prototypes. Meru has geographical, literary, symbolic, mythic and theological radiations of meaning. One's imagination wings back to the *Rāmāyana* where Sītā's necklace blowing against Ravana's dark forehead is described as "stars set against the crown of Meru."'

Another such archetypal myth is that of ambrosia being churned out of the ocean by the *Devas* and the *Asuras,* followed by a titanic war for possession of *amrita.* To the discerning reader it offers an insight into Hindu cosmogony: without the participation of the *Asuras* the nectar of immortality cannot be obtained. For, the gods cannot churn the ocean by themselves. Etymologically, too, *Asura* is a word with more than one meaning: both "a-sura" (anti-god) and "as-ura" (bright, energetic, strong). In other words, they are not necessarily evil. In the Vedas, Indra and Varuna are often addressed as *Asura,* the chief god. Interestingly, the chief of the Assyrian pantheon was Asshur, while their anti-divine forces were the Devas, a fact on which the renowned Hindi novelist Acharya Chatursen Shastri has woven his fascinating *Vayam Rakshāmah,* positing a clash between the two off-shoots of the Aryans in Mesopotamia and the Land of the Five Rivers.

Prof. Lal calls Meru "Hinduism's Garden of Eden". Theologically this is indisputable; but from the literary viewpoint, it is the isle of serpents that is more Eden-like:

> "Fragrant forests
> Washed by waves
> Echoing with birdsong . . .
> Fresh-water lakes
> Scented with
> Incense-breathing breezes . . .
> Beautiful forests

Filled with honey drunk bees . . .
Enchanting, lovely, soothing, holy. . . . "
(*Shlokas* 3-9, section 27)

"Incense-breathing breezes" and "echoing with bird-song" evoke *Paradise Lost, Book IV* immediately.

But the *Āstīka* is not just lyrical. As mentioned earlier, it is also highly imaginative and even horripilatory at places: "The *Āstīka* is a roaring *parva,*" writes Prof. Lal in his Preface to fascicule 6, "its *shlokas* constantly reverberating with the splendid fury of ocean storms and lightning flashing over giant sea-waves. . . . Vyāsa here deliberately underplayed terrestrial precision, letting his epic imagination soar to create an archetypal ocean." The description of the ocean that Vinatā and Kadrū pass by while going to see Ucchaihshravas is frighteningly-delightful (*romaharshana*):

"Roaring with the voices
Of invisible sea-animals;
Breeder of whirlpools;
Terror-striking creature;
Rolling high with winds
Of storm and anger;
Dancing with wave-
uplifted hands;
Heaving endlessly with
Moon-produced billows; . . .
Thousands of rival rivers
Rushing for its love—
They saw. Always full,
Always wave-dancing;
Reverberating with the roars
of makaras and timis—
They saw; space-vast,
Unfathomable reservoir." (*Shlokas* 8-10, 16-17, section 21)

It is, indeed, a singularly successful attempt at communicating the sense of billowing, monstrous waves, yet without any hint of chaotic movement, by using a mixture of dactyls and anapaests, rising and falling rhythms, within a four-line verse-form of controlled precision. The epic idiom of Vyāsa has been brilliantly transcreated. Here, for comparison, is the K.M. Ganguli rendering:

> "It is dark, terrible with the sound of aquatic creatures, tremendously roaring, and full of deep whirl-pools. It is an object of terror to all creatures. Moved by the winds blowing from its shores and heaving high, agitated and disturbed, it seems to dance everywhere with uplifted hands represented by its surges. . . . And they saw that unto it rushed mighty rivers by thousands with proud gait, like amorous competitors, each eager for meeting it, forestalling the others. And they saw that it was always full, and always dancing in its waves. And they saw that it was deep and abounding with fierce whales and makaras. And it resounded constantly with the terrible sounds of aquatic creatures. And they saw that it was vast, and wide as the expanse of space, unfathomable, and limitless, and the grand reservoir of water."

The vast gulf separating translation from transcreation is self-evident.

Lyricism, high-imagination and horripilation, however, are by no means the only qualities of the *Āstīka*: humour is present too in rare and subtle touches. There is the delicate Brahmin-baiting in section 28, *shlokas* 10, 12:

> "The Brahmin will stick in your throat
> like a fish-hook,
> The Brahmin will burn your liver
> like flaming charcoal. . . .
> You can tell a good Brahmin as one whom your stomach won't digest."

Hardly complimentary, gastronomically speaking!

There is also the amusing episode of the Vālakhilyas, a race of sixty thousand Tom-Thumb sages, engaged in penance while hanging upside-down from an Alamba tree. The branch snaps under the weight of Garuda and,

> "Before it hit the ground, Garuda caught it. He gazed in wonder at the giant bough and at the cluster of Vālakhilya rishis hanging head downwards from it." (30.2)

But these pygmies are the most austere of sages and woe betide him who dares to mock them, as Indra found out to his sore distress. Indra, carrying a mountain-size load of sacred wood for Kashyapa's *yajña*, comes across

> "some thumb-sized rishis carrying a single stalk of palasha. Poor rishis, starved to shadow-thinness; great was their distress when they fell in a dent in the path made by a cow's hoof." (31. 8-9)

Indra laughed, as anyone in such a situation would have done, and that tactless laughter resulted in his ignominious defeat at the hands of Garuda, born because of these thumbkin sages' curse.

There is also the hymn to Garuda, (23.16-28), interesting not only because of its majestic chanting, but also for the amusing sidelights it offers. Blinded by the splendour of the new-born Garuda, the gods mistake him for Agni, who sets them right. Then, *from a distance* the mighty gods pray to Garuda, pleading with him to restrain his blinding brightness. In the process, they unhesitatingly attribute to him epithets reserved only for the Most High, *viz.* Rishi, Prajāpati, Parameshthi, Indra, Vishnu, Brahmā, Agni, Vāyu, Truth above all Truths, All-that-was-not-and-all-that-is, etc. Out to gain succour through flattery, they go the whole hog. Yet, ironically, this is obviously lip-service which serves them ill, because soon we find the gods fruitlessly fighting Garuda and Indra futilely launching his *vajra* against one whom they have themselves described as "unconquerable protector" (*shloka* 19) and "unconquerably puissant" (*shloka* 23). Garuda, unfortunately for them, fully lives up to their fulsome praise and utterly routs them. Bitter are the fruits of glib flattery, especially when indulged in by the gods themselves.

Sauti begins his history of Āstīka with a singularly arresting image of the Yāyāvara (nomad) manes hanging head downwards in a cave from a grass rope being gnawed away by a rat. As they explain in the forty-fifth chapter where Sauti comes back to this story in greater detail, the rat is time gnawing away at the only thread by which the manes are hanging: Jaratkāru, their sole surviving descendant. Even that thread is half gnawed through because he is engrossed in ascesis instead of fulfilling his duties to his ancestors by begetting a son to continue the lineage and offer oblations to the manes, rescuing them from the foul hell into which they are about to be precipitated, to be followed soon by the wretch Jaratkāru if he continues to remain a witless celibate "who cultivates yoga, but lacks prudence and compassion" (45.27). These doomed spirits uncompromisingly enunciate that all their vigorous ascesis is of no use now, for the merit they have acquired dwindles away unless there is progeny to carry on the tradition.

"We who have the means
are like wretches who have none;
Shining stranger, friend,
who are you who weeps for us?
Who are you, Brahmin,
standing so near us,
Shining stranger,
why do weep for us?"

The plangent sorrow drawn out in these last six lines from the terse epigrammatic statement of an almost existential predicament is a splendid achievement of transcreation.

Hence the notorious dictum *putrārthe kriyate bhāryā* (the intention of getting a wife is to have a son) which turned women into mere wombs. That is precisely how Jaratkāru uses his wife, callously deserting her on the flimsiest excuse (she woke him up lest he should miss the hour for evening worship) once she is pregnant.

This particular image is repeated in the *Vana Parva,* chapter

96, where Agastya comes across his manes suspended head downwards in a hole and they explain that this is a result of his vow of celibacy. Being a sage of greater prowess than Jaratkāru, he does not have to search for a bride and face refusal because of his old age. He simply creates Lopāmudrā by putting together the best and the most beautiful portions of all beings on earth. The symbol also recurs in Vidura's discourse to Dhritarashtra after the war is over in the tale of the man-in-the-well that travelled to the West to become the parable of Barlaam and Josaphat.

Jaratkāru's predicament is only partially hinted at here: he travels the world over but fails to find a wife, not only because of his old age and poverty, but because of the peculiar conditions he lays down: she must be a virgin with the same name as his and must be pressed upon him as alms. The reason is interesting. We come across numerous instances where even kings bestow their daughters on sages, but these are always famous *rishis* with established hermitages. Here we have an ascetic who is a wanderer (*yāyāvara*), making his home at the place he reaches at dusk, with no following. Not a very engaging candidate as a prospective son-in-law!

Jaratkāru is also singularly hard-hearted and it requires some persuasion by his suffering ancestors before he agrees to break his vow of celibacy. He minces no words in making it painfully clear to his pleading manes that he is making a great sacrifice purely for their sake and not because he desires either wife or wealth. For him, the two seem to go together, since without the latter he cannot get the former; hence the pre-condition of the bride being gifted as alms.

Sauti proceeds to relate that Vāsuki offered his sister, also named Jaratkāru, to the ever-wandering sage who accepted her. And in the second *shloka* of chapter 15 Sauti slyly mentioned that the snake-king did this in order to neutralise the curse of Kadrū, the snake-mother, dooming all her progeny to death at Janamejaya's sacrifice, prompting Shaunaka to beg for the entire story in detail. Sauti rounds off the chapter by assuring his listeners that the son born of this union, Āstīka, duly discharged his debts to his manes by having progeny and that, thanks to Āstīka's birth, Jaratkāru also "went to the heaven of his ancestors"

(15.10). Agastya, on the other hand, voluntarily gave up his body after having a son and was caught up among the stars, instead of joining his no-longer-suspended ancestors.

6

The Āstīka Parva-II

Amrita, The Apple of Eris

We now come to myth which, along with that of Creation, constitutes the core of Indian Mythology: the Churning of the Ocean and the strife it occasions between the gods and the titans. Closely linked to this is the account of Garuda's tremendous prowess: the only hero who shrugs of Indra's infallible *vajra*, considers himself Vishnu's equal and gains immortality free from old age and disease without partaking of the ambrosia he is carrying. *Amritamanthana*, Garuda-Nāga strife and the bringing-of-*amrita* are recurring motifs in the Purānas and the epics, with parallels even in the Vedas which, after all, the *Mahābhārata* claims to paraphrase.

Sauti's narrative interweaves, characteristically, *amritamanthana, devāsura* war and Garuda's story, occupying sections 16 to 34 of the *Āstīka* sub-*parva*. Sauti starts off with the birth of the Nāgas and of Aruna and Garuda, whose internecine strife is prefigured in the rivalry between their mothers, Kadrū and Vinatā. Offered a boon each by their husband Kashyapa, the progenitor of all living beings, their choice parallels the Gāndhārī-Kuntī episode much later. Kadrū asks for a thousand snakes as her children, while Vinatā prays for two sons excelling Kadrū's children in every way. Their husband agrees, much to their delight.

Both of them deliver eggs: a thousand from Kadrū and two from Vinatā (Edgar Rice Burroughs would have been thrilled to come across evidence of such Martian oviparous traits). Gāndhārī, similarly, delivers a lump of flesh that Vyāsa divides into a hundred parts and stores in vats till they grow into a hundred sons. The same is the case with Sagara's queen Sumati, where the sage Aurva comes to the rescue in similar fashion. Kuntī, on the other hand, obtains three sons from the gods, and Mādrī two. Like these Nāgas and Vinatā's sons, the Pāndavas and the Kauravas are born enemies. The parallel is quite deliberate, starting with the fact that many of the major Nāgas share names with the Kauravas. As Danielle Feller Jatavallabhula (1997) notes, "In both instances we have one set of numerous and wicked brothers, and one of virtuous ones, who are limited in number ... in the end the 'good' brothers eliminate the 'bad' ones ... in a sacrifice ... in Janamejaya's *sarpa-sattra* and ... in the *rana-yajña*". There is yet another parallel in that the Garuda-Nāga enmity reflects the eternal strife between good and evil, the Devas and Asuras, who reincarnate as the Pāndavas and Kauravas to replicate this cosmic conflict on earth. In this manner, the very occasion of the recitation of the epic—the *sarpa-sattra*—is linked with happenings at the beginning of the world. Even the holocaust of the snakes is a consequence of Kadrū's curse in those distant times. Thus the epic narrative assumes a cosmic dimension with distinct Vedic echoes, reinforcing the *Mahābhārata*'s claim to be the fifth *Veda*.

Kadrū's snakes are hatched after five hundred years and Vinatā, out of impatience and jealousy (like Gāndhārī), breaks one of her own eggs to find a half-formed child who curses her to be a slave. This half-formed child departs to the heavens to become the charioteer of the sun. This theme of the malformed child is repeated with Jarāsandha and with Bhagiratha, one born in two halves, the other as a lump of flesh without a skeletal structure. It seems to be an adjunct of the thematic pattern in the epics regarding problems faced by kings in engendering successors to the throne.

After this *shloka* 21 there two *shlokas* which do not find place in the Bhandarkar critical edition but which deserve a place in any translation of the epic because of the lovely mini-myth they embody:

"When darkness-destroying, mighty Sūrya arose, he saw this pink son of Vinatā as resplendent as himself, shining with vitality. Impressed, Sūrya made him his charioteer and this son of Vinatā became immortal when he stepped into the chariot of the all-illuminating, infinitely powerful Sūrya."

How attractively it amplifies the bare:

"He is the charioteer of the sun, O Brahmins,
Named Aruna, seen early in the morning." (*Shlokas* 22-23)

Finally, Garuda is born and flies off to search for food.

Section 17 once again shows us how skilfully Sauti titillates the curiosity of his audience. He could have stopped short after mentioning that Kadrū and Vinatā saw Uchchaihshravas, the celestial horse and decided on a wager. But he prefers deliberately to draw attention to the horse by devoting two *Shlokas* to it, mentioning that it was "born from the ocean churned for amrita". Naturally, we find Shaunaka promptly rising to the bait and wanting to know, "Why and where did the gods churn the ocean for nectar, out of which, as you say, this lithe and lustrous horse was born?" (17.4)

Thus we are brought to *amritamanthana*, with Sauti immediately panning away from the Garuda story to a breath-taking view of

"a mountain called Meru,
a flaming heap
of splendour.
Sunlight falls on it
and scatters
at the summit
It is golden: it glitters:" (17.5)

This is a deliberate device to take the narrative on to a completely different and much higher plane, far above such matters as sorrowing manes hanging upside-down from grass ropes and ladies concerned over delayed hatching of eggs they have laid. The narration is now kept outside mundane time and place. For, it is on Mount Meru, which "mind cannot conceive of", that the gods meet in search of *amrita*. Notice how the transcreation conveys this sense of timelessness and of a problem far-removed from what has been the centre of interest till now:

> "It has stood high
> for countless ages:
> and once
> a gathering of gods
> met on its summit
> for consultation.
> They came in search
> of amrita,
> these strict-vowed gods." (17.9-10)

They are advised by Nārāyana, through Brahmā, to churn the ocean, obtain precious herbs and gems, after which ambrosia will emerge. In *shloka* 11 Nārāyana specifically describes the ocean as *kalashah*, i.e. "jar of curd", which is not translated either by Prof. Lal or by K.M. Ganguli. Only van Buitenen renders it with disastrously prosy accuracy as "The bucket of the Ocean". The description is very important because it provides the key to the understanding of this myth in Vedic terms: here is Vyāsa's popularised version of the Vedic Mystery of Soma-extraction.

In the *Sama Veda (Uttara)*, Soma is said to reside in the *samudra* (X.11.3), which is also termed *kalasha* (V.2-3), and is also described as rushing to the *samudra* with a roar (VII.4-1). Soma is pressed out with stones called *adri* which also means "mountain", and after being pressed out into the vessel (*samudra*) it *ascends* to the celestial regions, (*Rig Veda*, IX.40-2). Similarly, here we have Mount Mandara being used as the churning-rod to churn the ocean like a jar of curd for bringing up nectar, just as butter is produced from such churning.

The identification of Soma with *amrita* being clear, it becomes quite obvious how the receptacle housing it (*samudra*) was interpreted in the sense of the terrestrial sea. Similarly, the original sense of *adri* (pressing-stones) being forgotten, they would be thought of as *giri* (mountain), leading to the concept of the terrestrial ocean being churned with a mountain as churning-rod. Further, in *shloka* 19 we find, "A great roar from the whirling ocean churned by the gods and anti-gods, like clouds roaring at the dissolution of the world." This recalls the *Sama Veda* X.11.3 where Soma is said to reside inside the *samudra* and to make a terrible noise there. Further, *shloka* 28 says, "And gradually the milky waters of the churned ocean mixed with juices and resins, produced ghee." In the *Rig Veda* (IX.82.1) we have the idea of the birthplace of Soma (*yoni*) as being full of ghee. Finally, we have the juices and gums of different trees being crushed in the churning and mingling with the *samudra*, drinking which the gods become immortal:

> "the juices and resins of the different trees mingled with the ocean's waters.
> The gods drank the waters mixed with liquid essence of gold and nectar-propertied rasas, and became immortal." (18.26-27)

In the Soma-extraction process, the juice was mixed with milk in the *Soma-kalasha* (*samudra*) and it is significant that the gods are spoken of having become immortal by drinking the milky waters fortified with medicinal resins etc. The identification of this with Soma/*amrita* is quite clear. It is also significant that, according to the Vedas, Soma is hidden in the mountain (*girishtah, Rig Veda* IX.62-64) and from there it comes to the *kalasha*, which is *samudra*, on being pressed out. In Sauti's narrative, too, it is the minerals and herbs of the mountain that are crushed and run down to mingle with the milky sea to produce nectar.

These parallels, however, do not end here. In *shloka* 25 we find, "Then Indra, Lord of the gods, drenched the burning mountain with heavy showers." In the *Rig Veda* we find frequent references to Indra shattering the mountains to release the celestial waters and then placing the sun in the skies. Again, Soma is said to generate the heavenly luminaries after mixing with water (RV.IX.42.1). Similarly, here the churning produces Lakshmī, Vāruṇī, Soma, Uchchaihshravas and the Kaustubha gem, all of which proceed to the gods along the path of Āditya the sun (*shloka* 18.38). This is a re-iteration of the Rigvedic idea of the emergence of the heavenly bodies, particularly the sun, after Indra releases the celestial streams (RV. I.9-113).

Yet another parallelism is seen with respect to *shloka* 23: "Numberless fires from tre es grazing each other, blazed, making Mandara, like a black cloud, dazzle with lightning flashes." This detail of fire being produced by the churning is not mentioned in the *Bhāgavata* and *Vishnu* Purāna accounts. Indra quenches this fire by rain. Later we find Garuda quenching the fire encircling Soma/ *amrita* (32.23-25). Dange notes that in the *Jaiminīya Brāhmana* 1.287, Soma is also described as protected by fire-altars *(dhishnyas)*.

The point sought to be made through these parallels is that in this epic narrative Vyāsa is truly repeating Vedic truths and rituals in a form easily accessible to all and sundry.

However, strangely enough, Shaunaka never asks Sauti the obvious question: why were the gods confabulating so anxiously about obtaining *amrita*? It is in the *Vishnu Purāna* that the reason is given. The sage Durvāsā had once presented Indra with a divinely scented garland that the god placed on the head of his elephant, Airāvata. The rutting elephant threw down the garland and trampled on it, infuriating the sage to curse Indra with loss of prosperity (Lakshmī). Thereupon the gods sought Vishnu's advice and he counselled them to churn the milky ocean to recover Lakshmī.

The order in which the ocean throws up various products as well as their number differs from Purāna to Purāna. The *Mahābhārata* enumerates ten products: moon, Lakshmī, wine, white horse, Kaustubha jewel, Pārijāta tree, Surabhi the wish-fulfilling cow, Dhanvantari with *amrita*, Airāvata and Poison (the Bhandarkar edition drops the *shlokas* relating to Pārijāta, Surabhi, Airāvata and poison, and the entire Nīlakantha episode). The *Rāmāyana* has Dhanvantari, Apsarās, Vārunī, Uchchaihshravas, Kaustubha and Amrita. The *Agni Purāna* drops the moon, the horse and the elephant but adds the Apsarās, to have eight products. The *Vishnu Purāna* drops the horse, the elephant and Kaustubha and has the rest in the following order: Surabhi, Vārunī, Pārijāta, Apsarās, Moon, Poison (taken by the Nāgas), Dhanvantari with *Amrita*, and finally Shrī, in consonance

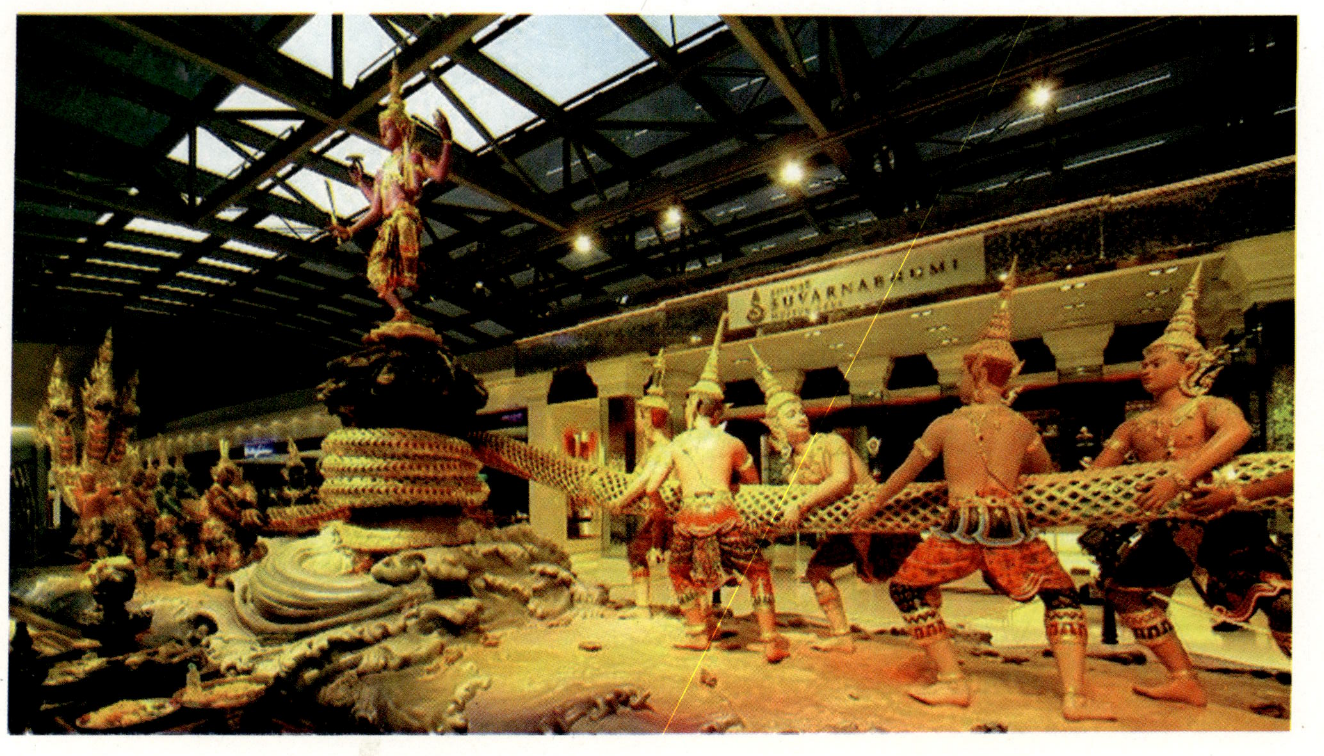

"Churning of the Ocean, Suvarnabhumi Airport, Thailand"

with its *raison d'etre* for the churning. The *Bhāgavata* replaces Moon by the Apsarās, the rest remaining the same.

There is also a slight difference between the *Mahābhārata* and the *Purānas* concerning the base on which Mount Mandara pivots. Here the gods approach the tortoise-king for the purpose. In the *Purānas* (e.g. *Vishnu, Bhāgavata)* it is Vishnu himself who incarnates as the *kūrma avatāra* for the sake of creating *amrita.* The entire account can be interpreted as a mythological an analogue of the basic creation myth where creation is said to begin with a lotus-stem growing out of Vishnu's navel as he lies immersed in yogic quiescence. In this case the Mandara mountain would be the lotus-stalk, standing on Vishnu-kūrma, and the act of creating *amrita* is one in which Vāsuki's help is essential. It is on Vāsuki/Ananta that Vishnu reclines while resting on the waters of dissolution, *pralaya.* In the *Mahābhārata* it is Ananta who is sent to uproot Mandara when the gods fail to do so, so that the churning can proceed. These three: tortoise (we recall that it is Kashyapa, which means tortoise, who is the father of all living things), serpent and the mountain are closely linked in the creative process. The serpent, particularly, is known in Indian mythology as a bringer of rain (*shlokas* 16-17 describe smoky vapour issuing from Vāsuki's mouth from the friction turning into rain clouds) and as a fertility symbol, much as in Egyptian Mythology.[1]

There is a curious problem posed by the transcreation of *shloka* 15. The gods hold Vāsuki by the tail and the Asuras by his head, "And Ananta, representing Nārāyana, periodically raised and lowered the snake's hood." Van Buitenen goes one better and translates: "Ananta stayed with the blessed Nārāyana and kept on raising the Snake's head and hurling it down again." Ganguli's version resembles Prof. Lal's. There is a half-*shloka* in the Bengal recension that clarifies the situation. It comes at the end of *shloka* 14 to say that Ananta, being a portion of Nārāyana, was able to bear the friction; and the Asuras seizing Vāsuki's hood and raising it, tugged repeatedly. Here Ananta is a synonym for Vāsuki, and it does away with the absurd picture of his hood being raised and lowered off and on by Ananta to no effect.

It is curious that the gods alone are said to drink the milky waters mixed with resins and gold and thereby become immortal much before *amrita* is churned out (*shloka* 27). The *Asuras* apparently looked on without following suit, possibly befuddled with the noxious vapours emitted from the mouth of Vāsuki that they were holding. Further, despite this immortality, the *Devas* (and not the *Asuras*, the powerful ones) get exhausted and plead with Brahmā to intercede with Nārāyana. Brahmā obliges and Nārāyana augments their energy. The ten 'gems' now appear from the ocean, as described previously.

The really curious fact is that the churning continues even *after* Dhanvantari has appeared with the *amrita*, which was the goal of the operation, till *Kālakūta*, poison, arises

> "like smoke-filled fire
>   and covered the earth.
> The three worlds reeled
>   with the deadly fumes." (*Shlokas* 42-43)

Suddenly Shiva appears and saves creation by drinking the poison at Brahmā's request and holds it in his throat, which turns blue. In the *Rāmāyana* this episode is described in greater detail with Brahmā praying to Shiva at length to intervene. It is significant that Vishnu the preserver is not the rescuer here but Maheshvara, author of the *tāndava nritya* heralding universal dissolution, who appropriately harnesses the destructive forces. In the *Vishnu Purāna*, poison is sixth in the order of emergence from the ocean, and is immediately followed by *amrita* and Shrī. The poison is, quite appropriately, taken by the snakes and there is no mention of its threat to creation or of Mahādeva. In the *Rāmāyana*, it is the *first* product of the churning: for a thousand years the churning goes on fruitlessly till Vāsuki, the churning-rope, can bear it no longer and spews out poison which threatens to engulf creation and requires Shiva's intervention. The appearance of poison is another aspect of the symbol that requires the churning to carried out by the gods and the anti-gods. In the *Bhāgavata Purāna* we find the gods approaching Bali, the *Asura* king, with the request for help in churning the ocean for *amrita*. In other words, the *sāttvika* by itself cannot create. That is why Brahmā, the creative demiurge, is red-complexioned to signify the *rājasika* stimulus. The Devas, *sāttvika-rājasika,* require the help of the *tāmasika-rājasika* Asuras for churning out the secret of life from the waters of creation. It is this indispensable coming together of opposites that is again symbolised in the poison appearing after or before the *amrita.* Here is the force of destruction that is as necessary for evolution as the elixir of immortality, because without change (which is another name for destruction) no evolution can take place. This is beautifully fused into a single composite symbol in the figure of the great deity Mahādeva, who is at once Shiva the benevolent and Rudra the destroyer.

We are now faced with a unique episode: Vishnu assuming the form of a bewitching woman to entrance the anti-gods into placing the *amrita* in her hands. Presumably, the titans had successfully seized the nectar after they shouted "Ours" (*shloka* 40) the moment it arose from the ocean. There is some confusion in the way the *shlokas* are arranged at this point. *Shloka* 45 has the Asuras full of despair on seeing Shiva's feat and most of the churned-out products going to the Suras. Thereupon they fight with the gods for Lakshmī and *amrita.* Yet *shloka* 46 has Mohinī being given the *amrita* voluntarily by the titans. Again, the *next shloka,* which starts off section 19, describes the titans attacking the gods in full armour, but *shlokas* 2-3 have the gods drinking *amrita* from Vishnu.

To solve this, the Bhandarkar edition omits *shloka* 45—along with *shlokas* 41-44 which relate to Airāvata, the poison and Shiva—and brings us straight from the appearance of *amrita* to the *Mohinī-mūrti.* But this does not explain why the Asuras should suddenly attack the Devas in the very next *shloka* (19.1). It would have been helpful, from the point of view of the narrative, to include a *shloka* that is available in the Bengal recension as the last one of section 18. It runs:

> "Then this *māyā*-manifestation of Nārāyana took the receptacle brimful with *amrita* and made the *daityas* and *danavas* sit in a queue with the *devas*; but she gave amrita only to the *devas* to drink which infuriated the *daityas.*"

Now *shloka* 1 of the next section comes as a natural corollary, as the Asuras rush towards the gods with weapons.

The second *shloka* of section 19 cryptically mentions Nara, with whose help Vishnu succeeds in depriving the Asuras of *amrita* which the gods drink quickly in the prevailing confusion. This is the first reference to the Nara-Nārāyana combination that is represented later in the invincible Krishna-Arjuna pair. The *Purānas* do not give any account of their origin except that they are born of Dharma and Ahimsā and term the pair *rishis*, seers. They are not always synonymous with Vishnu. Of them, Nārāyana is usually the centre of action. In the early *Vāmana Purāna* he produces Urvashī, the loveliest of *apsaras*, by rubbing a mango blossom on his thigh to show his prowess to the *apsaras* sent by Indra to tempt him. According to the late *Kālikā Purāna*, the two were born when Shiva in his Sharabha form split apart the man-lion incarnation Narasimha which was out of control. The sage Nara was born from the human part and Nārāyana from the lion portion. We also come across in the *Shānti Parva* (sections 343-6) Nārada's account of his meeting these mighty *rishis* at Badarikāshrama in the course of his peregrinations, when they show him the way to meet the Supreme Purusha at Shvetadvīpa.

The *Mohinī-mūrti* episode, occupying merely two *shlokas* in the *Mahābhārata*, has been elaborated by Kashiram Das in his Bengali re-telling of the epic into one of the most amusing and meaningful incidents of this *kāvya*. According to him, all beholders fall unconscious on seeing the incomparable beauty and Shiva, on regaining consciousness, runs after her, arms outstretched, begging for an embrace. She rejects his advances with a meticulous description of his old age, filthy, smelly body and laughs at his lack of self-control. Shiva threatens to kill himself and promises to leave family, fruits of penance, everything, for the sake of Mohinī. After this complete surrender, Mohinī embraces him and the Ardhanārīshvara manifestation results. It is a lovely myth depicting the union of Purusha and Prakriti (for Yogamāyā resides within Vishnu) and showing the profundity of Kashiram Das' assimilation of the philosophical implications of the incidents recounted in Vyāsa's revelatory epic. From this union, according to other *Purānas*, comes the South Indian deity Ayyappan.

Before the *Devāsura* war breaks out, there is the Rāhu incident, another mini-myth, serving to explain the eclipses of the sun and the moon. This incident is not mentioned in the *Vishnu Purāna*. Because Vishnu severed Rāhu's head before the *amrita* passed below his throat, the head remains immortal and periodically avenges himself on the Sun and the Moon, who had informed Vishnu of Rāhu's intrusion into the *Devas*' ranks, by swallowing them. As he has no body, the sun and the moon slip out through his throat. Interestingly enough, in the account of the children of Kashyapa, both Surya and Chandra are the names of two *Dānavas* born of Danu. They might very well have changed sides, as Lakshmi does, moving from the anti-gods to the gods in Purānik lore!

With the slaying of Rāhu, Vishnu abandons his Mohinī disguise and slaughters the titans *en masse*. He is identified with the god Nārāyana here in *shloka* 20 and we find Nara using the divine bow, whereupon Vishnu summons the discus Sudarshana. The parallel with Krishna with his discus and Arjuna with Gāndīva in the Khandava episode is, perhaps, deliberate. The routed *Asuras* flee into the bowels of the earth and the sea, and the *amrita* is handed over to "the diamed god" (Indra) for safekeeping, whence we will find Garuda spiriting it away. It is to destroy these demons that the gods first approach Agastya to drink the sea dry and later Arjuna to kill them. We also have a reference to Indra as the "slayer of Vala" in this last *shloka*, a valuable allusion to the Vedic myth of Indra destroying Vala to release the pent-up waters of creation or the herds of light taking us back to the *Rig Veda* (I.33) describing the battle of Indra and his human allies against the *Dasyus*. The parallels are too close to be accidental. There we have Indra searching out the fleeing *Dasyus* and striking off their heads, casting them out of heaven and earth, cleaving the mountains with his *vajra* to release the celestial waters. Similarly, here it is Nara who crumbles the mountains flung by the anti-gods with gold-tipped arrows. Just as the *Dasyus* were unable to escape Indra because he had set the Sun's rays to spy them out, so Nārāyana's resplendent discus (an obvious sun-image) annihilates the titans, driving some into the earth's bowels and others into the salt sea. This nectar of immortality is, indeed, the Indian counterpart of Greek mythology's apple of Eris that precipitated the ten-year long Trojan War.

The allusion to the *Dānavas* fleeing to the salt sea is not merely a poetic commonplace. It recurs in the *Vana Parva* section 105, where the Pāndavas hear the story of Agastya who was approached by the gods to drink the ocean dry in order to expose the Kālakeya Asuras who were terrorising the gods through guerrilla warfare and resting securely under the sea. Soon, thereafter, Arjuna destroys them during his trip to heaven.

Section 20 abruptly brings us back to Shaunaka's query in section 15, *shloka* 4 about *amritamanthana* and the birth of the celestial horse. From the empyrean heights, Sauti zooms down to two wives laying a wager over the colour of this horse. It is Kadrū who asks Vinatā to tell her what colour is Uchchaihshravas. Ironically Vinatā, asserting it is white, suggests they bet on it. Kadrū promptly agrees and lays down the penalty: the loser will become the other's slave. A clue to Vinatā's apparent over-confidence is offered by the meaning of her co-wife's name. The etymology of Kadrū is uncertain, but the prefix has a pejorative meaning and indicates that she was deformed in some manner. Dange[2] points out that according to the *Suparnādhyāya* (III.5.4) she is blind in one eye having lost it from the smoke of offerings (1.2.2). It is therefore natural for her to resort to deceit in order to win a wager depending on sharpness of eyesight, and equally inevitable on part of Vinatā to be so confident of her better eyes as to suggest a bet, confident that she will win. Her name also means "tawny", the colour of the earth with which snakes are closely associated. Another of her names is Surasā, fragrant like the earth, reinforcing the chthonic element and reminding us of her appearance to test Hanumān as he crosses the sea to Lankā in the *Rāmāyana*. The *Aitareya Brāhmana* (5.23) addresses the earth as *sarparājñi,* queen of snakes. Vinatā, the bent one, denotes the curved dome of the sky. Garuda's mother is named 'Suparnī' in the *Suparnādhyāya* and is identified with the heavens (*Dyauh*) while Kadrū is the earth, and they are said to compete over their looks. The *Taittirīya Samhitā* (VI.1.6.1 ff.), the *Kāthaka Samhitā* (XXIII.10) and the *Aitareya Brāhmana* (III.25) elaborate this stating that Kadrū defeated Suparnī in the contest and bade her bring Soma from the third heaven in order to set herself free. This passage also specifically identifies the one with earth and the other with the heavens and the metres *(chhanda)* with *sauparneyas* (children of Suparnī). The two older offspring, Jagatī and Trishtubh metres, fail, but the youngest, Gāyatrī, successfully brings the Soma taking "two pressings in her feet and one in the beak," just like Garuda carrying the tortoise and the elephant in his claws and the tree-branch in his beak.[3] But of this more later.

Just as the Dhārtarāshtras deprive the Pāndavas of their birthright through deceit, turning them into second-class citizens and finally force them into exile, similarly Vinatā and Garuda become the slaves of Kadrū and her snake-sons through a trick. Again, like Garuda, it is the Pāndavas who achieve victory finally: the biter is bit.

Kadrū, in order to win the wager and avoid becoming Vinatā's slave, commands her snake progeny to cover the horse's tail so that it appears black. Some of them who refuse to be a party to the deceit are cursed by Kadrū to be burnt alive in Janamejaya's *yajña.* Thus the narrative once again skilfully links up with the epic recital's beginnings. There is a passage of three *shlokas* in the Bengal recension, suspected to be an interpolation, which has Karkotaka pleading with his mother to have patience and placating her with the promise to enter the horse's body and cover its tail with his own black body. That is why not all the snakes were destroyed. In the *Pauloma* 11.18 it is quite categorically stated, "In the past, at the destructive snake-sacrifice of Janamejaya, *some* terrified snakes were rescued by a Brahmin." It is even clearer in 38.10 where Brahmā, sanctioning this curse, explains to the gods: "Snakes who are evil-minded are doomed. The virtuous will survive."

What is more interesting is that Kadrū's curse becomes effective only when Brahmā, noticing the vast numbers of the snakes and desiring the welfare of other creatures, concurs. Again, when Indra offers to grant Garuda a boon and he asks that the snakes should become his food, this has to be sanctioned by Vishnu (34.11-15). This is quite extraordinary, because nowhere else in the epics or *Purānas* do we come across such soliciting for ratification by higher authorities. Possibly, the fate of the snakes was of paramount concern to the trinity since two of them, Shiva and Vishnu, are intimately linked with them. We find a confirmation of this in the *Udyoga Parva*, sections 103-105, where Vishnu intervenes to save the Nāga prince Sumukha from Garuda and drastically humbles him when he rebels.

Two other instances of the peculiar nature of curses occur. One is in the *Paushya shloka* 126, where Uttanka tells King Paushya who has cursed him: "You said I would never be a father because I had declared the food unclean when it wasn't. But it *was* unclean. Your curse, therefore, is futile. I'm convinced of this." In the *Sambhava* sub-*parva* of the *Ādi Parva* (77.18-20) Kacha tells Devayānī, who has cursed him that the *Sanjīvanī vidyā* will be ineffective in his hands, that since she cursed him impelled by desire, though he was faultless, her aim would not be achieved and whomsoever he taught this secret lore would be able to utilise it successfully. Yet, when Kalmāshapāda is cursed for having served human meat to Vashishtha, it takes effect although the king was not in anyway responsible for the offence that had been perpetrated through Vishvāmitra's machinations. It will be noticed that these four episodes are all on a totally different plane from those in which we find curses being prolifically showered by Durvāsā and other sages, in so far as these four incidents relate to a supra-mundane level spatially and temporally belonging to the most ancient times (appropriately in the *ādi Parva*, the Book of the Beginnings).

After praising Kadrū for unwittingly becoming the mouthpiece of Fate and working for the welfare of all creatures, Brahmā summons their father, Kashyapa, and apprises him of what is in store for some of his children, urging him not to grieve as this had been ordained long back.

Brahmā, thereupon, grants Kashyapa poison-neutralising knowledge. This slight detail, not noticed by readers, is significant. In section 50 of the *Āstīka* it is a Kāshyapa Brahmin, i.e. one belonging to Kashyapa's *gotra* (clan) who is stopped by

Takshaka *en route* Parikshit's palace in order to protect him from snake-bite and to resuscitate him if bitten. This is, again, a parallel myth to that of Garuda, also a scion of Kashyapa and having the snakes for his diet. The difference is that where the Kāshyapa Brahmin is bribed by Takshaka not to proceed to save the king, Garuda frees Rāma and Lakshmana from the bondage of the *nāgapāsha*, the noose-of-snakes.

Dange[4] has attempted to interpret the Garuda legend in naturalistic terms by depending on this Kashyapa myth to argue that the Garudas and Nāgas were two warring factions of the same tribe with a snake-totem, practising snake-charming and treatment of snakebite. Vishnu appears to have brought about a reconciliation between them, according to the Sumukha-Garuda story in the *Udyoga parva* where Vishnu keeps the Nāga prince around Garuda's neck to be protected instead of being eaten by him.

Dange also argues that Garuda is a non-Aryan tribal bird-deity who got assimilated after much struggle, as symbolised in the conflict with Indra and the subsequent alliance with Vishnu. It is significant that despite being Kashyapa's son, Garuda and his progeny are not recognised as Brahmins because they indulge in destroying their step-brothers, the Nāgas (*Udyoga Parva*, 101). The story of the Garuda-Nāga rivalry was assimilated not only with the Kadrū-Suparni tale of the *Brāhmanas* but also with the ancient Rigvedic episode of the spiriting away of Soma. This will be discussed in the proper place, when we come to that episode in the epic.

Section 21 is wholly devoted to a superb evocation of the whale-tossed, *makara*-infested, thunderous-waved ocean that Kadrū and Vinatā pass on their way to see the celestial horse. Section 22 begins with a *shloka* that continues the aftermath of Kadrū's curse related in section 20. The snakes decide that disobedience would mean annihilation, while compliance might lead to revocation of the curse. Van Buitenen drops this as interpolated and finds himself unable to explain how Vinatā lost the wager (p. 443). Here is irony, for they do not know that the gods have eagerly sanctioned the curse and Kadr ̆never revokes it. *Shlokas* 5-12 are a somewhat weaker description of the ocean we have already found in the previous section. *Shlokas* 8, 9, 10 are identical with *shlokas* 6, 7, 8 of section 21 and are omitted in the Bhandarkar edition. Prof. Lal does not do so and ensures there is no monotony by couching the *shlokas* in section 22 in prose, toning down the entire description.

The minute details that Vyāsa provides to characterise his characters deserve attention. Kadrū, for instance, is characterised as "swift" (23.1) and speed is her basic feature: she wants a quick reply to her query about the colour of the horse (20.2) and with Durvāsā-like impatience curses her own children. Kashyapa would have had a hard time as her husband! Significantly enough, nowhere is he found living with Kadrū or Vinatā: he grants their wishes and promptly leaves for the forest!

Kadrū wins the wager and enslaves the dejected ("wretched-faced" according to van Buitenen) Vinatā. In the meantime, Garuda is born ("without any help from his mother", says the narrator; is there a sarcastic dig at Vinatā, recalling her disastrous helping out of Aruna?). He is immediately identified with Agni because of his dazzling splendour. This identification fits in with the Rigvedic parallelism, which has been discussed earlier. This is also one of the rare occasions when the epic gives Agni something of the pre-eminent status among the gods that he enjoys in the *Rig Veda*. The other such occasion is the Khāndava-forest conflagration. In the paean of praise that follows (23.16-28) the identification with Agni is extended to include the Sun, and we get the familiar image-structure common to most mythology: Sun-Fire-Eagle-Cloud-Serpent. Garuda, made to carry the snakes on his back, rises towards the sun, scorching them, whereupon Kadrū prays to Indra to intercede. Indra sends clouds and rain to save the *Nāgas* (*nāga* is a synonym for clouds as well). Later he protects Takshaka during the Khāndava conflagration and the snake-holocaust. There are fascinating similarities with Kukulkan, the Mayan Demiurge (a winged-serpent), the Assyrian Asshur (a winged solar disc), the Aztec war-god Huitzilopochtli who has an eagle's beak and a tattoo of two eagles destroying a serpent on his chest and the Egyptian Ra-Harus (hawk).

Section 26 again has an enthusiastic description of a storm at sea. It is clear that the poet who composed sections 20-26 in particular is a different hand from the others in his love for the ocean in its more rough moods as in the Old English poem "Seafarer". Nowhere else in the epics do we come across such lovingly detailed descriptions of the movement of the waters in the sea, not even in the *Rāmāyana* where the sea is being bridged:

> "The myriads of waves produced by the torrential downpour, the constantly-roaring clouds, the flashes of lightning, the violence of the wind—such chaos everywhere!—as if the sky was dancing in madness." (26.4)

Even Indra is addressed by Kadrū as

> "You the high-waved ocean,
> with *timis, makaras,* and other fishes." (25.14)

Vyāsa's masterly touches of detail are again visible in 23.15 where, despite being reassured by Agni, the gods and seers go to Garuda but speak to him "from a distance". How well it conveys their trepidation without wasting any explanatory periphrases!

Section 24 is generally regarded as an interpolation. Luckily, Prof. Lal has not omitted it unlike van Buitenen, and this allows us to savour the added enjoyment of the story of Aruna. It has already been related cryptically in section 16 in a few *shlokas* after *shloka* 21 which have already been referred to. Sauti now dangles the bait once more by making the bare statement that Garuda took Aruna on his back and flew with him to the east, depositing him there "for the Sun had determined to burn the worlds with his fierce rays."

The inevitable query follows, but this time it gives us a terrific jolt, for the questioner is not Shaunaka but *Ruru.* What has happened? It is the narrator's shrewd technique to wake up drowsy listeners, or those whose attention has been wandering. We have to go right back to the end of section 12 where the entire story of Āstīka is enquired of Pramati by his son Ruru, which Sauti is retelling. One could, of course, argue that this is a transmission-mistake and instead of Ruru we should have

"Shaunaka", as Ganguli has done in his translation. The problem is that Prof. Lal makes Sauti reply to Ruru, instead of attributing the answer to Pramati, as in the Bengal recension, which creates an anomaly. The scholar would point out that the very intrusion of Ruru and Pramati all on a sudden, and the complete lack of any connection between this episode and the next section warrants its complete rejection. On that analogy, sections 25-27 should also be omitted because *shloka* 24 of section 17 merely states that the moment he was born, Garuda left his mother and flew in search of food, which comes only in section 28. However, the reader's enjoyment is all the greater from including all these fascinating episodes, whatever the offence to the pedant. Sauti was, after all, entertaining an audience taking a breather from intensive application to ritual sacrifice.

The myth related now is directly linked to the *Amritamanthana* episode of Rāhu's beheading at the instance of Sūrya, as a result of which Rāhu devours him. Sūrya, finding himself alone in his difficulty, deserted by his compeers, retaliates by deciding to burn up all creation. The gods and seers rush to Brahmā who asks Aruna, with his huge resplendent body, to act as a shield by becoming Sūrya's charioteer. Aruna does so and the Sun is veiled by him.

'Vala' in 25.6 is a reference to Indra's piercing of the *Dasyu* Vala in the *Rig Veda* to rescue the celestial herds, or to Indra's rending open of Vala's castle or hole to obtain the hidden treasures. Vala is almost a synonym for Vritra, whom Indra destroys in order to release the pent up celestial waters. Hence he is termed both *Vritrakhada* (destroyer of Vritra) and *valamruja* (breaker of Vala) in the *Rig Veda mandalas* 3, 6 and 10 (e.g. 3.34; 6.39; 10.67). Hence Indra is often called *Vala-vritra-han* (slayer of Vala and Vritra) and *valabhida* (piercer of Vala).

In the very next *shloka* Indra is addressed as 'slayer of Namuchi', another Rigvedic reference to Indra's cutting-off his head with the foam of the waters. The name means 'not letting go', that is, withholding the celestial waters like Vritra and Vala.

In the annotation of 'Purandara' (25.8), another epithet applied by Kadrū to Indra, Prof. Lal explains it as "one of the thousand names of Vishnu". So it is, as also Shiva's and Agni's;

but here it is being applied to Indra and is a one word treasury of myth. In the *Rig Veda* Indra is described as such because he shatters the forts of the Panis and of Vritra. In the epic he rives open Diti's womb, cutting up her embryo into seven pieces to produce the Maruts (*Udyoga parva* 110).

Vasats in 25.15 is the *mantra* with which the sacrificial *ghee* is offered to the gods at the end of each sacred *shloka* and means 'carry up, bear', i.e. requesting the offering to be taken up. Curiously, van Buitenen does not translate the word, but explains it in connection with the *Pauloma* sub-*parva.*

Maināka (21.15) occurs in the *Rāmāyana,* Sundarakānda, where it has been related how mountains had wings at first but used to cause much destruction by their reckless alighting till Indra shore off their wings. Only Maināka, son of Himavant and Menakā, escaped by taking refuge in the ocean with the help of the god Pavana. The mountain is said to be located to the south of Kailāsha.

The only bit that escapes all efforts at annotation is 21.13, where there is a cryptic reference to *rishi* Atri vainly trying for a hundred years to plumb the depths of the ocean. Here is a myth that has been lost in the dark backward and abysm of time.

The seventh fascicule builds up Garuda, concentrating on appeasing his hunger (sections 27-30). It is in the very opening verses of section 27 that we have to acknowledge the immeasurable superiority of the Lal transcreation over even the most modern translation. Here are van Buitenen's and Prof. Lal's renderings for comparison. The Lal transcreation was already in print when van Buitenen published his in 1971:

LAL: "Fragrant forests
Washed by waves
Echoing with birdsong.
Lovely fruit trees
And flowering plants,
Enchanting palaces,
Lotus-filled ponds.
Fresh-water lakes
Scented with

Incense-breathing breezes.
Sandalwood trees
High on Malaya hill,
Shaking in the wind,
Raining down flowers.
And other trees too
Scattering their blossoms
As if welcoming the nāgas
With flowery rain
Beautiful forests
Filled with honeydrunk bees
And dear to the gandharvas,
Ravishing to the sight.
Enchanting, lovely, soothing, holy:
Echoing with birdsong."

VAN BUITENEN: "the island, which was encompassed by the waters of the ocean and resonant with the songs of birds. It was wooded with rows of groves that glistened with fruit and blossoms; lovely villas were laid out and lotus beds. Colourful lakes with tranquil water adorned it, while whiffs of pure breeze that wafted divine fragrances fanned it with cool air. It was lustrous with sandalwood trees that seemed to perfume space and, stirred by the wind, sent forth, a rain of flowers to strew showers of blossoms on the Snakes that dwelled there. It was a holy and lovely island, beloved of Gandharvas and Apsarās, who ever rejoiced in it; and awarble with all kinds of birds."

It is, indeed, a veritable Miltonic Garden of Eden. But the snakes want more, and command Garuda to take them elsewhere. Garuda's response is completely natural: he thinks it over and asks Vinatā why he is supposed to obey the snakes, which means that she has not yet had the courage to tell him of the real situation. Garuda, seeking to free his mother and himself from slavery, is set a typically impossible task, in the folk-tale manner, viz. to obtain *amrita*.

Vinatā designates the *Nishādas*, fisher-folk, as Garuda's food, giving no reason for the peculiar decision. The *Skanda Purāna* (IV.50.64-65) provides one reason: they are cruel people who sustain themselves on others' lives. The *Padma Purāna* (V.44.69) urges Garuda to eat them because they pollute the sacred waters. It is in the *Suparnādhyāya* that some sort of an explanation is given in VIII.16.2-3: the *Nishādas* are a divided nation who do not follow the Vedas, nor perform sacrifices or offer pure food to the gods. A euhemeristic conclusion from this could be that the episode is a symbolic account of the non-Vedic *Nishādas* being destroyed by the Vedic snake-totem tribe represented by Garuda. It is significant that a Brahmin dwells among them with a Nishāda wife, because, according to the *Manu* and *Yājñavalkya Samhitās* (X.8 and I.91), a Nishāda is counted among the sons born of a Shudra woman and a Brahmin, such as Vyāsa himself who, however, acquires the status of a seer.

In the *Padma Purāna* we find a little more detail about the Brahmin: he refuses to come out of Garuda's mouth unless his in-laws and his intimate friends are also allowed to escape. Kashyapa, to whom Garuda turns in distress, allows this. Dange has drawn a parallel between this escape of some Nishādas because of a Brahmin and the tale of Jimutavāhana that Harsha turned into the play *Nāgananda*. Jimutavāhana also saves the Nāgas from Garuda by offering himself in their stead. In the Buddhist Jataka, he is described as a Vidyādhara and a portion of Buddha, i.e. a Bodhisattva. Dange argues that the same folk-tale was used in different times by various communities to glorify themselves. Basically the exploit of a Nāga-hero who saved his people from Garuda, it was modified to a Brahmin/Buddhist protagonist to portray the superiority of Brahmanism/Buddhism. Otherwise, it really has no relevance to the main thread of narrative concerning the winning of *amrita* by Garuda.

Dange, however, misses the sly humour of Vyāsa when he ponderously states that the only reason for the existence of the passage is the glorification of Brahmins. If there is such propaganda, there is also delicious tongue-in-cheek baiting:

"He is the first-born of creatures,
The best of the four castes,

The father, the master, the teacher . . .
You can tell a good Brahmin as one whom your stomach won't digest." (28.7, 12)

Let us not forget that Vyāsa's father had deserted his mother, after forcing himself on her in mid-river, without the slightest compunction.

The destruction of the *Nishādas* is also a motif that recurs later in the *Ādi Parva.* Satyavatī is a fisher-girl who founds a *Nishāda* dynasty through her mixed-caste son Vyāsa, forcing the royal daughters-in-law of Hastināpura to accept impregnation by him. Soon, however, her granddaughter-in-law Kuntī supplants this by her own dynasty through Arjuna. In the process, she drugs and burns alive a Nishāda and her five sons in the house-of-lac at Vāranāvata. Her son Arjuna ensures that the unrivalled Nishāda archer Ekalavya loses his incomparable skill by sacrificing his thumb to Drona in a gruesome *guru dakshinā* while her nephew Krishna kills him.

Garuda's tactics (raising a blinding dust-storm, sucking up water from the ocean and shaking trees and mountains to terrify the Nishādas) are repeated by him when fighting the gods and the serpents guarding the *amrita.* It is, in effect, cyclonic:

"Like terror-stricken birds
scattering in swarms in the sky
when storms shake forests,
So the dust-blinded Nishādas
fled into the wide-open beak
of the terrible snake-eater." (28.19)

On Kashyapa's advice, he seizes the sages who have turned into tortoise and elephant. The story of these two brothers is an exemplary Mitāksharan homily on the dangers of partitioning joint family property (29. 17-20):

"Blinded by greed, many want to divide the family wealth; but this is unwise.
For, as soon as division takes place, they quarrel, blinded by

wealth. Enemies posing as friends come between them,
Exploiting ignorance and selfishness to set brother against
brother. Exposing each other's faults only confirms the
bitterness till the break-up point is reached,
And total ruin overtakes the separated brothers."

The episode is reminiscent of the Gajendra-moksha story in the *Bhāgavata Purāna* (VIII. 5) where the brothers are turned into quarrelling crocodile and elephant. The quarrel can also be interpreted in tribal terms, as by Dange, for the word *nāga* means both serpent and elephant. Again, the tortoise is a synonym for 'Kashyapa', father of the *nāgas*, and thus represents serpents as well. We have, therefore, a conflict between two *Nāga* clans, taking advantage of which yet another faction of theirs, which is superior by virtue of the mastery over poison-lore, achieves domination and supremacy (hence 'devours'). But this type of euhemeristic interpretation does not really lead us very far since both spatially and temporally the incidents cannot be "placed" in order to extract any significant anthropological or socio-historico-cultural inferences. It matters little whether the Nāgas and Garuda are different warring tribes, or factions of the same tribe, as Dange triumphantly claims to have proved. Accepting his claim as proven, so what? How does it enrich our reading of the epic?

It is, indeed, pleasurable to go on to the lovely description of the breathtakingly beautiful Alamba trees:

"Tall, stately trees
With gold and silver fruits
And gem-studded branches
Washed by the waters of the sea;" (29.41)

It is here that we are introduced to the unforgettable thumbkin *rishis*, the Vālakhilyas, hanging bat-like, upside down from one of the branches that snaps as Garuda alights on it. Their genesis is a peculiar one. In the *Vāmana Purāna* section 53, the *Shiva Purāna* section 49 and the *Skanda Purāna* I-26 and VII-19, it is stated that during the marriage of Shiva and Pārvatī, Brahmā got excited by the bride's beauty and ejaculated. Afraid and ashamed, he rubbed the semen into the ground, and the eighty eight thousand rishis were born from this. Nārada shunted them off to Gandhamādana mountain where they performed severe penance and became famous as followers of the Sun, representing its rays.

It is these seers who name the king of the birds 'Garuda' because he carries great burdens, but the etymology is not satisfactory at all. The word for weight, 'guru', cannot turn into 'garu'. According to Monier Williams, the name derives from 'gṛ' and 'udac' meaning 'swallower'.

Garuda is relieved of the *rishis* appropriately on Gandhamādana (where Nārada had sent them according to the *Shiva Purāna*) and disposes of the tree-branch in a snow-bound region with results that form one of the loveliest passages in the epic, beautifully transcreated:

> "The mountain cliffs, glittering as if with gems and gold, shook loose and rolled down on all sides.
> The falling bough levelled many trees whose dark-green branches, studded with golden flowers, looked like lightning-charged clouds.
>
> They fell on the ground,
> these gold-bright trees,
> They were coloured with the gold
> of mountain minerals,
> They looked like the long rays
> of the flaming sun." (30.27-29)

And so Garuda flies to attack the gods and take away the *amrita* single-handed. Ill omens terrify the celestials. Warned by Brihaspati, they draw up in battle array with terrible weapons clad in dazzling armour, and await Garuda.

The sheer pace of the narration, with its account of ominous portents terrifying gods, and their assumption of defensive array, sweeps along Sauti's audience in an irresistible surge:

"Thunder-voiced winds blew; thousands of meteors fell,
The cloudless sky roared;
The god of gods dripped blood;
The garlands on the necks of the gods
Faded into lustrelessness;
Masses of clouds vomited bloody rain;
Wind-blown dust dimmed the gods' crowns. . . .

Unmatched in strength, vigour and radiance, capable of disintegrating the cities of the anti-gods, displaying shapes as refulgent as blazing fires, resolved to guard the amrita, the gods waited.

They stood there, the gods,
Hundreds of thousands of maces
Fitted with iron spokes
  Shone
    On the battlefield!
The battlefield shone
  Like a second sky
    Radiant with sunlight." (30. 35-38, 51-52)

Characteristically, Sauti has slipped in a new thread while holding Shaunaka spellbound with the epic rhythm of his recital. He uses Brihaspati, mentor of the gods, for introducing this new element: the birth of Garuda out of the penance of the Vālakhilyas for chastising Indra, and endowing him with invincibility and chameleon-potency. The moment Sauti stops for taking breath with *shloka* 52, Shaunaka eagerly interrupts with a veritable shower of queries with which section 31 begins.

Section 31 deals with the story of the mystery behind Garuda's birth: it was not the simple granting of Vinatā's wish as stated earlier in section 16. Questioned by Shaunaka as to why the Vālakhilyas come into the picture, how Indra is at fault and what made Garuda invincible, Sauti proceeds to supply the answers "in brief". Upamanyu repeats this story to Krishna in the *Anushāsana Parva* (14.91-92) where we find the cryptic statement that, being insulted by Indra, the Vālakhilyas invoked Rudra through severe penance who granted them the boon of creating Garuda to deprive Indra of ambrosia. In Sauti's account, the furious *rishis* invoke the formation of a second Indra out of the sacrificial fire. There is a close resemblance to the myth of Tvashtā similarly creating Vritra to avenge the death of Trishirā at Indra's hands (*Udyoga Parva,* sections 9-10) and of Chyavana creating Mada when Indra attacks him for having given Soma to the Ashivinikumāras. The parallelism extends further when we find that Kashyapa persuades the sages to modify their intention in order to create a king of birds instead of gods. In the Vritra myth it is a wrongly pronounced invocation that produces a creature to be killed by Indra instead of killing him. Tvashtā, like Kashyapa, is also 'Prajāpati'. In the *Padma Purāna* (*Bhūmi Khanda,* section 23), Vritra is produced by Prajāpati Kashyapa by plucking out a hair on hearing that Indra has slain his son Vala, born of Danu. In the *Mahābhārata,* too, we find Vritra mentioned as one of the sons of Danu and Kashyapa (*Sambhava parva* 65.33). In the *Suparnādhyāya* there is no intercession by Kashyapa on Indra's behalf. Instead, on being approached by the furious Vālakhilyas, (Kashyapa is called *Tarakshya* here) he accepts half of their ascetic energy to create a bird to crush Indra's pride. It is also significant that Kashyapa should reassure Indra that he will have two brothers (Indra is his son by Aditi) to help him: "They will do you no harm, Purandara", he adds (*shloka* 31). That epithet is pregnant with implications: in the similar case of the birth of the Maruts, Indra had entered Diti's womb and carved up the embryo, fearing that it would supplant him. In the present case it is the mother herself, Vinatā, who is responsible for a similar deformation of one child, Aruna. In Diti's case, too, Indra's success is due to the mother's carelessness in not observing Kashyapa's injunction concerning purity. Vinatā also violates Kashyapa's warning that she must guard the foetus carefully and patiently.

The *Rig Veda* (III.48.4) has Indra forcibly seizing Soma from Tvashtri (identified with the Purānik Tvashtā) and quaffing it while the *Taittirīya Samhitā* (II.4.12) and the *Shatapatha Brāhmana* (I.6.3) relate how Tvashtri, whose son had been killed by Indra, refused to allow Indra to help at his Ṣoma *yajña,* whereupon Indra forcibly drank the Soma. The identification of Tvashtri with Indra's father is also very likely in the Rigvedic passage where he is said to crush his father and drink Soma (IV.18). There are obvious links with Kronos castrating Uranos and Zeus deposing him in turn, both being myths of sons destroying fathers, the former being sky, rain and lightning gods.

However, the other conclusion that these parallelisms hint at is that Garuda is a Vritra image---this time a successful one— since he does defeat Indra and is not killed by him thereafter. Instead, a reconciliation is effected. This will happen with Krishna and Arjuna vis-ë-vis Indra. Further, Indra wins back the Soma from Garuda, just as he liberates the celestial waters by slaying Vritra, albeit with Garuda's permission.

Yet, again, Garuda is an Indra-image right from the incident of his birth as a second Indra, willed by the insulted Vālakhilyas. In the *Rig Veda* (IV.26) Vāmadeva takes the form of Shyena, also called Suparna, and gets Soma for Manu. This Shyena is described as a bird who foils the attempts of the guardians of Soma to snatch the nectar away, exactly as Garuda does. Further, seeing him escaping, the archer Krishānu shoots him and a feather falls (IV.27.3) which is a precise analogue of Indra hitting Garuda with the *vajra* and Garuda honouring him by letting a feather drop. Both Garuda and Indra make the mountains tremble with their prowess. As Danielle Feller Jatavallabhula has pointed out, the theft of soma is a famous exploit that is mentioned in books 1,3, 4, 6, 8, 9 and 10 of the *Rig Veda,* the *Taittirīya, Maitrayānīya* and *Kāthaka Samhitās* and the *Shatapatha, Aitareya* and *Tāndya Brāhmanas.*[11] In the *Suparnādhyāya* Garuda is said to shatter nine times ninety fortresses of Indra to capture Soma, paralleling India's destruction of Sambara's forts of equal number (*Rig Veda* II.11; 14.6 and IV.26.3, where this is attributed to Vāmadeva). Significantly, in one passage of *Rig Veda* (IV.30.3), the gods fight Indra presumably as he tries to seize Soma. This is again paralleled in the gods fighting Garuda for the same cause. According to Macdonell's *Vedic Mythology* (p.151), the *Kāthaka Samhitā* has Indra himself in the form of an eagle capturing Soma. In Teutonic myths we have Odin as an eagle. Macdonell has pointed out the mythological parallels with the *Avesta,* where Verethraghna (the Vedic *Vritra-hana,* i.e. Indra) assuming the form of Varaghna, swiftest of birds, takes the Soma or mead to the gods; and with Zeus' eagle bringing ambrosia. The parallel motifs in the Garuda account argue in favour of a careful attempt to incorporate a non-Vedic deity into the Purānik pantheon. This is all the more substantiated in the *Suparnādhyāya* (XV.30.5) where Garuda asks Indra that he may enter the Vedas and the Brahmanas meditate upon him.

The episode, then, becomes an integral part of the surprisingly large corpus of Nāga myth that occupies so important a place in the very beginning of the epic, without having any obvious link with the Pāndava-Dhārtarāshtra story. A faint link is provided by Kuntī's maternal grandfather āryaka being a *Nāga* who rescues Bhīma and by Arjuna begetting a son on the *Nāga* princess Ulpī who resurrects him after he has been slain by his son Babhruvāhana. The *Mahābhārata* bears the impression of powerful formative forces exercised both by the Bhrigu clan (Shaunaka is the immediate audience) and the *Nāga* tribes in shaping the epic as we have it.

To recapitulate, Kashyapa reassures Indra, admonishing him not to take seers lightly, and so Aruna and Garuda are born to Vinatā. Aruna becomes the "forerunner of the Sun" and is described as "deformed" (*vikalānga*).

We now come to section 32 and the account of the Garuda-Deva battle that is narrated with gruesome relish. In the very beginning, however, we face another parallel with the Indra-Soma Rig Vedic account. First to meet Garuda is Bhaumana, a synonym for Vishvakarmā and Tvashtri, described as guarding *amrita* (as Tvashtri guarded Soma) and he is immediately slain by Garuda (as Tvashtri was by Indra). The gods who are mentioned as the first to flee in the four cardinal directions are the group of Ādityas, Vasus, Rudras, Nāsatya (Ashvins) Gandharvas and Sādhyas who are usually invoked together in the Veda, particularly the first three. The Sādhyas are associated with Brahmā, the Ashvins with *amrita* as its guardians, while the ādityas are gods of heaven, the Rudras of air and Vasus of earth (*vide* the *Shatapatha Brāhmana*) the implication being Garuda's omnipotence. Peculiarly, none of the major gods, except Indra and Vāyu, come into the picture at all in this battle. The majority of those mentioned cannot be traced elsewhere in Indian mythology and are nothing more than mere names to us: Ashvakranda, Renuka, Tapana, Krarthana, Uluka, Shvasana Nimishena, Praruja, Shvasana and Praliha—another instance of lost myths.

Having routed them, Garuda replicates another feat of Indra who destroyed nine times ninety fortresses of *dasyus*: seeing the *amrita* ringed with fire, he drinks up river waters with "ninety times ninety mouths" (32.24) and quenches the flames. The next encounter is with

> "A razor-sharp wheel, revolving endlessly.
> A blazing, sun-bright wheel! A fearful spectre!" (33.2-3)

This is a clear sun-image, which becomes significant when we recall that in the *Rig Veda* the sun is spoken of as a bird named *garutmat* and *suparna*. Agni, in the *Rig Veda*, is similarly designated and Garuda has been hymned by the gods and sages precisely in terms of Agni's resplendence in section 3. The indication is, therefore, of a solar myth, reinforced by the subsequent encounter with Vishnu, who himself is yet another solar symbol, and the carrying of the Vālakhilyas who reside in the sun's chariot.

Garuda's trick in reducing himself to miniscule size to enter through the wheel is duplicated in the *Rāmāyana* where we find Hanumān doing this to enter Lankā and to escape from Surasā (Kadrū), the snake-mother. Vāyu's duplication of Garuda's feat in dispelling the dust storm also prefigures the Hanumān-Vāyu nexus. Garuda's strategy of battle is faithfully ornithological: he invariably whips up a dust storm for gods and snakes alike; then, as they are blinded, rips them up. Taking up the *amrita*, Garuda speeds away and meets Vishnu. This encounter is recounted by Garuda himself in the *Anushāsana Parva*, section 13.43-52. Here we find Garuda being brought up to Vishnu's level by his offering him a boon. Vishnu, as usual, gets the upper hand by asking Garuda to bear him, while keeping his own word by placing Garuda on his flagstaff so that he remains above the god in terms of his desired boon.

The next episode is the futile flinging of India's thunderbolt, thus raising Garuda above Indra. Garuda says that he will pay due respect to the *rishi* from whose bones the *vajra* was fashioned, to the weapon itself, and to Indra as god of hundred sacrifices and allows a feather of his to fall, so that the weapon may not lose its reputation for infallibility. It is the beauty of this feather that leads to his being named Suparna, the lovely-plumaged one. In section 113 of the *Udyoga Parva* we find Garuda bereft of his wings because of Shāndili's curse, having mocked her penance, and being granted even more beautiful plumage and called "Suparna" by her on praying to be forgiven.

In the *Skanda Purāna* (IV.50-105) it is not Indra but Vishnu who fights Garuda as he flies away with the Soma, while in the *Suparnādhyāya* there is no such incident. Garuda is also the only creature to be granted immortality without hesitation. The parallel case of Hanumān comes to mind: as a child, after being wounded by Indra's *vajra*, he is blessed with life as long as that of Brahmā and invulnerability. The difference is that Garuda shrewdly asks for and obtains the boon that he should not grow old and should be free from disease too, thus avoiding a Tithonus-like shrivelling. Hanumān, however, does age, as we find in his encounter with Bhīma in the *Vana Parva*.

In the next section, 34, Garuda expatiates on his limitless prowess at Indra's request. The shrewd Purandara is always seeking to find some loophole in any enemy of comparable strength and is left stunned when, on asking the extent of Garuda's strength, he finds out that it is incomprehensible:

"The earth, her mountains, forests, oceans,
You too,
I can carry on a single feather of mine.
So listen to me Indra!
All the worlds put together,
Untiringly
I can carry, all moving and
unmoving things—
Such is my strength!" (34.4-5)

As he had done with Vritra, and Namuchi, Indra pledges

friendship with Garuda and immediately requests him to return the Soma for

> "Those to whom
> you give it
> will always be our enemies." (34.8)

He is hardly being truthful (which is quite typical, of course) since at Kadrū's prayer he has already succoured the *Nāgas* once from the sun's rays, strives to repeat this in vain in the Khāndava conflagration and later protects Takshaka during the snake-sacrifice. We now find deceit countered by deceit. The snakes who had enslaved Garuda through false means are hoist with their own petard when, as they perform their ablutions, the Soma is spirited away by Indra with Garuda's permission. In return, he grants Garuda the boon of feeding on the snakes. Garuda accepts Indra's boon, though he says there is nothing he cannot do (possibly in order not to have to fight the gods every time when attacking the nāgas), which is ratified by Vishnu who has both Garuda and Shesha as his vehicles.

After *shloka* 16 there is abrupt transition: Garuda is said to hurry to his mother, but in *shloka* 17 he is speaking to the snakes. Some account of the mother-son meeting after this unique feat would surely be natural. This is available in two *shlokas* that are dropped from the Critical Edition:

> 'Humbly addressing his mother, Garuda said, "Faithful-vowed mother, I have brought this nectar from the abode of the gods. Tell me what I should do now." Vinatā replied, "Son, I am pleased with your exploit. May you be immortal, ever youthful and beloved of the gods." '

Thereafter, Garuda asks the snakes to lick the *amrita* placed on the *kusha*-grass after their ablution, and gets them to release his mother from slavery. There is a shrewd bit of serpentine character analysis in a *shloka* coming after *shloka* 21 that has been omitted. Having completed their ablutions, this *shloka* says, "Vying enviously with one another to enjoy the Soma, they rushed towards it shouting 'I first', 'I first'."

Meanwhile, Indra has spirited away the nectar and, guessing counter-deception (the text uses this precise phrase), they lick the blades of grass, which slits their tongues into two. Here is a bit of folklore on how snakes got their divided tongues and speak in two opposing ways simultaneously, hence symbolising deception. It also explains why the *kusha* grass is held sacred having served as the seat for Soma. Thereafter Garuda and his mother happily pass their days in the forest merrily devouring snakes.

The chicanery going hand in hand with Soma is a motif that occurs not only here but begins to appear from the very birth of *amrita* when Vishnu tricks the *Asuras* into surrendering the nectar. There we have Rāhu attempting a counter-deceit by slipping in amongst the gods while they drink the *amrita* and, like the *Nāgas,* he is deprived of it when it is almost his. The gods, thereafter, rout the *Asuras* just as Garuda pounces on the snakes after obtaining *amrita.* In the later myth of Kacha and Devayānī the motif recurs. The gods send Kacha to Shukra, the Asura-preceptor, in order to learn the *sanjīvani vidyā* (knowledge of resurrection). The *Asuras* seek to delude Devayānī by repeatedly killing Kacha, but fail. He succeeds by winning the heart of Devayānī but, having obtained the secret, he deludes her and returns to the gods who are now able to defeat the *Asuras.*

The other recurrent motif is the conjunction of contrary forces for producing or obtaining the nectar of immortality. It is necessary for the gods to have the assistance of the anti-gods for churning the ocean. Further, it is their priest whom they approach for the secret lore of immortality. Similarly, the rivalry between the nāgas and Garuda is the cause of the *soma-harana.*

Prof. Lal's preface to this particular fascicule (vol. 8) raises some issues. He accuses Vyāsa of "fuzziness" in the concluding episode about the snakes getting forked tongues, and remarks, "though the story is pretty, Vyāsa, usually so careful in details, here nods." Prof. Lal fails to find any reason for the snakes licking the *kusha* grass when the *amrita* has been spirited away. The answer is provided in *shloka* 24: the power of *amrita* is so penetrating that the grass became sacred merely because it was placed on it, even though for a few moments. The snakes desperately licked the grass hoping-against-hope that some *amrita* might have oozed through the vessel onto the blades. It is remarkably true to human, if not to snake psychology.

In the preface there is a reference to "Indra's somewhat too neat acceptance of Garuda's might by making Garuda his 'flagstaff bird' ", which is cited as an instance of "hurried writing". However, the pact is not with Indra but with Vishnu. The "facile way" in which Indra's pact with Garuda regarding restoration of nectar occurs is merely a counterpoint to the manner in which Kadrū wins the wager.

Prof. Lal also complains that "the narrator, having so far developed his tale with such rewarding minutiae, decides to end it with such lackadaisical abruptness." But in *shloka* 4 of section 31 Sauti clearly tells Shaunaka: "I will give you the story *in brief*." Indeed, Vyāsa is very rarely to be caught nodding, and the critic must be doubly careful of his own ground before launching an attack. Modifying Alexander Pope on Homer we might say:

"Those oft are stratagems which errors seem
Nor is it Vyāsa nods, but we that dream!"

References

1. For interpretation of the myth on the lines of Vedic psychological experiences see *Secret of the Mahābhārata* (Bhattacharya, 1984).
2. S.A. Dange (1997) pp. 108-9.
3. Ibid. pp. 59-62.
4. Dange (1997) pp. 18-36.
5. D.F. Jatavallabhula, "The theft of Soma" in Brockington & Schreiner (1999), pp. 206-7.

7

The Āstīka Parva-III
The Snake Holocaust

Beginning with section 35, there is a shift in narrative perspective. As part of the constant to-and-fro oscillatory narrative technique of Sauti, there is a reversion to section 16, back to the birth of the snakes and the bird-sons of Vinatā. Shaunaka complains that Sauti has given them the names of Vinatā's sons, but not those of Kadrū, hastily adding that he wants to know only the important ones. Sauti proceeds to satisfy Shaunaka's curiosity with a tedious roll call over 11 *shlokas* preceded and succeeded by sly tongue-in-cheek comments:

> "I think it will bore you, the names of all the snakes. But let me give you just the chief ones. . . . I do not want to be tedious, so I omit the rest." (4, 16)

In this long list there are some names which recur in the epic: Takshaka, already familiar since the *Paushya*, will reappear a little later to assassinate Parikshit and then be saved during the snake-sacrifice; Karkotaka plays a crucial role in restoring the fortunes of the exiled king Nala; Kāliya is well-known as the snake worsted by Krishna as a child; āryaka is a maternal ancestor of Bhīma who gifts him jars of nectar when he is poisoned and thrown into the river by Duryodhana; Nahusha is Yayāti's father who becomes a python as a result of Agastya's curse and holds Bhīma powerless in his coils till his questions are answered by Yudhishthira; Vritra is Indra's main enemy in the Vedas imprisoning the celestial waters; Kauravya is the grandfather of Sumukha who is saved by Vishnu from Garuda, and the father of Ulūpī, Arjuna's wife. In the snake-sacrifice it is the families of Vāsuki, Takshaka, Airāvata, Kauravya and Dhritarāshtra who are mentioned specifically as the chief ones consumed. Dhritarāshtra and Kauravya suggest the coming Pāndava-Kuru confrontation and presage their destruction in the war-as-sacrifice.

In this section, Vyāsa creates another myth central to Indian mythology: that of Shesha encircling the world. Abjuring his kin, disgusted with their jealousy of Vinatā and Garuda, Shesha engages in severe ascesis. He asks for nothing from Brahmā except constant devotion to virtue. This steadfastness leads Brahmā to make him responsible for holding the world steady (i.e. adherence to virtue alone upholds the world). Shesha does this by entering the earth through a passage underneath it and holding it up. Brahmā compares this act of Shesha to feats that he himself and Valavid alone are capable of. Valavid is another name for Indra, referring to his piercing the *Asura* Vala with his thunderbolt. There is a cryptic reference following this to Garuda being made the helper of Shesha, thereby effecting a reconciliation between the two opposing forces and hinting that stability depends on such harmonious co-existence. It is significant that in the *Mahābhārata* it is Shesha who uproots Mount Mandara for the Churning of the Ocean, while in the *Bhāgavata* it is Garuda who carries it to the site when the gods and titans fail. As vehicles of Vishnu, they have assumed inter-changeable roles, and the Preserver resolves in himself their mortal enmity. The *Vishnu Purāna* refers to Shesha as the *tāmasik* form of Vishnu, named Ādishesha or Ananta, supporting the world in Pātāla and creating Rudra at the time of universal dissolution for destroying creation.

At the end of section 36 there is a 26th *shloka* omitted by Prof. Lal:

> "When Ananta had thus left, powerful Vāsuki was consecrated king by the Nāgas as Vāsava (Indra) had been by the gods."

We now come to a fascinating snake-meet where all hoods are put together for finding a way out of the terrible curse pronounced by Kadrū. Again, this parallels the conclave of the Kauravas following the marriage of Draupadī with the Pāndavas. What follows is very entertaining and is well summed-up in Prof. Lal's Preface: "The most naive and ludicrous suggestions are put forward, including a mass invasion and indiscriminate biting of all present at the sacrifice: Others want to go disguised as Brahmins in a manoeuvre vaguely resembling a messy cloak-and-dagger operation. One group, a shrewd one, knows that the chief priest is the kingpin, and suggests biting him—the humour here is mixed with elegant satire on the infernal mumbo-jumbo attending most Hindu rituals." There is another group of snakes, the virtuous and kind ones, who provide Sauti an occasion for inserting a didactic verse:

> "It does no one credit to kill Brahmins.
> That work succeeds
>   behind which is dharma;
> The use of adharma
>   defeats its own ends." (37. 19-20)

Others suggest turning into clouds to extinguish the sacrificial fire, thus looking forward to the memorable Agni-Indra confrontation in the Khāndava forest-burning episode later. Some snakes hark back to the *Soma-harana* feat of Garuda, doubtless still smarting from having been fooled out of the *amrita*, and want to steal the vessel containing Soma, without which no *yajña* can be performed. This same group would like to organise a mass biting of all at the sacrifice or defile the sacred victuals with excrement, which recalls Rāma's monkey-army doing precisely this to prevent Indrajit from completing his sacrifice, thus engineering his death at Lakshmana's hands. The real cloak-and-dagger suggestion is made by another group that suggests kidnapping the king and imprisoning him, or simply sending him the way of his father, by biting him to death. Vāsuki finds himself at a loss when asked to decide which course to adopt, "for praise or blame will fall entirely on me regardless of what I decide to do." (37.34)

In the midst of this welter of conflicting ideas, we come across in *shloka* 9 a reference to one of the most important myths: the gods resolving to recover Agni hiding in a cave. This takes us back to the *Pauloma* where, aggrieved with Bhrigu's unjustified curse, Agni hides himself till placated by Brahmā's modification assuring his purity despite having to consume all things as cursed to do. This story has its origin in the *Rig Veda* (X.51; III.124) and is repeated in the *Anushāsana Parva,* 85.

The solution is proffered by Elapatra (section 38) to counter doom by a pre-ordained rescue, for

"There is no refuge
When Fate dictates;
When Fate dictates,
Fate alone heals.
O best among snakes,
Our fear is Fate.
Let fate be our refuge." (38.3-4)

He relates the assurance given by Brahmā to the gods when this curse was pronounced that the virtuous snakes would be saved by Vāsuki's sister's son, Āstīka. This is repeated again in section 39, this time by Brahmā direct to Vāsuki who approaches him after the churning of the ocean is over, with the gods interceding on his behalf for having been of great help in that enterprise. The manner in which Elapatra reports Brahmā's words contains a shrewd hit at those frenetic advisers of Vāsuki who were all for a universal biting campaign:

"The always-biting snakes,
Snakes who bite for little reason,
Snakes who are evil-minded,
Are doomed. Only those who follow dharma
Will survive." (38.10)

The group that uttered the didacticism of *shloka* 20 of section 37 must have felt vastly reassured! Of course it is Brahmā who is behind all this:

"I myself, O Immortals, was the one who inspired the

speech that the snake Elapatra at the time recounted to him." (39. 8)

The manner in which Āstīka ultimately stops the snake-sacrifice looks back to the suggestion put forward in 37.25 that the snakes should disguise themselves as the king's *ritvijas* and demand, by way of *dakshinā*, that the sacrifice be stopped. It is through such unobtrusive means that the rhapsode holds together the massive corpus of the epic.

Section 40 begins with a curious and delightful bit of Sauti-baiting by Shaunaka. Right from the beginning Shaunaka has been somewhat doubtful of Sauti's excellence and accuracy as a reteller of the Purānas, and has repeatedly drawn comparisons between him and his illustrious father Lomaharshana, asking whether Sauti knows all the details as he did. Having been the victim of a number of sly hits in the preceding sections, Shaunaka tries to hit back here by posing an etymological problem to Sauti: the origin of Jaratkāru's name. Sauti explains that the word is a compound of 'decay' *(jara)* and 'huge' *(kāru)*, referring to the huge body of the rishi, which he "consumed" or decayed, through penances. Shaunaka, "unable to find fault," smiles in approbation and admits it was a test that Sauti has passed: "You are right. I have heard all this before." (40.5-6)

Sauti passes on abruptly to the account of Parikshit being cursed by Shringi. Parikshit is described in *shloka* 11 as the equal of Pāndu in his addiction to hunting. The analogy being drawn is between Pāndu incurring a curse while hunting, and Parikshit's similar situation. The next simile is that of Rudra's search for the sacrificial deer in heaven, a vedic myth. It recalls King Arthur's pursuit of the mysterious white hart that can never be caught. However, like the elfin golden deer that dooms Sītā, the deer chased by Parikshit also disappears ominously. The exhausted king comes across an unnamed sage who, like Upamanyu in the *Paushya*, is drinking the froth trickling from mouths of suckling calves. Addressing the sage, Parikshit gets no reply and, in anger, drapes a dead snake round his neck. Thereby he invites a curse from the sage's choleric son Shringi who worships Brahmā.

Hearing of the incident, Shringi curses Parikshit to be bitten

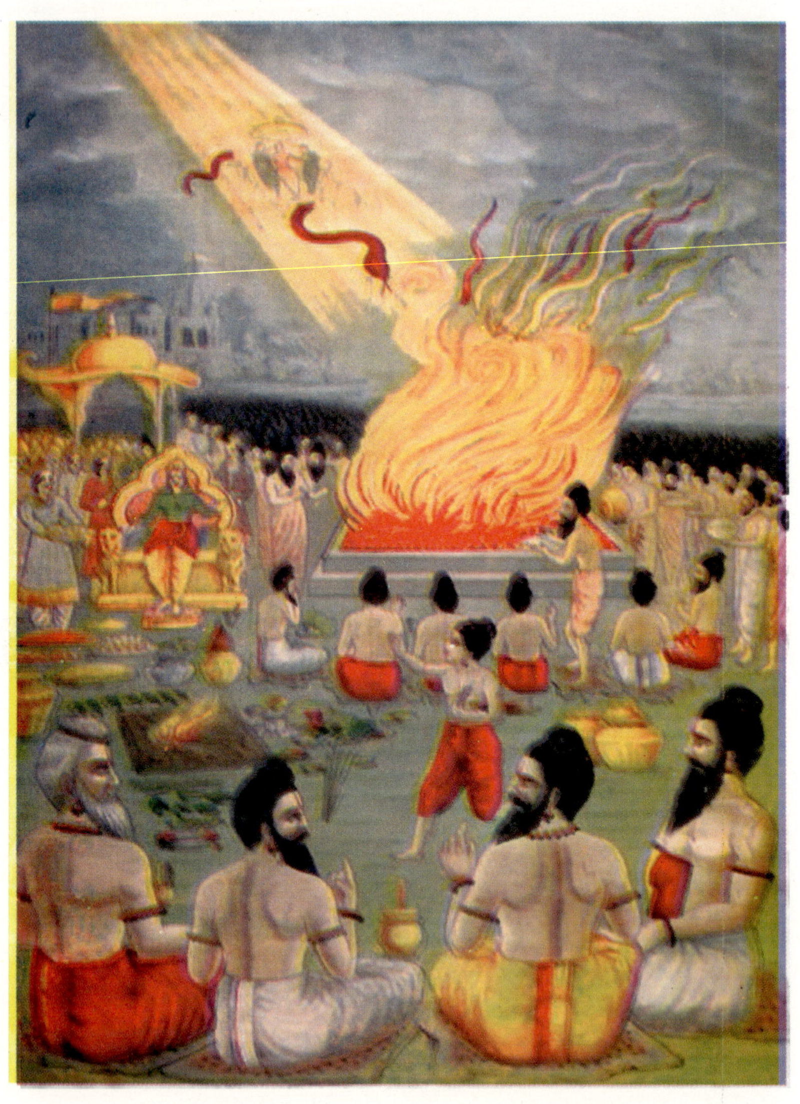

"Janamejaya's Snake Sacrifice"

to death by Takshaka and meets his father. His anger again flares up on seeing his father bearing the dead snake and he announces what he has done. The sage Samīka's response is literally an icy douche:

"If you destroy Dharma, my son,
  Dharma will destroy you.
If the king will not protect us,
  great sorrows will be ours." (41.22)

He advises that the faults of the protector should always be overlooked, for "the king establishes Dharma, and Dharma brings *svarga* in its wake" (*shloka* 29). He also quotes Manu: "The worth of one ruler of the destinies of men is equal to ten Brahmins loaded with Vedic wisdom" (41.31). For the first time we come across a direct statement placing Brahmins below Kshatriyas in social status. It is significant that this belongs to the post-Kurukshetra period, when the hey-day of Brahmin superiority is at an end and the Kali Yuga has begun. Samīka continues to pacify and advise his son in memorable verses:

"But even a grown-up son can benefit from a father's advice. . . .
You are very young, and your need for advice is therefore greater. . . .
But destroy your anger
Before your anger destroys you. . . .
Be serene; be patient; learn to forgive;
This will lead to success.
Goodness belongs to patient forgiveness,
In this world and the next.
Be self-controlled.
Learn to be patient and forgive.
Patient forgiveness will give you worlds
Beyond the reach even of Brahmā." (42.4, 5, 7, 9-10)

He apprises Parikshit of his fate and the king locks himself up in a palace raised on a single pillar, surrounded by physicians and mantra-adepts. We are now introduced to Kāshyapa, who has mastered the poison-lore and can nullify snake-poison. He proceeds to the palace to cure the king. The links with Garuda have been mentioned earlier in the confrontation between Takshaka and Kāshyapa. The remarkable degeneration in ethical values can be seen in Kāshyapa agreeing not to proceed to Parikshit on receiving adequate gold from Takshaka. The mercenary Brahmin is already on the epic scene, and Prof. Lal brings out Takshaka's sarcasm excellently.

> "But tell me, rishi, what do you hope to gain by going there? What wealth, O ascetically wealthy one?" (43.12)

Alas, Takshaka's sarcasm falls on deaf ears and rhino-hide.

In 42.39 Parikshit is referred to as "the sole representative of the Pāndavas", not just as "the immeasurably powerful Kuru monarch". It is a significant phrase because of the implications it carries of the tragic futility of the fratricidal war which left but a single descendent to the Pāndavas for enjoying the ashen fruīt of their stupendous efforts. Why Arjuna's son Babhruvāhana was not enthroned in Hastināpura remains a puzzle.

Takshaka secures entrance into the guarded residence of the king by deceit: snakes in the guise of hermits carry fruits to the king, in one of which he conceals himself in the shape of a worm. The king picks this particular fruit and what follows has excited some controversy among scholars. Parikshit says:

> "The sun is setting.
> I am no more afraid.
> May this insect, who is Takshaka,
> bite me.
> May my missdeeds
> be forgiven,
> May the words of the rishi
> become true." (43.32-33)

Saying this, smiling, he places the insect on his neck, drawing a parallel with his placing of the dead snake around Samīka's.

Does he say all this in a spirit of levity and defiance, on the assumption that the seventh day is ending and he is still alive? In that case, the references to the rishi are sarcastic and mocking, hence accompanied by smiles. The references to being impelled by fate and being in a trance (verse 34) would then seem to imply that by such mockery the king was inviting disaster. On the other hand, this could be a sincere expression of penitence and calm acceptance of what has been decreed, nobly desiring to honour the infallibility of a sage's word. This would be in consonance with 42.26:

> "King Parikshit, who looked like a god, would not have grieved so much for his own death as he did for his behaviour toward the rishi."

It is in the death-scenes that Vyāsa excels over and over again: Bhīshma on the bed of arrows; Karna, weaponless, struck down; Drona decapitated in meditation; Duryodhana grimly clutching on to life till the heads of Pāndava-progeny arrive. Here, too, the sheer poetry of Takshaka's leave-taking is breathtaking because of the use of an utterly unexpected image. Very sensitively Prof. Lal shifts to verse for *shloka* 3, section 44:

> "Even as they ran, they saw the king of snakes, marvellous Takshaka
> Flash through the sky
> Like a streak of lotus,
> Like the vermilion line
> In the centre-parting
> Of a girl's thick, dark hair."

Janamejaya is crowned king and in due course marries Vapushtama, daughter of the king of Kāshi. The Pāndava power had shrunk, for the king agrees only "after making enquiries." Janamejaya and Vapushtamā are compared to Pururavas and Urvashī, whose love has been immortalised by Kalidasa and not retold in the epic—a peculiar omission of a story that is so prominent in the Purānas and specially in the *Shatapatha*

Brāhmana. In the epic there is merely a reference to Pururavas' children by Urvashī in the genealogy of the lunar dynasty, as cryptic as the Rigvedic mention of Urvashī spending four autumns with mortals, and her being besought to return by Pururavas, around which the story was developed in great romantic detail later.

With section 45 Sauti veers back to the story of the 'huge-waster' Jaratkāru whom he had abruptly left controlling his sexual drive and roaming around without a thought of marriage in *shloka* 9 of section 40. The point-counterpoint has been well established: Vāsuki is eager to marry off his sister to Jaratkāru who has no intentions of getting married at all. So his ancestors have to step in, dangling head downwards from a grass rope, all of whose strands save one have been frayed and a rat is nibbling away at this solitary frail link which alone prevents them from being precipitated into a hole. This frail strand is the celibate Jaratkāru, being gnawed away by the Time-rat:

"Steadily devouring
   the wretch Jaratkāru
who cultivates yoga, but
   lacks prudence and compassion. . . .
When we plummet deep down
   with all our relatives,
Devoured by Time,
   Jaratkāru too will fall in hell
For tapasya, sacrifices,
   and other holy acts,
Are inferior, O child,
   to having a son." (45.27, 29-31)

The episode has been related already in sections 13-15 and is repeated here in somewhat greater detail, particularly the begetting of Āstīka. Jaratkāru's conditions for marriage are that the bride must be given to him as alms, *she must be willing,* he will not have to support her and she must be his namesake. Owing to his old age, he is unable to find a willing bride. The days of puissant sages are past, to whom kings were only too glad to gift their daughters. Finally, in desperation, he cries out his conditions in a forest, announcing himself as a rishi "devoted to awesome austerities" asked by his sorrowing ancestors to beget a son. The watchers posted by Vāsuki in 39.14 immediately report this and he bestows his sister on him, assuming the responsibility for maintaining her. Even then Jaratkāru adds a further rider, leaving a way open for himself: he will leave her if she displeases him. She proves herself to be a better wife, having greater regard for preservation of his dharma than for her own happiness, than Jaratkāru a dutiful husband. She awakens him so that he may not miss the time for the evening prayer, and the furious sage seizes upon this trifle to affect displeasure and desert her in her pregnancy, happy to escape the responsibilities of fatherhood. By way of self-justification Jaratkāru fulminates, "It is my firm belief that the sun dare not set so long as I am asleep," (47.26) thereby equating himself with *rishis* of yore such as Agastya. The text clarifies that Jaratkāru, bent on forsaking his wife, does not even listen to her explanations and her plea not to leave till the child is born.

When this is reported to Vāsuki, he anxiously enquires of his sister whether she is pregnant, though "I know it is not proper of me to enquire like this, but the gravity of the matter forces me to" (48.6). She reassures him by saying that her husband had answered her query on this by saying "There is." Āstīka is born and grows resplendent as golden-hued Shūlapāni, pike-wielder, lord of the gods.

Sections 49-50 recapitulate the entire episode of Parikshit's curse and death at the behest of Janamejaya with two additional bits of information: a sage named Uttanka is referred to as insulted. This takes us back to the end of the *Paushya* where it is Uttanka who urges Janamejaya to conduct the snake-sacrifice in order to avenge himself on Takshaka who had spirited away King Paushya's wife's earrings from him. Uttanka informs him that Takshaka had slain Parikshit and also bribed Kāshyapa not to attend on the king. *Shloka* 31 of section 50 ("how the king was assassinated and the seer Uttanka insulted by Takshaka") presumes that Janamejaya's queries in section 49 stem from what he was told in brief by Uttanka. That is the only explanation for the abrupt and imperative command in *shlokas* 3-4 of the preceding section 49:

> "You know all that happened to my father and how he died. After you have told me all about my father, I will do what is proper for me to do. Otherwise, I shall do nothing."

It is curious that this prince has not bothered to find out about the curious circumstances of his father's death so long. No wonder Uttanka taunts him in *shloka* 173 of the *Paushya* (when the king had just got back from a victorious expedition to Taxila): "You spend your time, O noble king, like a child, when urgent and important matters await your attention." It is significant that the ministers state, "All state affairs he (Parikshit) left in our hands" (49.23). Parikshit followed Pāndu in this irresponsible shrugging aside of a potentate's responsibilities at the advanced age of sixty and, unlike his forefathers, he is described as tiring easily being that old (49.26). Arjuna also, we are told in the epic, carried the Gāndīva bow till the age of sixty. We are well within the era of mortal realities with Parikshit who appears less a legendary hero and more a Kali Yuga king fully susceptible to all the foibles that the flesh is heir to. It is amusing to find the Aryashastra Bengali translation desperately trying to gloss this over by rendering the passage as: "At that time he was sixty years old; hence he was still young. However, being hungry and tired, he had become decrepit like an old man."

In 50.3 it is debateable whether Shringi is being described as worshipping his preceptor or the god Brahmā. Prof. Lal and Ganguli render *Brahmanam* as 'preceptor'; van Buitenen translates it as 'Brahmā'. Since we are already out of the realm of that level of myths where sages were said to be very close to the gods, it would be more correct to follow the Lal version. The dead snake is also described as being placed on the *shoulders* of the *rishi*, not on his neck as transcreated throughout.

The second bit of information given is a typical folk tale: Janamejaya wants to know, to verify the veracity of what his counsellors are relating, how the rejuvenation of the Takshaka-bitten tree was intimated to them. It seems that a firewood-collector on that tree was burnt to ashes by Takshaka's poison along with the tree (that is why Kāshyapa says in *shloka* 19 that Parikshit will be *burned* that day, instead of using the word *killed*) and was revived when Kāshyapa resuscitated it. This man reported the event to the ministers and thus Takshaka's role in setting-at-naught the only chance of Parikshit's escape becomes known. Janamejaya's entire energies are now focused on destroying Takshaka, though he goes about it in the roundabout way of annihilating the snake-race itself and *inter alia* Takshaka. The fact that he turns to his priests for advice (the days of great names such as Agastya, Vishvāmitra or Vashishtha as royal counsellors are long gone by) instead of seeking out the culprit bow in hand like Raghu or Dilīpa, shows the drastic cutting-down-to-size of the epic protagonists. It is significant that among the Pāndavas it is only Arjuna who is found consorting with the gods and fighting their battles in the tradition of the Ikshvāku and Paurava monarchs, and that too just once in the *Vana parva*, where the brothers could not be shown as merely wandering about aimlessly. No such exploit features during the reign of the Pāndavas either in Indraprastha or Hastināpura, and the gods hardly come into the picture except the gratuitous appearance of Indra at the very end by way of *deus-ex-machina* to give Yudhishthira his due reward.

It is in the very framework of the epic, this Janamejaya snake sacrifice, that the difference in milieu from the *Rāmāyana* becomes clearly evident. Where an *avatāra* is the hero, the entire atmosphere has about it the calm of pre-ordination, order and other-worldliness which cannot feature in a story about five brothers of doubtful parentage (hence the romantic aura of being sons of gods) out to win a kingdom guided by another avatāra who always behaves in an extremely human way. That constitutes the secret of the *Mahābhārata*'s powerful appeal to mankind down the ages.

Janamejaya's dependence on his priests and their insistence on a snake-consuming sacrifice, along with the description that follows of the building of the *yajña-vedī* (sacrificial-platform), indicates the era of the *Brāhmanas* and *Sūtras,* where rituals have taken precedence over the *Veda-Samhitās*. A point usually missed is that this is not the usual sacred ritual but one that partakes of the nature of black magic, *abhichāra.* The priests are garbed in black, and the rites are death-dealing. Much later, we will find that Drupada takes recourse to similar rites to obtain a killer of Drona from the sacrificial flames.

Again, it is not the priests who forecast the imminent danger to the projected *yajña,* as would have been usual in a story belonging to older times, but a lowly mason who is described as a *sūtradharah sūtah,* translated by van Buitenen as, "This Holder of the Cord, who was a bard of ancient lore." *Sūtradhara* does not merely refer to a cord-holder, i.e. carpenter or architect. The context would imply that he is one who has knowledge of the *Shrauta-sūtras* and *Smārta-sūtras* (manuals of sacred ritual founded on the Vedas, and on tradition). He, in addition, belongs to the *Sūta* caste, like Sauti. Sutas were attendants of kings, later charioteers like Karna's adoptive father, born of Brahmin and Kshatriya inter-marriage, and were professional bards reciting the heroic acts of their patron and his ancestors.

It is an indication of the flexibility and fluidity of the caste system as it prevailed then that the *sūta* could become an expert architect or carpenter without exciting any adverse comment, and utilise his combined lore of legendary history and astrological predictions to make announcements that were seriously acted upon by the king.

In section 52 we get a description of the havoc caused by the sacrifice as the *mantras* inexorably draw the hypnotised snakes to their doom (52.5-7):

"Sighing deeply
Hugely swollen,
Tails and heads entwined,
In thousands they fell
In the fierce fire.
White.
Black.
Blue.
Old.
Young. . . .

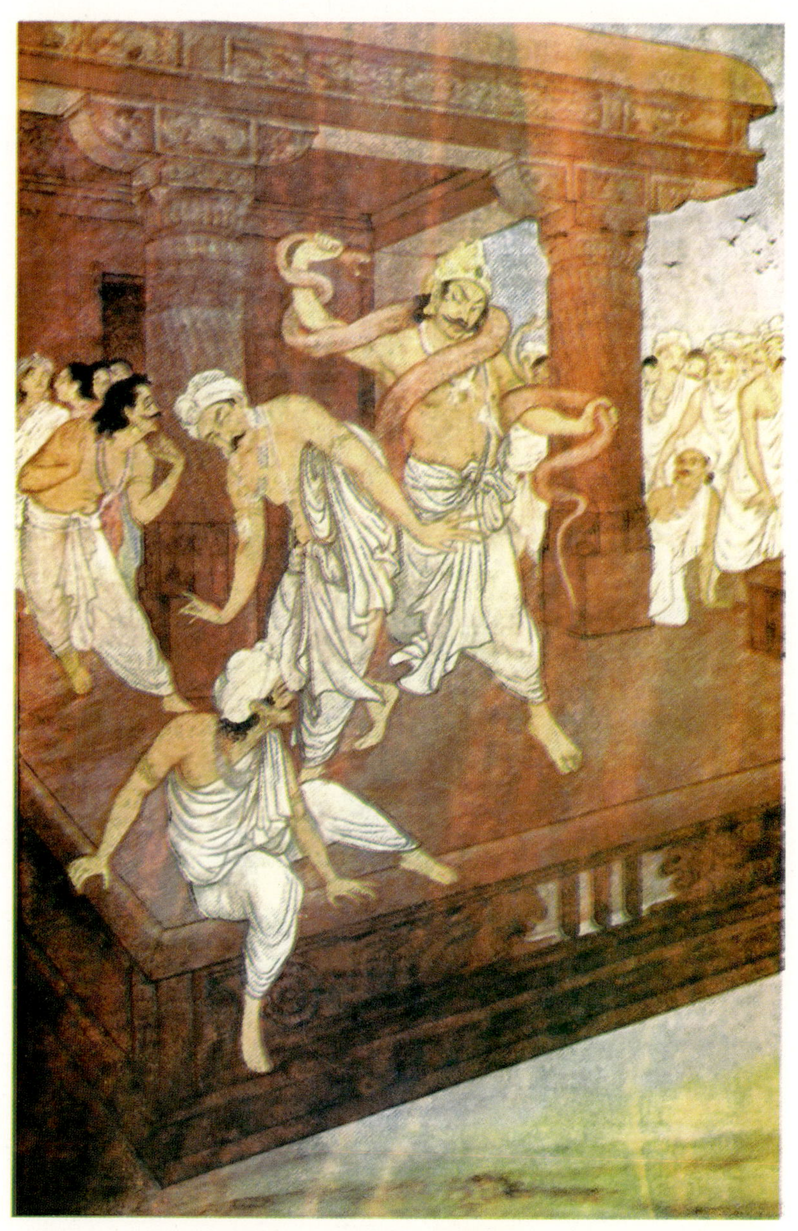

"Death of Parikshit" courtesy BORI

Krosha—
Long.
Yojana—
Long.
Gokarna—
Long.
Crying.
Falling.
Aflame."

The transcreation is an interesting five-finger exercise.

Shaunaka once again brings out the contemporaneity of the sacrifice by insisting that Sauti list the priests who officiated there so that "we may have a record of those who were familiar with the formalities of a snake-sacrifice" (53.3). This list is an extremely valuable bit of evidence that proves that this snake-sacrifice actually occurred. Van Buitenen points out (p. 445 of the Notes) that the *Panchavimsa Brāhmana* records a *sarpasattra* and enumerates the presiding *rishis,* in which a Janamejaya also features. The difference is that in this work, which is anterior to the epic, it is the snakes themselves who are the *yajamāna* (sacrificer). This prompts a very relevant query on part of van Buitenen, "Is it possible that at one time there was indeed held an anti-Snake Sacrifice, of which the Brahmana and epic preserve variant records ?"

In *shlokas* 5-6 Sauti's mentions four types of priests. The *Hotri* signifies the chief priest reciting from the *Rig Veda;* the *Udgātri* was the chief Sāma-vedic priest; the *Adhvaryu* headed the Yajur-vedists who, according the Monier-Williams, "had to measure the ground, to build the altar, to prepare the sacrificial vessels, to fetch wood and water, to light the fire, to bring the animal and immolate it" all the while repeating the hymns of the Yajur-veda; the *Brāhmana* was the most knowledgeable of the four, thoroughly versed in the three Vedas, whose function was to supervise the *yajña* and correct mistakes. Gradually the *Brāhmana* came to represent the Atharva-vedic priests. These four classes of priests together were termed *Ritvijs* or *Ritviks* (51.2) and each of them had four assistants, all named specifically, thus constituting a specialist body of sixteen ritualists. The seventeenth priest was the *Sadasya* whose status is somewhat dubious. His job seems to have been to observe and correct mistakes, much in the manner of the *Brāhmana,* and he possibly came into being when the *Brāhmanas* gave up their role as over-all-supervisor to concentrate on the *Atharva Veda,* handing over the supervisory functions to the *Sadasya.* The text very clearly states in *shloka* 5 that Chanda Bhārgava, who was the foremost of the *rishis* became the *hotri.* The rest include such famous names as Vyāsa, Uddālaka (*Paushya parva shloka* 33), his son Shvetaketu (responsible for prescribing monogamy in the *Sambhava parva,* section 122, and a major figure in the *Chhāndogya Upanishad*), Asita and his son Devala (who recites the epic to the ancestors in *shloka* 107-8 of the *Anukramanikā*), Nārada and Parvata (this uncle-nephew pair recurs frequently in the epic and has some vastly amusing adventures in *Shānti Parva,* section 30), and Shrutashravā, father of Janamejaya's *purohita* Somashravā (*Paushya parva shlokas* 14-21). Kahoda, another of the *sadasyas,* is Uddālaka's disciple and famous as Ashtāvakra's father. Atreya is a follower of Vāmadeva who believed in the *nirguna-brahma,* (*Anushāsana Parva* section 137 and *Vana Parva* section 55). As for Devasharmā, we only know of him as the husband of Ruchi who is prevented by his disciple Vipula from succumbing to Indra's blandishments in his guru's absence (*Anushāsana Parva,* section 40). The story has been memorably recreated in Bengali in Subodh Ghose's *Bharat Prem Kathā*[1]. It is unfortunate from the reader's viewpoint that these names have not been annotated in any translation. Nothing is known about Samathaka, Panchama, Kundajathara, Kutighata, Vatsya, Maudgalya, Shamasaubhara, Chandabhargava, Kautsya, Sarngarava and Pingala. Of the *ritviks* only Jaimini is mentioned elsewhere. One of Vyāsa's disciples who learnt the epic, he recites the *Brahmānda Purāna* to Hiranyanābha in this same Naimisha forest and is present in Yudhishthira's court in the *Sabhā Parva* along with Nārada and Parvata. Only the *Ashvamedha Parva* of Jaiminī's version of the epic is extant.[2]

As a result of their invocations, states Sauti, snake-marrow and snake-fat streamed in rivers (not "fed the river-like fire" as trancreated).

"Pitiful the screams of snakes
fallen in the fire,
pitiful the screams of those
falling in it." (53. 13)

Takshaka immediately rushes to Indra, who willingly protects him. There are linkages with Indra protecting the snakes when Garuda flies too near the sun with them on his back, and it recurs when Arjuna and Krishna burn the Khāndava forest. Yet it is curious, for Indra specifically grants Garuda the boon that snakes will be his diet and also helps Uttanka to enter the realm of Takshaka to recover the stolen earrings of Paushya's queen. From *shloka* 17 it seems that he has also particularly pleaded Takshaka's case before Brahmā. But we have seen in sections 38-39 that the gods approached Brahmā regarding the curse on the snakes in general and were assured by him that the virtuous would survive, but not

"The always-biting snakes,
Snakes who bite for little reason,
Snakes who are evil-minded. . . ." (38.10)

Takshaka apparently does not fall into any of these categories as he does survive and there seems to have been some behind-the-scenes special pleading in his favour on part of Indra.

The difference in the attitudes of Takshaka and Vāsuki is glaring. The one passes his time "in joyful luxury" (*Shloka* 18) being reassured by Indra, deserting his brethren, while the other's agony is inconsolable:

"Sweet sister,
My limbs are burning,
I cannot see clearly,
The points of the heavens are unclear.
Giddiness overwhelms me.
My mind whirls.
My vision is blurred.
My heart trembles.

I am numb.
I am falling
falling
in the fire. . . ." (53.21-22)

And so Āstīka is summoned, apprised of his mission and urged to rescue the snakes. He dispels Vāsuki's anxiety (the text says that he takes it upon himself) and proceeds to the sacrifice where, as directed by Janamejaya, he is refused entry. To gain his entrance, he lifts his voice in praise of the sacrifice. Āstīka would not be allowed to enter without the king's permission: no amount of flattery, in epic times, would persuade mere door-keepers to violate their ruler's express command.

Āstīka's paean in honour of the snake-sacrifice is another veritable library of purānik reference. He compares Janame-jaya's *yajña* to those conducted by other famous persons, starting right from the apocryphal ones of Soma, Varuna, Prajāpati, Indra and Yama, ending with that of Vyāsa. Inbetween he mentions Harimedhas, Rantideva, Gaya, Shashabindu, Vaishravana, Nriga, Ajamīdha, Rāma and Yudhishthira. Of these, the sacrifice of Soma (who, incidentally, is identified with Varuna in the *Rig Veda*) is referred to in Balarama's pilgrimage as being followed by the great Tārakamaya war between Devas and Asuras (*Shalya Parava,* 43.46–48). Yama is described as engaged in a lengthy sacrifice in the Naimisha forest in section 199 of the *Ādi Parva,* while an elaborate account of Varuna's sacrifice (Rudra is said to have assumed his form for the purpose) is given by Vashishtha in the *Anushāsana Parva.* In the *Pauloma,* section 5, Bhrigu is said to have been produced by Brahmā from Varuna's sacrificial fire. Indra's hundred sacrifices are mentioned in the *Shalya Parva,* section 49, while Harimedhas is said to have obtained a daughter from his *yajña* in the *Udyoga Parva,* section 110. Rantideva's generosity and munificence is celebrated in the *Shānti* and *Anushāsana Parvas.* He is reputed to have killed so many cattle to feed his guests (20,000 daily) that the blood formed a river named Charmanvati! Gaya's sacrifices are mentioned in the *Vana* (section 94), *Anushāsana* (section 65) and *Shānti* (section 234) *Parvas.* Shashabindu's name occurs as Sharavindu in the *Bhāgavata Purāna* where he is described as a great ascetic and powerful king with ten thousand wives and innumerable progeny. No reference to a sacrifice by him is found. Prajāpati's sacrifice is referred to in the *Agni Purāna* in connection with the holiness of Gaya-tirtha, and in the *Sabhā Parva* (section 3) where he performs this after a thousand yugas. In the case of Vaishravana (Kubera) the penance of hundred years is referred to in the *Padma Purāna* but not in the *Mahābhārata.* Nriga's *yajña* is famous because there Indra got intoxicated with Soma and the Brahmins danced with joy at his munificence (*Vana Parva* section 8). Ajamīdha is one of Bharata's great-grandsons, but there is nothing in the epic about his sacrifice.

Āstīka then goes on to praise Janamejaya's kingly virtues, equating him with Varuna, Yama, Indra, Khatvānga, Nābhāga, Dilīpa, Yayāti, Māndhātā, Bhīshma, Vashishtha, Krishna, Vasus, Dambodhbhava, Parashurāma, Aurva, Trita, Bhagiratha—a motley collection of sages, gods and kings, all extremely famous for their prowess. Aurva we shall come across in section 179 as he blinds the kings who seek to slay him, concealed in his mother's thigh. Trita is a Rigvedic character who invokes the Ashvins to rescue him from a well where he has been pushed by his brothers Ekata and Dvita, a story retold in section 35 of the *Shalya Parva.* Khatvānga and Dilīpa are identical, famed for one hundred sacrifices and included among the sixteen great kings of Bhāratavarsha in the *Drona Parva,* section 61. Nābhāga is praised for having gifted away the entire world to brahmins in the *Vana, Anushāsana* and *Shānti Parvas* (sections 25, 115, 96 respectively). The same section of the *Anushāsana Parva* celebrates Māndhātā. Yayāti we shall meet soon in the *Ādi Parva.* Dambodhbhava features in section 96 of the *Udyoga Parva* as the emperor who fought Nara and Nārāyana. The rest do not need annotation, except the inexplicable reference to Bhagīratha's awesome appearance that is not found anywhere else.

It is this recital of Āstīka's, spanning the entire range of Indian myths from a particular viewpoint, which convinces the king and the priests of his pre-eminence (56.2):

"He is but a boy,
 but he speaks like a wise old man.
He is no boy; he is old and wise.

I will give him a boon.
O Brahmins, give me permission."

We recall Āstīka's assurance to Vāsuki in 54.21: "I will speak sweetly to him, mixing blessings with words, so that he stops the sacrifice."

It is curious that Janamejaya should be so anxious to grant Āstīka a boon that he forgets that the main purpose of the sacrifice, the annihilation of Takshaka, is yet to be achieved, despite being doubly reminded by the *sadasyas* and the displeased *hotri*. This is part of Vyāsa's technique of character-delineation with swift strokes. Here is the surviving descendent of the Pāndavas, whose kingdom has shrunk practically to a principality, flattered grossly into making a desperate effort to measure up to that mythical standard by declaring, like those personages, "Ask any boon!" He forgets the warning of the Sūta that the sacrifice will be stopped by a Brahmin; he does not recall the implications of Shrutashravā's statement regarding Somashravā, the *purohita*, that he needs must give to a Brahmin whatever he demands. It is a bit of *hubris* at play succeeded by *hamartia* in *shloka* 16 when the *ritviks* confidently allow the king to grant Āstīka a boon although Takshaka is still in the process of being precipitated into the fire.

In *shloka* 11 of section 56 we find Janamejaya suddenly rising to the heroic stature of his ancestors in finding Takshaka being protected by Indra:

"If Takshaka is still in the abode of Indra,
Cast him into the fire with Indra himself."

Characteristically, as the *hotri*'s invocations drag both Indra and Takshaka to the sacrifice, the lord of the gods abandons his protégé, despite all his confident assurances that Brahmā has guaranteed his welfare:

"Purandara saw the sacrifice and, terrified, he cast off Takshaka and fled to his abode." (56.14)

The question that arises in the meantime concerns the *sūta* Lohitākshya (red-eyed, possibly from the sacrificial fumes) who, in *shloka* 6, states that Indra is sheltering Takshaka, and that he knows this "Because I know the Purānas." Is he the same person as the *sūtradhara sūta* of 51.15 who warned that the sacrifice would not be completed? This presumption is confirmed in 58.12-13:

> "the Sūta Lohitākshya, learned in masonry and foundation-laying, who before the sacrifice commenced,
> Had warned the king that a Brahmin would interrupt the rituals, he gave much wealth, food, clothing."

As the priests tell Janamejaya that Takshaka can be seen about to fall into the fire, "From the sky, somersaulting,/Paralysed, sighing deep sighs" (56.19), Āstīka demands his boon that the sacrifice be stopped. Janamejaya, despite his vaunt that "Even the most ungrantable/I will today grant" (56.17), desperately tries to bribe him with gold, silver, cattle till the *sadasyas* unanimously urge that Āstīka's wish be granted. Sauti throws in a bit of miracle to build up Āstīka by having him stop Takshaka's fall in mid-air merely by intoning thrice, "stop!" despite all the libations and invocations of the priests, much as Vishvāmitra had stopped Trishanku's fall from the sky in mid-air. And so this monstrous holocaust of an entire race is brought to an end by a Brahmin's persistence and a king's honouring of his promise.

Shaunaka once again, as in section 35, wants the names of the snakes consumed in the sacrifice, and Sauti obliges with the chief ones. These appear to belong to the families of Vāsuki, Takshaka, Airāvata, Kauravya and most of them to the family of Dhritarāshtra. It is perhaps a conscious parallelism that the maximum destruction takes place in Dhritarāshtra's lineage, as in that of his namesake in the Kurukshetra war. Āstīka returns, successful, to his mother and uncle and this enchanting sub-*parva* ends with the snakes promising not to bite anyone who invokes Āstīka. Sauti also reminds us in 58.30 that he is retelling what Pramati told Ruru, thus linking up with the *Pauloma's dundhubha* snake.

We meet Āstīka again in the *Āshramavāsika Parva*, section 35, where he praises the king for being steadfast to his word, thus enabling Takshaka to escape doom, and says that the snakes consumed in the sacrificial fire have reached the same abode as Parikshit's after his death. Āstīka leaves, promising Janamejaya that he will be present as a *sadasya* at his horse-sacrifice.

With the end of the *Āstīka* the framework of the epic is firmly established: it is during this sacrifice that Vaishampāyana recites the epic from which Sauti draws his material for the Naimisha forest recital. By having Vaishampāyana recite the epic in the presence of the composer, Vyāsa, its authenticity is set at rest as far as Shaunaka and his fellow-sages are concerned.

Casting a look back, notice how the *Āstīka* is constructed: Jaratkāru-Āstīka-redemption of the snakes; birth of snakes, Aruna and Garuda; wager of Kadrū and Vinatā on Uchchaihshravas; churning of the ocean; Kadrū's cursing the snakes; Garuda and *amrita*; Vāsuki's anxiety and Brahmā's advice; Parikshit, Samīka, Shringi's curse and Parikshit's death; Jaratkāru and his ancestors, his marriage, āstīka's birth; Janamejaya's query about his father's death, his decision to conduct the snake-sacrifice; Āstīka's intervention and the end of the sacrifice. Thus, the attempt that began with the *Paushya* sub-*parva* to build this framework is finally completed.

However, in the process, Sauti has forgotten to utilise Somashravā, introduced at the beginning of that sub-*parva* as Janamejaya's priest who can refuse nothing to a Brahmin. He is not even mentioned among the priests present at the sacrifice! What is more important, we have here considerable space devoted to the Nāgas who do not play any role in the rest of the epic but were obviously of great interest to hermits like Shaunaka dwelling in Naimisha forest, the resort of these snake-worshipping aborigines. It is significant that both Āstīka and Somashravā are born of Brahmin fathers and Nāga mothers, and are given honourable places in the Aryan Janamejaya's court, which would not have been possible once *Manusmriti* had laid down that children of Brahmins by non-Brahmin women could not belong to their father's caste. It is still upbringing that determines the person's caste, not his birth, as we shall see with Vyāsa himself.

Simultaneously, the authenticity of the incident is verified as the list of priests resembles one in the *Panchavimsa Brāhmana,* while the names of Janamejaya's brothers given at the beginning of the *Paushya* tally with the much older *Shatapatha Brāhmana* (13.5.4.1.) Further, the *Panchavimsa Brāhmana* (25.6) refers to a sacrifice conducted in the Naimisha forest that was never finished, tallying with the twelve year long *yajña* in which Shaunaka is engaged in that forest and at which the epic is recited by Sauti. This recital at the behest of a sage of the Bhrigu family has led Sukthankar to argue that the epic shows several signs of 'Bhriguization'.

The *Anukramanikā, shloka* 50, states that some begin the epic with the story of Āstīka, while others prefer to start with that of Uparichara (related in the next sub-parva, *Ādivamsāvatarana*). We have seen the one, and now proceed to the other, with Vaishampāyana as the original narrator whose recital is being reported verbatim by Sauti.

And so we leave the *Nāgas,* to encounter them only sporadically later when Garuda is forced to spare the *Nāga* Sumukha, Arjuna marries Ulūpī, Bhīma is rescued by Āryaka and is caught in the mortal coils of Nahusha-turned-snake.

References

1. Englished by Pradip Bhattacharya, *Love Stories from the Mahabharata,* Indialog Publications, New Delhi, 2005.
2. Englished by S.K. Sen, edited by Pradip Bhattacharya, Writers Workshop, Calcutta, 2009.

8

The Ādivamshāvatarana
Ineffectual Birth Pangs

Ādivamshāvatarana literally means 'descent of the first generations.' What we actually find is a curious medley of episodes consisting of several false starts on part of Vaishampāyana who tries hard to get on with the job of narrating the epic, only to be brought up short repeatedly by Janamejaya avid, like Oliver Twist, for more. It is interesting to watch how this happens.

It all begins with Shaunaka finally acknowledging that he is satisfied with Sauti's account of the Bhrigus, which had digressed into the elaborate snake-sacrifice history because of Shaunaka's curiosity. He now repeats the demand his *sadasyas* had made in the *Anukramanikā* that Vyāsa's epic be recited, including all the thrilling stories narrated to the *sadasyas* during the intervals between the various rites. This, incidentally, shows us how such epic-recitation proceeded. The occasions were sacrifices organised by kings originally, where the audience would be entertained and edified by retelling of myths and heroic legends suitably modified to stress the lineages of the officiating king. In such cases, the reciter was a priest, a Brahmin. Other occasions were gatherings of sages in forests for performing rituals, where storytellers *(sūta)* retold these. In the *Mahābhārata* we find references not only to these two types of tale-tellers, but also to rhapsodes or bards *(granthika,* XIV.70.7), whose work was chiefly to build up the warrior's morale by praising his lineage (singers, *gāyaka,* VII.82.2-3; II.4,7) and reciters of genealogical verses *(vaitālika,* II.4,7; XII.37,43). The epic itself, as we have it, is a combination of lays recited for glorifying the

Kuru race (Vyāsa's stated intention to Dhritarāshtra) and stories of ancient times. It is not a rhapsodic or dramatic delivery at all as we have in the *Rāmāyana* where the speakers are invariably indicated within the verses themselves. Here we have verse tales knit together by prose statements indicating the speaker, in the manner of the legends recited by priests and not rhapsodic lays accompanied with music.

Shaunaka wants to learn from Sauti all the subjects of the narrations. Sauti informs him that while other Brahmins narrated Vedic matters, Vyāsa recited the *Mahābhārata*. It has taken us 58 chapters to come back to this initial request with which we had started in the *Anukramanikā*! Sauti begins with a short introduction about the prowess of Vyāsa in which the transcreation of 60.4 is somewhat defective: "He achieved the unachievable, by ascetic discipline, by studying the Vedas, by vows, fasts, progeny, and yajña." The sense of the original is that the excellence achieved by Vyāsa cannot be surpassed by anyone through any of these methods enumerated in the *shloka*. The van Buitenen rendering goes quite awry: ". . . no one was to surpass him in austerities, in the study of the Veda, in the observance of vows and fasts, in progeny, or in temper." There is no question of the self-controlled Vyāsa being unsurpassable in progeny: he has only one son, Shuka. It is the Ganguli version that is faithful to the original: "And he readily obtained that which no one could obtain by asceticism . . . etc."

There is an interesting bit of material detail in 60.9 where Vyāsa sees Janamejaya surrounded by princes and priests seated on *kusha* grass, showing that the sacrificial area was covered with this grass, and lending vivid reality to Janamejaya's *yajña*.

It is Janamejaya who begs his ancestor Vyāsa to relate what he has himself seen of the fratricidal Kuru-Pāndava war. His specific query relates to the cause of their falling-out: "Did Fate blind them?" he asks. Vyāsa, in turn, commands his disciple Vaishampāyana to repeat the story exactly as he had heard it from his guru.

In section 61 we are given a summary of the *Ādi Parva* with cryptic references to the dice-game in the *Sabhā Parva*, the exile (*Vana* and *Virāta Parvas*) and the *Parvas* concerning the war itself. The summary is given in just 46 verses, and warrants a close look in comparison with the other summaries Sauti has already provided in the *Anukramanikā* and *Parvasangraha* sub-*parvas.*

Vaishampāyana follows up the major divisions of the story already indicated by Janamejaya in 60.18-20: the Breach (*bheda*), the War (*yuddha*) and the Victory (*jaya*). He begins with the Kauravas' jealousy of the superior excellence and popularity of the Pāndavas. There is merely a cryptic reference to the death of Pāndu, followed by the return of the Pāndavas from the forest to Hastināpura where they swiftly master archery and the Vedas.

The persecution of Duryodhana is seen as chiefly directed against Bhīma and 61.10-13 splits into three distinct incidents the single episode at Pramānakoti beside the Ganges: Duryodhana poisons Bhīma; binds him with ropes and throws him into the river; he survives despite being bitten by snakes in the river. The matter of Āryaka strengthening Bhīma by giving him nectar to drink is not mentioned. Vaishampāyana adds that it was Vidura's vigilance that protected them. Bhīshma, significantly, does not come in for mention at all despite his much vaunted efforts to maintain a just equation between the two branches of the family. Vaishampāyana also adds, doubtless looking back to Janamejaya's query in 60.20 ("Did Fate blind them?") that the Pāndavas "having been selected for grave purposes, were protected by Fate" (61.16).

The lacquer-house episode is sketched in outline, with the significant comment that Dhritarāshtra "possessive of kingship, sent the Pāndavas away in exile" to Vāranāvata. *Shoka* 20 states: "By his (Vidura's) help they escaped from the lacquer-house at night into a dense forest."

The killing of Hidimb is attributed not to Bhīma but to the five brothers in general, while his slaying of Baka is lauded as inspiring confidence among citizens. The emphasis in the Hidimbā episode is on their fear of Duryodhana, on uncompromising flight and the sense of complete isolation. The winning of Draupadī is mentioned, followed by Dhritarāshtra's exhortation that, to prevent internecine strife, they should shift to the Khāndava area. Vaishampāyana states how the five brothers engaged in extensive conquests till the world seemed blessed with six suns.

Now comes a very interesting passage in 61.40-41 referring to Arjuna's exile. Vaishampāyana makes it out as having been imposed by Yudhishthira, "for a certain reason", instead of showing it as self-imposed as in the detailed account of the incident subsequently. Does this enshrine the original version, revealing the psychological reason that is exposed at the end of the epic in Yudhishthira's bitter admonition to the dying Draupadī for having loved Arjuna specially? Further, the period of Arjuna's exile is stated as one year and a month (paralleling the twelve years plus one year exile of the Pāndavas) in the Southern recensions, but as twelve years and one month in other recensions that are undoubtedly influenced by the later exile of the brothers. Prof. Lal translates it as eleven years and a month, which occurs neither in the Southern nor in the Bengal recensions. K.M. Ganguli has it as eleven years and as many months.

The burning of Khāndava is now given in some detail, showing that it loomed large in the epic-scheme, followed by the building of the wondrous palace by Maya. Then, in just three more *shlokas* Vaishampāyana sums up the dice-game, the exile, the war and the victory. It is instructive to compare this summary with that given by Sauti in *shlokas* 110-138 of the *Anukramanikā.* Sauti begins with Pāndu's retiring to the forest and dying of a curse incurred by striking down a coupling stag. The begetting of the Pāndavas through the gods is mentioned and also a very revealing fact that is absent from Vaishampāyana's bare summary:

> "When the Kauravas saw them introduced as the sons of Pāndu, the nobler group among them shouted joyous approval. But some maintained that they were not the sons of Pāndu; others insisted they were. Some wondered how they could be the sons of Pāndu—for had not Pāndu died long ago?"—(*shlokas* 116-117)

Sauti completely omits the jealousy of Duryodhana and his machinations to kill the five brothers. Jumping straightaway to

Arjuna's winning of Draupadī and his consequent fame as an archer, Sauti attributes the successful institution of the Rājasūya *yajña* to his prowess alone. This shows how the viewpoint changed from one narrator to another. There is no reference to Bhīma's exploits or to Arjuna's exile and the burning of Khāndava forest. What Vaishampāyana limits to a single *shloka*, Sauti spins out to five, describing the wealth of the Pāndavas and their wondrous palace that so infuriated Duryodhana. Sauti also adds that Krishna allowed so much injustice to take place being furious with Dhritarāshtra for having permitted the dice-game. The logic is not particularly strong, nor is the point clear why Bhīma's offence in mocking Duryodhana as one of low birth in Maya's hall should become so grave by being committed in the presence of Krishna (*Anukramanikā*, 134). This stress on Arjuna and Krishna, absent completely from Vaishampāyana's summary, shows the difference in the attitudes of the two narrators, one twice removed and the other only once removed from Vyāsa's original composition. Sauti's summary does not even mention the exile but, like Vaishampāyana, it wraps up the battle and its consequences in a single *shloka*. Sauti's effort is distinctly lopsided and hardly gives one a proper idea of the epic's main incidents. The distortion that has taken place in the transmission becomes quite clear. Nevertheless, Sauti's greatest contribution is the Lament of Dhritarāshtra, a different version of which occurs in section 2 of the *Shalya Parva*, and raises the suspicion that the epic was originally the story of the tragic destruction of a royal dynasty by parvenus.

Janamejaya raises some very pertinent questions in the next section, 62, which also trouble the modern reader. To answer these, Vaishampāyana has to begin all over again in greater detail, warning the king to select a time for listening to this huge history, of which he has so far related only the beginning. The seven problems posed by Janamejaya are:

1. Why did the Pāndavas slay their own kin and, having done this prohibited deed (which is precisely Arjuna's objection in the *Gītā*), why are they honoured by people?
2. Why did they countenance victimisation by the Kauravas

when they were faultless and sufficiently powerful to retaliate?

3. Why did the immensely powerful Bhīma restrain himself (the reference is to Yudhishthira's repeated admonitions) despite being repeatedly wronged?
4. Why did Draupadī not destroy Dhritarāshtra's sons when insulted (this remains unanswered, as, indeed, does her own question to the assembly)?
5. Why did the brothers follow Yudhishthira in his addiction to gambling despite being deceived (referring to the second dice-game resulting in the exile, following the one in which Draupadī was insulted)?
6. Why did Yudhishthira patiently suffer unjustified oppression?
7. Why did Arjuna bear such persecution when, with Krishna's assistance, he could have annihilated all his enemies?

Vaishampāyana does not supply direct answers to these questions. He launches into an elaborate panegyric on the epic, the third one after the *Anukramanikā* and the *Parvasamgraha*. Indeed, nowhere in the body of the epic will we come across direct answers to any of these pertinent queries except in the *Gītā* in so far as the first one is concerned. The reader will have to find out the answers himself through an interpretative study of the character of the Pāndavas and the circumstances in which they find themselves.[1]

Vaishampāyana begins with what is virtually a fresh introduction to the merits of the epic justifiable from the point of view that this is really the first recital. What Sauti has narrated along the same lines in the first two *parvas* is really a re-hash of this and therefore what is given in *shlokas* 14-53 of section 62 is not really an exercise in tautology, but the original recital. At the outset, he informs us that,

"The epic has
one hundred thousand shlokas
by Satyavatī's son,
infinite-energied Vyāsa." (62.14)

Twice it is stressed that it equals the Vedas (62.16,49) and once it described outright as "this Veda of Krishna", *kārshanam vedamimam.* This has a double reference: to revealed truth by the seer Krishna Dvaipāyana and to the *Gītā* by Vāsudeva Krishna.

There are a number of points that have already been made by Sauti in the first two *parvas*: *shloka* 19 is paralleled in *shloka* 266 of the *Anukramanikā*; *shloka* 33 in *shloka* 254 of the *Anukramanikā*; *shlokas* 23 and 28 in *shlokas* 381 and 391-2 respectively of the *Parvasamgraha*; and *shlokas* 37 and 24 in *shlokas* 263 and 26 of the *Anukramanikā* respectively. It is here that, for the first and the last time, we come to know that Vyāsa took three years to complete the epic, rising daily at dawn (62.55,66). Another lovely image is added to those describing the *Mahābhārata* in the first two *parvas*:

"Like the mighty, bhagavān ocean,
like the mahā mountain,
the Mahābhārata
is a mine of gems."(62.52)

Shloka 54 supplies another etymology of the epic: it recounts the wonderful, exalted origins of the Bharatas. *Shloka* 270 of the *Anukramanikā* attributed the name to its being heavier than all the four Vedas.

Shloka 34 comes as quite a surprise with its reference to Shiva, Pārvati and "many-mothered" Kārttikeya along with Keshava as forming part of the epic's subject matter. These are the only gods mentioned by name, raising the suspicion of the *shloka* being an interpolation by Shaivites. It has been omitted in the Bhandarkar edition.

The reason for Vyāsa composing the epic is brought out in *shloka* 27:

"To extol the Pāndavas
and other Kshatriyas, famous
for their learning and heroic deeds, . . ."

In other words, a specific bardic or rhapsodic function was being discharged, particularly in the four rainy months (verse 32).

Shloka 64, also classed as spurious, dates itself by referring to gifting a copy of the epic, thus alluding to a period when it had come to be written down in a number of copies as distinct from oral transmission.

The entire panegyric culminates in the famous lines of 62.57 which end this section:

> "O bull-brave Bharata,
> what is in this epic
> on Dharma, Artha, Kāma, Moksha,
> may be elsewhere.
> What is not in this epic,
> is nowhere else."

Shloka 24 of this panegyric is of particular interest:

> "It is recited in the present,
> it will be recited in the future;"

This looks back to *shloka* 26 of the *Anukramanikā*:

> "Some poets have already sung this story; some are reciting it now before others; and others will sing it in times to come."

Besides the fact that the reference to 'singing' reinforces the rhapsodic character of the Kaurava-saga that the epic originally might have been, as stated in *shloka* 27 by Vaishampāyana, the repeated mention of the timelessness of the *Mahābhārata* raises a number of issues.

In the first place, this is of a piece with the cyclic view of history which we find in the Purānas: the four ages, *Krita, Tretā, Dvāpara* and *Kali* (referring also to throws of the dice starting with four for *krita,* the luckiest throw, and ending with one in *kali,* the losing die) recur in cycles ending in universal dissolution at the end of a *kalpa* (a day of Brahmā, lasting one thousand yugas) after which another such Brāhmic day starts. In each *kalpa* the Divine incarnates in a different form to help the earth emerge from the waters of nescience: as a fish, a boar, or a tortoise etc. In each such spell of creation, the institutions remain the same; only the people change. This is brought out in great detail in the third part of the *Vishnu Purāna,* chapter 3, where Krishna Dvaipāyana's father, Parāshara, explains to Maitreya that in every Dvāpara yuga Vishnu incarnates in the form of Vyāsa (the arranger) to split the Veda (esoteric knowledge) into four parts each, in turn, being subdivided into numerous branches to ensure the widest dissemination. Parāshara explains that in the Satya yuga Vishnu appears in the form of sages such as Kapila to spread wisdom; and in Tretā he incarnates as King to subdue the unruly and protect the three worlds. In the seventh Manvantara, which is in progress, there have been twenty eight Vyāsas up to the time of Parāshara's recital as follows: Brahmā, Prajāpati, Shukrācharya, Brihaspati, Sūrya, Yama, Indra, Vashishtha, Sarasvat, Tridhāmā, Trishika, Bharadvāja, Antariksha, Varni, Traiyyāruna, Dhananjaya, Kratunjaya, Jaya, Bharadvāja, Gautama, Haryatma, Vājashrava, Trinbindu, Riksha, (interestingly, the text says he is subsequently called Vālmīki), Shakti, Parāshara, Jātukarna, Krishna Dvaipāyana. The twentyninth will be, most intriguingly, the infamous Ashvatthāmā, Drona's son, condemned by Krishna to wander as an outcaste after his ineffectual attempt to destroy the sole descendant of the Pāndavas, Parikshit.

This 'dates' Parāshara effectively vis-á-vis the *Yoga-Vāshishtha Rāmāyana* where Vashishtha tells Rāma that Vyāsa has been born ten times already and will be born a further eight times and write his *Mahābhārata.* He speaks, therefore, of only eighteen, not twentynine Vyāsas, and goes only up to Jaya, the eighteenth Vyāsa. This particular Vashishtha, in other words, is nine cycles anterior to the Parāshara reciting the *Vishnu Purāna* and eleven cycles before Krishna Dvaipāyana Vyāsa.

As in the *Anukramanikā,* we are told here (62.26):

"Diseases will not afflict him,
  nor fear of the other world,

who listens to this history
without cynicism"

recalling *shloka* 251 of the *Anukramanikā*:

"The study of the Bharata is an *act of faith*. One line *read with reverence* washes away the reader's sins." (emphasis mine)

The attitude of the listener is of all importance in deriving benefit from the epic. That is why Vaishampāyana insists that Brahmins ought to read it in a disciplined manner.

Section 63 is concerned with the story of King Uparichara Vasu, which recalls *shloka* 53 of the *Anukramanikā*: "Some read the Mahābhārata from the first mantra, others begin with the story of Āstīka; others begin with Uparichara. . . ." The natural question any reader would ask is, "Why begin with the tale of Uparichara?" Vaishampāyana, we find, has not yet truly launched into his theme, the story of the Kauravas. Like Sauti at the beginning of section 60, having introduced the epic Vaishampāyana provides the king with an introduction to Vyāsa. Uparichara turns out to be the maternal grandfather of Vyāsa, having accidentally fathered Satyavatī, or Matsyagandhā (fish-odorous), on an Apsarā-turned-fish.

The story of Uparichara is one that offended the Victorian prudery of its first translators. They either omitted the 'shocking' portions or Latinised them. Among the modern translators van Buitenen, following the Bhandarkar edition, gives an extremely cryptic version, "And while he roamed the lovely woods, his seed burst forth", while Prof. Lal, faithful to his promise to give us the epic in full as it stands, translates the seven *shlokas* preceding this, which build up to it in the manner of an inevitable orgasm by weaving a web of sensuous allurement. Approached by his wife Girikā in her most fertile period, the king is sent by his manes on a mission to hunt deer for their funereal rites. We never get to know what happens to the mission, for the king is unable to get his wife out of his mind in this forest peopled with trees,

"beautiful, sacred, loaded
with fragrant flower and sweet fruit.
Heady bee drone
and kokila song
filled the forest.
It was spring,
the forest as lovely as
the gardens of Kubera.
Desire stirred in him.
Girikā was not near.
Desire maddened him.
He roamed aimlessly; he saw
A ravishing ashoka
densely-foliaged, but
so thick with flowers
the branches were hidden.
He sat in its shade,
drinking in flower scent
blended with fragrance of honey.
He sat there, breathing,
soft winds blowing; and,
maddened with visions of Girikā,
There, in the forest, he
had an erection; but,
eschewing a fruitless emission,
ejaculated on a leaf." (63.43-49)

This is part of the totality of the *Mahābhārata* that Vaishampāyana has asserted in 62.53 while stating that what is not in it cannot be found anywhere. In omitting such portions "for obvious reasons" (as M.N. Dutt put it in his Victorian translation, quoted by Prof. Lal) the translators and editors were literally bowdlerising Vyāsa precisely along the lines that Bowdler had followed when vandalising Shakespeare. As Prof. Lal comments in his Preface, "Masturbation—if indeed that is what Uparichara did—will not seem a very 'obvious reason' in the twentieth century, so I have retained the passage in its entirety."

The story, however, appears to suffer from all the defects of an amateur storyteller: it is made up of several disjointed episodes such as the Uparichara-Indra episode; the Uparichara-mountain episode; the Uparichara-Girikā-Adrikā episode. The story simply refuses to get off the ground smoothly. Its components, moreover, are quite disparate: there is folk-tale in a fish delivering a human child; there is anthropological data in the origin of the flag-staff worship of Indra; there is the typological myth-structure where India's splitting-open of mountains to release the celestial waters is paralleled in Uparichara riving-open the mountain Kolāhala to let the river Shuktimatī through, along with her son and daughter whom he appropriates, just as Indra seizes the herds of light he releases from the hold of Vritra and Vala.

The favours Indra bestows on King Vasu have their origin in the god's fears that through his austerities Indra will be supplanted as their king. Vasu becomes king of Chedi as a result of Indra's boon, and does not take up asceticism thereafter. We are not told anything of his life previous to this ascesis: he appears to be a king without a kingdom, presumably engaged in austerities, abjuring all violence, in order to obtain one. Vaishampāyana merely tells us that Vasu belongs to the dynasty of Puru, without mentioning his father, which is extremely unusual in an epic where the emphasis is on the dynasty of Puru. It is possibly the only such instance. Elsewhere in the *Purānas* we find in the genealogical lists that he is descended from one of Kuru's sons, Sudhanus, being fourth in descent after him. Shāntanu, who marries Vasu's fish-born daughter Satyavatī, is descended from Viduratha, another son of Kuru, being sixth in descent after him, thereby marrying an agnate cousin. On the other hand, the story of Vasu handing over Adrikā's daughter to the fishermen looks like an effort to lend some royal ancestry to Satyavatī since Shāntanu marries her. The fact of nothing being mentioned of Vasu's ancestry itself hints at this sort of manufactured legitimacy at which the Brahmins were adept, accounting for the numerous interpolations in the Purānas and the innumerable inconsistencies.

Dr. S.N. Pradhan, in his *Chronology of Ancient India* (p. 64), points out that in the Kumbhakonam recension of the epic, attempts to invest Satyavatī with royal ancestry are made quite transparent. Thus, in chapter 53.19 of the *Anushāsana Parva* of this recension, Vyāsa is stated to have been born to Satyavatī, daughter of a Dāsa. Again, in the *Ādi Parva* 64.114, of the same recension, Satyavatī is found recalling that she was the daughter of Uparichara Vasu in her *previous birth.*

Another interesting feature is the profession followed by Satyavatī, namely of ferrying people across the river. According to the *Anushāsana Parva,* 48.21, where inter-caste marriages and their offspring are described, Bhīshma states that the child fathered by a Nishāda on a Magadha Sairandhra woman was termed "Madguru". The term *sairandhra* means an orphan working as domestic servant. Bhīshma goes on to explain that a synonym for *Madguru* is *Dāsa* and that the offspring of such a union earn a living by plying ferries. Now, Gandhakālī, or Satyavatī, is of uncertain parentage, brought-up by the Dāsa chief and plies a ferry as her daily work—all of which fit in exactly with the description given by Bhīshma. She was, therefore, the product of such a union between a Nishāda and a female domestic menial from Magadha. It will be recalled that the kingdom of Magadha was established by Uparichara Vasu's son Brihadratha. It is, therefore, quite conclusive that the attempt to make Satyavatī a daughter of Vasu is a later, post-Vyāsan attempt to raise the status of the sage by making him the son of a princess instead of a low-caste Dāsa woman.

An extremely interesting bit of additional information is provided about Gandhakālī in the *Harivamsa,* I.20.49-71. Here we are told that king Ugrāyudha of the Dvimidha dynasty (brother of Ajamidha, an ancestor of the Kauravas) demanded of Bhīshma, after Shāntanu's death, that Gandhakālī be sent to him and offered considerable wealth in return. Enraged, Bhīshma attacked the Pānchāla king and killed him. There is only a reference to this killing without the interesting background in the *Shānti Parva,* 27.10. Satyavatī must have been one of the renowned beauties of her time! The Kuru-Pānchāla enmity, therefore, has her as the *cherchez-la-femme.*

The delectable description Indra gives of the Chedi country successfully lures Vasu away from his penances, especially when the god gifts him a celestial sky-ranging chariot. It is because of this flying crystal chariot that Vasu is named "Uparichara". This chariot has an interesting history: it descends from Vasu to his son Brihadratha and thence to Jarāsandha, from whom Krishna takes it after having him slain by Bhīma (*Sabhā Parva*, section 24). In that account we find Krishna summoning Garuda to perch on the pennant on the chariot, a whole *shloka* being devoted to the description of this wonderful flagstaff. Indra, in the Uparichara episode, presents the king with a bamboo rod by way of sceptre that Vasu adorns with gold cloth and flowers and has it worshipped annually in an Indra-festival *when Indra appears in swan (Garuda?) form.* Dange has pointed out that according to the *Brihadsamhitā* it is Vishnu who presented the victory-staff to Indra, who passed it on to Uparichara, and it enabled Indra to rout his enemies. Now, Vishnu's standard has Garuda on it, as we have seen in the *Āstīka* sub-*parva*. In other words, this hints at Garuda assisting Indra, which is reinforced by Krishna calling on Garuda to perch on the flagstaff of the crystal chariot gifted by Indra to Vasu. This king, in other words, is an Indra-image on earth, with the bamboo rod being a Garuda or swan pennant (a parallel is seen in the celebrations around the Maypole in Europe). In the *Harivamsa* we meet another such king, Paundra Vāsudeva, who styles himself Vishnu's incarnation on earth, imitating all the godly panoply.

This concept is built up with Vasu's encounter with the mountain-demon to free the river from his clutches and by an episode in the *Shānti Parva*, section 335. There it is stated by Bhīshma that Uparichara (again nothing is given about his ancestry) practised non-violence and had been granted an empire by Vishnu, of whom he was a famous worshipper. Pleased by his devotion to Vishnu, Indra shared his seat with the king. Once again the link-up between Indra and Vishnu recurs, which we have noticed in the Garuda story. Uparichara is said to be the last king who will know of the scriptures composed by the seven sages named Chitrashikhandi, having studied it under Brihaspati. This king seems to have been famous for his pledge not to kill any animal. That would explain the complete omission of all mention concerning the deer he had set out to hunt when he got distracted in the forest by thoughts of his wife. Yet, curiously enough, in section 337 of the *Shānti Parva* Uparichara is cursed by sages for interpreting the word 'Aja' as 'goat' (as the gods also interpreted it for the purposes of sacrifice) instead of as 'seed' (as the sages preferred to interpret it, arguing that animal sacrifice was not permissible in the Satya yuga). At this decision in favour of animal sacrifice by the king, the sages curse him to fall to the lower regions from the heavens. The gods help Uparichara who pleases Vishnu by his unfailing devotion even in *Pātāla*. Vishnu has Garuda restore Vasu to the ethereal regions, so that he becomes 'Uparichara' again. Here Garuda is once again specifically linked with Uparichara. It raises a strong possibility that the flagpole Indra presented to the king would have had a Garuda-pennant on it, transferred to the chariot that ultimately returns to the original owner Krishna-Vishnu, who had given it to Indra for destroying demons, whence it came to Uparichara and from him to Brihadratha and Jarāsandha. It seems that this chariot had been used by Indra and Vishnu jointly (being a unique chariot which could carry two warriors in addition to the charioteer) during the famous Devasura war known as 'Tārakāmaya', fought over Brihaspati's wife Tārā who eloped with his disciple Chandra helped by the Asuras (*Sabhā Parva*, 24.15,16). The Indra-Vishnu nexus is completed when Vishnu is made Indra's brother Upendra as one of the Ādityas born of Aditi and Kashyapa.

On the other hand, in Krishna's taking of the chariot gifted by Indra to Vasu, we see a mythical representation of the Krishna-cult superseding that of Indra. This can be traced very clearly beginning with Krishna's Govardhana miracle, where he replaces the annual worship of Indra, referred to in the Uparichara story, with that of the cow. Indra bestows upon him the title of "Upendra". In the *Mahābhārata* itself we come across accounts of Krishna's battle with Indra for the Pārijāta tree, which he succeeds in taking away for Satyabhāmā. By identifying Krishna as a full incarnation of Vishnu, this cult finally supplanted that of Indra completely, leaving practically no trace of it. The younger brother, mentioned occasionally by Indra in the *Rig Veda*, ultimately cast the eldest completely in the shade.

Uparichara, we notice, is described as addicted to hunting (63.1), which clashes with the subsequent attribution of non-violence to him, both here (63.3) and in the *Shānti Parva* (section 335). This predilection seems to be inherited by his descendants as a fatal flaw. Through Satyavatī, he is Vyāsa's grandfather and through him the ancestor of Pāndu, fatally addicted to hunting, and of Parikshit, whose doom comes upon him in the course of a hunt. In all three cases, the operative motif is one of loss of self-control in the course of a hunt in the forest. It is pursuit of a violent objective, the killing of inoffensive deer, which boomerangs in death through another form of self-destroying violence: lust. This second motif, however, operates only partially for Uparichara and Parikshit, since in the case of the former the violent objective is eschewed in favour of sensual gratification; while in the latter the element of lust does not occur. In Pāndu they combine, with fatal results.

The twins born of Adrikā's accidental artificial insemination by Uparichara are the virtuous and truthful king Matsya—presumably ruler of the fishermen or of that kingdom of which Virāta becomes king—and a daughter later called Satyavatī whom Vasu quickly allots to fishermen. It could be an indication of gender bias or her fishy odour being too much for him. It does not, however, repel the sage Parāshara, who is so powerfully stirred by her beauty that he must have coitus with her in mid-stream while being ferried across the Yamunā.

It is interesting to study Satyavatī's reactions. Her immediate response is to point out the completely exposed situation: "Holy one, there are rishis standing on both banks of the river. They'll see us. How can I?" (63.72). Parāshara counters this by creating a dense fog. Satyavatī is taken aback and blushes (the *Āryashāstra* translation glosses this by saying that she blushed at the desire for intercourse arising in her despite having lived a self-disciplined life so long). Her next ploy is the standard double-edged appeal of her not being an independent person but subject to her father (not Vasu, but the head-fisherman) and the problem of despoiled virginity. The first excuse is obviously half-hearted and Parāshara does not even bother to counter it. He merely assures her that her virginity will remain unimpaired, whereupon her father would not come into the picture at all. Satyavatī eagerly responds to the sage's offer of a boon, by way of return for her favours, by asking for the piscean body-odour to be replaced by enchanting fragrance, indicating the simplicity and utter femininity of her desires as befitting a simple fisher-girl:

"And she, ecstatic with her boon,
Conceived that same day
From her intercourse with Parāshara."—(63-83)

Thus, Krishna born-on-the-island *(dvaipāyana)* is engendered. Following this, after *shloka* 85, the Bengal recension has four *shlokas* where the Dāsa king of the fisher folk is delighted with the fragrance of Satyavatī's body and finds out from her that it is a boon bestowed by Parāshara. She does not mention anything about Vyāsa.

Little is written about Satyavatī in the epic, but obviously she engaged the imagination of later redactors in *Harivamsa* and even more so in *Devī Bhāgavata Purāna* (II.2.1-36). The *Devi Bhāgavata Purāna* (II.2.1-36) provides extremely interesting psychological insights into Matsyagandhā's character by recounting in detail the conversation between her and Parāshara, developing this adolescent virgin's remarkable character at length. When Parāshara grasps her right hand, Kālī smiles, ever so much in control, so mature, and says (my translation):

"What you are about to do,
befits it your ancestry, your ascesis or the scriptures?
Your family name is spotless;
of Vashishtha's clan are you.
O dharma-knower, what is this you crave
enslaved by desire?
Best of Brahmanas! Rare is human birth on earth.
Specially rare in men is Brahmana birth.
Best of twice-born! You are highborn, virtuous,
scripture-versed, dharma knowing.
O Indra among Brahmins,

my body stinks of fish,
yet why do un-Aryan feelings arise in you?
O twice-born! Your wisdom's doubtless most prescient,
but what auspicious marks you see in my body
that you crave me thus?
Does desire so possess you
that your own dharma you forget?"

So saying, she mused:

"Oh! mad to possess me
this *dvija* has lost his senses.
He'll upset the boat and drown.
He's desperate; his heart's pierced
by Kama's five arrows;
He's unstoppable."

Musing thus, the girl told the great sage,

"Great one, be patient
till we reach the other bank."

She said, Parāshara heeded her well-meant advice.
Her hand he left and sat quiet.
But reaching the other side,
the sage, desire-tormented,
seized Matsyagandha again
for intercourse.
Quivering, annoyed, she spoke to the sage before her:

> "O best of sages! My body stinks.
> Can't you sense it? Making love
> ought to delight both equally."

As she spoke, in a flash she turned
fragrant-for-a-yojana,
Yojanagandha, lovely, beautiful.
Making his beloved musk-fragrant, enchanting,

the sage, desire-tormented,
seized her right hand.
Then auspicious Satyavatī
told the sage bent on coitus,

"From the bank all people
and my father can see us.
It is daylight.
Such beastly conduct doesn't please me.
It disgusts me.
Hence, O best of sages, wait till nightfall.
Coitus is prescribed for men
only at night, not in daytime.
In daylight it's grievous sin;
if seen, brings great disrepute.
Grant this desire of mine, wise one."

Finding her words logical,
the generous sage at once
shrouded all in mist by his powers.
As the mist arose
deep darkness shrouded the bank.
Then the desirable woman
spoke to the sage in dulcet tones:

"I'm a virgin, O tiger among twice-born.
Enjoying me you'll depart where you will.
But infallible is your seed, O Brahmin.
What of me? If today I'm pregnant
what shall I tell my father?
When, enjoying me, you leave,
what shall I do? Tell me!"
Parāshara said, "Beloved, today
having delighted me,
you shall again be virgin.
Yet, woman, if you fear,
ask what boon you will."
Satyavatī said, "Best of twice-born,

ever you honour others.
Act that neither my father nor anyone
knows anything. Act that
my virgin status isn't ruined.
May your son be
like you wondrously gifted.
May my body be
forever fragrant;
May my youth be
forever fresh, ever new."

Assuring Kālī of her son's fame as arranger of the *Vedas* and author of the *Purānas*, Parāshara swoops upon the consenting maiden. Later we will find Surya doing the same with adolescent Kuntī. Having sated himself, the sage bathes in the Yamunā and leaves, never to have any contact with her again.

This fisher-girl's striking character emerges from this interaction. Though she has but just reached puberty, a sage, howsoever famous he might be, does not overawe her. Instead, she reads him quite a lesson in propriety, resisting his advances with remarkable presence of mind. Noticing his violent passion, she takes care not to refuse him outright, lest in forcing her he should capsize the boat. She buys time until they have crossed, hoping his passion will have cooled by then. Reaching near the other shore, she voices her irritation and disgust at his animal lust and draws attention to her own repulsive body-odour more than once. With a maturity and frankness that astonishes us even in the twenty first century, she points out that coitus ought to be mutually enjoyable. Even after becoming musk-fragrant she does not give in, objecting to beastly coupling in daylight in public. Once again, the sage bows to the logic of her arguments and raises a screen of mist. Yet she does not give in and raises the ultimate objection: what will be her status when he has deflowered her and departed? No one will point a finger at the high-caste sage; but what about her? With a maturity that is astounding for an uneducated, pubescent girl, she harbours no illusions that the sage might wed her. Hence, she obtains assurances of regaining her virgin status and the fame of the illegitimate offspring. Only after these practical aspects have been taken care of does she allow the eternal feminine to come forward, desiring to remain forever young, forever fragrant—a gift that was Helen's, and one that perhaps women of all time, everywhere, have craved.

The 'miracle' of unimpaired virginity has been explained by Dr. Esther Harding in *Woman's Mysteries* (p. 103) as the quality of being "one-in-herself": "A girl belongs to herself while she is virgin-unwed—and may not be compelled either to maintain chastity or to yield to an unwanted embrace. . . . This liberty of action involves the right to refuse intimacies as well as to accept them." Dr. Harding points out that the word "virgin" actually connoted precisely the opposite of what it has come to mean now. Such goddesses as Ishtar, often addressed as "the Prostitute", and Aphrodite were called virgins. It refers not to a physical condition but to an inner state, a psychological attitude: "It may be used of a woman who has had much sexual experience; it may be even applied to a prostitute. Its real significance is to be found in its use as contrasted with 'married'".

When Satyavatī mentions that she is ruled by her father, she is referring to the concept that the woman is not her own mistress but the chattel of her father who has the right to transfer her, as property, to a husband. In breaking away from this and asserting her liberty of action, she gains the "one-in-herselfness" in so far as even after having completed the relationship Parāshara has sought for and she has accepted, she does not become dependant on him, cling to him or insist that the moment be made eternity through formalised marriage. Both break-off without any regrets or lingering backward glances and mushy sentimentality. There is no anguished query about the child to be born, nor any hopes expressed of meeting again. It is an extremely functional, clean-cut relationship with a specific purpose and no strings attached—highly modern in fact. The contrast between this "virgin" Satyavatī and the "married" Jaratkāru clarifies how powerful this quality of virginity is. It is because of this unique wholeness and completeness of character that Satyavatī can continue to preside over the destinies Shāntanu's lineage long after his death.

Kuntī appears to be another such liberated "virgin", also having had a child of her own will beyond the trammels of marriage, and even within that institution choosing to have three sons by persons other than her husband. Both Satyavatī and Kuntī emerge as far stronger characters, independent and liberated, than their doting, lust-ridden husbands. To quote Dr. Harding again, "the woman who is virgin, one-in-herself, does what she does not because of any desire to please, not to be liked, or to be approved, even by herself; not because of any desire to gain power over another to catch his interest or love, but because what she does is true . . . she is not influenced by the considerations that make the nonvirgin woman, whether married or not, trim her sails and adapt herself to expediency. . . . dependant on what other people think" (p. 125). We shall see this when she forces Vyāsa to father sons on her reluctant daughters-in-law.

Vaishampāyana goes on to state in 63.89 that Vyāsa taught the four Vedas and the epic to his disciples Sumanta, Jaimini, Paila, Shuka and Vaishampāyana himself. In the *Vishnu Purāna*, part 3, chapter 4, Parāshara expands this cryptic statement to explain that Paila was taught the *Rig Veda*, Vaishampāyana the *Yajur Veda*, Jaimini the *Sāma Veda* and Sumanta the *Atharva Veda*. Further, Vyāsa taught the *Purāna* to Lomaharshana of the Sūta clan. Each of these disciples further split up the Vedas and Purāna among their disciples, and so it went on till there were innumerable sects forming a veritable forest under the single Veda-tree. Besides this, each disciple was assigned recitation of a version of the epic to a particular audience. One of the most intriguing puzzles for the Indologist is Jaimini's retelling of which only the *Ashvamedha Parva* is extant, differing considerably from Vyāsa/Vaishampāyana's version via Sauti's transmission.[2]

Having mentioned the birth of Bhīshma after this, Vaishampāyana abruptly jumps to the sage Animāndavya, carrying in his body the stake on which he was impaled, who cursed Dharma to be born as a Shudra. Thus Vidura is born. However, no mention is made of Vyāsa fathering him on a nameless serving-maid. Curiously, Vaishampāyana picks Sanjaya for mention next to Vidura and before Karna and Krishna, followed by the births of Sātyaki, Kritavarmā, Drona (pot-born), Kripa (reed-born),

Dhrishtadyumna (fire-born) and Draupadī (altar-born). The story of Animāndavya is retold in detail later in the *Ādi Parva*, as also of these other heroes. What is curious is the mention in *shloka* 117 that both Shakuni and Gāndhārī "were adept in worldly matters" since no such indication is found concerning the latter. Subala, their father, is said to be the incarnation of Nagnajit, a disciple of the Asura-king Prahlāda (*shloka* 115).

Shlokas 124-125 tell of the sons of Dhritarāshtra of whom Yuyutsu, also called Karana, is specifically mentioned as born of a Vaishya woman. The sons of the Pāndavas are now mentioned and Vaishampāyana throws in Shikhandi to complete hurriedly a somewhat haphazard list, admitting that

"I could not remember all their names,
Even if I lived for ten thousand years.
What I give you is a list of the principal heroes."—(63.131)

Janamejaya, however, is not discouraged, and insists on a detailed account of at least the purpose for which these mighty warriors were born. This provides the narrator with an opportunity for deifying his heroes and investing them with apparently unnecessary divine paraphernalia. This, of course, would be in the bardic tradition of building up the image of the concerned dynasty, which can be made into gods only if their enemies are elevated to the status of titans.

Vaishampāyana first provides a picture of a veritable Satya Yuga, Golden Age, stressing by implication the defects, the evils that were occurring in his own time. It provides fascinating insight into the social conditions obtaining at that time. In the first place, the very beginning of the new race, after Parashurāma had destroyed all Kshatriya males, occurring through a mixture of two castes: Brahmin men and Kshatriya women, to produce children who were accepted as Kshatriyas in society, which would be unthinkable by Vaishampāyana's own time. In that age,

"No one died untimely.
None had sexual relations
before coming of age. . . .

No Brahmin sold the Vedas . . . no Brahmin
read them aloud before Shudras.
The Vaishyas used bullocks to plough
and would not yoke cows.
Lean cattle were carefully fed.
Nor were cows milked
till calves had first their fill.
Traders did not use false weights." (64.17, 20-22)

The implication is, of course, that in Janamejaya's time promiscuous sex, mercenary Brahmins like Kāshyapa who was bribed by Takshaka, cruelty to cattle and cheating in trade were current. These were considered the most heinous crimes, the golden age being envisioned in terms of negations of them all. Into that golden era were born the anti-gods, seeking overlordship of earth. Brahmā, on being approached by the distressed Earth, commanded the gods to send out parts of themselves to be born on earth and fight the titanic forces. The gods, in turn, approached Nārāyana who also agreed to incarnate. He is described, *inter alia*, as having the *shrīvatsa* symbol on his chest, which cannot be translated as "auspicious wheel-mark." Recent iconographic studies have identified it as a hieroglyphic representation of a child, signifying the child of the mother goddess Lakshmī (*Shrī-vatsa*). It would not be a circular mark, but in the form of a roughly sketched human figure as is still drawn in red in all Hindu houses on auspicious occasions, particularly in case there is any act of worship. In *shloka* 52 the phrase "whose eyes . . . are slanted" signifies not any Chinese facet but that Vishnu's eyes are always gazing down at the tip of the nose in the standard yogic meditative gaze.

It is Indra who requests Vishnu to descend on earth and not Brahmā, as is usually the case. This Indra-Vishnu nexus that has been growing since the *Āstīka* is brought to a culmination here, to be reflected on the mundane level in the Arjuna-Krishna relationship based upon the archetypal Nara-Nārāyana duo. With Vishnu's acquiescence at the end of section 64 the *Ādivams hāvatarana* ends. Van Buitenen prefers to extend it by another six *shlokas* of section 65 till Janamejaya asks his next question on how gods, anti-gods, men etc. were created and which would logically be the beginning of a fresh chapter. These six *shlokas* merely describe the gods incarnating in the lineage of seers and royal sages and the failure of the anti-gods to slay them even in infancy owing to their celestial prowess.

Vaishampāyana has been unable, even by now, to get to his main story because of the persistent interruptions by Janamejaya who obviously wants to invest his ancestors and their fratricidal war with as much of supranormal ramifications and superhuman glory as possible. We will see how the king continues to hold-up the narrative flow chapter after chapter until he has succeeded in his attempt to satiate all those present with the divine ancestry of the Pāndavas.

Although the *Sambhava* sub-*parva* begins with section 65, the account of the descent of the first generations actually continues right up to section 67. It is, therefore, appropriate that we continue to deal with that portion of the *Sambhava* as forming part of the *Ādivamshāvatarana* before passing on to the story of Shakuntalā.

Following Indra's consultation with Nārāyana, the gods are born in the lineages of Brahmin and royal sages and proceed to destroy the titans and other evil creatures. Vaishampāyana ends here and would have gone on to his main theme, but Janamejaya once again interrupts him in *shloka* 7: "I am eager to know more about the births of the Devas, Dānavas, Rākshasas, Gandharvas and Apsarās, Yakshas, humans and all other creatures."

What follows is a typically Purānik account of the birth of the twelve ādityas, of whom Vishnu the youngest was the greatest (65.16), the lineage of the Daityas born of Diti, Dānavas of Danu and other types of anti-gods, at the end of which Vaishampāyana admits, "Their sons and grandsons are so many that it is beyond my power to enumerate them" (65.38).

Curiously, although he refers to forty sons of Danu in 65.22, he enumerates only thirty-four. Two of these titans are named Sūrya and Chandramā, so Vaishampāyana explains that these should not be confused with the identically named celestials (65.27). However, it could also be evidence of these deities being originally titans who were later absorbed in the pantheon, just as the Greek sun god Helios became Apollo and the moon goddess Selene became Artemis. There is a slight mistake in translating 65.36 where the four sons of Shukra are rendered as "Atri and three others". The correct version would be "Tvashtādhara, Atri and two others". In *Shloka* 39 we come across a new piece of information: so far we knew from the *Āstīka* that Vinatā had only two sons. Now we are told that she had six: Tarkshya, Arishtanemi, Garuda, Ārunī, Vāruni and Aruna. Similarly, we find two new names of Kadrū's snake-sons: Kurma and Kulika (65.41). There seems to be some confusion in his mind regarding the progeny of Pradhā and Kapila, as he attributes Gandharvas and Apsarās to both, and even *amrita* is said to be born of Kapilā. Having completed this account of Kashyapa's progeny which, Vaishampāyana assures the king, leads to accretion of "much wealth and fame, the genealogy of the other mind-born sons of Brahmā is taken up.

The eleven sons of Sthānu, that is Brahmā, are enumerated first, who are "known as the eleven Rudras". The Vālakhilyas are mentioned as Kratu's children, though in the Purānas they are born from Brahmā's involuntary ejaculation during the wedding of Shiva and Pārvati. Similarly, Kumāra is categorically mentioned as the son of Agni, not Shiva (*shloka* 24). There is a sudden paean to Vishvakarman in *shlokas* 29-31, followed by a repetition of Kashyapa's progeny interspersed with a reference, quite out of place, to the birth of the Ashvins, adding that Garuda, Aruna and Brihaspati are counted among the Ādityas. Harking back to the preceding chapter, as many as three verses from *shloka* 43 are concerned with Shukra, the seer-poet and teacher of yoga who is termed the preceptor of both the gods and the demons presiding over the monsoons as a planet.

The text appears to be somewhat garbled in *shloka* 50 where Aurva is said to have one hundred sons with Jamadagni as the eldest, while in *shloka* 48 Jamadagni is Richika' son. *Shloka* 53 contains an obscure reference: "The mind-born sons of Lakshmī were the sky-ranging horses". Van Buitenen feels that this may refer to Gandharvas. It may also refer to Uchchaihshravas, the celestial steed. The birth of animals and trees is described and, once again, the progeny of Vinatā and Kadrū are mentioned. Clearly, the repeated reference to the *Garudas* and *Nāgas* shows the predominance of these two clans in the matrix producing the *Ādi Parva.* There is also an indication of three species of elephants—a synonym for whom is *nāga*—in *shlokas* 64, 67 and 68 namely, Airāvata, Mātangi, Shvetā.

Janamejaya, however, is not satisfied. He persistently leads Vaishampāyana back to the origins of the dynasties, now specifically hinting that the various incarnations be identified, thereby enabling him to acquire a celestial ancestry. And so, Vaishampāyana begins all over again in section 67, entering into a fanciful exercise of equating mortals with their supposedly other-worldly existence. Not all the kings he mentions, however, occur again in the epic, as they should considering their asurik or divine origins. In making Hiranyakashipu reincarnate as Shishupāla there is a deliberate attempt to lift the Pāndava story out of the naturalistic world into a cosmic sphere of conflict between Vishnu and this Asura repeated in each *yuga.* Vaishampāyana's account includes such curious manifestations as the royal sages Paurava, Rishika and Manimat being originally the Dānavas Sarabha, Arka and Vritra. Dhritarāshtra is said to have been originally a Gandharva prince named Hamsa, but Pāndu *is not provided with any godly pre-existence.* He is merely mentioned as Dhritarāshtra's younger brother and sandwiched between him and Vidura who is described as Atri's son, not as Dharma (67.86-87). It is a curious omission, unless we interpret *shloka* 86 as saying that the younger brother of the Gandharva Hamsa was reborn as Pāndu. The fact that Janamejaya does not remark on this is also remarkable. The sons of Dhritarāshtra are uncompromisingly made into incarnations of *rākshasas,* but Vaishampāyana runs out of re-birth material where the 101st son Yuyutsu and the daughter Duhshala are concerned, leaving them high and dry without any heavenly origin. The hundred names given here appear differently in various recensions, and even in section 116. *Shlokas* 108-9 contain high praise of their achievements and prowess, as well as their being versed in the arts and sciences and experts in warfare, which clashes oddly with the gratuitous attribution of *rākshasa* origin. Shikhandi, the shield used by Arjuna to slay Bhīshma, is also said to be originally a *rākshasa.*

It is interesting to watch how Janamejaya's lineage is built up: Arjuna is an emanation of Indra, whose prestige is further enhanced by having Nārāyana as his friend. Soma, the moon-god, allows, very reluctantly, his son Varchā to be born as Abhimanyu to Arjuna. One wonders why the bard forgot to give Subhadrā a similar divine origin. Much later she replaces Ekanamsā in the triad worshipped in the Jagannātha temple. Janamejaya, being Abhimanyu's grandson, can thus trace his lineage back to Soma, adumbrating the entire origin of the Pāndavas who are a lunar dynasty. This does appear to be instant genealogy creation since Varchā is not mentioned anywhere else in the Purānas as a son of Soma. One can sense here the compelling desire of a parvenu dynasty, only two generations old in kingship, to legitimise itself with a genealogy drawn direct from gods. Otherwise, they would have remained content to be known as the Paurava dynasty, which traced its origin to Soma anyway. It is because there was considerable debate surrounding the birth of the Pāndavas and their inability to produce indubitable proof of Pāndu being their father that the need arose for having a fresh ancestry. Naturally, the easiest way to do this was to draw on the readily available divine pantheon, with the unquestioned doctrine of avatarahood being stretched to include all the gods, instead of being restricted to Vishnu. In medieval times such creation of a divine origin was seen in the case of the Rajput clans.

The twelve verses devoted to Abhimanyu single him out as the most important figure in this account of the descent of the generations and the reason is baldly stated (67.126): "Your majesty, I have given you accounts of the births of your father and his father."

Draupadī's five sons, who have no achievement to their credit and whose sole claim to fame is that they are Ashvatthāmā's victims, are made out to be the Vishvadevas, important Vedic deities. Siddhi and Dhriti (Success and Endurance) are respectively Kuntī and Mādrī, though it would be more appropriate to reverse the nomenclature: Mādrī is successful in outwitting Kuntī by using her charm to have twins at a stroke, and Kuntī is the symbol of calm endurance and relentless effort in the epic. It is through Kuntī that the Pāndavas are related to Krishna, as she is his father's sister, given away to her childless uncle as her father Shūrasena had promised to give his sister's son, childless Kuntibhoja, his first-born. Hence Prithā becomes Kuntī, who is engaged by her adoptive father to look after Brahmins and guests. Like her father, she also gives away her first born.

We now have thirteen verses devoted to the birth and prowess of Karna. Brought up by Rādhā and Adhiratha, he is named Vasusena The long bit on Abhimanyu was obviously spun out with an eye on the kingly audience, but the elaborate description of Karna cannot be justified in similar fashion unless we recall the argument that the epic was originally a celebration of Kuru valour.

The Critical Edition rejects both the Abhimanyu and Karna portions in this chapter as interpolations not occurring in most of the manuscripts. Besides, there is no explanation for these two particular warriors being singled out. The former may be explicable, as we have seen above, but not the latter.

To this is added the incarnation of Nārāyana as Vasudeva, accompanied by his eternal companion, Shesha-nāga in the form of Balarāma (the emphasis on the nāgas recurs yet again), the sixteen thousand Apsarās and Shrī-Rukmini as his wives. Pradyumna, Rukmini's son, is said to be an emanation of Sanatkumāra while in the *Bhāgavata Purāna* he is bodiless Madana re-incarnated by Shiva's boon on the prayer of his distraught wife Rati. Draupadī is described as an emanation of Shachi, Indra's wife, in order to fit in with Arjuna, Indra's son. This is a distinct departure from the account Vyāsa gives later to Drupada making her Shrī reborn. Obviously, Sauti or Vaishampāyana is trying to resolve the embarrassment of having Vishnu's wife wed Indra's son. In this epic she is also one of the very few women with dark complexion (her great grandmother-in-law Satyavatī-Gandhakālī being another): her skin has the sheen of beryl (*vaiduryamanisannibha* 67.159). It is curious that Gāndhārī should be said to be an incarnation of Mati (wisdom). This becomes all the more ironical when Gāndhārī voluntarily assumes blindness: it becomes a powerful symbol illuminating the entire Pāndava-Dhārtarashtran conflict.

With this we come to the end of the protracted account of the "downcomings" (67.164) of the godly and titanic forces, setting the cosmic background for embellishing the violent story of the envy-riven dying house of the Bharatas.

The cyclical narrative technique is seen towards the end of the epic when, in the *Svargārohana Parva*, section 4, Indra shows Yudhishthira many of the protagonists assimilated into their original celestial forms. Thus the narration achieves a closure in a complete circle.

References

1. See P. Bhattacharya: *The Mahabharata TV Film Script: A Long Critique* (Writers Workshop, 1991)
2. Translated into English by S.K. Sen, edited by Pradip Bhattacharya, Writers Workshop, Kolkata, 2009.

9

The Sambhava Parva-I

Shakuntalā

The story of Dushyanta-Shakuntalā, immortalised by Kalidasa as an exquisitely romantic love-episode, hardly occupies the place of importance in the epic that a reader approaching the *Mahābhārata* through the *Abhijñāna Shākuntalam* would expect. Vaishampāyana relates it in response to Janamejaya's insistence that the glory of the kingly ancestors of the Kurus be recounted. Since they trace their ancestry to the famous Bharata, he naturally devotes some space to his origin. Prof. Lal in his Preface to the twelfth fascicule makes valuable points such as Vyāsa's economy and realism against Kalidasa's elaborate lyricism and sentimentality. As for the heroine herself, though Prof. Lal says, "She belongs to an impressive gallery of self-confident and very vocal Hindu ladies of the past who combined moral righteousness with sensual glamour: Devayānī . . . Gāndhārī. . . , Draupadī," Gāndhārī shows no hints of any "sensual glamour" or sex appeal.

Vaishampāyana styles Dushyanta the founder of the Paurava dynasty, which is a misnomer since he has not gone back to Puru, a mistake that will be remedied in the subsequent sections dealing with Yayāti and his successors. Section 68 is the only place where we find some details about this king as a person. He appears to be physically enormously strong:

> "His body was like a thunderbolt;
> He could lift Mandara mountain, with its woods and forests,
> if he wished, with his two arms."—(68.11-12)

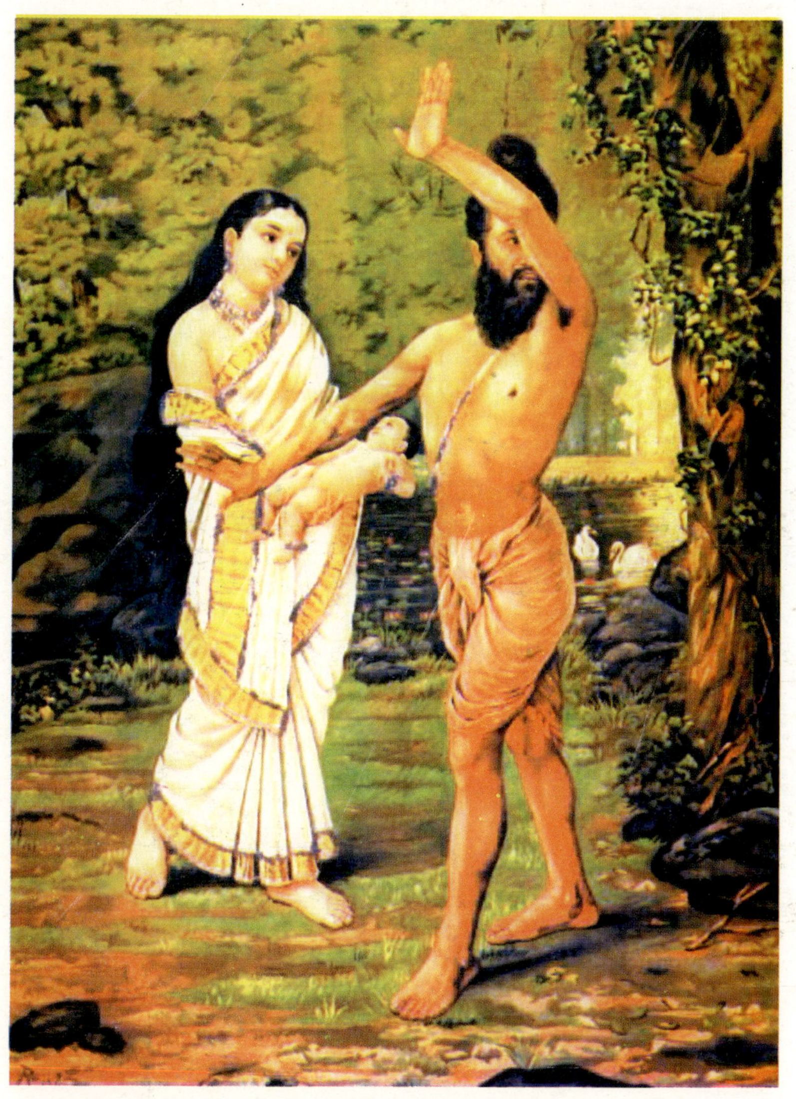

"Vishvamitra rejects Menaka and Shakuntala" by Ravi Varma

He is an all-round warrior, having mastered all four types of mace fighting, namely *prakshepa* (throwing the club at an enemy at a distance), *vikshepa* (where the enemy is nearby), *parikshepa* (protecting oneself with the club when encircled by enemies by rotating it all round) and *avikshepa* (attacking with the pointed end surmounting the club). He is also adept at elephant and horse riding. His prowess as a ruler is stressed by his command over the far-off *mlechchhas* (barbarians).

Such details concerning the precise type of weaponry in which the king is adept and his qualities as a rider are rare indeed in the epic. It is significant that the chariot is not mentioned, perhaps indicating that during his time it was not yet in vogue. We hardly come across a single person famed as a fencer other than Sahadeva. The club or mace is quite a favourite weapon (Bhīma, Duryodhana, Shalya, Jarāsandha, Balarāma), despite its unwieldiness, and could indicate a primitive type of culture. It is archery that comes to occupy the pre-eminent place in the epic war, along with the javelin *(Shakti)*.

Dushyanta, like his successors, engages in a massive hunt that seems to be an organised expedition to clear a wilderness of fierce beasts. It looks forward to the hunts that the Mongol Khans used to organise periodically that were veritable holocausts. The king is mentioned as driving off in a chariot of such speed that it seemed winged. In hunting, he uses arrows, javelins, scimitar and club (he is again described as "expert in whirling the club" in 69.23).

Following the holocaust, Dushyanta reaches the hermitage of Kanva, described in terms almost identical to the description of the Edenesque snake-isle of the *Āstīka parva.* In the meeting of Dushyanta and Shakuntalā, it is peculiar that at no stage do we find him introducing himself. In the Bengal recension we find part of a *shloka* in-between *shlokas* 6 and 7 of section 71 where the king introduces himself as the son of the royal sage Ilīna, who, in terms of the highly confused genealogy in the epic, is a grandson of Matināra (section 94), also called Ilīna. It is interesting how Vyāsa hints at the playboy in the king:

"(the king) Did not see any rishi near.
He heard her talk to him.

He saw she was lovely, sweet-smiling,
She was enchanting."—71.12

The Bengal recension has him propose to her immediately, justifying himself with the argument that she cannot be a Brahmin's offspring because he is self-disciplined and can be attracted only to a Kshatriya woman. Vishvāmitra, of course, was a Kshatriya who successfully fought a protracted battle with the gods and the sages to be accepted as a Brahmin seer, and Shakuntalā was born to him from Menakā, the celestial courtesan. Menakā, in response to Indra's request to seduce the sage, narrates some of Vishvāmitra's famous exploits. The first reference is to his causing the death of Vashishtha's sons, which will be narrated in detail later in the epic. It was on the banks of a river, called Kaushiki after him, that he achieved Brahminhood, as we shall find in the *Vana Parva.* He named this river 'Pāra' because his wife had safely crossed the twelve years of famine, thanks to the efforts of the royal sage Trishanku, also called Matanga, living as a hunter in the forest. It was while doing this that Trishanku killed Vashishtha's cow to provide food to Vishvāmitra's wife and children, thereby incurring the third sin (the two earlier ones being adultery and his father's wrath) because of which he was named Trishanku. In gratitude, Vishvāmitra became his priest when everyone else had refused and forced all the gods to accept the sacrifice. When the gods threw Trishanku down as he rose to reach heaven in his earthly body, Vishvāmitra proclaimed he would create a parallel galaxy for the king beginning with Shrāvana. This made Indra quickly provide the king with a seat in heaven to make Vishvāmitra desist from creating a parallel pantheon.

Menakā makes an extremely powerful plea for exemption, listing the awesome prowess of the royal sage:

"His righteous anger can burn the worlds.
His kick can make the earth totter.
He can uproot the mahā-mountain Meru and hurl it far.
He can cover the ten points of the universe
in an instant."—71.42

Yet, the only assistance she seeks from Indra is that the wind should lend a hand in simulating a realistic striptease! There is, surely, implied sarcasm in this conjunction of the mighty rage of the sage and his complete enslavement through the most simply arranged artfully artless disrobing. The confidence Menakā has in her own charms is undoubtedly boundless, since she appears to be reciting the dangers she will be incurring only to show her own superiority in overcoming them with such ease, through pretended bashfulness in deliberate nudity.

In the tradition of these *apsarās,* like Adrikā with Uparichara and Urvashī with Pururavā, Menakā also leaves the sage after delivering the child, as she does later with Pramadvarā. Like Satyavatī, Shakuntalā is a fruit of lust and this double taint from two sides of the family marks the Pāndavas and the Kauravas like a curse of Greek mythology, heralding their doom. We shall analyse this when we come to Pāndu.

Dushyanta himself is moved purely by lust. When Shakuntalā, worldly-wise with an innate maturity, demands that her son alone must inherit the crown, as the Dāsa-king will insist later for Satyavatī, Dushyanta immediately agrees. Vaishampāyana's comment is significant (73.17): "The rājā, without thinking twice, agreed." That is why he refuses to recognise her when she arrives with her son Sarvadamana at his court. Having had his fun, he is not in the least interested in keeping his word. As we shall find elsewhere in the epic, a lie told while making love is said to be excusable. Strangely enough, he is quite unconcerned about possible repercussions from the offended foster-father Kanva. Vyāsa does not whitewash the king at all by inserting any such excuse as a curse by Durvāsā and the lost signet ring that Kālidāsa invents. Kanva himself does not consider this marriage of convenience, carried out to persuade the girl to satisfy the king's lust, improper between willing parties if both are Kshatriyas, as is the case here.

A valuable portion of Dushyanta's speech is devoted to the eight types of marriage sanctioned in the scriptures: *brāhmya, daiva, ārsha, prājāpatya, asura, gandharva, rākshasa, paishācha.* There is some contradiction here because Dushyanta says that the first six, including *asura,* are ordained for Kshatriyas (73.9) but in the next verse he says that the *asura* form is for Vaishyas and Madras, and even equates it with the *paishācha*, as not to be practised (73.11). He replaces the *asura* with the *rākshasa* for Kshatriyas. Bhīshma recounts these in section 102 before abducting Ambā, Ambikā and Ambālikā, but drops the *prājāpatya* and *gandharva* forms, introducing *svayamvara* (self-choice) as another accepted form of marriage.

An important indication as to Shakuntalā's extremely realistic and unromantic response to Dushyanta's solicitation is in *shloka* 16 where she sets out the pre-condition and says: "If you agree, let us make love". The original quite uncompromising and baldly uses the word *sangama* (coitus). She is obviously not seduced into romantic sentimentality by his flattery. She treats him as an equal, not a superior, and this independence and strength of character comes out even more fully in her confrontation with the king in his court. She does not argue concerning the scriptures when Dushyanta is narrating the reasons for the *gandharva* rite being blameless. She simply says that if she truly can choose for herself according to the scriptures, she will accept him provided he accepts her pre-condition. Here is a young woman of great foresight, quickly seizing the sudden opportunity to carve out a kingdom for herself through her yet to be engendered son. She is mature enough not to fall into the usual trap of being overcome by her suitor's royalty into becoming his mistress for an instant and then sighing over what-might-have-been. She ensures that his momentary weakness is turned into a life-long relationship for her and her child on the most legitimate basis. The orphaned woman is extremely careful of her position and will not be deluded by the unctuous flattery of a royal playboy. There is none of the mushy sentimentality of Kālidāsa, with Shakuntalā lost in sighing over memories of a faithless lover-husband.

Vyāsa categorically states that when Shakuntalā faces the king with their son, "He remembered all" (74.20) yet denied her. Shakuntalā now launches a frontal attack on him and through her mouth we find some of the most direct utterances of the status of wives in the ancient Indian ethos:

"A wife
   is a man's half;
A wife
   is a man's sakhi, his love-and-loving friend;
A wife is the threefold root:
   Dharma, Artha, and Kama;
A wife
   is one who ferries the husband across. . . .
A wife
   is like a mother in illness and sorrow. . . .
The man
   who has a wife
      is trusted
         by all;
The wife
   is a means
      to a man's
         salvation. . . .
No man,
   not even in anger,
      should displease his wife;
Happiness, joy, virtue,
   everything
      depends on her.
She is the hallowed soil
   in which he is born
      a second time."—74.44, 46-47, 54

Having recounted the importance of the wife, she goes on to speak of the wife's crucial place in a man's life because he is reborn in her:

"A man himself
   is born as his son;
so a wife who has a son
   should be treated
      as one's mother."—74.51

Shakuntalā, well versed in the scriptural texts, is repeating here a doctrine of the *Aitereya Upanishad,* chapter 2:

"when he casts it (the seed) into the woman, 'tis himself he begets. . . . She the cherisher must be cherished."[1]

The next phase of her attack concerns the benefit and delight of having a son, quoting in *shloka* 62 from the *Parāshara Grihyasūtra* 1.18.2, as noted by van Buitenen, 'When he sees his son he murmurs, "From each limb hast thou come forth, thou art born from my heart, thou art myself with the name of son, live thou a hundred autumns."' There are a number of extremely touching verses here:

"Is any happiness greater
than what a father feels
when his small son,
though grubby and dusty,
runs towards him
to be clasped in his arms?"— 74.56
"The touch of sandal paste,
of women,
of water,
is not half as pleasing
as the embrace
of one's own son."— 74.60
"Far away from home,
a man picks up
another man's son,
smells his head
and feels his being
fill with happiness."—74.65

This portion of her argument she rounds off with an unanswerable mirror image:

"This boy
is flesh of your flesh,

being of your being,
  Like your image in a lake
you see before you
  a part of yourself."—74.69

Now she shifts to a welcome personal note of anguish, lamenting how she was deserted by her parents and now is being rejected by her husband. The woman in her finally comes out with her plea that the son be accepted even if she has to go back. Dushyanta callously seizes on the reference to her parents and alleges that she is a lying slut in defaming the first of the apsaras and the finest among rishis in this manner. Shakuntalā has referred to Menakā in *shloka* 73 as born of Brahmā and as the loveliest *apsarā*, which is what Dushyanta flings back in attacking her as a liar. He roundly abuses her as a slut of mean birth and bids her leave.

Put on her mettle, Shakuntalā's approach changes, and we find a splendid burst of pride:

"My birth, Dushyanta,
  is nobler than yours.
You walk on earth,
  I roam the sky."—74.87-88

She holds up a mirror to him, virtually calling him a swine:

"A pig delights in filth
  even in a flower-garden;
a wicked man finds evil
  even where there's good"—74.94

and reels off a string of homilies differentiating the good man from the wicked, which effectively classes him as of the latter type. Again she launches into a series of homilies, each urging against rejection of a son, and advising him, to hold on to Truth that is the highest dharma:

"If you and falsehood unite,
  if you disbelieve me,
I will go, now, by myself.
  I do not want you."—74.111

She ends with a calm prophecy of the inevitable succession of her son to his throne, even without his help.

We do not know how this king would have reacted to this burst of injured pride and the calm conviction in her son's right, for the *deus-ex-machina* of a celestial announcement resolves the problem. Much in the manner of Rāma in his testing of Sītā and her banishment, Dushyanta points out that he had decided against accepting Shakuntalā and her son because:

"Had I acknowledged him
  at Shakuntalā's words,
my subjects would have suspected me,
  my son would not have been thought pure."—74.122

He further explains to Shakuntalā that he was afraid of the legitimacy of their son being suspect because there were no witnesses to their marriage and, with typically male face-saving arrogance, he forgives her all the plain speaking, but does not apologise for the abuse he showered on her. The Bengal recension, however, carries a *shloka* after 123 where he asks her to forgive his harsh words, for that is the conduct proper of a wife devoted to her husband. It also has eight *shlokas* after 124 where Dushyanta presents Shakuntalā to his mother Rathantarya, who foretells Bharata's splendid career.

This brings us to the end of section 74, after which another genealogical account begins. By itself, the story of Shakuntalā has little bearing on Janamejaya's desire to know the story of his ancestors, except in so far as it relates the prowess of Bharata, the eponymous ancestor of the Pauravas, who came to be known as the Bharatas after him, and later as the Kauravas, after Kuru one of his famous descendants. However, in the character of Shakuntalā it gives us an extremely rare picture of a nubile orphan; mature and self-assured enough to fight for her rights and to plan out her future at the shortest notice, quick to seize Dame Fortune by the proverbial forelock. Dushyanta appears as an unmitigated opportunist always seizing the quickest and easiest way out of a situation. There is indeed, a vast difference from Kālidāsa's world. As Prof. Lal points out, "But that is part of the difference between the epic, classical world and the more relaxed, post-classical, perhaps more refined but certainly more hedonistic world of the later dramatists (Kalidasa, Bhasa, Bhavabhuti, Harsha)!"

The Shakuntalā episode, however, raises a serious genealogical problem. Vishvāmitra is said to be her father, but this seems to be quite impossible because the Vishvāmitra who fought with Vashishtha and gave up his kingdom to become a sage comes much later. According to the Purānas and the *Harivamsa,* Vishvāmitra's predecessors are as follows: Dushyanta-Bharata-Vitatha-Bhumanyu-Vrihatakshtra-Suhotra-Hastin (who founded Hastināpura) and Vrihat (who founded the Kanyakubja dynasty). Then, Vrihat-Janhu-Ajaka-Balakashva-Vallabh-Kushika-Gādhi-Vishvāmitra. Thus, according to this version, Vishvāmitra is one of the distant descendants of Dushyanta, instead of being his father-in-law! Acharya Chatursen holds that the purānik statement of Vishvāmitra being Shakuntalā's father is without foundation and a mistake. Pargiter, in his *Ancient Indian Historical Tradition,* gets round the problem by positing more than one Vishvāmitra, taking it as a *gotra* name and suggesting it is the well-established tradition of Vishvāmitra being Shakuntalā's father that is correct. Pargiter points out that Vishvāmitra's ancestor Jahnu belongs to the early period of the Haiheya, Aikshvāku and Paurava kings, much anterior to Bharata. Hence the *Mahābhārata* account (*Ādi Parva* 94 and *Anushāsana Parva* 4) making Vishvāmitra a descendant of Ajamīdha, son of Suhotra and great-grandson of Bharata, is wrong. It clashes with the immediately succeeding section 95 of the *Ādi Parva* where Shakuntalā is described as Vishvāmitra's daughter. Pargiter suggests that the error arose out of the *Rig Veda,* the *Aitareya Brāhmana* and the *Sānkhyāyana Shrauta Sūtra* where Vishvāmitra is termed "leader of the Bharatas" as the priest of the Bharata king Sudasa of the North Pānchāla dynasty, who is considerably after Bharata and Dushyanta. It is this Sudasa who drove Samvarana out of Hastināpura. His priest, carrying the *gotra* name of Vishvāmitra, was possibly confused with the first Vishvāmitra, father of Shakuntalā, and therefore he and his ancestor Jahnu were arbitrarily inserted into the Ajamīdha dynasty, making Jahnu one of his sons.

Dr. S.N. Pradhan, however, rejects this theory and places Vishvāmitra squarely as a Bharata on the basis of synchronisms worked out in great detail, showing the sage to have been a contemporary of Viduratha, whom he places fourth in descent after Kuru, son of Samvarana. The problem remains quite mind-boggling!

Reference

1. Sri Aurobindo, *The Upanishads*, p. 361, vol. 12, Centenary Edition

10

The Sambhava Parva-II
Lust and the Quest for Immortality

We now meet four of the most memorable characters of the *Mahābhārata*: Kacha, steadfast in his pursuit of esoteric lore in the face of a woman's blandishments; Devayānī, lovely, aggressive, knowing exactly what she wants and how to get it; Sharmishthā, princess-turned-maid, beating Devayānī at her own game; and Yayāti, hungering for sex, proud of his virtues, meteor-like flashing down from the heavens.

The theme of Vaishampāyana's narration is actually Yayāti, for he devotes half of chapter 75 to an account of his old age and how he exchanged it for the youth of his son Puru hoping to sate his lust, in vain:

"He enjoyed both his wives. . . .
He dallied with the apsarā Vishvāchi. . . ..
And still the kāma of the mahā-illustrious king
O rājā, was not satiated. . . .
No pleasures satisfy desires.
Like ghee poured in yajña,
They inflame desire." (75-47-49)

It is Puru who carries on the dynasty that comes to be named after him. This itself is significant, for Puru is born of Sharmishthā, daughter of the Asura king, and thereby not the fruit of an inter-caste *pratiloma* marriage, like that between Yayāti and Devayānī which was frowned upon as improper. The issue of such a marriage were debarred from inheriting their father's property. It is quite possible that this ordinance came into being from Yayāti's time, as he is one of the most ancient rulers of the Bharatas.

Vaishampāyana comes to Yayāti in the process of reciting the genealogy of the Bharatas afresh. As we begin section 75, we face the disconcerting probability of yet another ineffectual attempt to run through the Paurava dynasty, which Vaishampāyana has been trying to do since the *Ādivamshāvatarana*:

> "And now, O defectless one, about Prajāpati Daksha, Vaivasvat Manu, Bharata, Kuru, Puru, Ajamīdha,
> Yādava, and other kings of the Paurava race—let me recite before you their famous, inspiring, auspicious,
> Long histories, bringing wealth, fame and long life."

The ten sons of Prachetā are cryptically said to have burnt large trees. This interesting myth is related in section 15, part I of the *Vishnu Purāna.* These ten Prachetās had engaged in the worship of Vishnu for thousands of years immersed in the ocean, because of which the earth became overcast with forests of huge trees in the absence of a ruler. Seeing this, the wrathful ten loosed fire from their mouths, burning up the prolific vegetation till Soma pacified them and gave them, in marriage, Mārishā or Vārkshi, a nymph born of the trees. From this union issued the mighty Prajāpati Daksha, ancestor of all humanity. Wishing to people the earth, Daksha produced five thousand sons, the Haryashva, whom Nārada persuaded to renounce the world. Next came the thousand Sabalashvas, who were prevented similarly from carrying out their father's wishes. Daksha finally settled for daughters, fifty according to the epic, and sixty in the *Vishnu Purāna.* The extra ten are bestowed, in the *Purāna,* as follows: four to Arishtanemi, and two each to Angirā, Bahuputra and Krishāshva. Through Daksha's daughters we are once again back to Kashyapa, but this time the genealogy comes straight to humanity. Manu, grandson of Kashyapa through Vivasvat, the sun, fathered the race of humans (75-14).

Manu is said to have had ten sons and a daughter Ilā, a curious phenomenon in Hindu mythology, being the only person who is at once male and female, hence described as both the father and the mother of Pururavā. In section 147 of the *Anushāsana Parva,* Ilā is the daughter of Manu who later becomes the male Sudyumna, a transformation that we find Shikhandi and Bhangāvasana also undergoing. According to the *Bhāgavata Purāna,* Vashishtha turned Ilā into a man at Manu's request. The transformed Sudyumna blundered into the charmed Kumāra forest and was turned back into a woman. In this condition Ilā met Budha, son of Soma and Tārā, who married her and birthed Pururavā. Vashishtha intervened once again and persuaded Shiva to restore īlā to manhood. The boon, however, was a peculiar one: he would alternate between the two conditions, remaining a man for a month and becoming a woman for the next, and so on. It is after her that the area now known as Mesopotamia was originally named Elam, or Ilāvarta, as argued by Acharya Chatursen in his magnum opus *Vayam Rakshāmah.* Bhangāsvana is another instance of a man becoming a woman, whose story Bhishma recounts to Yudhishthira in the *Shānti Parva.* Ilā's son Pururavā may be said to be the founder of the Paurava dynasty, for Yayāti's son Puru is also named after him.

Pururavā has been immortalised by Kālidāsa in his *Vikramorvashi* and the story of his dalliance with Urvashī is one of the most important myths from the point of view of significance and symbolic import. First mentioned in the *Rig Veda* (X.95), this relationship expands into a complete story in the *Shatapatha Brāhmana* (11.5.1). Pururavā is the first of the mighty kings who consort with the gods, like Uparichara Vasu, Nahusha and Yayāti later. All of them, curiously, are his descendants. Because of his marriage with Urvashī, Pururavā is able to bring three types of fire from the Gandharvas for use in sacrifices (75.23). The *Bhāgavata Purāna,* part 9, gives details of how this took place and names the three fires as Pranava, Nārāyana and Agnivarna born of the flame Jātavedas kindled by the king at the beginning of the Tretā Yuga. The *Mahābhārata* alludes to the death of this king from the curse of sages whose wealth he looted (75.22) in his arrogance. This is an incident which we find only in the *Vāyu, Matsya* and *Padma Purānas.* It is the sort of outrage that power-drunk monarchs will perpetrate time and again, as in the cases of Haiheya Sahasrārjuna and Vishvāmitra.

Nahusha, Pururavā's grandson, is the next important king, his father Āyu not having left much of a mark. Nahusha is an important figure in the epic and the Purānas since the gods unanimously elect him to officiate as Indra when Purandara goes into hiding having incurred grievous sin by slaying the Brahmin Trishirā. Nahusha will recur in snake-form to question his descendant Yudhishthira in the *Vana Parva.* He taxed the sages and forced them to carry him on their backs like beasts of burden. It is precisely this outrage that led to in his fall from Indra-hood, as he was proceeding to woo Shachi in a palanquin borne by the sages.

Yayāti is the second son of Nahusha who succeeds to the throne because the eldest, Yati, becomes a hermit. This is a recurring motif in the Paurava dynasty: Shāntanu becomes king because his elder brother Devāpi, suffering from skin-disease, turns ascetic; Dhritarāshtra, the elder, is disqualified from kingship, though he effectually does hold the throne as Pāndu is more interested in living in the forest; Karna, the eldest Kaunteya, is disqualified by illegitimacy. Vaishampāyana expatiates on Yayāti's famous plea to his sons to assume his decrepitude and give him their youth, but there is a curious prevarication in *Shloka* 40 where Yayāti tells Yadu that,

"Once, during a long sacrifice
The rishi Ushanas cursed me
With loss of my sex-pleasures."

This suppresses the truth that it was his giving in to Sharmishthā's plea to father children on her that resulted in this curse. Fittingly, it is the fruit of this union that brought about the curse that becomes the means of his salvation. Puru, Sharmishthā's youngest son, agrees to the proposal and thus inherits the throne.

It is necessary to take a look at another pregnantly cryptic allusion in *shloka* 14: "Later the Brahmins were united with the

Kshatriyas." The reference is to Parashurāma's extermination of all male Kshatriyas, even the embryos, so that the women had to approach Brahmins in order to beget children. Thus, the two races fathered by Manu were united and every Kshatriya had a Brahmin ancestor.

At this stage, once again, Janamejaya breaks the narrative flow by wanting to know how Yayāti could marry the daughter of a Brahmin. Incidentally, he refers to Yayāti as tenth in descent from Prajāpati, which is incorrect unless Prajāpati is taken as referring not to Daksha but to Prachetā.

Janamejaya's query throws the narrative back into cosmic dimensions that we had left behind with the churning of the ocean. Here, once again, is a war between the titans and the gods that gives rise to the quest for immortality. Presumably, this is before the ocean was churned for the nectar, but it is vain to try to find any chronological order in the inexorable cyclic arrangement of Hindu myths, particularly those relating to such archetypal conflicts.

In this *Devāsura* war the gods are at a loss because the Asura-preceptor Shukra is able to resuscitate slaughtered *Asuras* through his magical powers. Brihaspati, the Deva-guru, is ignorant of this art of life-restoration. Indra persuades Brihaspati's eldest son, Kacha (this is the only episode where we hear of him) to act as a spy and ferret out the secret from Shukra through his daughter Devayānī. It is part of the carefully interwoven relationships that form the tapestry depicting the clash between good and evil in the epic, that Krishna, destroyer of evil, should trace his ancestry to the asura-preceptor Shukra through Devayānī and her son by Yayāti, Yadu, who founded the Yādavas. The gods stress, repeatedly, the importance of Devayānī:

> "Revere also Devayānī, who is
> Mahā-ātmaned Shukra's favourite daughter. . . .
> Pleasing Devayānī
> By your conduct, sweetness,
> Kindness, generosity, and self-control
> You will discover the secret." (76.15-16)

Kacha accepts the assignment and is accepted by Shukra as his disciple, knowing full well that he is the son of Brihaspati, his opponent. Here is a superb instance of devotion to knowledge surpassing all considerations of rivalry. The abrupt fall from such high ideals during the Pāndava period will be seen when Drona ensures that Ekalavya will not surpass Arjuna in archery by misusing his rights as a guru. On the other hand, Drona accepted his enemy Drupada's son Dhrishtadyumna as his disciple knowing that he had been produced to kill him.

Kacha, following the shrewd advice of the gods, concentrates on pleasing Devayānī:

> "Daily the youth pleased her,
> The young Devayānī,
> With songs and dancing,
> And instrumental music.
> Daily he pleased her,
> The young Devayānī,
> With flowers and fruits
> And a menial's obedience." (76.24-25)

Kacha in the prime of his youth is counterpoised by Devayānī, a virgin in the full bloom of youth. This delicate balancing, deliberately done in order to bring out the mutual attraction, is carried on into *shloka* 26 where it is Devayānī who entertains Kacha *in private,* a very significant pregnant phrase:

> "And Devayānī,
> When the two were alone,
> Attended upon the strict-vowed youth
> With songs and sweet speech."

The third line brings out Kacha's strict adherence to the vow of celibacy, despite the blandishments of the forward Devayānī, who does not hesitate to attend upon him even in privacy. This aspect of her character will be revealed in greater prominence when she tackles Yayāti and Sharmishthā.

It is when half of the thousand-year apprenticeship of Kacha

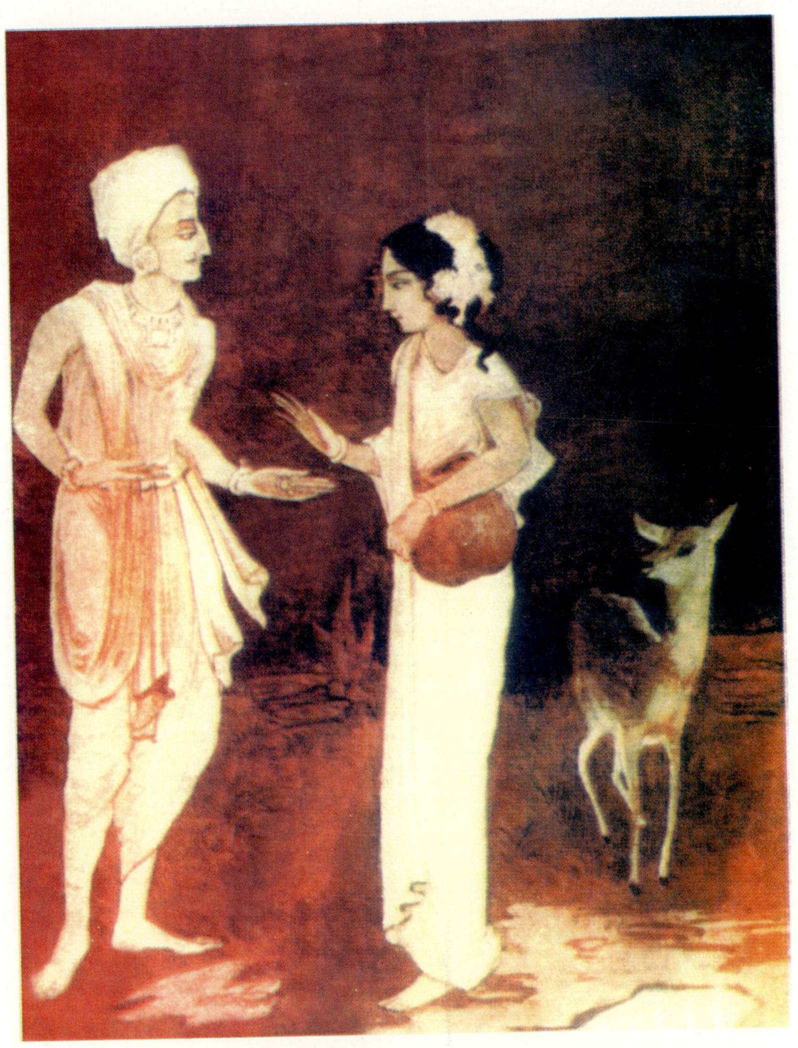

"Kacha and Devayani" by Abanindranath Tagore

is over that the anti-gods get wise to his intentions and carry out repeated attempts to destroy him, only to be frustrated by Devayānī who persuades her father to resurrect him, for, she says, "The truth is, father/I cannot live without him." (76. 32)

The first time he is hacked to pieces and fed to wolves; the second time he is ground to paste and mixed in the ocean; the third time he is burnt to ashes and drunk by Shukra mixed in wine. Significantly, we do not find Shukra taking any preventive steps by way of warning off the *Asuras*, nor does Devayānī suggest this (possibly she is smugly secure in the knowledge that her father will invariably bring him back to life for his spoilt child). Shukra is obviously a little annoyed with her repeated pleas and seeks to hold up an ideal of divine indifference before her with fulsome flattery:

"I have revived him again and again.
He is always killed. It's no use
Why should you
Grieve for a mere mortal?
Brahmā, Brahmins, gods,
Indra, Vasus, Ashvins, anti-gods,
All the three worlds revere you
At the three prayer-times through my prowess." (76.45-47)

Devayānī's response is typically feminine, but shrewdly laced with appropriate reference to Kacha's lineage to show that he was not "a mere mortal" and was also a dutiful disciple of Shukra's, so that the guru cannot absolve himself of all responsibility for one whom he has taken under his tutelage.

"His grandfather is the ancient rishi Angiras,
His father the rich in ascesis Brihaspati—
For those rishis' son and grandson
Shouldn't I grieve, shouldn't I weep?
He was a brahmachāri, dutiful,
Rich in tapasyā . . .
Oh, I will starve and die. . . .
Dear father, I love handsome Kacha."—76.48-49

Shukra immediately responds as a doting father would, quickly finding scriptural justification for anger against Kacha's murderers for the sin of Brahminicide. He begins to imagine that by repeatedly slaying his Brahmin disciple the *Asuras* wish to inveigle him into participating vicariously in the sin, thereby threatening his very Brahminhood: "The sin of Brahmin-murder would burn even Indra." This is particularly appropriate because Indra did incur this sin by slaying Vritra and Trishirā and had to give up his kingship, resulting in Nahusha's elevation to that seat.

Shukra, however, does not follow this up, as one would expect, by a curse on the *Asuras*. He merely uses the knowledge he possesses to resurrect Kacha, this time within his stomach, and poses the dilemma to Devayānī: if Kacha lives, he dies. Her response, once again, is true to character. She wants both to be hers and will not be deprived of either father or lover. As she says, "I burn in the fire of two griefs".

Shukra adopts the only way out: allow Kacha to rive open his stomach and then be resurrected through Kacha's use of the treasured secret. Shukra's words show how right the gods were in their advice to Kacha: "Devayānī is your *bhaktā*, you have triumphed" (76.57). But he adds a caveat:

> "If you are not Indra disguised as Kacha
> Accept from me the science of Sanjīvanī." (76.57)

Indra was notorious for his manifold exploits in disguise, chiefly amorous, but this also explains why Indra did not approach Shukra. Only the Brahmin Kacha could succeed, for

> "No one can emerge alive
> from my stomach.
> Except a Brahmin.
> Therefore, listen:
> Come to life as my son." (76.58)

Yet, Shukra is apprehensive and he urges Kacha not to be ungrateful and forget the mangled remains of his guru. Kacha faithfully and gratefully resurrects Shukra and reads him a homily on the disciple's devotion. This swallowing and regurgitation is the core feature of initiation rites of which an instance is graphically represented on the Douris Kylix (drinking cup) depicting Jason ("the healer") half-in and half-out of the maw of a huge serpent.[1]

The first act of the resurrected Shukra is to enact the first mandate against drinking of liquor by Brahmins, equating it with the sin of Brahminicide. His next step is to inform the *Asuras* that Kacha has succeeded in learning the secret lore. They do not attempt to destroy him again. One wonders why. An attempt on his way back would have been only natural.

Section 77 gives us the Devayānī-Kacha confrontation. Here is a woman boldly demanding return of her love; a woman used to getting her way without question. She devotes the first *Shloka* to praising his virtues, the next to declaring her admiration for his father, the third attributing to him knowledge of her feelings all through, ending with the blunt:

"Your vow is now over. I am your *bhaktā*
  I love you. Accept me
Take my hand in yours
  with the proper mantras." (77.5)

It is a direct proposal that would admirably befit a liberated female of today. She will go through precisely the same exercise when Yayāti appears on the scene. Bernard Shaw would undoubtedly have seen in her his ideal concept of the Life Force working through the predatory female to capture the helpless male victim. We do not come across the likes of this lovely, aggressive, utterly self-centred woman in the *Mahābhārata*.

Kacha, very firmly but respectfully, rejects her advances. Devayānī tactlessly, yet so true to her supremely egotistic nature, reminds him that he owes his life to her. Here is an offer to barter marriage against a past service done—the worst gambit to win a man's heart. Kacha now raises the spectre of incest. The original is quite baldly direct, stating that both Devayānī and Kacha have dwelt in the same womb (***kukshi***):

"Gracious one, where you lived,
in the womb of Shukra,
I, lovely lady, lived too."—77.13

He follows this up by pointing out that thereby she is his sister according to dharma. He begs her to bid him a fruitful journey back to the gods. Devayānī's response is a curse:

"If you, Kacha, spurn me
who have importuned you myself,
moved by dharma-artha-kāma,
useless will be your learning,
your life fruitless."—77.16

Kacha responds, "Devayānī, I have voiced the dharma of seers" and he calmly foretells her future:

"Since kāma motivates you,
your kāma will go unfed;
no son of a rsi will take
your hand in marriage" (77.19)

He also analyses her curses logically and finds a saving feature:

"Useless will be my learning
according to you. Very well.
But it will fructify
in those to whom I give it." (77.20)

And so Kacha disappears from this glorious pageant. The Kacha-Devayānī episode is significant in more ways than one. Devayānī importuning Kacha is paralleled in Sharmishthā soliciting Yayāti . Kacha resists, is glorified by the gods and given a share in the sacrificial offerings. Yayāti succumbs, is cursed with senility, rises to heaven and is driven out of it. We will study Yayāti's predicament in its proper place.

Dange has shown that this myth is a parable of initiation. As in the vedic sacrifice of Soma, Kacha is repeatedly killed, only to be re-born.[2] Again, as in the *upanayana* (sacred thread investiture ceremony), where the pupil is symbolically "swallow-ed" by the preceptor, made part of himself as an embryo, and then regurgitated to emerge as the "twice-born", so Kacha is swallowed and disgorged by Shukra. In the *Rāmāyana* there is the incident of Hanumān entering the maw of the snake-mother Surasā (Kadrū) and successfully emerging unscathed to receive her blessings for the success of his mission to Lanka. He has passed a crucial test. We have already pointed out the parallel with similar Greek rites. The *sanjīvanī mantra* that is the means of Kacha's resurrection is like the Gāyatrī mantra taught to the initiate by the guru. A similar episode is that of Mārkandeya, who is swallowed by Vishnu-as-a-baby whom he finds floating on a banyan tree leaf and is disgorged by him, related in the *Vana Parva.* However, we should not confuse this swallowing-and-regurgitation symbol of initiation with Vātāpi metamorphosed into a goat by Ilval being eaten by sages who die as he rips open their abdomens to emerge resurrected at Ilval's summons. Nor is it to be equated with Kronos swallowing up his new-born children who emerge full grown when Zeus makes him vomit, although the tales share the motif of death and resurrection. Zeus himself swallows his wife Metis who emerges in a different form from his head as Athene armed *cap-a-pie.*

In a way, Devayānī, "the path of the gods", is identifiable with Sanjīvanī/Gāyatrī itself, being the means of Kacha's rebirths, for without her this *mantra* would not have become his, nor could he have been reborn. In the *Shatapatha Brāhmana,* both the Devas and the Asuras are found soliciting Gayatri to join them, as she stands between them. But she chooses the gods, leading to the defeat of the titans. Devayānī also serves as the bridge between the gods and the secret of immortality lying with the *Asura* guru. By taking Kacha's side against the anti-gods she ensures the ultimate victory of the gods. In the *Maitrāyani* and *Taittirīya Samhitās,* Devayānī is the name of the fire-altar while Shukra is the *yajña* as also Soma, the divine nectar. That shows how Devayānī came to be termed the "daughter" of Shukra. Shukra himself, we find in the *Shānti Parva,* section 289, was swallowed by Shiva, emerged through his *linga,* and was called his son by Pārvati, with Shiva's sanction. Kacha is repeating the same initiatory cycle of being swallowed and regurgitated by the guru. The atrocities Kacha suffers at the hands of the *Asuras* parallel the purificatory rites, torturing the flesh, which the initiate to the Greek and the Egyptian mysteries had to go through, and later the aspirant to knighthood in medieval Europe. The successful bearing of such ordeals was the test after which the initiate was considered reborn as a member of the esoteric sect, fit to receive the secret knowledge, as Kacha finally does.

The exact parallel to this story occurs in the *Rig Veda's* Soma-sacrifice. *Amsu* is the hair-like fibre of Soma that stands for the sacrificer. Its crushing and filtering into a purified flow of nectar represents the crushing of man's crude nature and transforming these into the delight of immortality called *amrita*. *Kacha*, meaning hair, provides the hint of this esoteric sense.

By way of interesting information, according to the *Devi Bhāgavata*, 8th part, the name of Devayānī's mother (and this is the only place she is mentioned) is Urjasvati, daughter of Priyavrata (eldest son of Svāyambhuva Manu, the first man) and Surupā.

Another point of interest is the feature of sexual temptation that forms part of the tests set to the novitiate. Devayānī sings and attends upon Kacha in private, but he does not succumb to the sexual invitation. While leaving her, he clearly states that he would like her to remember that he never transgressed the dictates of dharma during his stay. In the *Paushya* we have seen how Uttanka rejected the request of his guru's household to have intercourse with his wife in the guru's absence. This refusal to give in to temptation brings both Uttanka and Kacha success in their endeavours. The feature of the novitiate's temptation by sirens also forms part of the ancient mysteries and the medieval cult of knighthood, where chastity was the paramount virtue prized in the aspirant along with infinite patience, perseverance and implicit obedience to the preceptor's commands. The quest for immortality is fruitless unless lust is conquered.

Rabindranath Tagore's treatment of the story in his *Bidāya Abhishāp* takes the form of a dialogue between Devayānī and

Kacha at the point of his final departure from Shukrācharya's hermitage. Through Devayānī's artful questioning Kacha is made to reveal that when he arrived at the hermitage it was she whom he approached first and she persuaded Shukra to accept him as his pupil; that unasked he would gather flowers for her, tend the domestic pets, and entertain her with song and dance. The matter of the repeated killings by the Dānavas is comparatively unimportant, the emphasis being on Devayānī's desperate attempt to elicit some declaration of love from the departing Kacha. The crucial resurrection of Kacha inside Shukra's stomach and his gaining the knowledge of the Sanjīvanī mantra thereby are merely referred to. Tagore uses these instances to make Kacha admit a debt of gratitude to Devayānī as his saviour, and the reference to gratitude makes her flare up in anger. Devayānī's assertion is that winning a woman's heart is well worth a thousand years of ascesis and that it is in no way less of a boon than the Sanjīvanī mantra. Tagore balances the one against the other: love of a woman for a man on one side; and duty on the other, which is also love of a different sort, love for his fellow-beings passing the love of woman, which makes Kacha return to the Devas. It is interesting that where, in Vyāsa, it is Devayānī who reminds Kacha that he owes his life to her and demands marriage in return, Tagore makes Kacha acknowledge the debt spontaneously and has Devayānī spurn the offering of gratitude and passionately demand love. Tagore hints delicately that Kacha does love Devayānī, but builds him up by having him sacrifice this love at the altar of duty. His Kacha is not the heartless stern ascetic of Vyāsa who curses Devayānī back. Tagore's Kacha, instead, blesses her in response to her curse, saying that she will find happiness and glory and that the gloom oppressing her heart will fade. Thus, in effect, he does not discard the proffered love. He accepts it and gives the return in the form of a Brahmin's boon though, regretfully, he must depart. Nor does he indulge in hair-splitting to prove that her curse will not frustrate the application of the secret he has so laboriously won. His only response is the calm bestowing of the boon of a future happiness and glory. Instead, it is Devayānī herself whose curse is so framed as to make the knowledge fruitless if used by Kacha, but not if he teaches it to others.

By and large, therefore, Tagore lifts the theme to the heights of a lyrical dramatic-romance, enthroning love on a romantic plane, unlike the down-to-earth physical attraction and demand for marriage that characterise Vyāsa's story. Characteristically, Tagore ignores objective data, such as the attacks on Kacha and his repeated resurrections, to concentrate on developing the subjective aspect of Kacha and Devayānī's responses to each other, using external incidents and features only as vehicles to bring these out. It is fascinating to watch the artful manner of Devayānī's questioning which gradually, yet inevitably, leads to Kacha's confession of his love for her; the way in which Devayānī dramatically poses before Kacha the crucial choice between knowledge and love; then her misinterpretation of his devotion to duty as deliberate deception on his part, taking it as if he had coldly used her to achieve his ends, exploiting her weakness for him (which is indeed what Vyāsa's Kacha does); culminating in her cursing him with the frustration of being unable to apply the knowledge he has thus falsely won; and, finally, Kacha's supreme act of love, expressed in forgiveness and giving the blessing of happiness. There is also the hint that, blinded by desire, Devayānī is unable to perceive that Kacha simply does not have the freedom of choice to choose between her and the mantra as she wants him to. His course of action was predetermined and his freedom was confined to the romantic interlude which he inserted into an otherwise stern ascetic discipline. It is this hint that, along with the entire presentation of Tagore, lifts the rather tricky and cold Kacha of Vyāsa to heights of romantic feeling and nobility. In the process, Tagore is also guilty of a gross anachronism when he has Devayānī cite as an example one of her far-off descendants, Samvarana, who suffered untold suffering to win Tapatī. His Devayānī could never have become the hectoring woman who forces Yayāti into marriage and makes the Asura-king give her his daughter as a slave.

We pass on now to the tale of Yayāti which forms one of the most poignant episodes in the epic and is also peculiarly timeless in its appeal. For, here is a man with whom we can easily identify ourselves—a man overawed and virtually forced into marriage by the imperious Devayānī; a man who gladly responds to the submissive Sharmishthā's plea to beget children on her (three to Devayānī's two); a man hungry for sensual gratification, untrammelled by domineering wives and the bonds of marriage, desperately engaged in an existential search to glut the body's desires; a man who achieves peace finally and rises to heaven by realising that lust is insatiable and yet falls from there because of the universal human frailty, pride.

The two episodes are loosely linked through the *deus-ex-machina* of Indra. The gods, reinforced with the knowledge Kacha has brought, urge Indra to lead them against the titans. On the way, Indra catches sight of Devayānī, Sharmishthā (the *Asura* king Vrishaparvā's daughter) and their companions sporting in a lake. In the form of a strong breeze he mischievously mixes up their clothes, and the tragic drama is on! It is again the arrogant Devayānī who abuses Sharmishthā for daring to wear her clothes and addresses the princess as "disciple", arrogating to herself the status of her father as preceptor of the *Asura*-lord. Sharmishthā's reply is devastating. She describes Shukra (who was also called *kāvya,* son of *kavi,* chanter-poet) as her father's bard, singing the king's praises in hope of largesse:

> "You are the daughter of a professional praise-chanter, I am the daughter of one whose praises are chanted. Your father begs, my father bestows alms. You are an alms-beggar's daughter, I an alms-giver's daughter.
> "Beat your breast, beggar-girl! Shout, rent, curse! Weep away! I can harm you, you can't harm me! And I won't even quarrel with you—you are not my equal." (78.10-11)

Devayānī, livid, starts tearing the garment she is wearing, which belongs to Sharmishthā. The outraged princess pushes her down a well and flees.

Yayāti now appears on the scene, inevitably in the course of a deer-hunt and gives us the first picture of what Devayānī looked like. So far, she has been the conventional slim-waisted, large-eyed, moon-faced lady as seen through Kacha's chaste eyes. Here, we find a king seeing a woman and struck, above all, by her copper-bright nails, to which he refers twice. He also calls her *shyāmā,* dark complexioned, unusual for a Brahmin lady but quite typical of the *Asuras.* We recall that the only other dark ladies we know in the epic are the fisher-girl Satyavatī who rules Hastināpura and imperious Draupadī, doom of the Kshatriyas:

"Lovely dark-blue complexioned lady, *Shyāmā,*
Who are you
With nails like burnished copper,
And ear-rings like divine gems?
Why are you alone? Why are you weeping?"—78.17

Devayānī takes him up on this admiration of her nails and offers him her "right hand/with burnished copper-bright nails. . . . Take my hand and lift me up." She had once before asked Kacha to take her by the hand; he had refused. Yayāti does not, and finds himself trapped into a misalliance, for Devayānī deftly uses his rescuing her by grasping her right hand (she takes care to present the right hand to him in *shloka* 22) as a symbol of his having accepted her hand in marriage.

There are number of gaps between *shlokas* 19 and 20 and again between 22 and 23 that need to be filled in for obtaining the full flavour of the story. These have been dropped in the critical edition, but their absence hampers the smooth flow of the narrative. For instance, how does Devayānī know that Yayāti is a king in *shloka* 22? The two verses that precede it state:

"Who are you,
Handsome, virile, strong,
What brings you here?
Why are you asking me this?
"Lovely lady," replied Yayāti,
I am Yayāti, son of Nahusha.
Exhausted on a deer-hunt
I paused near this moss-covered well."

Devayānī insists that he marry her, but he refuses as she is a Brahmin's daughter. With supreme assurance she responds that he may well reject her words, "But I'll get my father to order you. Then you will have to agree." Yayāti quickly, politely, takes leave of the "tapering-thighed lady", once again a telling observation from a *Kshatriya.* Kacha appears never to have looked below her face.

What follows once again brings out Devayānī's complete dominance over her father, as we have seen earlier where she insists that he revive Kacha yet again, despite his advice that it is fruitless. Shukra, knowing his daughter's faults, says that she has probably brought this misfortune upon herself by her own foolishness. Look at Devayānī's reply, typically in character, browbeating him into doing what she wants, viz. presenting an ultimatum to the *Asuras*:

"Fault or not,
first listen to me, father! . . .
Father, tell me. . . .
  am I a hired chanter's daughter?
a beggar's daughter?" (78.41, 45)

She succeeds in hurting Shukra's pride, but the seer is still sufficiently self-controlled to try to calm her by reassuring her of her father's pre-eminence in Creation and reading her a lesson on forgiveness as a supreme virtue (a theme that will run all through the epic through Yudhishthira):

"Svyambhu Self-Born Brahmā himself,
  pleased with me, told me
I was lord of all there is on earth
  as well as in heaven. . . .
Devayānī, whoever
  without anger rules anger,
is the greatest conqueror
  known on earth.
And he who rules anger
  with forgiveness—like a snake
casting off its skin—
  he is really a man. . . .

Take two men: one performs yajñas
every month for a hundred years,
the other has learnt to rule his anger.
The second is the greater man."—78.49; 79.3, 4, 6

Now he makes his mistake:

"Boys and girls who
can't tell right from wrong
quarrel needlessly. Wise ones
don't follow their example." –79.10

This immediately spurs Devayānī into a display of obduracy and she counters Shukra's advice in three verses elaborating on the ill effects of staying in envious and inferior company. adeptly quoting homilies back at him, flatly refusing to stay within the *Asura* realm:

"I think it's wretched to respect
one's enemies in high estate,
when one is oneself demeaned
Death is preferable, wise men say." (79.18)

The clever harping on the insult to Shukra's status arouses his anger and he announces to Vrishaparvā that the slaying of Kacha and the insulting of Devayānī (he does not mention her being thrown into the well and she also does not mention it to him; was she too ashamed of her helpless plight?) leave him with no alternative but to leave the kingdom. He is, however, not very much in earnest, for he suggests that the king placate Devayānī if he wants Shukra to stay on:

"My life depends on her.
Go if you will, anti-gods,
and placate her. Just as Brihaspati
seeks Indra's good, I seek yours."—80.11

He even takes it upon himself to report to his daughter that the king has declared Shukra to be his overlord. But Devayānī is not content with this. She needs royalty to humble itself before her, not just her father:

"Bhrigu's son, dear father," she said,
  "if you are really lord
of the anti-god king and his wealth,
  let him personally say so before me."—80.15

Now comes yet another verse missing from the critical edition that is narrative logic requires:

"Vaishampāyana said: hearing this from Shukra, Vrishaparvā and his courtiers prostrated themselves on the ground before Devayānī."

Even in this confrontation between Devayānī, Vrishaparvā and Sharmishthā, it is once again the latter who emerges with the greater dignity and nobility. Hearing of the demand that she must become Devayānī's attendant, Sharmishthā says:

"With all my heart. . . .
  Neither Shukra nor Devayānī
must leave the anti-gods
  through any lapse on my part."—80.22

Contrast Devayānī's petty gloating with Sharmishthā's royal calm:

"But I am the daughter" replied Devayānī,
  "of a hired praise-chanter,
I am the daughter of a beggar.
  And you are the daughter
of a highly respected person.
  Why should you be my maid?"
''When one's family is in trouble,"
  replied Sharmishthā, "one tries
to be of help. I will follow you

wherever your father bestows you."—80.25-26

Devayānī patronisingly pats her father approvingly:

"I now see that your powers
are not fruitless, your knowledge is potent."—80.28

Doting Shukra, Vaishampāyana tells us, was delighted "When he heard his daughter speak to him in this manner." One is not left with a very high opinion of this doting father, despite his much-vaunted ascetic prowess.

Sharmishthā's last sentence is the concern of the next episode, the seduction of Yayāti. Actually, there is no employment of feminine wiles: it is more of an *āsurik* marriage in reverse, with the woman virtually carrying off the man. The scene is a repetition of that in section 78: the women are amusing themselves, Yayāti arrives again in pursuit of deer, tired and thirsty, the only difference being:

"Sweet-smiling shuchismitā Devayānī,
Voluptuously reclining,
Paragon of beauty,
Loveliest of them all, varānganā,
And Sharmishthā beside her,
Gently massaging her feet." (81.6-7)

Yayāti has not recognised in this regally accoutred Devayānī the forlorn maid he had pulled out of the well, catching her by the right hand glowing with burnished copper-bright nails. He is particularly drawn to Sharmishthā, the lady "of lovely eyebrows" and intrigued that she should be massaging another's feet. There are a few verses in some recensions where the obviously enchanted Yayāti launches into an elaborate description of the beauty of Sharmishthā and her regal bearing: "Never have I seen so lovely a lady on earth—not Devī, Gāndharvi, Yakshī or Kinnarī. With lotus-like large eyes like Shrī; with all auspicious marks, bedecked with ornaments."

Devayānī's reply to his question is superbly trite and casual, quickly dismissing his curiosity in order to concentrate on him:

> "Fate," replied Devayānī.
> '"Fate is behind everything. . . ."

She tries to inveigle him into conversation but the moment he hints at departure, she throws aside all feminine modesty and guile and states, "Stay here and be my lord." By way of inducement, she adds:

> "With me are a thousand maids
> and my personal maid Sharmishthā." (81.17)

Yayāti and Devayānī now engage in a wordy battle, the one trying to escape, the other determined that he shall not. She brushes aside his objection to an inter-caste marriage by pointing out that Brahmins and Kshatriyas have inter-married before. This may be an anachronistic reference to what will happen in the Tretā Yuga after Parashurāma's annihilation of all Kshatriya men. Since Indian mythology is wholly cyclical, this really does not matter, as that particular Tretā Yuga might belong to a cycle preceding the *yuga* in which Yayāti and Devayānī are fighting out their battle of possession and freedom. Devayānī cuts short the entire argument with her firm, supremely confident declaration:

> "I chose you," said Devayānī, "You did not ask
> for me. My father shall approve
> you shall marry me.
> Why be afraid? You are getting without asking."—81.27

Devayānī summons Shukra, tells him that she will marry none else, and he, without even asking Yayāti whether he is willing, immediately bestows his daughter on him, freeing him from the taint of inter-caste marriage and counselling him to treat Sharmishthā well but not to call her to his bed. Shukra is very careful of protecting his daughter's interests and only too eager to hand over the extremely difficult job of pandering to her spoilt whims and fancies to a monarch. Kacha was undoubtedly wise in not marrying her. Yayāti is soon to regret his weakness bitterly.

The only way to deal with a lady who browbeats a great sage, treats the *Asura* king like dirt and arrogates another king to herself, is to bypass her. This is precisely what Sharmishthā does. She has noticed Yayāti's admiration of her beauty. Besides, as the daughter of a king, she is his equal and he feels more at ease with her. She has little difficulty in persuading him to have intercourse with her. He admits:

"I know you are nobly-born,
In the race of the Daitya anti-gods.
Your beauty is ravishing.
There isn't the least fault in you."—82.14

But Shukra's injunction makes him hesitate. Sharmishthā deftly gets round this by quoting a *shloka* (82.20) little known to us today: "Five kinds of lying are excusable; when joking, when enjoying a woman, at the time of marriage, when facing death, and when one has lost all of one's wealth." The verse is important enough to be repeated by Krishna in section 70 of the *Karna Parva* while dissuading the furious Arjuna from killing Yudhishthira.

The next *shloka*, 22, is quite controversial as there are many different readings. Ganguli translates:

"O king it is not true that he is fallen who speaks not the truth when asked. Both Devayānī and myself have been called hither as companions to serve the same purpose. When, therefore, thou hadst said that thou wouldst confine thyself to one only amongst us, that was a lie thou hadst spoken."

Van Buitenen's version is:

"The one who lies when questioned in a suit
Him they call a liar, king.
But when a common purpose is at stake

It's then a liar is injured by his lie."

It is the Ganguli version that fits the context, for it looks back to the lie permissible during marriage.

Gratuitously, Yayāti suddenly mentions a vow of his to grant whatever is asked, thereby making his final capitulation all the more "honourable" for him. Sharmishthā takes the cue and pleads with him to protect her dharma by making her a mother. She also indulges in a bit of legalistic casuistry that provides Yayāti his final justification for doing what he has obviously been wanting to: a slave has nothing of his own; she is Devayānī's slave; Devayānī belongs to Yayāti; hence she is also his. Their union is significantly described: "They lovingly came together and lovingly parted" (82.33).

Yayāti's reference to his vow does not seem all that abrupt if we take into account five verses between *shlokas* 23 and 29 which have been omitted in the critical edition. These run as follows:

"Kāvya bestowed me along with Devayānī and has also asked you to see to my welfare. Without my asking, you are giving me gold, jewels and gems. So what is left in your becoming my husband indeed? O king, cows, jewels, land and whatever else is asked of you by anyone, you grant freely. Among such gifts, giving of a son and of oneself are supreme. And the gift of one's body surpasses all. Thrice you have announced in the city-streets that you will grant anyone whatever he desires. If you reject my request, it will prove you false to your declared word. Hence, O king, like Vaishravana keep your promise."

Whatever the excuse, it remains an undeniable fact that Yayāti succumbs to lust and its fruits are dreadful. Devayānī, who is immediately suspicious, confronts Sharmishthā with a direct accusation of having given way to her sexual desires and having had a son by a person of doubtful origin. Sharmishthā quibbles on the words *rishi* and *dvija,* claiming that she was visited by a radiant Veda-knowing, twice-born man who fulfilled her desires for a son. Since Kshatriyas are also twice-born like Brahmins, she is quite sincere when she says "this is the truth" (83.4).

Besides, kings were also referred to as royal sages, hence she can rightly call her son the progeny of a *rishi*. But it is the children who betray Yayāti by calling him father in Devayānī's presence. And what hurts her most is not that she has been duped and bested once again by Sharmishthā, but that she has been able to have three sons by him against her two. So, even in sex-appeal Sharmishthā has proved herself superior. This plunges Devayānī into a veritable hell of jealousy and frustrated pride. What makes it worse is that when she abuses Sharmishthā, the princess calmly answers back, as she had done in the unprovoked attack earlier,

"I am not afraid of you.
When you chose him as your husband,
I chose him too. Lovely lady
According to dharma, a *sakhi*'s husband
Is one's own husband."—83.22

In the face of Devayānī's crude assault, Sharmishthā addresses her as "sweet-smiling lady", "lovely lady". Devayānī, living example of the saying that hell hath no fury like a woman scorned, rushes pettishly to her father, with Yayāti anxiously in tow. See what an exaggerated view she takes of the situation, as if all creation centres round her alone:

"Adharma's defeated dharma!
The low rise, the high fall.
I have been insulted
By Vrishaparvā's daughter.
This king here, Yayāti,
Has three sons by her;
And me—unfortunate me—
I have only two."—83.30-31

This fury at having been outwitted in the number of sons is repeated much later in the epic by Kuntī against Mādrī, hectoring Pāndu for pleading the younger wife's case who has proved to be so cunning in getting twins at one go. The complaint Devayānī makes is almost the same that she had made in the earlier incident, except for the last *shloka*: a sense of outraged pride, grossly inflated. Dharma here, of course, is whatever Devayānī considers befitting her status and worth. Shukra seems merely to be a puppet of hers, to be used for chastising those who do not regard her in the same light that she herself does. Shukra promptly curses Yayāti to fall victim to invincible decrepitude. Yayāti's repetition of the justification Sharmishthā had advanced is summarily brushed aside: Shukra tells him he ought to have obtained his approval, for Yayāti is his dependant and, having knowingly broken his pledge, he is guilty of the sin of theft. However, Shukra is not as hard-hearted as his daughter. He agrees that Yayāti may exchange his senility for the youth of any of his sons and grants that that son will inherit the throne. This makes it clear that Shukra was the accepted lawgiver for not only the Asuras but the kingdoms of mortals as well.

Now, in section 84, comes one of the most pathetic scenes in the epic: the senile Yayāti pleading with his sons to exchange their youth for his old age, unashamedly acknowledging his unsated lust and being rejected contemptuously by one after another. Each is cursed by Yayāti. Yadu is cursed that none in his line will be rulers: royalty of the Yādavas is never mentioned in the epic. Turvasu's line will become extinct, as indeed it does after a last reference in *Shatapatha Brāhmana*. Druhyu is exiled to the seas and to be known as Bhoja, the western rulers. Anu is barred from performing *yajñas* and cursed with senility. Ushinara and Shivi are the famous Ānavas. There is a peculiar instance of time-collapse here. Yayāti's sons are all small children—at least not teenagers—when Devayānī discovers his *faux pas* and Shukra curses him with instant senility. Yet, the moment he returns from Shukra, the sons speak to him like grown young men! The version given in the *Udyoga Parva* avoids this peculiarity by not bringing in the curse at all and simply refers to Yadu and others having displeased their father.

Yayāti asking his sons for their youth becomes an archetype in itself, which is stressed in the reiteration of the same formula by the king as he is rejected by each son:

"Child of my heart
  yet you
Will not give me your youth."

This form of a test set to the aspirants for kingship or a hidden treasure they have to find, with the elders usually failing because of their egotism and the youngest winning it through his humility, is a motif recurring time and again in folk tales throughout the world.

Puru, no doubt wiser because of the curses incurred by his elder brothers through their obduracy, accepts Yayāti's senility and bides his time patiently, to be rewarded with the kingdom and win renown as the founder of the Paurava dynasty.

But what is more important is the appealing figure of Yayāti, who realises that lust is insatiable, a priceless realisation which, unfortunately, is not handed down to the succeeding generations who continue in themselves this taint of lust:

"Kāma never ends,
Kāma grows with feeding,
Like sacrificial flames
Lapping up ghee.
Become the sole lord of
The world's paddy-fields, wheat-fields,
Precious stones, beasts, women—
Still not enough.
  Discard desire.
This disease kills. The wicked
Cannot give it up, old age
Cannot lessen it. True happiness
Lies in controlling it."—85-12-14

The critical edition and van Buitenen's translation are all the poorer for leaving out these Upanishadic lines, looking forward to the immortal exhortation to cut the tree of desire with the sword of non-desire, which the *Gītā* will pronounce.

The fact that Yayāti is met by a deputation of his subjects consisting of representatives from all the castes is an indication that the monarch could not rule whimsically as a tyrant. His subjects lodge their protest against what they consider a whimsical and unjust setting aside of the elder progeny in favour of the youngest. Yayāti has to explain the situation to them and to invoke the sanction of Shukra before they allow Puru to be made king. The tendency towards the law of primogeniture is already in evidence among the people.

Another curious feature is that Yayāti is said to have dallied with the *apsarā* Vishvāchī after his rejuvenation, although in his plea to Shukra he had put forward his infatuation with Devayānī as his excuse for wanting to remain youthful. Nor is there any mention of Sharmishthā. Presumably, Yayāti steered clear of the twin sources of his predicament and turned to a pleasure-giver without any strings tied. But when he proceeds to the forest after retaking his old age, it is peculiar that his queens are not mentioned as accompanying him. One would expect at least the virtuous Sharmishthā to follow him, if Devayānī had reverted to Shukra's home in a huff (she is not said to have returned with Yayāti after Shukra cursed him). One would also expect a tempestuous outbreak by her when her sons are passed over by Yayāti and the detested Sharmishthā's progeny made his successor. Yet Vaishampāyana is tantalisingly silent on her reactions to this final blow where she is wholly worsted by her rival. However, in section 75 Vaishampāyana has Yayāti enjoying *both* his wives as also the *apsarā* after his rejuvenation and describes him as achieving heaven along with his wives, neither of which is mentioned in the extended account that follows. Her not returning with Yayāti proved her undoing, for she could at least have briefed her sons appropriately and won the crown for them. But, as before, her self-consuming pride stood in the way of her achieving her cherished desires. In more ways than one, she reminds us again of a similar red-blooded beauty, arrogant, ruling males by her flaming loveliness and steel-will, yet ultimately frustrated in all her most prized attempts to win happiness: Eleanor of Acquitaine, first Queen of France, then Queen of England, wife of Henry II, in whose unbending egotism she met her match. And Elizabeth Woodville, Edward IV's Grey Mare, who destroyed York and Lancaster, yet united them ultimately in Henry VII's marriage to her daughter Elizabeth, at the cost of her sons' lives.

Thus, Vaishampāyana satisfies Janamejaya's curiosity about the inter-caste marriage of his ancestor (76.1) which had interrupted his account of the Descent of the Generations. Like Sauti, Vaishampāyana now slips in an adroit reference to Yayāti having been flung down from heaven, which inevitably prompts the insatiable Janamejaya to insist on yet another digression enabling us to savour a unique episode in Indian mythology that is only feebly paralleled in the Trishanku myth. It is true that both Yayāti and Trishanku are suspended in limbo when Indra refuses to harbour them and the ascesis of sages prevents their being precipitated on earth; and ultimately both do achieve heaven. But Yayāti's story has been related with a poignancy that makes it the tragedy of all men who aspire to bliss. Where Trishanku remains an individual king sponsored by Vishvāmitra to enter Indra's realm in his mortal body and serves more as an illustration of the sage's powers than as a symbol of man's eternal effort to capture Ananda in this mortal coil, Yayāti is Everyman who has reaped the fruits of his toil but falls victim to his innate hubris and loses all that he had so painfully built up, till fellow-men come to his rescue. Through their joint human endeavour, not because of any intervention by a seer of supernatural powers, he is able to regain his lost happiness. This is particularly significant because, as the falling Yayāti tells Ashtaka:

"I fall from heaven,
my excellence humbled
for slighting my fellow men."—89.1

But he has not yet learnt his lesson and is still blindly proud. He has been asked repeatedly by Ashtaka to reveal his identity:

"Who are you, O youth
falling in the sky,
handsome like Indra,
shining in self-splendour?
Who are you

falling like the sun falling
scattering masses of clouds
as it falls? . . .
Had you asked first
who we were
we would not be uncivil
and ask as we do now,
Who are you, O handsome one?
Why do you fall here?"—88.7, 8, 10

Yayāti's response is in line with his swollen pride in the merit of his austerities and his self-love that prompted the transference of his senility to Puru:

"I am older than you,
so I did not greet you
first. It is said
that he who is older
or superior in learning
is revered by Brahmins."—89.2

Ashtaka immediately snubs him, much as Ashtāvakra will snub Janaka when his youth is held against his meeting Dandin:

"According to you, O rājā,
a man old in years
deserves instant respect.
Only those who are superior
in learning or asceticism
are worthy of reverence."—89.3

The retort is all the more deserved because Ashtaka has already paid Yayāti the compliment of equating him with those honest and virtuous persons among whom he is falling, for in such company he cannot be harmed even by Indra. He has also addressed Yayāti as Shakra, Arka (i.e. Sun) and Vishnu and referred to his 'enviable beauty'. Yayāti is once again guilty of what Indra had accused him:

"You belittle your superiors,
your equals, and your inferiors,
without knowing their merits"—88.3

His reply to Ashtaka is also disjointed, for his fall has definitely confused him as much as those who are seeing him fall (88.8). He launches into a monologue that is full of implied self-criticism and fatalism:

"Ill deeds cancel good deeds.
Pride is the road to hell. . . .
I was virtuous once—
All gone—irrecoverable."—89.4, 5

So it is not enough to be virtuous, but once must also be wise:

"Be wise and virtuous—learn from me.
Who finds heaven?—
He who has wealth yet does yajña,
He who is learned yet humble,
He who, knowing the Vedas, is ascetic.
Shun pride of wealth,
Shun vanity of Veda-knowing. . . .
Power, effort, are vain and useless.
Fate is the lord—remember this,
And shun pride, and cast off grief."—89. 5-7

But from this fatalism Yayāti proceeds to the equanimity celebrated in the *Gītā*:

"The wise are always equable,
Not sorrowing in sorrow, not rejoicing in joy. . . .
O Ashtaka, I do not fear fear,
I do not grieve over grief.
I know I am what I am,
What the Great Ordainer made me."—89.9-10

Prof. Lal has dropped a *shloka* after *shloka* 12 that is included in all recensions, including the Bhandarkar Critical Edition. This runs:

'Vaishampāyana said, "And when his maternal grandfather, repository of all virtues, Yayāti, had spoken thus, Ashtaka again addressed him, suspended in mid-air." '

Yayāti's description of the various heavens to which he had ascended step by step again reveals the flaw of pride:

"I have lived in many realms,
I was adored by the gods,
I shone like the gods,
I was powerful like the gods."—89.19

He has not only stayed in Indra's heaven, but ascended to that of Prajāpati, "A difficult realm to attain" (89.18) and finally to that of the "god of gods". But, true to character, the cause of his fall is seen to be that basic feature of lust, even in celestial realms:

"for millions of years I made love
to apsaras in the Nandana-gardens,
under clustering, lovely trees
ornamented with flowers
shedding delicate scent upon us. . . .
Then a fearful-faced messenger came
and shouted loudly, thrice:
Lost! Lost! Lost!
And I fell from Nandana."—89. 20-21

This is, indeed, a faultless transcreation, bringing home to us all the throbbing anguish of Yayāti's heartbreaking plangent lament in brilliantly evocative verse, far surpassing all other efforts. Look at van Buitenen's prosaic modern translation:

"For a myriad centuries.
With Apsarās I played, and contemplated

The most fragrant blossoming, beautiful mountains.
The Envoy of Gods of awful aspect
Cried three times "Fall!" with the lengthened accent. . . .
And then I fell, meritless, from paradise."

Under Ashtaka's indefatigable questioning (for Yayāti will fall to the ground the moment he has finished answering his questions) Yayāti mentions the terrifying earth-hell, again something experienced by everyman at one time or another when he faces, perforce, the existential predicament of man in this universe. And this hell is particularly the home of those who boast of their own virtue, these who are egotists, who are reborn time and again in

"This is the earthly hell
Which seems to offer no release."—90.7

What follows is the concept of birth and re-birth as believed in then:

"What falls from heaven, O king,
Becomes subtle essence in water;
Water becomes sperm, sperm creates life
In woman's womb after her period. . . .
A man's being is latent in subtle form
In the sperm that enters the womb;
Life-force, impelled by his karma,
Pulls being into life on this earth. . . .
O lion among kings, a man dies,
But his subtle essence remains;
He remembers good acts, evil acts,
As if in a dream; swifter than wind,
He assumes a new form.
To virtuous wombs go the virtuous,
To wicked wombs the wicked.
The sinful become worms and insects."—90.10, 14, 18-19

These concepts underlie all Hindu scriptures: water being the carrier of life; man's *ātman* being immortal and caught in the cycle of birth-death-rebirth under the karmic law. What is happening here is a regular catechism on the basic doctrines of Hindu philosophy, which will be re-iterated in the *Shānti Parva*, but the focus here is on pride:

"The wise say: Seven massive gates,
Asceticism, charity, serenity,
Self-control, modesty, simplicity,
And compassion for all creatures
Lead to heaven.
Pride cancels all these. . . .
Study, control of speech,
Agnihotra, performance of yajña—
These remove fear. Mixed with pride,
These four create fear."—90.22, 24

Yayāti's attack now centres squarely on the ego:

"I gave so much,
I performed many yajñas,
I am learned,
I keep my vows"—
    All vanity, all pride.
    Fearful.
    Give it up, absolutely.—90.26

From pride Ashtaka moves on to the manner in which a hermit, a *muni*, can acquire virtue, and elicits a detailed account of a *muni*'s characteristics from Yayāti. This appears to be an attempt to propagate a certain type of view of the forest-dwelling mendicant's life in the context of many conflicting opinions prevailing at that time, as referred to by Ashtaka in 91.1. *Shloka* 2 concerns the *brahmachārī* (celibate student), *shloka* 3 the *grihastha* (householder), *shloka* 4 the *muni* (hermit), *shloka* 5 the *bhikshu* (mendicant) and *shlokas* 6-7 the proper frame of mind for retiring to the forest.

Shloka 14 as transcreated by Prof. Lal runs:

Who will not revere
the eater of simple food,
the non-injuring one,
the holy-hearted one,
the ascetic-merited one,
the abstainer from violence
even when violence is sanctioned by dharma?"

This is also the sense of the K.M. Ganguli translation. However, the Bhandarkar version, followed by van Buitenen, and the Aryashastra edition give a considerably differing text that runs:

"Who will not respect the one who cleans his teeth, cuts his nails, always bathes and grooms himself and, though black of complexion, is white in his acts?"

The Ganguli-Lal text fits in more with the context.

Ashtaka's next query raises an interesting age-old controversy that will be re-iterated in the *Gītā*: who gains salvation first, the man of knowledge or the ascetic? Yayāti favours the man of knowledge, for the ascetic takes time to acquire wisdom. This, however, is according to the text followed by Prof. Lal and Ganguli. The other version, in the Bhandarkar edition, declares the *muni* to be superior since he is free of desires though living amid desire-ridden people, as against the forest-dwelling householder who, though blessed with long life, may fall victim to passions and have to try all over again for release; the way to salvation is to eschew whatever causes hurt and to follow dharma without thought of gain.

It is quite obvious that all this is very much of an interpolation, right from section 90 till 92.5, because then suddenly Ashtaka wants to know who this falling person is (92.6) although Yayāti had already announced his identity in 89.1. Now we enter another fascinating territory: the appearance of four grandsons of Yayāti through his hitherto unmentioned daughter Mādhavī. The story forms part of the gripping Gālava-Garuda episodes in the *Udyoga Parva,* sections 119-22, where Gālava, like Uttanka with Veda, insists that Vishvāmitra must accept something by way of *guru-dakshinā.* He is asked to procure eight hundred one-black-eared horses. Yayāti gifts Gālava his daughter Mādhavī who is blessed with the ability to regain her virginity after every marriage. She is, in other words, like Satyavatī, one-in-herself, independent, not craving to possess or be possessed by another human being. In succession, Gālava sells her to three kings: Haryashva, Divodāsa (famed in the Rigvedic battle of kings), and Ushīnara, in return for two hundred such horses from each. Mādhavī gives birth to Vasumanas from Haryāshva, Pratardana from Divodāsa and Shibi from Ushīnara. Gālava then presents her and the six hundred horses to Vishvāmitra who fathers Ashtaka on her. This is a unique story in the epic that deserves to be studied from the sociological as also psychological angles in depth. Subodh Ghose first attempted this in a masterly short story forming part of his famous *Bharat Prem Katha.* Recently, Bhisham Sahni has written a Hindi play, *Mādhavī,* on her tragic tale and Dr. Chitra Chaturvedi has a splendid Hindi novel *Tanayā* about her.[3] Incidentally, the three kings are joint authors of *sūkta* 179, *mandala* X of the *Rig Veda.*

In the text, however, Vasumanas introduces himself as the son of Ausadasvi or Rausadasvi, not Haryashva. He and Shibi are the only ones who mention the names of their fathers. The sudden appearance of the other three besides Ashtaka is also unexplained. Each of them gifts to their common maternal grandfather the heavenly regions earned by his karma. Yayāti steadfastly refuses to accept gifts like a Brahmin, i.e. alms like a mendicant. Four times he resists the temptation, firmly saying, "I cannot enjoy worlds earned by others./So I cannot take your offer", thereby rising in our esteem. So far he has been a pitiable figure, first browbeaten by Devayānī, then succumbing to Sharmishthā's blandishments, and then enslaved by his lust, callously shrugging off his decrepitude on to his youthful son and assuming his youth like a vampire, finally thrown out of heaven for his overweening pride. But here, faced with the dread prospect of the earthly hell, he clings fast to his principles and becomes a figure worthy of admiration, phoenix-like rising from the ashes of his pride and lust.

At this stage, in the Bengal recension, we find Mādhavī entering, just after Yayāti has told Ashtaka in *shloka* 13 that five golden chariots have appeared to take them all to heaven. In a passage of nineteen *shlokas*, Mādhavī informs Vasumanas that Yayāti is their grandfather, learns from him the cause of his fall, and gifts to her father the heavenly regions won by her and her four sons through their meritorious acts. In section 121 of the *Udyoga Parva,* Gālava also appears and gifts him his merit as well. The brothers were performing the *Vājapeya Yajña* in the Naimisha forest at that time, the venue of Sauti's recital.

What comes now is Ashtaka's amazement that Shibi should outstrip them all in the race for heaven. Yayāti explains Shibi's all-surpassing merit. Here it seems to be a re-telling of the story narrated to the Pāndavas by Mārkandeya in the *Vana Parva,* section 198. There too the four brothers are told by Nārada that Shibi will be the only one to reach heaven if there is space for only one passenger in the celestial chariot, because of his complete selflessness.

It is peculiar that Ashtaka should ask Yayāti yet again in 93.36 who he is. This is an indication that the intervening verses are interpolations. Yayāti reveals himself as their maternal grandfather finally, and once again relates his glorious deeds, including gifting of countless cows to Brahmins—which is again mentioned in section 196 of the *Vana Parva*—ending with an exhortation to stick to Truth and Dharma. And thus Yayāti finally achieves immortality through his grandchildren's generosity, having abjured Pride and Lust.

The tale of Yayāti is not just a dynastic history or a moral fable. As a dynast, too, he is a watershed in Indian proto-history. All five sons are repeatedly mentioned in the *Rig Veda* and the *Purānas.* Of them, the Yādavas stemming from Yadu and the Yavanas originating from Turvasu, are the most important besides the Pauravas. Krishna will be born in the Yādava clan, to weave the web that will annihilate the entire solar and lunar dynasties, but for a few feeble survivors.

Yayāti himself serves as one of the most important homiletic lessons in Indian mythology and legend. Nārada narrates the story of his fall because of his overweening pride to Dhritarāshtra in the *Udyoga Parva*, vainly attempting to show him the dangers and folly of pride. That episode becomes a fascinating exercise in narrative technique, being something like a four-ring circus: Sauti is narrating what Vaishampāyana told Janamejaya, having learnt it from Vyāsa, about Nārada telling the story to Dhritarāshtra. And, within the story itself, we have dramatic dialogue between Yayāti, Ashtaka and Mādhavī, to introduce yet another level in this highly complex Chinese-box structure.

Another interesting point is the alliance with the *Asuras* that comes to a head with Puru's kingship. His ancestor is Budha, born to Soma of Tārā, the cause of the Tārakamaya war between the gods and titans with the latter espousing Soma's cause. Budha's son is Pururavā, whose son Āyu marries *Asura* Svarabhānu's daughter. Āyu's grandson Yayāti marries the *Asura*-preceptor's daughter but hands over his kingdom to his son by Sharmishthā, the *Asura* king's daughter. It is significant that in the *Rig Veda* (VII.8.4) Puru is called "Asura-Rākshasa," just as in the Purānas other kings of the Lunar dynasty, such as Madhu, Lavana, Kamsa and Jarāsandha are called *Asuras*. Thus, the epic war that takes place is largely among *Asura*-affiliated clans, since by this time the solar dynasty culminating in Rāma had already declined to little more than a mere shadow of a name. In this context, the infusion of daivik blood through the birth-by-proxy of the Pāndavas revives an ancient and eternal conflict between the titans and the gods on a human level. Yayāti is the watershed in this history.

References

1. Robert Graves, *The Greek Myths-2*, Penguin 1960, p. 219 note 4. The cup is dated to the early 5th century BC http://en.wikipedia.org/wiki/File:Douriscup_83d40m_Athene_aegisWingedLionessOwl_pythonVomitsJason_fleeceInTree_Vatican.jpg
2. S.A. Dange, *Myths from the Mahabharata*, vol.1, Aryan Books, New Delhi, 1997
3. P. Bhattacharya, *Love Stories from the Mahabharata*, Indialog, New Delhi, 2005. Bhisham Sahni, *Madhavi*, Rajkamal Prakashan, Delhi, 2005, English translation by Ashok Bhalla, Seagull, 2009. Chitra Chaturvedi, *Tanaya*, Lokbharati Prakashan, Allahabad, 1989.

11

The Sambhava Parva-III

Yayāti, Yima and Eochaid Feidlech

The Yayāti myth is not, however, limited in significance to purānik history. This biography of one of the earliest of kings ruling over the entire known world, which he distributes among his five sons, has remarkable Iranian and Celtic parallels. These have been investigated at length by George Dumezil who has shown that the Iranian and Celtic counterparts of Yayāti, the First or Universal King, are Yima-Jamshid and Eochaid Feidlech, with Uparichara Vasu serving as the purānik parallel in the *Mahābhārata* itself.[1]

There are a number of themes common to these four figures. The first of these is that of the Universal Monarch presiding over the division or the progressive peopling of the world. Yima-Jamshid increases the dimensions of the earth thrice to accommodate the ever-burgeoning population in a post-diluvian world where death and sickness are unknown. He also includes in his ark-like *vara* the three strata into which human society is divided for the Iranians: the priests, the warriors and the tiller-breeders. There is, however, no division of the kingdom in his case. Yayāti's assigning of the four peripheral regions to his elder sons and the fifth—which is also the central part—to the youngest (*Ādi Parva* 87.5) is close to what we find in the biblical and the koranic lore. There Noah curses two out of his three son who become progenitors of the white, black and yellow races (Shem, Ham and Japhet respectively in the Islamic version). Similarly, the Yādavas, Yavanas, Bhojas, Mlechchhas and Pauravas stem from Yayāti's five sons: Yadu, Turvasu, Druhyu, Anu and Puru respectively. Eochaid Feidlech, king of Ireland, also curses his three recalcitrant sons, even killing them in a battle, and ordains that none of them shall succeed to his throne.

This division of the empire corresponds to the common Indo-European concept of the world consisting of the four cardinal points and the centre. In the Purānas this is represented through the *lokapālas,* the guardians of the directions: Indra ruling over the North and also representing the quality of greatness; Varuna guarding the West, standing for beauty; Kubera, lord of wealth, in the East; and Yama, the epitome of restraint and discipline, in the South. The Iranian division of the world into five or seven *kishvars* is similar to this, as is the Celtic splitting up of Ireland into *coiceds* (fifths). In China, as Perry points out[2] this took a different shape as the San Huang (three august ones) and the Wu Ti (five sovereign sages), the latter corresponding to the five elements and powers: earth, wood, metal, fire and water; yellow, green, white, red and black. Huang-ti, Chuan-hu, Kao-sin, Yao and Shun were the corresponding Wu-Ti.

The other function of the First King is to divide society into various functional strata. In the case of Yayāti, of course, there is no such stratification because the function-wise division pre-exists. A hint of such division is to be found in Yima's *vara* where the seeds of the priests, the warriors and the tiller-breeders are conserved by him. What Yayāti does provide us with, however, is a union, in himself, of the three meritorious functions of the Ideal King: amassing merits by distribution of wealth, conquests, sacrifices and truth-telling (the last two being parts of the same function of treading the path of the Truth and the Right). It is because of these merits that he ascends to heaven. When he falls from there because of his sin of pride (just as Jamshid's becoming false to the truth of his own being leads to the loss of the *xvarrah,* the divine glory, and his descent to beneath the earth) he falls among his grandsons, each of whom represents one of these supreme merits: Vasumanas' riches and generosity, Pratardana's prowess, Shibi's veracity and Ashtaka's assiduous practice of *yajña.* Their unusual joint engagement in celebrating the *Vājapeya* sacrifice is also significant because this ritual includes two rites that are reproduced in Yayāti's experience: a symbolic ascent to heaven and a chariot race that the king must win. This part of Yayāti's story is concerned with his re-ascension to heaven in a chariot race, which Shibi wins because Truth is pre-eminent among the monarch's functions. The point to be noted is that by the four grandsons gifting their peculiar merits to Yayāti, he comes to re-acquire the sum of the types of meritorious functions that were present in him in a natural synthesis during his kingship. Such reconstitution enables him to reverse his fall from heaven and restores him to the celestial regions. Yayāti recalls this synthesis in himself, which is peculiar to the Universal Monarch:

"I conquered the earth;
  fed and clothed Brahmins, . . .
I gave away to Brahmins all the earth. . . .
Sky and earth stand
  because of truth.
Fire burns
  because of truth
Never once
  did I
  speak a word not true.
Be like the wise: love and worship truth."—93.38, 40

In keeping with the supreme status accorded to Truth, it is the veracious Shibi who outstrips them in the heavenly ascension.

It is interesting to see how, in the Iranian account, Yima's royal farr *(xvarrah),* "the flame of Glory" leaves him thrice and is seized in succession by Mithra (the priestly function), by Karasaspa (the warrior) and by Oraetaona (the tiller-breeder), in consonance with the three strata of human society. The synthesis of the triple functions in Yima is thus split up and returns separately in the *Denkart* account quoted by Dumezil. The first descent of this royal glory is to Freton who teaches men agriculture; the second is to Saman Karasaspa, the warrior-hero; and the third to the priest-magician Osnar minister of King Kai-Us (Kavya Ushanas).

The difference in the Yayāti and the Yima myths is, however, marked. Yima's "glory" is inherited by three heroes in successive generations, but Yayāti's merits are annihilated by his Lucifer-like outburst of egoism, not to be passed down to anyone. On the other hand, Yima has no redeemers such as Yayāti meets in his four grandsons who jointly synthesise the four meritorious functions which restore him to heaven. In the Iranian myth, therefore, we come across a case of splitting up and dispersion of the *xvarrah,* the essence of Universal Monarchy, while Vyāsa presents us with a myth of reconciliation and fusion.

Yet, as Dumezil points out, the basic approach remains the same, although the end may be synthesis in one case and division in the other. Yima-Jamshid's proud boast is made before the gathered dignitaries consisting of the social strata he had founded and it results in the corresponding parts of his royal glory departing from him. Yayāti, on the other hand, confesses his fault of pride before his gathered grandsons, representing the First King's functions together and, consequently, receives back the categories of merits he had lost. This inversion itself depends on the nature of what is lost by the one and won by the other. The *xvarrah* was not something that could be won by anyone: it was a gift of Ahura-Mazda to Yima which could be lost by him, but could not be won back.

Yayāti's merits, however, are essentially earned by him, being the fruit of his karma, and though lost can be obtained again by fresh karma on his part or on that of his descendants. The other dissimilarity lies in that Yayāti's sin is in an other-worldly existence while that of Yima takes place during his terrestrial reign. Again, while Yayāti's fall and redemption are limited to his post-earthly life, Yima's loss of glory puts an end to his reign (and presumably his life) and benefits three later generations. Moreover, Yima obtains the *xvarrah* by ascending to heaven temporarily during his reign to receive it as a gift from God, whereas Yayāti's ascension is the usual one after death for a person who has acquired the requisite merit. Yima's sin does not have any repercussions on his ascension, as this is not envisaged at all and seems to have occurred only once in his experience. However, like Yayāti, the effect of the sin is to condemn Yima to a subterranean (or earthly) hell.

The other theme that invites Indo-European comparisons is

that of deferred decrepitude. The remarkable feature of Yima's reign is the absence of old age and death. However, this is something that applies as much to all his subjects as himself, while in the case of Yayāti it is limited to him and his sons only. Later in the *Ādi Parva* (section 199) we will find mortals free of death during Yama's long sacrificial ritual in Naimisha forest so that the earth groans under the increasing burden and the gods are dismayed to find no difference between them and mortals. Both Yima and Yayāti enjoy unblemished youth for a thousand years. Dumezil seeks to equate the increasing of the earth's size by Yima with the banishing of his sons by Yayāti, both being based on the theme of arrested senility, to suggest that these might be later embellishments of the original simpler tradition setting forth the peopling of all lands, starting from the centre outwards in a centripetal movement, resulting from a surplus of youth in the society. The common theme, thus, is that of semi-permanent youth creating problematic situations in the kingdom that leads to an extension of the earth or the colonisation of the peripheral regions of the kingdom. A parallel Indian myth not noted by Dumezil is that of Prithu-Vainya extending the earth thrice over to accommodate the numbers of subjects.

Yayāti's violent differences with his sons over their refusal to age in his stead not only recalls Admetos' failure to persuade his son to die in his place in *Alcestis,* but also has links with the Iranian monarch Kay Us (Vyāsa's Kavi Ushanas). Besides these, we find two remarkable parallels in Scandinavian mythology in the stories of King Aun *(Ynglinga saga)* and Halfdan the old *(Flateyjarbok)*. Aun, at the age of sixty, is granted a reprieve of ten years for every son he sacrifices and dies from old age when he is prevented from sacrificing his tenth son to Odin. This extended life, however, is not free from decrepitude. Aun, at the later stages, is confined to bed and drinks from a horn like a nursling, though he is free from sickness by Odin's grace. After him, dying of senility without illness was termed "sickness of Ani" *(anasott)*. There is, therefore, the same theme of deferred death through the replacement of the king by his son, but the feature of arrested age and an extended youth, which characterise the Yayāti myth, are missing. In the Halfdan story, the death of his nine sons ensures a guarantee by the gods that although he would live only his normal life span, his dynasty would be famous for three hundred years.

The career of Yima presents similarities with the reign of Uparichara Vasu too. Both kings are given a crystal chariot traversing the skies; they establish an annual celebration (the Navroz festival by Yima and to honour Indra by Vasu). Again, these two archetypal symbols of monarchy lose their glory and are precipitated below the earth because they prefer butchered food or sacrifices. Yima, it seems, taught his subjects to eat meat (the flesh of the ox, according to *Yasna* 32.8 quoted by Dumezil). The difference is that, like Yayāti, Vasu achieves a re-ascension to the celestial regions by worshipping Vishnu who has Garuda rescue him from the deep pit. Yima, however, is condemned permanently.

It will be apparent from these parallels that the themes that appear in a unified form in the Yima-Jamshid myth—the First King, the division of the world, the special favour of the Divine, the loss of special status because of Luciferan *hubris,* the deferred decrepitude, the re-appearance of the kingly functions in subsequent generations and the founding of an annual festival—are found in the *Mahābhārata* separately in the Yayāti and Uparichara Vasu stories. Here, therefore, is Vyāsa's version of an ancient Indo-Iranian tradition about Earthly Kingship.

References

1. G. Dumezil, *The Destiny of A King* (University of Chicago Press, 1973)
2. J.W.Perry, *Lord of the Four Quarters* (Collier, NY, 1970, p. 210-211)

12

The Sambhava Parva-IV

Lust in Action

Sections 94 to 128 of the *Sambhava* in the *Ādi Parva* continue and bring to a shattering climax the theme of lust that was initiated with Nahusha and elaborated in the history of Yayāti. But here it is no longer the conflict between Lust and the Quest for Immortality that concerns Vyāsa. For, with Kacha and the legendary figure of Yayāti such a soaring aspiration has also passed away. What we find is a pitiless baring of the tainted generations of Kurus from Shāntanu onwards, all afflicted with the same disease—lust that speeds them on inexorably to their doom, bringing home to us the theme of Shakespeare's 129th sonnet:

"The expense of spirit in a waste of shame
Is Lust in action. . . .
Mad in pursuit and in possession so. . . .
A bliss in proof, and proved, a very woe."

The tragedy—and it is no longer one on a heroic scale—of Shāntanu, Vichitravīrya and Pāndu is that of all men, whether prince or pauper:

"All this the world well knows; yet none knows well
To shun the heaven that leads men to this hell."

Such predetermined damning through a family taint is almost Grecian in its fatalism, the only difference being that the gods do not intervene directly to play a malevolent role. Thereby Vyāsa's account remains an even more appealing human document in which it is human failings that invite the ultimate penalty, not something imposed gratuitously by a sadistic and callous President of the Immortals in his cat-and-mouse game with mankind:

> "In tragic life, God wot,
> No villain need be! Passions spin the plot:
> We are betray'd by what is false within"—George Meredith,
> "Love's Grave"

Sections 94-95, however, strain the reader's patience and logical faculties to the extreme. Here Vaishampāyana gives us two widely varying genealogies of the Pauravas in response to Janamejaya's insistent queries. In Section 94 the lineage is peculiarly garbled. On the one hand Vaishampāyana states that of Puru's three sons, Pravīra, Ishvara and Raudrāshva, it was the first who was the dynast. Yet, he carries Pravīra's line only up to the second generation and comes back to describe Raudrāshva's progeny, calling his son Richeyu-Anādhrishti "sole lord of the earth" (94.12), continuing to trace his lineage as follows: Anādhrishti-Matināra-Tamsu-Ilina-Dushyanta-Bharata-Bhumanyu-Suhotra-Ajamīdha-Riksha-Samvarana-Kuru-Ashvavān-Parikshit. After this there is yet more confusion as the lineage now shifts to Ashvavān's brother Janamejaya followed by Dhritarāshtra, after which there is another break and we pass on to Pratīpa-Shāntanu. Now, in Section 95 the lineage is as follows: Puru-Janamejaya-Prāchinvat-Samyāti-Ahamyāti-Sārvabhauma-Jayatsena-Avāchina-Ariha-Mahābhauma-Ayutanāyin-Akrodhana-Devatithi-Ariha-Riksha-Matināra-Tamsu-Ilina-Dushyanta-Bharata-Bhumanyu-Suhotra-Hasti-Vikunthana-Ajamīdha—again a break. Then, Samvarana-Kuru-Viduratha-Anasvas-Parikshit-Bhimasena-Pratishravas-Pratīpa-Shāntanu.

It is clear, therefore, that the only common point from which the lineage can be traced with any accuracy is Matināra, who is at one point Puru's grandnephew and at another in the fifteenth generation after him. The second common point is Samvarana, as there appears to be some sort of a break in-between Bharata and him. These peculiar gaps have baffled all scholars who have sought to draw up an intelligible genealogy, even such names as Pargiter, Pradhan and Bhārgava having admitted failure. Pradhan concludes that the Kurus were cut off from the Bharatas by a long time-gap and were practically a new dynasty. Even between Dushyanta and Tamsu, there is a break, for in the different *Purānas* he is variously termed as the son of Raibhya, Ilīna and Tamsu. Therefore, by the time we reach Shāntanu, he can be called a Paurava only by stretching the imagination.

There is yet another break after Bharata, who appears to have adopted Bharadvāja's son Bhumanyu (94.22) and the lineage is now a mixed Brahmin-Kshatriya one. Dushyanta's lust appears to have tainted his progeny, for Bharata is unable to have suitable sons, just as his descendants Vichitravīrya and Pāndu fail to procreate. Bharata's nine sons are unsuitable to rule and their three infuriated mothers kill them—a unique incident in Indian mythology. Bhumanyu's grandson Ajamīdha, also mentioned in the *Rig Veda*, originates two dynasties: through Riksha come the Kurus and through Nīla the Pānchālas. The latter attack their cousin Samvarana, son of Riksha, and he has to flee his kingdom until Vashishtha helps him to regain his empire. Another branch of the Kurus is that of Uparichara Vasu in Chedi, which produced such potentates as Brihadratha, Shishupāla and Jarāsandha and was linked to the line of Samvarana through Shāntanu's marriage with Vasu's daughter Satyavatī, the 'fishy' issue.

In this confusing genealogical list an extremely important fact is apt to be lost sight of. This occurs in 95.20, concerning Mahābhauma's son Ayutanāyin, where, explaining the origin of his name, it is said, "He was so called because he performed a *purushamedha* sacrifice in which the fat of ten thousand males was required". This explicit statement to ten thousand human sacrifices tucked away casually amid the welter of names is not to be discounted as unbelievable. The supporting evidence is available not only in the Shunahshepa episode, but in the more grisly one of Somaka. This king sacrifices his only son Jantu and makes his wives inhale the smoke from his burning limbs so that

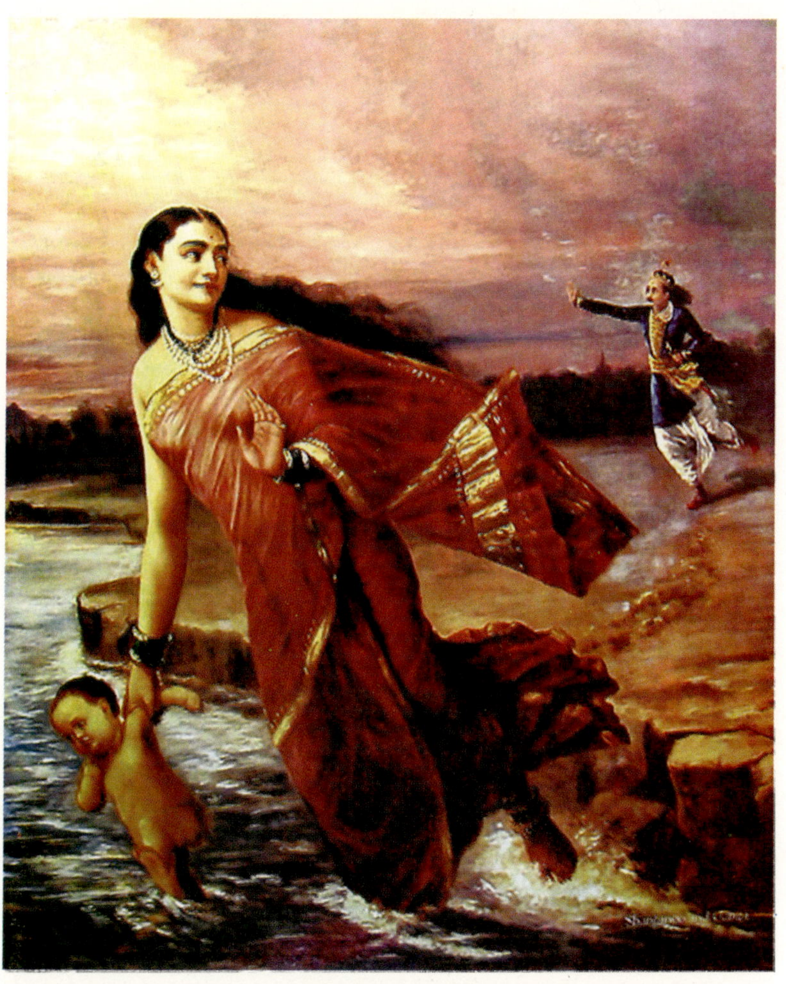

"Ganga with son leaves Shantanu" by Ravi Varma

they can give him several sons. It is described in pitiless detail in the *Vana Parva*, section 128.

The genealogy has to be repeated in Section 95 because Janamejaya feels it has been related in brief and he must have all the detailed particulars. That is how, finally, the real story gets under way with a fresh garbled genealogy. It will be recalled that, according to the *Anukramanikā*, some begin the epic with Manu, i.e. section 95 where Janamejaya wants to hear of his ancestry beginning from Manu (95.3). In this fresh account we find five chronicle verses namely 95-9, 27, 30-31, and 46, concerning Yayāti's sons, Tamsu's progeny, the exhortation to Dushyanta to acknowledge Bharata as his son (74.110-111) and the pseudo-etymology of Shāntanu. Bharata was so named because Dushyanta agreed to maintain him (verse 31). *Shloka* 46 states that Shāntanu is so named because his touch brought serenity to "old men touched by this king's hands." In 97.18 his name is explained wrongly as "the child of controlled passions" as he was born to his parents in their old age. The epic also spells his other name wrongly as "Mahābhīsha" instead of "Mahābhīshaka," which means "the great healer or physician," and fits in very well with the sense of "Shāntanu" given in 96.46. The *Matsya* and *Vāyu Purānas* refer to him as "Mahābhīshaka", which was obviously corrupted to Mahābhīsha in the epic. That is why one can find no trace of that name in the solar dynasty of Ikshvāku. Further, 95.45 merely states that Devāpi, the eldest son of Pratīpa, became a hermit and therefore Shāntanu became king. In the *Udyoga Parva* (149.17-28) it is stated that the Brahmins and other subjects of Pratīpa objected when he tried to consecrate Devāpi as his successor because he was suffering from skin disease. Thereupon Devāpi took to the forest. The next son, Bāhlīka, preferred to take up the kingdom of his maternal uncle, i.e. the Shibis. It is then that, with Bāhlīka's permission, Shāntanu became king at Hastināpura.

The *Brihaddevatā* and the *Bhāgavata Purāna* refer to a twelve-year drought during which Shāntanu requested Devāpi to resume the kingdom, but he refused and performed sacrifices to remove the drought. This is also borne out in Devāpi's Rigvedic hymn (X. 98), which is preceded by Mahābhīshaka's hymn (X.97).

Thus, both were vedic *rājarshis,* seer-kings. According to the *Purānas,* Devāpi is still alive and will restore the Paurava dynasty in the new Satya Yuga.

95.48 is the only place where Satyavatī is named Gandhakālī, possibly a combination of her other names, Matsyagandhā/ Yojanagandhā and Kālī (dark). It is in *Shloka* 75 that Draupadī's five sons are named. We learn that Yudhishthira had another wife Devikā, the Shaibya princess, and their son was named Yaudheya; that Bhīma married the Kāshi princess Balandharā and fathered Sarvaga on her; that Nakula married Karenumati of Chedi (a link with Uparichara Vasu's lineage) and their son was Nirāmitra; that Sahadeva's Madra wife (his mother was also a Madran) was Vijayā and their son was Suhotra. Adding Abhimanyu and Ghatotkacha, this makes eleven sons of the Pāndavas, not counting Irāvān by Ulūpī and Babhruvāhana by Chitrāngadā to Arjuna who are, strangely enough, not mentioned here. Of them, seven died in the war. Is it not puzzling that the others did not even participate in the Kurukshetra war? the Puranas never refer to the surviving Pandava sons by their other wives. Surely, with such famous fathers they ought to have founded renowned dynasties? Even Jaimini, who brings in the next generation in his *Ashvamedha Parva,* does not know them. Why did the rhapsode introduce them? In this fashion, Vaishampāyana is finally allowed to bring his account down to Janamejaya and his two sons. Then, without interruption, he launches into the full story of the Pāndavas, starting with the birth of Shāntanu in section 96.

This sequence itself begins with lust. The Ikshvāku monarch Mahābhīsha (here there is another interesting fusion of clans as the solar dynasty king is re-born in the lunar clan as Shāntanu) stares fixedly at Gangā in Brahmā's presence when, "gusty winds/ Uplifted her moon-white dress" (96.4). Like Yayāti, Mahābhīsha has been unable to pass beyond sexual urges and suffers for it like him, condemned to the earthly hell through re-birth as Shāntanu. He is not alone. The object of his lust is also to accompany him, for lust arouses a response in what it desires:

"Gangā, queen of rivers, saw

Mahābhīsha lose control of himself,
And left, thinking deeply of him."—96.10

Brahmā promises him release only when he is disgusted with what he has desired; in other words, when his lust has eaten itself up:

"When Gangā stirs you to anger,
Shall your curse be lifted."—96.8

Nothing in the *Mahābhārata*, however, stands in isolation. Every event forms part of a pattern in the incredibly rich and involved tapestry that is this epic. As Gangā leaves Brahmā's abode she is requested by the Vasus, cursed by Vashishtha to be born on earth, to be their mother, and they choose for their father Mahābhīsha-Shāntanu. The reason for the curse is again blind infatuation:

"Because his lotus-eyed wife asked him,
 Dyaus did what he did,
unmindful of the strict-vowed rishi,
 oblivious of the sin of stealing."—99.27

Significantly, when they approach Gangā, the Vasus conceal the real cause of their misfortune and make it appear as Vashishtha's whimsicality:

"We have been cursed by Vashishtha
For the most trivial of faults.
We crossed the rishi's path, unaware
He was doing his sandhya worship.
He cursed us: Be born as men!" (96.13-14)

It is difficult to understand why Gangā wantonly solicits Pratīpa by sitting on his right thigh and demanding intercourse. Pratīpa, however, is untainted with the lust that has affected Gangā and Mahābhīsha. He politely refuses:

"Beautiful one," said Pratīpa,
"I have never lusted for another's wife,
Or for women outside my caste.
This is dharma, this is my vow." (97.6)

Gangā persists:

"I am not ugly", she said,
"I do not bring ill fortune, O rājā
No one has cast a slur on me,
I am not unfit for sexual enjoyment.
I am celestial, I am beautiful,
I love you. Take me, my lord." (97.7) Shāntanu, significantly, lusts for women who are not of his caste. Both Gangā and Satyavatī are not *Kshatriyas.* Both are river women. One is celestial, the other a fisher-girl; one far superior, the other far inferior. It is Shāntanu's son by Gangā who sets up a unique and wholly different paradigm at the opposite extreme of Yayātian lust. He abjures women wholly, a terrible resolve, and is therefore named Bhīshma, the terrible.

Pratīpa adds, as another reason for his refusal, the interesting information that women to be sexually enjoyed should be seated on the left thigh, the right being reserved for children and daughters-in-law, and Gangā has sat on his right thigh. She extracts from him the promise to marry her to his son with one condition: he must not question her actions.

With Shāntanu we are introduced to the other facet of character that goes hand-in-hand with sexual lust: the lust for blood. Shāntanu spends most of his time hunting, and it is while engaged in satisfying this blood-lust that he meets Gangā, desires her and, swept away by his blind infatuation like Dushyanta, does not think twice before accepting her conditions. It is not, however, a one-sided affair. Gangā is similarly afflicted:

"He stood there,
Entranced,
All his body
In horripilation.

With both eyes
He drank in her beauty,
And wanted
To drink more.
She saw him,
In shining splendour.
She was moved
With tenderness and affection.
She kept gazing
 and gazing
  and longed to gaze
   even more." (97.28-29)

It is ironic that Shāntanu, "the child of controlled passions" (97.18) should be such a slave of passion:

"Captivated by her skilful love-making,
The rājā was not conscious of
The months, seasons, years that rolled by." (98.11)

In Shloka 13 he is said to have enjoyed her sexually in every possible way. Vyāsa's emphasis is squarely on the baldly sensual nature of the attachment. It is only when Shāntanu's addiction to sensual gratification is conquered by his concern for the fate of an infant that the spell *la belle dame sans merci* has cast can be broken. Like the ensnared knights-at-arms, Shāntanu is left wan and forlorn, less of a man than he was before meeting Gangā. He is truly but the dry husk of a hero, a hollow man, his manliness sucked out by her like a succubus. It is, therefore, quite inevitable that he should be unable to control yet another passion for a pretty fisher-girl in his late middle age. It is peculiar that while Gangā ensures that the seven Vasus and herself are freed from Brahmā's curse, Shāntanu-Mahābhīsha has to stay on in this earthly hell despite the god's assurance that he will achieve salvation the day he displays anger towards Gangā, which he does in protesting against her drowning their eighth son.

The throwing of seven children into the river, one after another, is a ritual myth paralleled in Kamsa killing seven sons of Vasudeva. Possibly this indicates an ancient fertility cult where the vegetation god-king had to die annually, so that his blood could fertilise the earth-goddess-queen. Gradually, with the advent of a powerful king, who refused to be sacrificed annually, the surrogate-tanist tradition grew up which we can see in Kamsa's killing of a child annually and in his fear of being slain and supplanted as king by Krishna the cowherd, who is very much of a fertility and vegetation god. In the present instance, there are also clear parallels with the Egyptian ritual of throwing infants into the Nile for propitiating that life-giving river. The Greek myth of Thetis drowning or burning up seven sons she has from Peleus, till he stops her as she strives to make Achilles immortal by burning away his mortality or by immersing him in the river Styx is yet another closer parallel.[1] Like Gangā she is a river goddess and takes her son away from his father to be brought up to be a hero. What we have here is not a simple myth but a tale rich in anthropological material. There is also a parallelism between Bhīshma, the eighth son, and Krishna, Devakī's eighth child, both being the protagonists of the opposing camps. In one case, Gangā kills seven of her own sons; in the other Kamsa dashes out the brains of Devakī's sons. Karna, who is floated down the river Moses-like by the unwed Kuntī, consistently opposes and insults Bhīshma and is Duryodhana's mainstay is a parallel to Krishna who is the Pandavas' friend, philosopher and guide.

In 98.19 Gangā identifies herself to Shāntanu as the daughter of sage Jahnu. The reference is found in the *Rāmāyana's* account of Bhagiratha bringing down Gangā from the heavens. En route she sweeps away the hermitage of the royal sage Jahnu who angrily drinks her up in a single gulp. On Bhagiratha's entreaties, he allows her to re-emerge from his ear. Hence, she is known as Jāhnavī, Jahnu's daughter (*ādikanda,* canto 43).

Section 99 brings out another contradiction. In 98.20 Gangā explained to Shāntanu that the Vasus had to be born on earth for a trivial fault. But in 99.31 she reveals that this was not a minor transgression, being the theft of Vashishtha's wish-fulfilling cow. We recall that this is precisely what Vishvāmitra had attempted with disastrous results and that Trishanku had lost kingdom and caste by killing Vashishtha's cow. Further, in 96.21-23 the Vasus had stated that they would leave a son for Shāntanu formed of one-eighth of each of them. But in 99.38 and 44 Dyaus, the Vasu who actually stole the cow on his wife's prompting, is cursed to live out a long life on earth, much as Mahābhīsha appears to eke out a mediocre human existence as Shāntanu, despite Brahmā's assurance to the contrary.

Vaishampāyana now proceeds to eulogize Shāntanu in fulsome terms, having his immediate audience in view. He is made out to be a perfect monarch, with no defects, but for a revealing *Shloka* where the basic flaw is deftly stressed:

> "For thirty-six years
> king Shāntanu enjoyed
> the company of women,
> then retired to the forest."—100.20

Though in 100.15 it is said that no animal was slain needlessly, only eight *Shlokas* later Vaishampāyana describes Shāntanu pursuing a wounded deer during a hunt—surely not a needful slaying? The account of Shāntanu's ideal reign, in which the four classes pay due respect in hierarchy and all kings seek to emulate Shāntanu's exemplary conduct in generosity, holding yajñas and extending protection to the helpless and his being the storehouse of all virtues including self-control appears to be very much in the nature of a command performance, for his subsequent conduct does not show either any self-control or selflessness, or even any manliness or sense of priorities. He places his own lust above the welfare of his kingdom, and the results are indeed disastrous as they culminate inexorably in the Kurukshetra holocaust where Shāntanu's dynasty is wiped out. The surviving Pāndavas are only his surrogate descendants, with no blood relationship with him.

Vyāsa, with typical brevity, puts across the essence of the meeting between Shāntanu and the black-eyed fisher-girl, which has been captured admirably in the transcreation. The king is led to her by a lovely fragrance and the reader will recall the encounter between this girl and the sage Parāshara who metamorphosed her obnoxious fishy-odour (because of which Uparichara had quickly given her away to the fishermen) into the fragrance of a lotus emanating for a *yojana* from her. Shāntanu's reaction parallels that of Parāshara:

"She was fragrant,
beautiful,
smiling.
Shāntanu saw her,
and desired her." (100.49)

But the *kshatriya* king differs from the *rishi* in his desire to possess for himself this beauty, unable to simply enjoy and pass on. Hence, he asks the fisher-chief for her (he does not mention marriage, but the head fisherman does). It is significant that here, where we find the first reference to Satyavatī's father, she should uncompromisingly be termed the daughter of the king of the fisher folk and not his adopted child, as he later makes out for Devavrata's benefit. The flaw in Shāntanu's character is stressed again:

"The fire of desire
ravaged his body. . . .
Desire maddened him
He kept thinking
Of the daughter of the Dāsa chief." (100.56-57)

Yayāti's warning to eschew desire has fallen on deaf ears. It is significant that here Satyavatī is not known as Uparichara Vasu's offspring but is uncompromisingly described as a fisherman's daughter. The royal ancestry was obviously a later addition, invented after she had become the queen.

Devavrata is introduced to us in superlatives only: as knowledgeable in the scriptures as Kāvya Ushana Shukra and Brihaspati, expert in weapons as Parashurāma and like Indra in battle. Devoted to his father's welfare, he notices Shāntanu's dejection, for the king keeps thinking of the black-eyed fisher-girl. Notice Shāntanu's hypocritical reply:

"I wonder, son of Gangā
  should anything happen to you
what will happen to our dynasty? . . .
It isn't that I wish to marry
  again. . . .
Should you die in battle,
What will be the fate
  of our race, our dynasty?
This is the cause of my sorrow. (100.64-65, 71)

This cuts no ice with the astute, sensitive Devavrata who ferrets out the true reason for the king's grief from his minister and approaches the fisher-chief. It is here that we learn that her name is Satyavatī and she is not the daughter of the fisher-chief but of one left unnamed: "the daughter of a man whose virility equals yours" (100.85). It is peculiar that the foster-father does not mention that Uparichara Vasu is her biological father, which raises strong suspicions that the entire story was made up subsequently in order to grant some royal ancestry to this low-born girl who rose to be a queen. She herself tells Shāntanu that she is the daughter of the chief of the fisher-folk who refers to her throughout as his daughter except when he refers vaguely to someone else being her father. The fisher-chief is exceptionally shrewd and drives a hard bargain. Knowing that the king is hopelessly in thrall, he does not rest content with Devavrata's promise to abdicate his rights to the throne, but points out the danger of a fratricidal war in the next generation. Now Devavrata takes the vow of celibacy that gives him the name of Bhīshma, because attaining heaven without the help of progeny was unthinkable, as we have seen in the case of Jaratkāru. But Bhīshma confidently declares that he will attain heaven without sons: "Sonless, nonetheless I will find heaven" (100.103). Ironically, that fratricidal war which the fisher-chief plotted to avoid inevitably takes place, with the redoubtable Bhīshma initially enigmatically detached and ultimately an active participant in the holocaust. Shāntanu is gracelessly glad with his son's sacrifice and blesses him with the power of dying only when he wishes to. What a curse it turns out to be as it condemns him to lie in indescribable torment on a bed of arrows through the carnage of the Kurukshetra war. Shāntanu truly cuts a sorry figure.

Section 101 begins with an interpolation that buttresses the argument that the entire story of Satyavatī's birth was added by court-poets:

"Satyavatī was the daughter
 of the rājā of Chedi;
she had been reared
 by the Dāsa-rājā".

The entire episode of her intercourse with Parāshara is suppressed, only to be revealed when Vyāsa has to be called upon for *niyoga* purposes. One wonders whether the strict-vowed Bhīshma would have still sacrificed so much for a fisher-girl who had already had a child. It is significant that this is never mentioned during Shāntanu's lifetime. It would possibly have shattered whatever semblance of self-respect he might have had left in him.

The fruits of this lustful union are two inconspicuous sons: Chitrāñgada and Vichitravīrya. The former is quickly slain by his Gandharva namesake. It is curious that Bhīshma, the invincible warrior, not once came forward to help his step-brother, and that no steps are taken by him, nor urged by Satyavatī (which is even stranger) to avenge his death on the Gandharva king. The lack of any reprisal by Bhīshma suggests that the tragedy was self-invited by a rash, immature youth, over-confident of his prowess, killed in a self-invited fair duel that would leave no excuse for any blood-revenge. Or does it indicate the none- too-strong condition of the so-called empire left behind by the "redoubtable" Shāntanu? After all, the immediate neighbours were the Pānchāla and the Magadha kings, yet we find no reference to their having been conquered by Shāntanu or any of his successors. Their world-conquests seem to have been limited to petty surrounding principalities—a very shrunken world indeed! Vaishampāyana, of course, duly describes Chitrāñgada as having defeated all kings, without mentioning a single one. Similarly, when he described Shāntanu's greatness, he had conveniently omitted to mention a single king subject to this "emperor" who ostensibly commanded the whole world. In like fashion, he dubs Vichitravīrya "a mighty archer" in 101.4 although he is put on the throne "still a minor" (101.15) with no evidence of his celebrated archery anywhere. To be doubly sure of the dynasty's continuance, no doubt under Satyavatī's instructions, Bhīshma provides him with two voluptuous brides:

> "Both his wives were tall.
> Black, wavy hair.
> Fingernails and toe nails
> Painted red and pointed.
> Hips round and full.
> Swelling and large breasts.
> Sweet-smiling, beautiful,
> With all auspicious marks
> On their bodies. . . ." (102.65-66)

Here, lust once more enters the field. Himself a fruit of lust, Vichitravīrya, "driven by passion became a kāmātmā/a victim of his own lust" (102.64) and died without issue after enjoying his wives for seven years (like his father did with Gangā), struck down by consumption, said to attend upon sexual excesses.

This is the end of Shāntanu's dynasty through a Nishāda maiden. What a selfish and short-sighted king he was! He never made any attempt to get his full-grown son Devavrata married. Indeed, we never find him showing any special concern or affection for his successor. Yet he has no shame in hypocritically worrying what will happen to his dynasty should Devavrata be slain in battle. Nor does he think ahead to what might happen if his children by the new queen die as minors, or, more important, that he is far too old to look after a new generation. He blithely passes on the entire burden to the uncomplaining Bhīshma, content to frolic in bed with his fisher-girl. What a pitilessly drawn picture of a renowned Kuru ruler! What is even more interesting is that Vaishampāyana completely forgets to dovetail the Mahābhīsha story into Shāntanu's and there is no reference to Shāntanu returning to Brahmā's abode after death as

Mahābhīsha. That story, therefore, also seems another command-performance meant to invest Janamejaya's ancestor with some celestial glory. It is quite sloppy patchwork, not at all characteristic of Vyāsa who is most attentive to the smallest details and is most likely an interpolation.

Bhīshma had initially intended to marry all the three-princesses of Kashi—Ambā, Ambikā and Ambālikā—to Vichitravīrya. His abduction of the princesses is in accordance with the *rākshasa* rite of marriage. The passage where Bhīshma describes the various modes of marriage (102.12-17), is comparable to Dushyanta's description of these to Shakuntalā. However, here the Gandharva and the Prājāpatya modes are missing.

The first mode is gifting the girl to a guest (*brāhma*); the second is to bestow her with ornaments (*daiva*); the third is to exchange her for a pair of cattle (i.e., selling the bride, the *Ārsha* mode); the fourth is to be sell her for money (*asura*); the fifth abduction (*rākshasa*); the sixth by mutual agreement, which may either be the *gandharva* or the *svayamvara* (the latter is not mentioned in the *Manusamhitā*); the seventh by drugging the bride (*paishācha*). Bhīshma also mentions two other variations, where marriage takes place with the parents' consent and where wives are obtained in return for helping at a *yajña.* The last one is a variation of the *ārsha* form, while the former could be the Prājāpatya.

The reaction to Bhīshma's entrance into the *svayamvara* hall is revealing:

"Some exquisitely lovely girls
  in the hall, saw him
bearded; giggling, *He is old,*
  they fled from the place. . . .
Old, wrinkled Bhīshma
  from whom the ladies run!
Bhīshma the brahmachārī
  comes here. . . . Why?" (102.7, 9)

Bhīshma, therefore, is aged by the time Chitrāñgada dies, which shows that he must have been past his teens when Gangā handed him over to Shāntanu. Anyhow, the taunts have the salutary effect of exposing us to the first duel between two human warriors: Bhīshma and Shalva. It is a relief to find a hero who really fights like one, instead of having to hear interminable eulogies about one's prowess without any incident to prove it. There is a happy image in the midst of this fight:

"Their ornaments and armours,
  O Janamejaya,
dazzled like meteors
  that flash across the sky." (102.22)

The episode concerning Ambā's refusal to marry Vichitravīrya, a minor, and Bhīshma escorting her to her chosen husband Shalya, is disposed of in a few *shlokas* here, but forms a sub-parva in the *Udyoga Parva,* sections 173-392, where her re-birth as Shikhandi and assumption of male-sex are described.

In 103 verses 1 and 24 Satyavatī is described as "hungry for sons", looking forward to Pāndu's obsession. The dynasty has to continue, but Bhīshma is quite adamant in keeping his vow of celibacy:

"I will give up the three worlds;
I will give up the kingdom of heaven,
I will give up more than the three worlds and heaven.
But I will not give up truth. . . .
Let doom overtake the world!
  Immortality cannot tempt me,
nor lordship of the three worlds!
  I will not break my vow." (103.15, 19)

Here again, in *shloka* 24, Satyavatī has been described as "hungry for (grand) sons", a telling epithet: Pāndu inherits this trait, craving son after son. The full version of this *shloka* would be:

"Repeatedly urged by
  the grieving mother,

hungry for grandsons,
but whose words strayed from Dharma. . . ."

It is her greed for successors that will prove her undoing. In the *Devī Bhāgavata Purāna*, Book VI, Vyāsa refuses to beget sons on Vichitravīrya's widows since they are like his daughters and intercourse with wives of others is a grievous sin. *Niyoga* was permissible only at the instance of the husband (as in Kuntī's case, ordered by Pāndu), not of the mother-in-law. Vyāsa even tells his mother that preserving the dynasty by adopting such heinous means is improper (VI.24.46-48). Satyavatī once again displays her mastery of *realpolitik*. Desperate to propagate her lineage, she argues that improper directives of elders ought to be obeyed and such compliance attracts no blame, particularly as it will remove the sorrow of a grieving mother. It is when Bhīshma urges Vyāsa to obey his mother that he gives in and engages in what he describes as "this disgusting task" (VI.24.56). Vyāsa wonders whether progeny born of adultery, *vyabhicharodbhava* (VI.25.28), can ever be the source of happiness for him. How prophetic!

In response to Satyavatī's frantic demands, Bhīshma specifically addresses her, for the first time, as Queen in 103.25. Earlier, in 100.107 and 103.13, he has called her "Mother". Now, possibly in order to bring home to her that the responsibility for choosing the lawful and righteous course of action for the welfare of the kingdom lies with her alone, Bhīshma gives her the regal title. It is also here that Bhīshma appears, for the first time, in the guise of the repository of all ancient traditions, as he proceeds to narrate an account of the birth of Dīrghatamas, a seer who composed some of the loveliest *suktas* in the *Rig Veda.* This feature of Bhīshma's character will be fully exploited in the *Shānti Parva,* where he will educate Yudhishthira in all the duties of a monarch through a vast repertory of legends and stories, example and precept.

Bhīshma narrates the extermination of *Kshatriyas* by Parashurāma as many as twenty-one times, a story that is told to Yudhishthira in sections 116-17 of the *Vana Parva.* The operative *shloka* in this account is:

"With all Kshatriya heroes dead,
the Kshatriya ladies
solicited Veda-knowing Brahmins
and conceived by them;
Dharma impelled them,
not lust." (104.5-6)

The point, of course, is that with Shāntanu it is lust, not Dharma, which impelled him, as with Vichitravīrya and later with Pāndu. Lustful intercourse does not, ultimately, lead to birth of such progeny as can carry on the dynasty. The lustless *Kshatriya* women gave birth to sons who rejuvenated the class, but the lustful Shāntanu is unable to procreate a single dynast.

What follows is a rare and an extremely fascinating insight into the social mores prevalent in pre-epic times. The story of Mamatā and Brihaspati shows a society, at least among Brahmins, where the younger brother could have sexual relations with his elder brother's wife without social stigma. Mamatā does not oppose Brihaspati desires because it is against Dharma, but only because she is already pregnant by his brother. She admonishes him:

"Your semen should not be wasted.
But how can two babies
live at the same time in one womb?
Do not lust for me now." (104.12)

Her implied admonition is that intercourse is to be resorted to for procreation, not to gratify lust. Hence where the semen is likely to go waste it should not be indulged in. Brihaspati, however, is unable to control his lust and forces himself on her (note that Mamatā does not resist physically, as it is his right to enjoy her if he so wishes; she merely points out the drawbacks and submits). He persists, although the unborn child in her womb also requests him to desist on the same grounds. When this plea goes unheeded, for lust, as Shakespeare wrote, is "Savage, extreme, rude, cruel," the child takes direct action and blocks the entrance to the womb, so that the seed spills out. This brings Brihaspati to his senses. On seeing the precious life-producing semen wasted, typically he curses the blameless foetus, being still in the grip of his frustrated lust. Therefore, the child is born blind, paralleling the blindness of Dhritarāshtra sown in the unwilling lustful field of Vichitravīrya's queen shrinking away from awful Vyāsa.

This son of Utathya and Mamatā, named Dīrghatamas (dwelling long in darkness) is known as the son of Uchathya in the *Rig Veda* (1.158) and the *Brihaddevatā* (4.11-14.21-25). In the latter, the story is similar, except that it is servants who throw him into the river, not his sons, and he floats to Anga where the king rescues him. Here, again, we come across a cryptic and unexplained reference to the practices of the cow-race:

"Veda-learned, mahatmā Dīrghatamas
learnt from Surabhi's son
the practices of the cow-race
and publicly indulged in them." (104.24)

The only hint of what this might connote is in the next *Shloka*:

"The other rsis of the asrama
saw him overstep the limits
of what they held as decency,
and were indignant."

Possibly this is a reference to a sect practising unrestricted sexual intercourse in public without regard for degrees of kinship, with sexual desire as the only criterion. This is of a time when the social and familial set-up was still fluid and not bound down to rigid norms. Thus, Dīrghatamā's wife can flatly refuse to look after him and have him thrown into the river by her sons. In the process there is another bit of information provided by the *rishi* about this esoteric cult to which he belongs: "Take me to the Kshatriya,/and you will be rich" (104.29). Dīrghatamas is a professional impregnator, valuable because he is a famous sage and *Kshatriyas* were anxious to rejuvenate their feeble race by having their wives impregnated with virile Brahmin seed to produce progeny capable of glorifying the dynasty. His wife, of

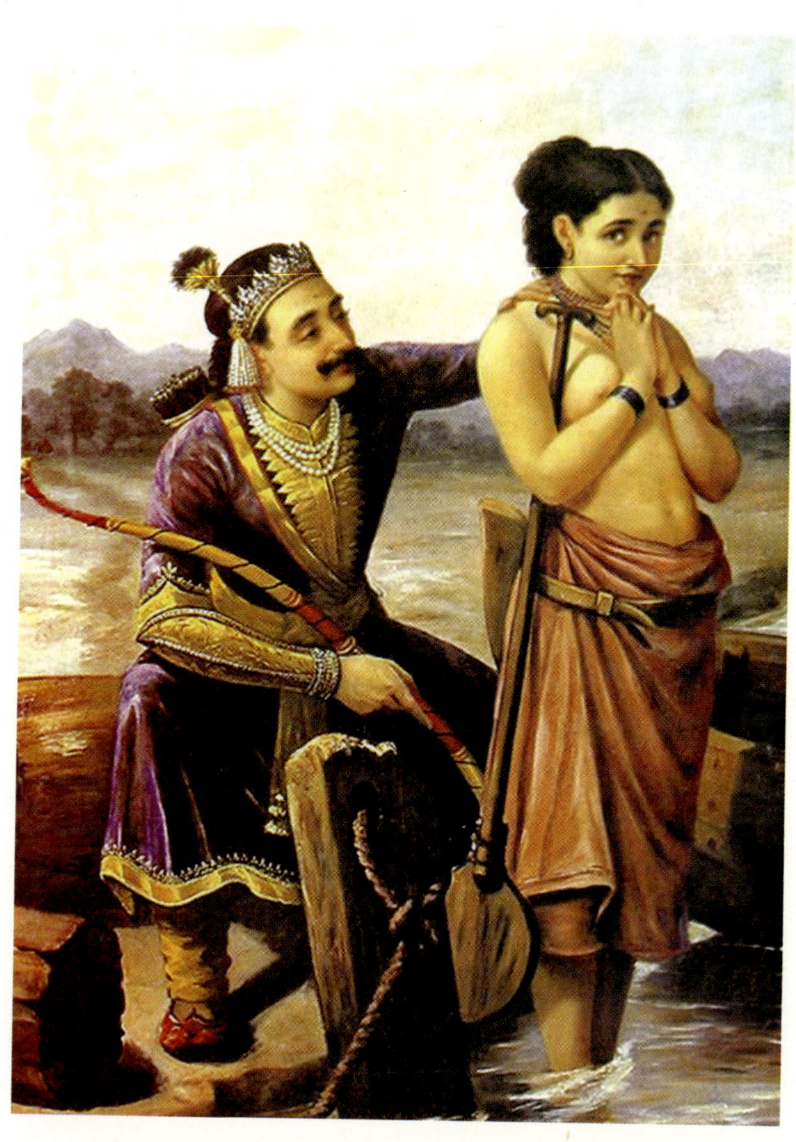

"Shantanu with Matsyagandhi" by Ravi Varma

course, refuses to use her husband as a stud-bull. It is now that Dīrghatamas lays down the first law against freedom of women:

"Every woman must stay with one husband
    throughout her life.
Whether he is dead—or alive—
    she must not seek union
with another man. If she does,
    she will be counted corrupted." (104.31-32)

It is a similar law of monogamy that Shvetaketu lays down in 122.17-20 by rebelling against the tradition. His father Uddālaka, on seeing his wife taken away for coition in his presence by another Brahmin, explains to him that the "sanātana dharma" is:

"All women of the four castes
    are free to have relations
with any man. And the men,
    well, they are like bulls." (122.4)

Shvetaketu's doctrine is a little more balanced, in so far as he lays down that the unfaithful husband is also to be cursed. This is basically the foisting of a patriarchal system on what was originally a matriarchal one that gave total freedom to women, and is typical of a nomadic herdsmen culture worshipping the sun and the bull as against the agricultural ethos based on moon and cow worship.

Dīrghatamas is rescued by a king named Bali of Anu's dynasty and we find yet another parallel with what will follow. Bali wants his wife Sudeshnā to have children by the sage. She, disgusted with his blindness and old age, sends her servant instead, just as Ambikā does to Vyāsa. In both cases worthy progeny are born from the substitute. Sudeshnā is sent a second time when the king learns of the truth and has five sons by the ascetic: Anga, Vanga, Kalinga, Pundra and Suhma. All five are eponymous kings and refer to modern Bhagalpur (in Eastern Bihar), South Bengal, South Orissa, North Bengal and Central Bengal respectively.

Blind Dhritarāshtra and Dīrghatamas are prolific begetters, while royal Pāndu and Kalmāshpāda are barren.

Bhīshma suggests that Satyavatī may request some renowned Brahmin to impregnate her daughters-in-law. He has given her two alternatives: one is the tradition where younger brothers-in-law could have intercourse with the wife; and the other where *Kshatriya* women could solicit Brahmins. In both cases, however, his emphasis has been on Dharma, not lust, being the motivation. It is because of lust that Brihaspati's seed is wasted; and Sudeshnā fails to beget children out of her fascination for externalities rather than looking to the purpose of the act. Bhīshma, very diplomatically, does not urge any particular course of action: "Having heard this, mother, do as you please" (104.50). In 105.2 Bhīshma specifically urges Satyavatī :

"Choose a merit-laden Brahmin,
offer him wealth,
let him procreate children
in the field of Vichitravīrya."

Now Satyavatī reveals her secret, in the process slipping in a reference to her father being Uparichara Vasu (105.6), but contradicting it a couple of verses later by saying that she is a Nishāda's daughter (105.10). This, again, raises the suspicion that all such references to Satyavatī being Vasu's daughter are interpolations by Vaishampāyana who has his royal audience in mind. Kālī, the dark-complexioned, suggests that Krishna her dark son should impregnate her daughters-in-law, and Bhīshma agrees. Vyāsa appears and the manner in which he is greeted is typical of ancient Indian tradition and so eloquent:

"Milk gushed from her breasts,
Wetting, annointing him." (105.25)

Prof. Lal has very correctly rendered the original *prashrava*. Earlier translators, and even the most recent van Buitenen, have rendered it as "tears," losing most of the emotionally charged force of the cryptic utterance. This episode follows an ancient folk-lore tradition, most memorably brought out in the story of Shankhamālā by Dakshinaranjan Mitra Majumdar in his *Thākurmār Jhuli* (Grandmother's Bag). There, for determining who the real mother is, the rival claimants are asked to direct streams of milk from their breasts to the king's lips. Only the true mother succeeds as the milk gushes automatically to her son.

It is ironic that the fruit of one lustful union, Vyāsa, should be asked to sow in the lustful field of Vichitravīrya, who is himself an issue of middle-aged lust. It is in keeping with the impatience and unwise haste characterising this failing that Satyavatī cannot wait till her daughters-in-law have purified themselves by a year-long vow, as advised by Vyāsa. She, of course, puts forward reasons of security of state to justify the short-cut required. Vyāsa then posits a different type of ordeal:

"If Kaushalyā-Ambikā can stand my smell,
  my fearful, stern looks,
my dress, my body,
  she will have an excellent son."—105.45

Satyavatī plays a dirty trick on Ambikā. She leads her to believe that Bhīshma will be visiting her, by cunningly referring to the plan suggested by him and referring to a visit by her husband's elder brother. This indicates the taint of lust remaining in Ambikā, of which Vyāsa wanted her to be purified. The result is a blind son: Dhritarāshtra. Vyāsa informs his mother that the son will have the strength of ten thousand elephants, the only evidence of which we find when he crushes the iron statue of Bhīma after the war is over.

Now Satyavatī urges him to impregnate Ambālikā, since a blind man cannot rule the kingdom. This itself is supremely ironic, for it is the blind Dhritarāshtra, the first born, who actually becomes king while Pāndu irresponsibly takes to the forest. Ambālikā, also, fails to respond with equanimity so that her son is born of sickly pallor.

Satyavatī solicits for a third issue, but this time Ambikā, recalling Vyāsa's body odour (inherited from his mother) and appearance, tricks her by sends her maid instead. This nameless servant welcomes and honours the sage. Thus the wise Vidura is born:

"With his permission, she attended on him
carefully, respectfully, and loved him secretly
as he desired. The strict-vowed maharshi
was delighted with her love-making."—106.26

Thus, Satyavatī fails in her efforts to obtain normal and healthy grandchildren, despite the intervention of the greatest sage of the time, because she neglects to take into account this family taint of lust, doubly reinforced through herself.

So far, Janamejaya has been unusually quiet, but he is unable to restrain himself when Vaishampāyana refers to Vidura being the incarnation of Dharma because of *rishi* Māndavya's curse. Janamejaya's query leads to the only digression in this narrative.

Māndavya's story is a peculiar one. He is a seer engaged in austerities with uplifted hands under a tree, observing a vow of silence. It is strange that the king should sentence a sage to death along with thieves without ascertaining why he remains mute. It seems the decision was taken purely on circumstantial evidence of the loot having been found in the hermitage. He appears to be an ideal sage, like the one afflicted by Parikshit, and is satisfied when the king apologises. However, the stake on which he was impaled is embedded within him as it cannot be extricated. Hence he is named Ani-Māndavya. This results in another dispensation being handed down. The sage learns from Dharma that this is the retribution visited upon him for having, in a previous birth as a child, pierced flies with grass-blades. Dharma has weighed the pain and the value of the life of a sage and that of a fly equally, but Māndavya thinks otherwise:

"Venial was my crime, O Dharma,
terrible my punishment.
Worse than mass-murder, it is said,
is the killing of a single Brahmin."—108.15

Māndavya prescribes that nothing done by a boy under twelve

shall be classed as *adharma*, for till that age awareness of Dharma does not arise. He goes on to amend this and prescribes that "Below the age of fourteen/no one commits a crime" (108.17). He also curses Dharma to be born in a *Shudra's* womb as punishment for his injustice.

Section 109 paints a picture of the felicity of the Kuru kingdom following the birth of these three children. We find that Shudra-born Vidura is treated on par with his two brothers, gets the same Kshatriya training from Bhīshma, and is the one to whom the Protector of the Kurus turns for advice regarding matrimonial alliances. There is a hint in *Shloka* 10 of the rivalry between the southern Kurus (Bhīshma's line) and the northern (the Pānchālas). This rivalry is the basis of the alliances that take place and ultimately lead to the war. The Pānchālas and Matsyas ally themselves with the Pāndavas against the Kurus, Madra, Sindhu, Gāndhāra, Avanti. It is an interesting ranging of Southern and Western Aryans with Duryodhana against the Eastern and Central Aryans with Yudhishthira. The latter were always at the centre of the great empire-building efforts, first by Māndhātā, then by Bhagiratha, followed by Bharata, with the Haiheya Kārtavīrya Arjuna in-between in a disastrous attempt that only resulted in a great catastrophe for *Kshatriyas*. The former, on the other hand, were at the periphery, hence averse to being moulded into integral parts of an empire that Krishna was aiming at building through the Pāndavas. Hence the confrontation.

It is significant that both the Gāndhāra and Madra kings are initially reluctant to marry their princesses to Dhritarāshtra and Pāndu. Each of them obtains something in return. Gāndhāra ensures that his son Shakuni stays on at the Kuru court to influence its policies through his nephews. Madra obtains a substantial dowry for bestowing Mādrī on Pāndu, quoting a convenient *kuladharma* (family tradition). Prithā alone is freely bestowed by her foster-father in a *svayamvara*, thereby forging an alliance of Hastināpura with the powerful Yādavas on which the Pāndava destiny is to pivot.

Prithā parallels Satyavatī in a peculiar way: she, too, has had a child and yet retained her virginity. The story of the *mantra* gifted her by Durvāsā is introduced here in order to prepare the ground for the subsequent godly impregnations and to mention Karna and his upbringing by Adhiratha and Rādhā. "He will be himself" is a very significant prophecy the sun god makes about him. We are also told of his cutting-off his natural armour and ear-rings and gaining the infallible weapon from Indra disguised as a Brahmin. Thus Vasusena, born with riches of celestial armour and earrings, became Vaikartana, the cutter-off.

In section 113 an account of Pāndu's "world-conquest" is given. The campaigns are all limited to the Gangetic belt: Magadha, Mithilā, Kāshī (why he needs to do this is not clear as his mothers are princesses of Kāshī), Suhma and Pundra. These appear to be old rivalries and enmities, and by subjugating them Pāndu is re-asserting the Kuru supremacy lost after Shāntanu:-

"Those who had previously looted
the wealth of the Kauravas
now pay tribute to Pandu,
Lion of Hastināpura."—113.38

He returns with a load of treasure including animals, gems, shawls, hides etc. There is repeated reference to the joy of citizens, showing the nature of the monarchy of that time which concerned itself directly with the reactions of its subjects.

Pāndu now retires to the forest to relax with his queens. Like Yayāti and Shāntanu, his lustful ancestors, Pāndu is addicted to the indiscriminate slaughter of animals, for, as Shakespeare wrote, lust is "murderous, bloody, full of blame/Savage, extreme, rude, cruel". Perversely killing a deer-sage in the act of copulation, he is cursed to die in intercourse. It is now that Vyāsa explicitly voices the underlying theme that he has been stressing from the story of Nahusha onwards. Pāndu learns too late the lesson that,

"Noble blood is of little help.
Deluded by passions, the best
of men turn wicked, and reap
the punishment of their karma."—119.2

He laments,

"My father was deep in dharma,
his father was too,
But kāma was his ruin, he died
while still a youth.
And in the field of his lust
I was sown
By a truth-honouring rishi,
bhagavān Krishna Dvaipāyana. . . .
And I am a victim of the hunt!
My mind is full of killing,
shooting down deer."—119.3-5

The tragedy of lust's malevolent attraction is precisely what Shakespeare put so memorably:

"All this the world well knows; yet none knows well
To shun the heaven that leads men to this hell."

Pāndu himself, despite his desperate resolve to seek moksha by renouncing all pleasures, is overtaken by his karma when

"passion overpowered him,
it seemed that he wanted
To commit suicide, as it were.
First he lost his senses,
then, clouded by lust,
he sought the loss of his life." (125.12,13)

He dies in raping Mādrī although "she fought against him fiercely." Of these generations of Kurus, consisting of Nahusha (who fell because lust for Shachi robbed him of his good sense), Yayāti, Mahābhīsha-Shāntanu, Parāshara-Satyavatī, Vichitravīrya-his wives-Vyāsa, and Pāndu, we can say with Milton,

"They, fondly thinking to allay
Their appetite with gust, instead of fruit

Chewed bitter ashes."

What Pāndu says in his guilt-driven resolve to adopt a hermit's life (119.6-21) is an excellent picture of the life and character of the ideal sanyasi, the keystone being equanimity, non-violence and poverty. It is strange that when his resolve to undertake forest-life and renounce kingship is made known, we do not find either Bhīshma or Vidura coming to see him to find out the reasons and to dissuade him. Is it because, like Devāpi, he has some skin disease (leucoderma?), whence "Pāndu"? This peculiar inaction of Bhīshma will be seen to recur time and again where the interests of Pāndu and his children are concerned vis-é-vis the active enmity of Dhritarāshtra and Duryodhana. As for Satyavatī, she is totally out of the picture and even Vyāsa is not invoked to tackle this exigency. It is some itinerant sages who forecast children for Pāndu and advise him to think hard and clearly to find out the means to achieve that end.

This elicits a lecture from Pāndu to Prithā on the different types of sons that is repeated in the *Anushāsana Parva*, section 49. These six types are: one's own son; son born to one's wife by an accomplished person; son born to one's wife through another by payment; son of a remarried woman by her second husband or to a woman through *niyoga*; son born to the wife before her marriage; and son of an adulterous wife. These six are classed as heirs and kinsmen in the *Manusamhitā*. Pāndu then mentions six others who have no such rights: the son given away in adoption; the son who, out of gratitude, calls himself thus; the son conceived before marriage (how does this differ from the son born to the wife before marriage?); the son born of incest; and the son of a lower caste womb.

What follows is a series of stories that Pāndu and Kuntī narrate in support of their clashing points of view. The first one is the little-known tale of Sāradandāyanī that has exact mythic parallels in Sumerian, Babylonian and Assyrian mythology. Seeking a child, she stands at the crossroads and solicits passers-by. This myth is linked with the cult of the triple-formed moon-goddess Hecate of the crossroads that spread to Greece from Mesopotamia with identical rites. Later, in medieval times, it was perverted into a meeting-place for witches and black magic.

Both in 120.37 and 122.28 Prof. Lal has Pāndu appeal to Kuntī to beget children by soliciting a worthy person as he has lost his procreative powers—more a case of azoospermia than impotence (*hinah prajananāt svayam*), whatever Iravati Karve might argue in favour of the latter in her *Yuganta.* Moreover, Pāndu is repeatedly described as roaming in the forests like Airāvata in 'musth' with two she-elephants, and he dies in the very act of raping Mādrī.

To return to this fascinating exchange between husband and wife, each countering the other's argument with a tale dug out of hoary antiquity, Kuntī narrates the story of Vyusitāshva and Bhadrā (section 121). She points out that Bhadrā was able to have seven sons by lying with the corpse of her husband. The story itself is pervaded with grim irony, once again linking up with the theme of "The expense of spirit in a waste of shame/ Is lust in action". Vyusitāshva is another of those intriguing names of which we find no mention anywhere besides what Kuntī tells us; although he was obviously a famous king since a chronicle-verse is devoted to him (121.14) and his *yajña* was so successful in pleasing the gods that they themselves performed it for him. The chronicle *Shloka* is quoted by Kuntī to prove that she is not just pulling this story out of a hat to justify her stand, but that it is vouched for in the *Purānas.*

The irony lies in the close parallels between this king's life and that of Vichitravīrya. Both were over-addicted to sex and died from the resultant consumption:

> "So strong was their passion
> So frequent their indulgence,
> that he soon fell a victim
> to consumption;"—121.17-18

It is rather tactless of Kuntī to dig up a legend with such uncomfortable analogies to her father-in-law's fate. Pāndu, no doubt, feels irked, particularly as she urges him "come to me,/ let us have a child", presumably with the idea that even if he dies in the process, she will be able, like Bhadrā, to have sons from his corpse. Pāndu is too much of a realist to class himself with such superhuman heroes of old with yogic powers for progenition beyond death. Very tactfully he admits that she is right and yet points out its impracticality:

"What you say, Kuntī,
is true. Auspicious lady,
God-like Vyusitāshva could afford to do
what you said he did."—122.2

He proceeds to give us another fascinating picture of sexual mores in ancient Indian society. The stress is again on the freedom enjoyed by woman, which came to be restricted more and more as Aryan civilisation advanced, till she became a mere chattel, first of the father, then of the husband, and finally of her children :

"in the past, women
were not restricted to the house,
dependant on family members;
they moved about freely,
they enjoyed themselves freely.
They slept with any men they liked
from the age of puberty;
they were unfaithful to their husbands,
and yet was not adharma,
for the practice of those times
was promiscuous intercourse."—122.4-5

Pāndu adds two facts that are even more pertinent:-

"The mahā rishis have praised
this Purāna-dharma;
the northern Kurus still practise it. . . .
the new custom is very recent"—122.7, 8

For this reason, the Aryans settled around the Sarasvatī-Yamunā had started looking down upon their northern brethren, and eventually would even class them with *mlechchhas* and non-

Aryans. Later, it is this northern Kuru tradition that Yudhishthira quotes to Drupada to bolster his decision that Draupadī will wed all five brothers.

As Bhīshma had narrated the story of Brihaspati and Mamatā, Pāndu gives Prithā the story of Shvetaketu, son of Uddālaka whom readers will remember from the *Paushya* sub-*parva* as Ārunī. When Shvetaketu is outraged at his mother being taken away by a Brahmin in his father's presence, Uddālaka explains:

> "This is the Sanātana Dharma
> All women of the four castes
> are free to have relations
> with any man. And the men,
> well, they are like bulls."—122.13-14

Dīrghatamas was one of such bull-men and possibly this is what his following of the practices of the cow-race implied. Like Dīrghatamas, Shvetaketu also lays down the law imposing monogamy, making it applicable equally to the husband and the wife, while Dīrghatamas had left the husband totally out of it in his anger at being thrown out by his wife.

The story may seem to have little relevance to the point in issue, but Pāndu very cleverly chooses his material. The third dictate of Shvetaketu is that:

> "Third, the faithful wife who,
> commanded by her husband
> to procreate children, refuses,
> is guilty of infanticide."—122.19

Swiftly he piles on this two more examples: Saudāsa's wife Madayantī having a son by Vashishtha, and Vyāsa fathering children on Ambikā and Ambālikā. Like a true bureaucrat he finally says, "With these precedents before you,/you should do as I say" (122.24).

Pāndu has provided her with three examples (Saradandāyani, Madayantī, Ambikā-Ambālikā) and the muted threat of incurring the sin of infanticide should she refuse to obey her husband in this matter. But knowing his wife's strong will, his last approach is one of abject begging (though he is still vain enough to point out that his fingers are like lotus-leaves):

"Sweet lady,
I fold my palms
joining the tips
of my lotus-leaf fingers
and I implore you in anjali—
listen to me!"
Be gracious to me!—122. 29

One can almost sense the changing expressions on Kuntī's face as Pāndu speaks from *shloka* 24 to 30, for in each verse he changes his tone and approach as if in response to what he sees in her eyes and on her face. In *shloka* 24 he firmly points out that she should do as he says for the advice he is giving is not against dharma. Obviously the response must have been a sullen silence, for he quickly changes to blandishment, "Sweet queen, devoted wife," and goes back to his reliance on the time-honoured tradition that

"when a wife's fertile period
arrives, she must go to her husband
And have intercourse with him;
at other times she is free."—122.25-26

This, of course, is the pre-Shvetaketu tradition that Pāndu is advocating. Kuntī, possibly, continues to be unresponsive as she has already told her husband: "Not even in thought will I / be embraced by another" (121.5). The irony lies in the fact of her already having lain in the embrace of Durvāsā/Sūrya, as we will find out later. In that light, she doth protest too much, sounding primly self-righteous.

Pāndu switches to the implied threat of sin (it is a virtual see-saw between admonition, threat and wheedling) if a wife does not obey her husband's command *even if it is a sinful one,* thus going one better on Shvetaketu who restricted the wife's implicit obedience to the husband's command to procreate children. Such threats, however, have no effect on the redoubtable Kuntī, and the desperate Pāndu ultimately turns to the only course left open: a direct appeal for grace, which is what would have won him his case at the very beginning. We should not forget that Kuntī chose him out of all the assembled royalty as her husband and this deep love for him is what drives her throughout. But husbands are always slow to learn that to get the wife to do what they want the best way is to become a suppliant. It is only then that she graciously responds:

> "O excellent Bharatas! Great adharma
> it is for a wife to be
> repeatedly asked a favour; shouldn't a wife
> anticipate her husband's wishes?"—122.32

Kuntī displays admirable one-upmanship over Pāndu. He had begged her to solicit some eminent Brahmana; she informs-him that she has the power to summon any god he may wish to have as his surrogate. Like Satyavatī revealing her secret weapon, Vyāsa, only in the last extremity, Kuntī reveals the mantra she possesses, but not the effects of its first test. We will see how Kuntī always has the last word where Pāndu's desires are concerned.

Shloka 123.1 provides the link-up between the birth of the Pāndavas and the Dhārtarāshtras: "At the time that Kuntī summoned undecaying Dharma, Gāndhārī was already a year advanced in pregnancy." The implication is very important: Duryodhana is a year old in the womb when Yudhishthira is conceived. Unfortuantely, he is born later—quite a conundrum for primogeniture! This takes us back to section 115 where Vaishampāyana stated that Dhritarāshtra had one hundred sons by Gāndhārī and one more by a Vaishya concubine (Yuyutsu). Janamejaya, true to character, poured forth a volley of queries, quite dissatisfied with such a bald account:

"How did Gāndhārī give birth to a hundred sons? How many years did it take? How long did they live?

How did he have his hundred-and-first son by his Vaishya wife? What was Dhritarāshtra's attitude to his loving, faithful and virtuous wife Gāndhārī? . . .

Tell me all this in detail, O tapasyā-wealthy one. I am never tired of listening to your accounts of my friends and kinsmen."—115.3-4, 6

Vaishampāyana's account begins with a confusing statement. He attributes the hundred sons of Gāndhārī to a boon from Vyāsa, whereas in 110.9-10 he has told us that Bhīshma specifically chose her as Dhritarāshtra's consort because she had obtained this boon from Shiva. This once again shows the sort of contradictions in minutiae that are inevitable in epics handed down by word-of-mouth.

In true epic fashion she carries the embryo for two years, as Vinatā had done, and like Vinatā it is jealousy that drives her to a premature delivery. Hearing that Kuntī has already delivered a son, she aborts herself in a fury of frustration to deliver a mass of flesh out of which Vyāsa produces a hundred sons and one daughter. We recall that this is what had happened long back with Sagara's wife Sumati where Aurva had formed sixty thousand sons from the lump she had delivered. Vinatā had similarly broken one of her eggs in impatience and been cursed with slavery. We are also told that Yudhishthira, though conceived a year later, was born before Duryodhana, who was born on the same day as Bhīma. It is interesting that Duryodhana is said to have brayed like an ass immediately after birth. Kumāra Vyāsa, in his Kannada *Mahābhārata,* has Gāndhārī married to a donkey first because an early widowhood had been foretold for her. The prophecy is fulfilled when the ass dies, but Duryodhana's braying on birth provides a curious link-up with this first marriage of his mother.

K.L. Jain draws our attention to four verses dropped by the editors of the critical edition which state that the Madra king married his ten daughters, including Gāndhārī, to Dhritarashtra and that the one hundred sons and one daughter were born from them. The Jain *Shatrunjaymahatmaya* (10.641-3) has the same account.[2] It is not, therefore, an abnormal one-woman show.

The Brahmins advise Dhritarāshtra to destroy his first-born whose birth is attended with evil omens and it is here that the key to the blind king's character is unobtrusively provided. In 115.29-30 he concedes Yudhishthira right to the throne, as he will over and over again as lip-service, but asks, "After him, my son Duryodhana/But will he also become king?" They urge him to sacrifice this child for the sake of the kingdom, "But rājā Dhritarāshtra loved his son./He rejected their advice" (115.37). This is precisely what he will do time and again in the face of the advice of Vidura, Bhīshma and Krishna, constantly letting his son have his way while mouthing his love for Yudhishthira.

It is after this that Vaishampāyana comes to the story of Pāndu's curse and the birth of the Pāndavas by proxy. The first god Pāndu chooses is Dharma, for who would dare to question the legitimacy of a son born of the god of Law and Justice! The Prithā-Dharma encounter is one of the finest instances of Vyāsan delicacy and brevity in delineating subtle human relationships. We have only to compare Prof. Lal's version with the other translations to see how immeasurably superior the transcreation is. Ganguli renders it as:

> 'Smiling he asked, "O Kuntī, what am I to give thee?" And Kuntī too smiling in her turn, replied, "Thou must even give me offspring."

Prof. Lal's transcreation captures the exact delicate nuances of the original:

> 'He laughed.
> "Kuntī, what can I give you?"
> She laughed,
> "A son".'—123.4

Here is someone well known to Kunti, for she is totally at ease with him, and he with her. We see the difference when Vāyu appears. Kunti smiles shyly and there is no smiling greeting on his part. There is enough reason for positing, as Iravati Karve did, that this Dharma is none other than Kuntī's brother-in-law Vidura, the first by right to be summoned under the custom of *niyoga.*

In some recensions this splendid brevity is spoilt by an interpolation that, though a lovely *shloka* in itself, is not Vyāsan at all. This *shloka* is worth including, however:

"In that finest of mountains, hundred-peaked Satashringa, with its numerous deer-forests, most fortunate Kuntī summoned Dharma for the sake of Pāndu. In her fertile period, having bathed and purified herself, wearing spotless raiment, the celebrated lady, the pious and lovely hipped one, lay with Dharma."

After the birth of three sons, when Pāndu urges Kuntī to have more, she characteristically refuses, bluntly reminding him of what is not advisable according to the scriptures, in which she is very well versed:

"The wise do not sanction
 a fourth conception, even in crisis.
The woman who has intercourse
 for a fourth is svairinī, a loose woman;
the woman who has intercourse
 for a fifth is bandhakī, a prostitute."—123.83

Here, again, the irony is that self-righteous Kuntī has had intercourse with four persons and Arjuna is actually her fourth conception!

She follows this by admonishing Pāndu for asking her to do that which he knows to be *adharma.* Yet, the same Kuntī forces Draupadī to live out her entire life with five brothers, because of which Karna calls her a public woman in the dice-game episode. In many recensions we find an eighty fifth *shloka* which is typical of Pāndu's weak character. At this direct refusal from Kuntī, he quickly retreats, saying, "What you say echoes the sacred scriptures." His greed for sons is only another facet of the fatal flaw in his character.

Kuntī's adamantine will is revealed yet again when she turns

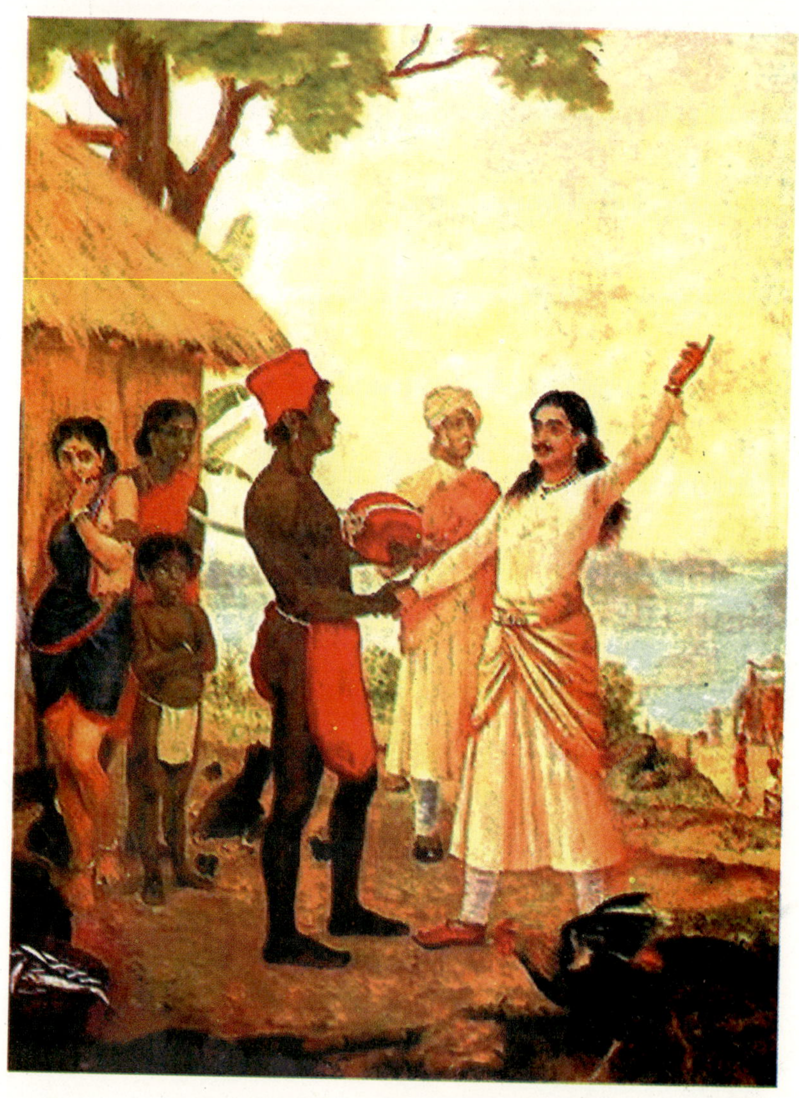

"Bhishma's vow" by Ravi Varma

down Pāndu's request to help Mādrī beget more children by use of the *mantra.* Mādrī's initial request itself is significant. She is jealous of her co-wife and does not approach her begging the favour, but goes to her husband to complain that he is discriminating between his wives and that he should ask Kuntī to oblige her. Pāndu's reply is again characteristically vain and hypocritical, He has never shown the slightest interest in Mādrī having children by proxy, being fully wrapt-up in getting Kuntī to agree to such a process repeatedly. But now he says:

"Mādrī, I have often thought
of this; yet I refrained
from telling you ; I was not sure
if it would please you or displease you."—124.7

And he adds with hollow bravado:

"I know that if I ask Kuntī,
she will not refuse me."

He can hardly admit that she has already refused his request to have more sons and that even getting her to agree to have these three has been a monumental task in which he succeeded only by begging in abject surrender. Kuntī agrees and Mādrī cleverly makes the best of it by summoning the twin Ashvinikumāras. When the insatiable Pāndu again requests her on Mādrī's behalf, he meets with a flat refusal that also reveals the smouldering rivalry between the two wives. Kuntī's reply shows the hidden bitterness and hunger for superiority that we would never have suspected to be part of her character:

"She deceived me", said Kuntī
"With one mantra I gave her,
she managed to get two sons.
I am afraid she will get
more sons than I. Scheming woman!
What a fool I was!
How was I to know

she would summon the Ashvins,
and obtain twins?
Don't come to me again, my lord,
saying 'Grant her a favour.'"—124.26-28

A couple of things are interesting and worthy of note here. Firstly, Kuntī does not seem to have any qualms about having sons by proxy once she has been bested by Mādrī. She is now thinking in term of her status only and not her husband's welfare, out of concern for which she had originally agreed to this process. One would have expected Pāndu to take advantage of this and suggest that Kuntī go ahead and have more children by Ashvins or others. But the fact that he does not dare to make any such suggestion shows his awareness of his wife's indomitable will. Once she has refused to have more sons, he is powerless to make her change her mind. It is also possible that, having parted with the *mantra*, Kuntī no longer has that magical power in her. She never uses it again.

The other significant point is that Kuntī does not straightaway summon Indra by her *mantra.* First Pāndu engages in severe austerities, propitiates the king of the gods and obtains from him the assurance of having a sun of unparalleled valour. It is only after this that he tells Kuntī to use her incantation.

Thirdly, the question naturally arises: if the three sons of Kuntī were born of the gods Dharma, Vāyu and Indra, why should she refuse to summon further gods and speak of herself as having had intercourse with three *men* and point out that a woman having intercourse with four or five *men* loses her reputation? Surely, the very idea of starting the process with Dharma was that no one would be able to condemn the practice? This gives credence to Iravati Karve's argument that Yudhishthira was the son of Vidura, for the *niyoga* custom made it customary to approach the younger brother-in-law first of all. Similarly, the fathers of Bhīma and Arjuna are metamorphosed into gods by Pāndu, or the attending hermits, in order to lend weight to their birth, as their claim to the throne remains precarious in view of his long absence from the capital. It is surprising that he does not seek the advice of Bhīshma, the guardian of the kingdom, in the matter and that we find no accounts of any visits by any of the of the royal family, including his mother, to the forest to see how the sometime king and his wives are faring. In this, Pāndu resembles his ancestor Devāpi, Shāntanu's elder brother, who had also retired to the forest and was never heard of thereafter, despite his younger brother's insatiable lust for hunting in the forests. This neglect of Pāndu and his consorts suggests that he was not very highly thought of by Bhīshma and Satyavatī, otherwise why would they allow a blind man to sit on the throne? Or was it because a blind figurehead made it easier for Bhīshma to take care of the Kuru interests wholly untrammelled by the whims of the unstable Pāndu?

Section 124 introduces an important element in the Pāndava story. This is the Vrishnis or Yādavas, who send a priest of the Kashyapa clan to carry out the purificatory sacraments and rites for the Pāndavas. It is again curious that the Kaurava clan should remain utterly indifferent to Pāndu's fate and the upbringing of his children. The alliance with the Vrishnis will be the Pāndavas' major strength during the war. This particular passage is omitted in the critical edition of the epic and in the K.M. Ganguli version too but is available in the Lal transcreation.

Another interpolation at this point is the story of King Shuka coaching the Pāndavas in weapon-craft, with Yudhishthira excelling in spear-throw, Bhīma in mace-fight, Nakula and Sahadeva in sword and shield, while Arjuna is already made into an unbeatable hero, which hardly tallies with all the training he has to undergo later under Drona.

An important chronological clue is provided in 124.53: "The Pāndavas were separated/from each other by a year's difference." To this we have to add 125.2, which states that Arjuna was fourteen years old when Pāndu died, a victim of his violent lust.

Characteristically, Kuntī accuses Mādrī of the death, describing her husband as self-restrained (125.20) possibly because she had never been able to move him to passion. The jealousy between the two wives stems from Kuntī's consciousness that Mādrī is more attractive and from Mādrī's annoyance at having to take second place to one less gifted in beauty. Kuntī's frustration slips out ultimately:

"I always was careful with him,
my self-restrained husband!
Mādrī, you should have
been careful. . . . Why, why,
why did you tempt him
in the loneliness of the forest? . . .
Princess of Bāhlīka!
You are fortunate indeed—
you had the chance to see
his face radiant in intercourse."—125.20, 21, 23

The last *shloka* shows that when Pāndu was roaming the forests like a rutting elephant before the curse, he possibly devoted himself to Mādrī and not Kuntī. And thus Pāndu passes from the epic, pathetic in his insensate greed for sons so that he can glut himself on their offerings in the land of the pitris; so human in his inability to control his mental or physical desires. After all, he was the fruit of the seed sown in his father's lustful field that was left unpurified because of Satyavatī over-ruling Vyāsa's advice for a year-long purificatory vow in her hunger for grandsons. No wonder Pāndu was quietly removed from power and encouraged to engage in dalliance in the forest!

It is supremely ironic that the sages, in their address to the Kauravas (126.26 ff.), should repeatedly stress (five times in fifteen *shlokas*) that Pāndu had renounced sensual pleasures and lived in true *brahmacharya* (hardly a case of turning necessity to glorious gain!)

The difference between the characters of the two wives comes out again in their conversation following Pāndu's death, as Mādrī argues that she must be allowed to follow her husband:

"My lord, the best of the Bharatas,
wanted intercourse with me,
and I could not satisfy his kāma.
Let me do so in Yama's realm."—125.41

Even more significant is Mādrī's admission that she would not be able to bring up Kuntī's children as her own, for she lacks that firmness of will which conquers the ego's petty jealousies:

"Noble lady, could I bring up your children
  as if they were mine ?
And if I do not,
  will not the blame be mine?"—125.42

She is confident that Kuntī will treat her two sons as her own. The sages urge them that their duty lies in staying alive to look after their sons' welfare for "Dhritarāshtra, eager for power,/ will not deal fairly with your sons" (125.47). Kuntī accepts this well-considered advice, showing her maturity and concern for her children's future. But Mādrī remains, first and last, the *kāmini:*

"My passion is not quenched.
  Elder wife, let me go with him. . . .
My passion is still not satisfied."—125.40, 59

She is afraid of the responsibility of bringing up children, and prefers to be her husband's bed-mate only. She also points out that Kuntī has Kuntibhoja and the Vrishnis to help her, conveniently forgetting her brother Shalya.

Now comes a curious speech by her to Yudhishthira, where she tells him that she is not his true mother, but was only his nurse to wean him. This throws interesting light on the family life of Pāndu and his wives. Kuntī was so busy getting pregnant every year, that the first-born was naturally brought up by Mādrī, and would know her and love her more than his real mother. However, this hardly explains why such a condition should prevail for sixteen years, for that is Yudhishthira's age when Pāndu dies. *Shlokas* 45-70 of this section have been dropped as interpolations in the Critical Edition possibly on grounds of such inconsistencies. The last four *shlokas* describing the cremation of Pāndu are also suspected interpolations. Part of these passages, however, consists of a splendid tribute to Kuntī by Mādrī as she seeks permission to commit *sati:*

"You are blessed. There is none , O Vrishni lady,
like you, for you have the valour
strength, vigour, and brilliance
of five sons around you, . . .
Devi, you are my light,
my guide, most pujā-worthy,
Superior in status, purer in virtue." (125.66,67,68)

The permission is given:

In a broken voice Kuntī said,
"I give you permission.
Today you will unite with your husband
in heaven—be happy with him. . . .
enjoy him forever in heaven"—125.70

Section 126 raises some problems. *Shloka* 32 provides an important clue to judging the authenticity of text. The sages say that Pandu died "seventeen days back". In 125.33, Mādrī is described as entering the flames of the funeral pier and in 126.35 the sages confirm this while presenting the remains of the bodies and urge performance of funeral rites by the family. But 127.21 says:

"And the remains of the body,
with the new dress on,
lying on the luxurious bier,
looked as if brought back to life."

This does not mean that the bodies of Mādrī and Pāndu had been embalmed and kept intact for seventeen days till they were cremated in Hastināpura. Hence, the commentator Nīlakantha had taken all references to "body" as referring only to the bones. The passage in 127.22-24 refers to the remains as being burnt and the rites ending with performance of the horse sacrifice.

An important chronological clue has been omitted after 126.9 in the critical edition. These two verses give the ages of the Pāndavas when they entered Hastināpura: Yudhishthira is 16, the rest following at intervals of a year each. Considering that the princes are well into their teens and reputedly well-versed in weapon-craft and the scriptures during their upbringing in the forest, Bhīshma's anxiety about securing a proper teacher for them is difficult to understand, unless we accept that the *shloka* stating that Pāndu died when Arjuna was 14 is not authentic. A number of *shlokas* following 126.9 dropped from the critical edition give the duration of the Pāndavas' stay at Hastināpura, in the House of Lac, in the forest with Hidimbā, in Ekachakra and then at the Pānchāla court, followed by the return to Hastināpura, the stay at Indraprastha, the exile, the war, ruling at Hastināpura and finally the departure, at which stage Yudhishthira is said to be 100 years old. The authenticity of these verses is doubtful.

Section 128 gives the first hint of the impending holocaust when Vyāsa, finding everyone grieving for Pāndu, advises his mother to retire to the forest in order to escape the heart-rending agony of witnessing the destruction of the dynasty. Prof. Lal's translation once again brings out the immense difference between the transcreation by a sensitive poetic sensibility and the translation by a conscientious but prosaic personality as in the other extant versions. In 128.6, Prof. Lal's "the green years of the earth are gone" carries the delicate fragrance of a nostalgic vignette weighed down by a deep tragic awareness of irretrievable loss, which only poetic metaphor can convey. Against this, compare the Ganguli and van Buitenen versions, which are bald, but alas not as the mountain tops are bald:

"The world hath got old"—Ganguli
"earth herself is aging"—van Buitenen

Again, take Prof. Lal's version of *Shloka* 9:

"Do not be a witness
to the suicide
of your own race."

Notice how Prof. Lal's replacement of a single word "annihilation" in the Ganguli version transforms the entire impact of the line, making it so much more appealing in its anguished warning and plea. And the change is vital, for it is suicide that the Dhārtarāshtras commit, as Pāndu had done, losing their senses in their blind envy and rakshasan egoism. In 128.13 we learn of the deaths of Satyavatī and her daughters-in-lawafter they had performed awesome austerities.

Shloka 128.14 marks the point where we finally plunge into the Pāndava-Dhārtarāshtran story, leaving behind all the preliminary build-up. In this *shloka* the reference to the Pāndavas performing the various vedic sacraments now suggests that the passage in section 124 describing this being done by a priest sent by the Yādavas may not be authentic. However, no royal family could have left it so late for carrying out these sacramental rites, such as wearing of the sacred thread, etc. It is, therefore, not clear to what rites this *shloka* is referring, unless we reject the verses laying down the ages of the Pāndavas between 13 and 16 at this stage because of the clean break in the narrative sequence.

Here we take leave of the lustful generation, with the death of Satyavatī, Ambikā and Ambālikā, the lustful field in which Shāntanu and Vichitravīrya sowed fruitless seed. This family taint is carried on through Dhritarāshtra into his 100 sons, who are all "murderous, bloody, full of blame/Savage, extreme, rude, cruel," and like Pāndu they also commit suicide by deliberately arranging a fratricidal holocaust. The Pāndavas, be it noted, are not fruits of lust. Kuntī, unlike Mādrī, had never seen her husband's face "radiant in intercourse," and was not sullied by his lustful embraces. Her sons are born through use of a divine *mantra*, after due purification of herself and they are completely free of this family taint which began with Nahusha. It is interesting that Kuntī's sons should so completely overshadow Mādrī's although the Ashvins are by no means inferior to Dharma and Vāyu in the Hindu pantheon. Is the cause to be sought for within the characters of the mothers? Nakula and Sahadeva are mere followers of their elder brothers, much as Mādrī was nothing more than the bed-mate of Pāndu, finding her salvation in giving him sexual pleasure.

References

1. www.theoi.com/Pontios/NereisThetis3.html
2. Jain, p.484.

13

The Sambhava Parva-V

Kuntī

There is little doubt that the figure which easily dominates sections 121-128 is Prithā, whom we shall meet henceforth as Kuntī, as she was called after her adoptive father Kuntibhoja of Druhyu's dynasty. It is she who bows to the frantic plea of Mādrī and takes up the difficult and dangerous task of bringing up five teenagers in a hostile court, lacking powerful friends, without resources, and dependant on the tender mercies of the Dhārtarāshtras. She lets Mādrī esertyop cape that burden by immolating herself on the funeral pyre of their husband and shoulders this monumental responsibility. Even more than Satyavatī, she is a *kanyā*, a "virgin" in the Jungian sense. Though formally married, she is not a slave to her husband, but very much of an independent entity as we see in the exchanges regarding Pāndu's desire for children. The initial hint is provided in the boon given by Sūrya that she will remain a virgin despite having a son by him. The state of virginity refers to an inner state of the psyche, where it remains free and untrammelled by any slavish dependence on a particular man. This feature is further stressed in the manner by which she has three sons by three different gods and then refuses to continue the process. Actually, Mādrī presents the precise picture of the "married woman" as opposed to the "virgin" Prithā. Mādrī is the type of woman who, in the words of Dr. M. Esther Harding, "has a psychological attitude to life which makes her dependent on what other people think, which makes her do and say things she really does not approve. . . . She is not one-in-herself but acts always as female counterpart or syzygy to some male. . . . The woman who is psychologically virgin is not dependent in this way. She is what she is because that is what she is."[1]

The other Kuntī-like character we shall meet is Draupadī, adept in the *chāndrāyana vrata,* whereby she regains virginity before living with each of her five husbands. To quote Dr. Harding again, "as virgin, she is not influenced by the considerations that make the nonvirgin woman, whether married or not, trim her sails and adapt herself to expediency . . . the woman who is virgin, one-in-herself, does what she does not because of any desire to please not to be liked, or to be approved, even by herself; . . . but because what she does is true. Her actions may, indeed, be unconventional." Kuntī's conduct is by no means that of the conventional wife personified in Mādrī. In her we see in a clearer fashion what a "virgin" can be of which Satyavatī was only a hint and Draupadi will be a further extension.

What a splendid job Kuntī makes of carefully grooming her and Mādrī's children for kingship through manifold dangers, practically all on her own with occasional assistance from Vidura, is the theme of the succeeding sections. Up to the marriage of Draupadī it is largely Kuntī's story: the story of her shrewd guidance at every step to gather powerful allies around her five children till they are enabled to claim their rightful inheritance. Throughout she remains completely in the background, her guiding touch being wholly unobtrusive, yet firm and unmistakable.

We begin with the account in section 128 of the ruthless baiting of the Dhārtarāshtras by Bhīma who shakes them down from trees like ripe fruit, nearly drowns them in ponds, mercilessly thrashes them, dragging them by the hair, till Duryodhana poisons him in a picnic feast. Here the transcreation takes on a gnomic folk tale-like balladic rhythm, which lends it special distinction:

"His speech was like nectar,
  His heart like a razor,
He rose like a brother,
  like a bosom friend." (128.46)

Shloka 57, referring to the effect of snake-bites on the poisoned Bhīma, provides an interesting ayurvedic detail: the *sthavara* (vegetable) poison fed to Bhīma is neutralised by the *jangama* (animal) snake-venom.

Shlokas 64 and 65 are a typical instance of the breakdown of English vocabulary when it has to tackle the incredibly complex family relationships of Hindus. āryaka, the snake-king to whom Bhīma is taken by the *Nāgas*, is not just the grandfather of Kuntī's father Shūrasena (128.64), but is his maternal grandfather, and Bhīma is his "dauhitra's dauhitra" (maternal grandson's maternal grandson). This particular narrative is a good example of how the reality of the poisoned Bhima being rescued from the river and revivified by a tribe having the snake totem is converted into a magical tale by the wandering rhapsode for gripping his audience.

Here Bhīma is given the magic potion, which gives him the strength of ten thousand elephants. He drinks eight vessels of this potion and returns not only safe and sound but, much to Duryodhana's chagrin, far stronger than ever before. The Bhandarkar Edition's editors have omitted this entire incident. It remains, however, relevant as it affords an insight into the actual situation of the Pāndavas in Hastināpura.

Yudhishthira immediately runs to Kuntī for advice on not finding Bhīma. She turns to Vidura voicing her fear of foul play by Duryodhana. He cautions her against charging Duryodhana:

> "Protect your other sons.
> If you accuse wicked-ātmaned Duryodhana,
> he may decide to harm them." (129.17)

We never find Kuntī approaching Bhīshma for protection in such an extremity. He remains a curiously detached and aloof figure. Kuntī's reliance on Vidura, her brother-in-law and possibly the father of Yudhishthira, is understandable in a situation where they are in Hastināpura purely on sufferance, with no friends or influence. On Bhīma's return, Yudhishthira cautions his brothers not to mention the incident to anyone:

"And let us all, from today
learn to look after
each other." (129.35)

And in this Vidura is their discreet advisor.

Following this, the Bengal recension gives a *shloka* that the critical edition drops, but is valuable in building up the atmosphere of constant danger surrounding the Pāndavas: "Duryodhana had Bhīma's charioteer strangled, but in this too Vidura counselled Prithā's sons to keep silent." This is repeated in verse 41, showing how they were living virtually on the edge, with no protection available from Bhīshma.

The other person who aids the Pāndavas is another son of a maidservant, Yuyutsu. When Duryodhana once again seeks to poison Bhīma, Yuyutsu intimates the Pāndavas. However, here we have a bit of heroics, as Bhīma ignores the warning and eats the poisoned food, effortlessly digesting it.

Now comes a peculiar anachronism. In 129.40 Vaishampāyana says that Karna assisted Shakuni and Duryodhana in thinking-up various plots to get rid of the Pāndavas, who silently controlled their anger. Yet, Karna joins them only in section 138. This is a *shloka* that does not belong to this particular section, but is a statement holding true for the entire *Sambhava* and *Sabhā parvas.* Why Karna should have been thus singled out as a wicked counsellor is difficult to understand, since the story hardly shows him machinating at this early stage. The true Kautilyan schemer is Shakuni.

Though blind, Dhritarāshtra notices the growing animosity and decides they have had enough of games and ought to undergo some discipline. He engages Kripa, born in a reed-clump, as guru for the princes. Naturally, Janamejaya asks for the story of this peculiar birth which occupies section 130. Bhīshma, we find, is by no means satisfied with Kripa as a guru for the princes, despite his fame, for,

"Only the most intelligent,
only the most illustrious,

only the expert in war-craft,
   only the equal of the gods,
Should be guru to the children.
   Such was Bhīshma's resolve.
So, he chose Bharadvāja's son,
   wise Drona. . . . " (131.2-3)

Interestingly, both Drona and Kripa, preceptors of the Kauravas, are fruits of lust. The sages Sharadvat and Bharadvāja ejaculate spontaneously at the sight of naked *apsarās* bathing, and from the semen ejaculated on a reed-clump and in a pot, these two are born. Sharadvat was born armed with arrows. Seeing the ravishingly lovely Jānapadī clad only in a single sheer cloth, his semen, falling on a reed, splits into two, from which the twins Kripa and Kripī are born. It is lusty Shāntanu who adopts these progeny of a *rishi*'s loss of self-control as "children of his compassion"; hence their names. Sharadvat learns of this and comes to teach Kripa the arts of war.

Bhīshma, however, is anxious to impart special training to the princes and that is how Drona arrives. It is again Janamejaya's persistent search after details that elicits from Vaishampāyana the story of Drona's birth and career. In the description of the Bharadvāja-Ghritāchī encounter the unquestioned superiority of the transcreation over all other translations is glaringly evident. Here is the stilted prose of Ganguli, where English is still very much of a foreign tongue:

> "With an expression of pride in her countenance, mixed with a voluptuous languor of attitude, the damsel rose from the water after her ablutions were over. And as she was gently treading on the bank, her attire which was loose became disordered. Seeing her attire disordered, the sage was smitten with burning desire."

Van Buitenen circumvents the problem by omitting all details and confining himself to:

> "He saw an Apsarā alighting, Ghritāchī herself, who had just

bathed. A sudden breeze blew her skirt way, whereupon his seed burst forth."

Here is the superb Lal transcreation, completely successful in its succinct poetic brevity, suggestive force and unforced naturalness of expression:

"There, from the waters
  rose the *apsarā* Ghritāchī,
young, confident,
  lovely, sensual.
As she rose, her dress
  slipped and fell—
he saw her, and sexual desire
  inflamed the rishi."—131.11-12

Vaishampāyana now introduces the crucial story of the Drona-Drupada animosity that sows the seeds of the eventual holocaust, with Drupada deliberately ranging himself against his one time friend-turned-enemy. Drona approaches Drupada having failed to obtain wealth from Parashurāma. The Drona-Drupada meeting is a rewarding study in the nature of friendship. Drupada knows very well that his onetime playmate has come to ask for favours, not impelled by any desire to meet a childhood friend. The brutal arrogance of his response shows that a great deal of time has elapsed since Parashurāma humbled the pride of *Kshatriyas* and gave the earth to Brahmins. Hence, Drona obtaining weapons from this mighty Brahmin warrior must be as much of a gratuitous interpolation for image-building as Devavrata having Parashurāma as his tutor. Bhīshma, Drona and Karna, all three are reputed to be disciples of Parashurāma in the late Dvāpara-yuga, although that avatar was sent into retirement in the earlier Tretā-yuga itself by the new avatar, Rāma. Drupada disdainfully points out:

"Foolish man!
  Do you think great kings
can be friends with ill-starred

and moneyless people like you?
If we were equally favoured
we could have been friends.
Time, which corrodes everything,
corrodes friendship too."—132.5-6

Shakespeare would have violently disagreed of course! Drupada goes on to explain that he had befriended Drona at one time out of a particular motive: he needed a playmate and a companion during his studies. The motif of omnipotent time has once again been articulated.

Drona perforce swallows his rage and proceeds to Hastināpura to stay secretly with his brother-in-law Kripa (he married Kripa's twin sister) whom his son Ashvatthāmā assists in coaching the Pāndavas. Drona shrewdly impresses the princes with his prowess in recovering a ring and a ball from a well. The news is conveyed to Bhīshma who immediately appoints Drona their preceptor. Drona's account of his reasons for coming to Hastināpura are a pitiable narrative of the poverty-stricken condition of a Brahmin, not much different from what we still see in the country:

"One day Ashvatthāman,
seeing a rich man's son
drink milk, began to cry.
The four points of the sky
started swirling around me. . . .
Though I traversed the length and breadth
of the country, I could not find
one milch-cow!"—133.37, 39

Here he is referring to the fact that he could not find anyone with sufficient cows to be able to gift him one without incurring loss himself, which throws up a stark picture of the widespread poverty in the land. Drona continues:

"Some boys offered
Ashvatthāman pishtodaka,
Powdered rice mixed in water.

He drank it. 'Milk! Milk!'
he shouted, and danced in joy. . . .
They grinned at him,
and he kept on dancing.
O Bhīshma, that sight
I remember so vividly!"—133.39-41

This impels Drona to approach Drupada. Here Drona repeats verbatim what Vaishampāyana has narrated in section 132, the repetition serving to show how the insulting words had burned into Drona's consciousness. Carefully and zealously Drona nurses this wound till Arjuna, as guru-dakshinā, throws the bound Drupada at his feet. Drona is no forgiving Brahmana: he releases Drupada, but keeps half his kingdom.

The peculiar teacher-taught relationship we find here forms a violent and rather sad contrast to what we have seen in the *Paushya* sub-*parva.* Here we have no disinterested pursuit of learning and no Āyodah Dhaumyah putting his pupils through the most difficult of tests. Instead, there is Drona who becomes a tutor purely out of selfish reasons to take revenge, not out of a sense of dedication to knowledge. He teaches the Kauravas so that in return, by way of guru-dakshinā, he can demand that they bring Drupada before him as a prisoner. What is never explained is why, if he is indeed such a matchless warrior, he cannot make mincemeat of Drupada on his own.

Drona's is a truly rootless personality, in line with his peculiar birth. Here is a Brahmin who has abjured his dharma and adopted an alien calling befitting a *Kshatriya.* Never do we see him content and happy. Was not this the case with another such dharma-fallen Brahmin, Parashurāma? The manner in which Drona manages to pay special attention to his son even while teaching him with the princes is fascinating. He does not give him any special lessons that would violate his ethics as a teacher, since to a guru all pupils are equal. Drona indulges, instead, in cunning sophistry. He gives Ashvatthāmā a wide-mouthed pot while the princes get narrow-mouthed ones to fill water, so that he arrives for his lessons earlier and thus gets more, but not different, instruction. When Arjuna gets wise to this and also manages to hurry back earlier, Drona has no objection to giving him extra lessons as well. After all, it is only Arjuna, among all the princes, who unhesitatingly promises to fulfil his guru's secret wish when Drona asks for such an undertaking. From this point (134.7) onwards, it is Arjuna who comes to the forefront. Bhīma is no longer heard of till we get to the House of Lac.

134.11-12 are out of place *shlokas*, referring to Karna as a pupil of Drona rivalling Arjuna and making fun of the Pāndavas at Duryodhana's behest. Since Karna does not make an appearance till the tournament, this is definitely a spurious passage.

Prof. Satya Chaitanya has pointed out (in a personal communication) what most readers miss: how keen Drona is that Arjuna does not outstrip Ashvatthāmā. Noticing Arjuna's special gifts, he specifically forbids the cook to serve Arjuna food in the dark. By chance, once the lamp goes out, but Arjuna finds his hand automatically conveying food to his mouth. Realising what force of habit can achieve, he begins to practise archery by night as well, becoming the most proficient among the brothers. It is then that Drona promises him that none will be his equal. The contest Drona arranges is also revealing. Arjuna alone displays the total concentration that sees only the head of the bird-target, while Yudhishthira and the rest see everyone present. This appears to be the high-point of Drona's teaching, for when he hears Arjuna's response, he feels Drupada is as good as finished. However, he imposes another test on his students by crying to them to rescue him from a crocodile. While the others, even Bhīma, stand petrified, it is Arjuna who responds immediately to shoot the reptile and rescue Drona. He receives the divine weapon *Brahmashira* as reward which he will use to counter Ashvatthāmā in the *Sauptika Parva.*

But, amid this edifying account of ideal teacher-student relationship, what leaves a bitter taste is Arjuna and Drona's treatment of Ekalavya, son of the Nishāda ruler Hiranyadhanu. From the *Harivamsa* we learn that he was born to Vasudeva's brother Devashravā who, for some reason, gave him away to the Nishādas and that he lived on the Raivatak mountain. Thus, it is internecine strife between the Yādavas and Pāndavas, just as

Sātyaki and Kritavarma are ranged on opposite sides in the war despite both being Yādavas. Ekalavya is yet another cousin whom Krishna kills (*Udyoga Parva* 48.77), but no details of this are available anywhere. Drona refuses to accept him as pupil because he has the interests of the Kauravas at heart (134.31). How far we are from the vast tolerance of Shukra who accepts Kacha as his pupil fully knowing the purpose of his visit. The young Nishāda surpasses everyone merely through his unmitigated and devoted application to archery in front of a clay image of Drona. The jealousy of Arjuna is utterly despicable and would have elicited a severe reprimand from a guru like Āyodah Dhaumyah:

"You once embraced me
  and joyfully told me
no pupil of yours would
  equal me in bow-skills.
And now there is one. . . .
  . . . excelling everyone.
How can this be?" (134.47, 48)

Drona, however, is nowhere near Dhaumyah in either Veda-knowledge or moral stature. He knows Arjuna is his only hope of achieving his petty goal of humbling Drupada. Hence, he basely takes advantage of Ekalavya acknowledging him as guru to demand his right thumb as *guru-dakshinā*. Ekalavya rises far above both his guru and the royal Arjuna by cheerfully complying and thus losing his self-taught skill. Ekalavya ends up fighting on the side of the Dhārtarāshtras in the great war. The revolting sop thrown to him in *shloka* 58, where the gratified Drona shows Ekalavya how to shoot with his middle and third fingers, is an interpolation designed to show Drona in a better light. As Prof. Lal writes in his Preface to fascicule 17, "It is difficult to think of anything more shabby than this joint violation of the code of teaching ethics. Vyāsa sees life steadily, whole and unsentimentally; yet there are occasions when one wishes he did not, and this is one of them." It is, however, such instances that gradually lead up to the tremendous debunking at the end of the epic when Arjuna finds himself unable to use the Gāndīva bow to drive off staff-wielding bandits abducting the Vrishni women he is escorting, for "Dharma, cultivated, preserves; Dharma, violated, destroys."

In a number of *shlokas*, e.g. 135.22, 137.18, 140.39, 141.7-8, the third Pāndava is called by names other than Arjuna: "Phālguni" (born when the full moon is in the asterism Phalgun in February-March) "Bībhats˘(he who has never committed a loathsome act in battle), "Pākshāsani" (son of the punisher of the *Daitya* Pāka, i.e. Indra) and "Gūdākesha" (thick-haired, or he who has conquered sleep, referring to Arjuna's archery practice by night).

Drona's instruction having been completed, he proposes a tournament to show-off the training received by the princes to the people and the court. An open-air arena is constructed with special seating arrangements for women (136.11) where the entire population collects. In the description of the tournament, Prof. Lal faces tough competition from R.C. Dutt's version in Locksley-Hall metre. For instance, comparing 136.19-20 it is difficult to say which version is better:

Dutt: "Came the saintly white-robed Drona, white his sacrificial thread
White his sandal-mark and garlands, white the locks that crowned his head."

Lal: "White his robes
White his sacred thread
White his hair
White his beard
White the flower-
Garland on his body
White the sandal paste
Smeared on his body."

In 137.8, 12 Arjuna is first introduced by Drona as Indra's son, and lauded as such by the public, which strikes Prof. Lal as peculiar: "How does Drona know that Arjuna is Indra's son? If Kuntī has revealed the secret, it is not right that he should make it public. Perhaps he is merely drawing a heroic comparison. The text gives no clear indication why Drona makes this apparently tactless remark." If, however, we go back to 126.27 we will find that the sages bringing Kuntī and her children to Hastināpura inform the court and all the citizens of the true parenthood of each of the Pāndavas. This was the only way of granting them some sort of elevated status and legitimacy in the public eye in view of the curse imposed on Pāndu. The so-called divine origin of each of the Pāndavas is, therefore, well-known to the people of Hastināpura and Drona is by no means committing a *faux-pas* here.

The display becomes gripping when Bhīma and Duryodhana begin a mock-duel with maces that swiftly turns into a serious battle, with the spectators also beginning to take sides. Drona deftly controls the situation and prevents a riot by having Ashvatthāmā stop the fight. The introduction of the resplendent Arjuna in 137.9 is another instance where the comparison of the transcreation with other translations is highly instructive. Dutt's elaborate Locksley-Hall metre precludes the pregnant terseness that is the essence of Vyāsa's poetry; the prose of Ganguli and van Buitenen is much too verbose:

"Then he stepped forth proud and stately in his golden mail encased
Like the sunlit cloud of evening with the golden rainbow graced."—Dutt

". . . donning his golden mail, appeared in the lists even like an evening cloud reflecting the rays of the setting sun and illumined by the hues of the rainbow and flashes of lightning."—Ganguli

". . . wearing a golden cuirass, Phalguna made his appearance like a rain cloud with a golden sun, iridescent as the rainbow aglow with lightning, red like twilight."—van Buitenen

The Lal transcreation effortlessly captures all the beauty of Vyāsa's Sanskrit without sacrificing any of the brevity or the suggestiveness:

"Phālguna-Arjuna stepped forward
in gold armour, before the crowd;

he shone like a cloud
shot with sunset-light,
he dazzled with rainbow-
iridescent lightning."

Note the happy phrase "shot with sunset-light", evoking a picture of clouds streaked with golden sun-rays, not effulgent with sunlight. Similarly, "dazzled with rainbow-iridescent lightning" is far more arresting in its vivid multi-hued brilliance than the meek elegance of Dutt's "with the golden rainbow graced" or the prose versions.

The roar of delight that goes up from the spectators at Arjuna's entry prompts Dhritarāshtra to voice a rare tribute to the Pāndavas, rare because here it is sincere. The translation of this *shloka*, 137.18, has the king merely say that he is blessed in having these three fine flames of Kuntī. It is curious that Mādrī's sons are not mentioned and this possibly indicates that they were never of much account. Arjuna's feats in putting twenty-one arrows into a cow-horn dangling from a swinging rope and simultaneously shooting five arrows into the jaws of a moving iron-boar leave Robin Hood far behind!

Vyāsa now introduces Karna, making sure that his entrance transfixes his audience. The hero strides in "like a walking cliff' with such a tremendous slapping of arms that all the princes are alarmed. Arjuna comes out in a very poor light indeed as earlier in the Ekalavya incident. He cannot brook anyone as his equal and in this he is typically Indra's son, for that king of the gds was notoriously jealous of anyone attempting to equal him through ascesis, and had no hesitation in foiling such attempts through trickery. Karna's reply is noble, restrained, dignified:

"This arena is open to all,
it is not your private show. . . .
Why speak words, O Bharata?
why use the weapon of weaklings?
Speak in arrows!
Give me the chance
to slice your head off
in the presence of your guru."—138.19-20

Arjuna is hoist with his own petard! He gets out of the situation thanks to Kripa who points out that such a duel can take place only between opponents of equal nobility. The confrontation between two of her sons is too much for Kuntī who faints and, when revived by Vidura, is bewildered and can do nothing. The line-up behind each is also interesting: Kripa and Drona stand with Pārtha, while Karna is supported only by the sons of Dhritarāshtra.

As the two heroes face each other, Vyāsa gives us one of his loveliest descriptive passages, which Dutt renders thus:

> "Now the clouds with lurid flashes gathered darkling, thick and high,
> Lines of cranes like gleams of laughter sailed across the gloomy sky."

The sheer beauty of the Lal transcreation leaves other renderings far behind:

> "Clouds obscured the sky.
> Lightning flashed.
> Indra's bow
> Scattered rainbow clouds.
> The clouds laughed.
> Their teeth showed
> Like white cranes flying."—138.23

The pettiness of Bhīma is exposed by the manner in which he mocks Karna's supposedly low birth (139.6-7) and Duryodhana's furious retort is the rare instance where Vyāsa lets him stand forth as a champion of the underdog. He shrewdly mentions to Bhīma "I know how all of you were born", which shuts him up completely. Karna is crowned king of Anga and becomes Duryodhana's source of strength vis-ë-vis Arjuna. Significantly, even Yudhishthira feels that Karna is unrivalled in the world, for he had duplicated all the feats of Arjuna without having had the benefit of Drona's tutelage.

We do not usually realise the age difference between Karna and Arjuna in their first meeting. Arjuna was fourteen when the brothers came to Hastināpura and has not yet outgrown his teens. Karna was born before Kuntī married Pāndu. At the very least, Pāndu would have exiled himself a year after this and Arjuna would, at the earliest, be born four years later. Karna, therefore, is at least five years older than Arjuna. We have here a young man in his early twenties challenging a stripling.

In the course of his retort to Bhīma, Duryodhana refers to the birth of Karttikeya, who is known as the son of Agni, Gangā, Rudra and the six Krittikās, which will be related in detail in section 225 of the *Vana Parva*, to the making of Indra's *vajra* out of the bones of rishi Dadhīchi (also in the *Vana Parva*, section 100), and to Vishvāmitra achieving Brahminhood (*Ādi Parva* section 174 ff.). The hurried and simple coronation of Karna as king of Anga, as opposed to the highly elaborate ceremony which is required (as in Yudhishthira's coronation in the *Sabhā Parva*), suggests that this was probably more of a symbolic gesture than a real conferment of kingship. The magnificent build-up Karna has been given, however, hardly seems justified later. In the battle with Drupada that follows in section 140, he is ingloriously routed. We find this in *shloka* 140.24: "Badly mauled by Drupada, Karna jumped down from his chariot and fled." This could easily be an interpolation by a pro-Arjuna and anti-Karna bard, but for the fact that nowhere in the epic, besides this tournament, do we find Karna displaying his much-vaunted prowess and he is invariably worsted by Arjuna in every confrontation.

In section 140 the battle with Drupada is described in typical epic mode:

"He pierced Duhshāsana with ten arrows,
  Vikarna with twenty,
Shakuni with thirty flesh-shredding arrows.
With twentyeight arrows
  he pinned down Karna and Duryodhana.
Karna left his chariot and fled.
He wounded Subāhu with five,
  And routed others,
    and roared aloud his war-cry."—140.23-24

Arjuna succeeds in capturing Drupada "as Garuda grips a snake/from the whirling sea-depths" (144.61), thus completing his *guru-dakshinā.*

An interesting passage occurs in 141.9-12 where Drona again gives Arjuna the divine weapon *Brahmasira* which had given in 128.18-21 after Arjuna had rescued him from the crocodile. The former is more likely to be an interpolation since Drona's extreme satisfaction at the humiliation of Drupada and taking over half his kingdom would find natural expression in bestowing such a unique gift on his favourite disciple. This section is concerned with the conquests of the Pāndavas, with not a word about any exploits of the Dhārtarāshtras. Arjuna conquers Yavana and Sauvira kings, all kings of the east with the help of Bhīma and also the south, thereby expanding the Kuru kingdom. We are also told that Sahadeva became proficient in political science (*nīti*) and Nakula as a chariot-warrior, while Bhīma further perfected his knowledge of fighting with the mace under Balarāma, Krishna's brother, till he equalled Dyumatsena in expertise. We know nothing about this mysterious reference beyond a cryptic statement by Bhīshma in the *Sabhā Parva* (38.682) that Krishna had fought Dyumatsena after demolishing many mountains. The only other king of the same name is Satyavān's blind father and he was never famed for any such expertise with the mace.

The success of the Pāndavas now evokes the first attack of jealousy in Dhritarāshtra. He is unable to sleep out of envy and anxiety over how to put a stop to their meteoric rise. He seeks the advice not of Vidura or Bhīshma, but a Machiavellian minister, Kanika, and tells him frankly that he cannot bear the constantly increasing popularity and prowess of his nephews. Kanika's advice is in the *Nītishāstra* tradition and almost straight out of the *Arthashāstra,* and for this reason the entire section has been dropped as spurious in the Critical Edition. This is also one of the very rare instances where an animal fable is related to illustrate Machiavellian policy in the epic. Madeline Biardeau has pointed out[2] that the Brahmin minister's name may have a pejorative connotation as it means "little speck, of little worth", suggesting that a worthless advisor has been consulted. On the other hand, the *āpaddharma* section 140 of the *Shānti Parva* has none other than the acme of dharma, Bhīshma himself, giving practically the same advice to Yudhishthira on what to do in times of distress. According to Bhīshma, such is the teaching of Kaninka (Kanika?) Bharadvāja who we find being quoted by Kautilya too. The normal dharmic rules do not apply where the throne is in danger. Because of such advice Yudhishthira recoils in horror and decides to become a hermit, unwilling to dirty his hands as a king needs must.

In *shloka* 24 Kanika mentions the four means of tackling an enemy (money, conciliation, discord and force). The epic itself quite naturally falls into such segments: discord, efforts at conciliation, use of force.

Kanika's Kautilyan advice is made memorable by his use of remarkably homely images:

> "Let him see through others,
>   not let others see through him.
> As a tortoise hides its limbs,
>   he should hide his plans.
> But when he is set on something,
>   let him carry it through.
> No use half-extracting a thorn—
>   the only result is an abscess." (142.8-9)

The tortoise image is a fascinating turnabout of the famous metaphor in the *Gītā* where the yogi is described as one who draws in his senses as the tortoise does its limbs.

Shloka 142.15 refers to the three, five and seven strategies. The wily minister is talking abut the different types of resources an enemy has that should be done away with. The three resources are fortresses, confidence or morale and strategies. These are to be countered by attacking the fortress, undermining confidence through fifth columnists who will extol the prowess of the king, and discovering the secret strategies by using spies. The five resources are ministers, kingdom, fortress, treasury and army. The seven are conciliation, bribery, dissension, force, poison, fire and imprisonment.

Prof. Lal sensitively shifts to a familiar, colloquial idiom evoking delightful echoes of the *Panchatantra* and the *Hitopadesha.* This is particularly so in the fable Kanika relates of the jackal outwitting the tiger, wolf, muse and mongoose to feast on a deer all by himself. This story resembles one in *Panchatantra* where the jackal Mahachaturaka shrewdly plays n the psychology of a lion, a tiger, a leopard and anther jackal in order to feast on a dead elephant's corpse The central thesis of Kanika's speech is: destroy your enemy by any means, even if he seeks your protection (142.13). Twice, in *shlokas* 51 and 58, he stresses that the enemy must be destroyed at all costs, by curses, mantras, bribes, poison, treachery, and stealth, battle or any other means, even if he happens to be his son, brother, father or guru. Ironically, this is precisely the advice put into practice by Krishna in the battle of Kurukshetra to kill Bhīshma, Drona and Karna. *Shlokas* 62-64 might be straight out of Kautilya.

"Scoundrels and fake ascetics make
  fine spies in others' kingdoms.
Plant them in public gardens,
  entertainment houses, temples. . . .
And wherever people gather.
  Let them circulate in these places,
let their words be soft,
  their hearts sharp as razors."

The sheer ruthlessness is terrifying:

"Great Bharata, never show anger
  when rebuking a wrongdoer.
Smile before you strike an enemy,
  smile while you strike him.
After you have struck him,
  show pity, grieve, even weep. . . .
Remember also to burn down
  your enemy's house after killing him." (142.54, 55, 57)

Here is advice to smile and smile and still be a villain so

memorably portrayed by Richard Crookback. But there is also mature political wisdom in plenty:

> "The king
> who relaxes after signing a treaty
> With an enemy, is like a man
> who opens his eyes after falling
> from a tree-top where he was sleeping. . . .
> Like a she-mule inviting
> her death by conceiving,
> A king who trusts an enemy
> who is already in his bands
> invites his own doom.
> Consider the future as arrived,
> or you will overlook
> important details while planning.
> Intelligence and hard work
> go hand in hand with success." (142.73-74, 81-83)

In the midst of this cold calculating advice, it is indeed refreshing to come across such delightfully down-to-earth images as:

> "A crooked stick
> is excellent to pull twigs
> and pluck sweet fruit. Crooked means
> are excellent enemy-catchers.
> Let an enemy ride you; and
> when the time comes, throw
> him over like a clay pot
> and smash him on the stones.—142.20-21

Best of them all is this one straight out of a barber's repertory:

> "Be like a razor,
> sheathed in velvety leather.
> Slice off hair coolly
> when the time comes."—142-88

Shloka 142.72 gives an interesting bit of advice ("When misfortune strikes/seek consolation in the Purānas") which reminds us of Sanjaya doing precisely this to console the grieving king in the *Anukramanikā* (220-48), by reeling off the names of nearly a hundred great kings of the past who suffered much. We recall *Deor's Lament*, where the poet consoles himself by recalling examples of tragic suffering in the past saying, "that sorrow passed away, so may this". And Virgil's immortal lines of course:

O passi gravira dabit deus his quoque finem
"Fiercer griefs you have suffered; to these too God will give ending."

Kanika, in keeping with the image of him such advice creates, does not tell Dhritarāshtra what he must do to tackle the Pāndavas. Like Krishna telling Arjuna at the end of the *Gītā*, "Do as you wish", Kanika is careful that no responsibility can be fixed upon him in future: "Act in such a way that you/need no more fear the sons of Pāndu." He sidles out on this parting cue, leaving behind an understandably disturbed and thoughtful blind monarch. All this poisonous counsel will bear fruit in the plot of the House of Lac.

References

1. M. Esther Harding, *Woman's Mysteries,* p. 125-26; also P. Bhattacharya, *Panchakanya* (2005), *Revisiting the Panchakanya* (2007)
2. *Hinduism* (OUP, 1989, p. 57)

14

The Sambhava Parva-VI

Kuntī-Bhīma: The House of Lac, Ghatotkacha and Ekachakra

The Richard Crookbackian machinations of Duryodhana, Vidura's ever-alert protecting hand, the dharma-obscuring doting love of Dhritarāshtra, Yudhishthira's unruffled calm and sagacity, the common man's love for the Pāndavas, Bhīma's Herculean prowess, Hidimbā's *grande passion* for the second Pāndava—these form the stuff of the gripping human drama played out in the Jatugriha, Hidimb and Baka sub-parvas of *Sambhava parva.* Out of the seething maelstrom of clashing interests and passions, two figures emerge distinct and prominent: one is the extraordinarily strong-willed and highly intelligent Kuntī, who is the behind-the-scenes guiding and controlling Grey Eminence of the Pāndavas right up to the winning of Draupadī; the other is Bhīma. From the very beginning, as we have seen in section 128, it is Bhīma who aroused the rancour of Duryodhana:

"He thought: Wolf-waisted Bhīma,
  son of Kuntī, second Pāndava,
surpasses us in strength.
  I must somehow destroy him.
The man's so powerful,
  single-handed he dares
to challenge a hundred of us.
  I must break his strength."—128.27-28

Right from this time till Draupadī's *svayamvara*, it is Bhīma who acts as the lightning conductor for all the plots and dangers faced by the Pāndavas and their mother. The ten thousand elephants' strength that he gained through the beneficence of āryaka, the *Nāga*-king, now stands him in good stead, and Vyāsa exploits his superhuman prowess fully to thrill his audience with *romaharshana* accounts of his mighty feats vis-a-vis Hidimba, Baka and the suitors at the bridegroom-choice ceremony of Draupadī.

The suspense generated by Kanika's Kautilyan advice to Dhritarāshtra in section 142 is skilfully brought to a head by Vyāsa in the first eleven verses of the next section where he swiftly sums up its consequences. This summary is very interesting because it shows what happens when a narrator tries to compress an elaborate episode: he invariably misses out something important, remembers it towards the end and somehow tags it on anywhere in his recital with splendid *sang-froid*. Thus, Vidura gets to know of Duryodhana's plan to burn the Pāndavas alive and informs Kuntī (this, by the way, is not confirmed in the detailed version which follows); they escape in a boat he arranges. At this point Vaishampāyana (or is Sauti the culprit?) suddenly recalls that he has forgotten to mention the most important fact of all, namely the burning of the *lākshā griha*, the house of lac, and how the Dhārtarāshtras were deluded by the burnt remains of a Nishāda woman and her five sons. So, he abruptly tags this on at the end of his synopsis with a *sang froid* that Prof. Lal puts across superbly:

"Well, it so happened that
a tribal woman of the Nishādas
came to the house of lac and
was burnt alive with her five sons."—143.10

Shloka 5 describes the boat prepared by Vidura as *yantrayukta*, which inspires the Aryashastra editor to exclaim enthusiastically that this proves the existence of motorised boats. *Yantra* applies to any mechanical contrivance and would refer to oars and sails.

Shlokas 15-16 show that the Dhārtarāshtras are implementing Kanika's advice literally. After hearing of the supposed death of the Pāndavas, he and his sons sorrowfully perform the funeral rites in terms of the Kanikan verse 142.55: "After you have struck him,/show pity, grieve, even weep."

It is again Janamejaya's curiosity that prompts Vaishampāyana to narrate the complete story from verse 19.

In the next *shloka*, Karna is described as *vaikartanah*, "the cloud-scatterer's son" which looks backwards and forwards. It recalls the tournament where Arjuna stands in the cool shade of the clouds, while Karna dazzles all eyes in the sun's rays; and the incident after Bhīma's insulting references to Karna's low birth when "Karna looked up at the sky, at the sun in the sky" (139.8). It also looks forward to Karna's anti-Arjuna obsession, particularly because Arjuna is "the cloud-gatherer's son" just as Karna *vaikartanah* is "the cloud-scatterer's son".

Vyāsa now brings in the common populace to show that they want Yudhishthira as their king. Their logic is quite straightforward: Dhritarāshtra was not allowed to become king in the past because he was blind, so there is no question of his ruling the kingdom now either. Bhīshma voluntarily renounced the throne and would not accept it now. Hence, they select Yudhishthira as the most suitable. *Shloka* 27 describes Yudhishthira as *tarunam vriddhashīlinam,* i.e. "though a youth, mature in conduct as the aged".

The stratagem suggested by Duryodhana, Duhshāsana, Karna and Shakuni is to exile the Pāndavas to Vāranāvata. Dhritarāshtra's objections make an interesting study. He starts by recalling the piety of Pāndu, referring to quite unbelievable qualities such as indifference to the world's pleasures, while we know that his basic weakness was pleasure. He points out that Pāndu was specially courteous to him and devoted to him. Therefore, he owes a debt of gratitude to his brother's progeny. His next objection is that Yudhishthira is faultless and loved by the people, and, most important "he has many friends", for

"Pāndu took good care of
 his counsellors and soldiers,
and their sons and grandsons.
 Since they benefited so much,

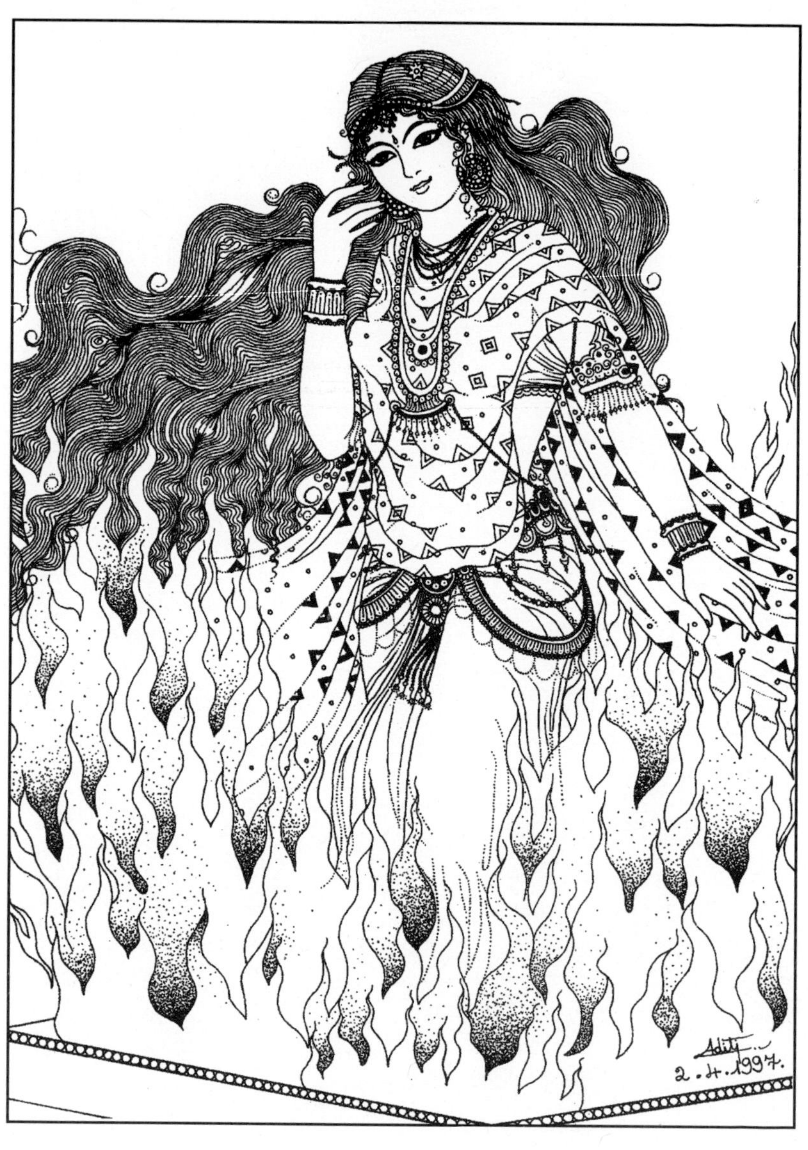

"Draupadi emerging" by Aditi

Don't you think, my dear son, *tāta,*
that if I do what you tell me,
they might turn against us,
even kill us, to protect Yudhishthira?"—144.11

This is sound political sense, with none of the mushy sentimentalism that he was hypocritically showing, Kanika-like, at first. Even Duryodhana agrees, but points out that risks have to be taken.

The strategy they now adopt follows Kanika's advice in section 142 almost word for word. First, while the treasury and the officials are under their control, the Dhārtarāshtras, conspire to win the people to their side through bribes and favours (145.1). Then they inveigle the Pāndavas into opting to visit Vāranāvata during the festival of Pashupati by having its attractions praised sky-high by courtiers. Here is the first mention of Shiva whose presence will grow in the background till it looms over the holocaust that is the epic's theme. The Dhārtarāshtras lull their enemy into a sense of security through soft words and simulating friendship, then burn them alive. Thereafter, they shed copious crocodile tears, leaving no ritual unobserved.

Duryodhana, however, is not above duping his father. He pretends that his only desire is to exile the Pāndavas so that in their absence he can be crowned, whereafter they will be brought back. Dhritarāshtra quickly grasps this specious suggestion and states that this is what he too had in mind, but that he never expressed it because Vidura, Bhīshma, Drona and Kripa would never agree and might even turn on him in anger and slay him. Duryodhana's reply gives a shrewd estimate of the weight carried by each of these Kuru notables, and reveals what a good judge of character and situation he is:

"Bhīshma", Duryodhana replied,
"never takes sides; Drona's son
is on my side; and Drona, I know,
will be on the side his son is.
Sharadvat's son Kripa
will follow Drona and his son.

How can he repudiate Drona
 and his nephew Ashvatthāman?
Though Kshattā-Vidura depends on us,
 secretly he is a Pāndava-lover
Let him join them.
 Alone, he can do us no harm."—144.20-22

Duryodhana's appreciation of the situation holds true till the very bitter end, for all the first three fight on his side, while Vidura is of no account. Bhīshma's loyalty remains to the Kauravas born of Dhritarāshtra, not to the *niyoga*-born Pāndavas.

Vidura's intelligence service, we find, is far superior to Duryodhana's: he even knows the precise date on which the house of lac is to be set on fire. Duryodhana's Kanikan stratagem does not succeed in duping either the Pāndavas or the public. The people of Vāranāvata send Dhritarāshtra a brutally frank message:

"Your purpose has been fulfilled,
 the Pāndavas burnt to death.
Your grand plan accomplished, O king,
 you are now free to enjoy,
with your sons, the Kuru kingdom."—143.14-15

Yudhishthira, even before proceeding to Vāranāvata, perceives the intention behind Dhritarāshtra's honeyed words suggesting an outing for them:

"Yudhishthira read Dhritarāshtra's
 mind, but felt he had no choice,
being without allies, and said,
 "Whatever you say."—145.13

The Pāndavas leave only after having performed all rites prescribed for obtaining their royal inheritance (*shloka* 21). The deplorably ineffective intelligence system of the Kauravas will be exposed again when they fail to spot the Pāndavas during their two spells of exile. That of Vāranāvata is excusable because of the misleading evidence of the burnt remains of the Nishāda family; but there can be no justification for their failure to spot Bhīma in Virāta's court where he was perpetually showing-off amazing feats of strength.

The Vyāsan counterpart of Shakespeare's *Richard III* (IV.2) is to be found in section 146, where Richard-Duryodhana bribes and flatters Tyrrel-Purochana to commit the horrid deed, even pressing his right hand and calling him by the patronymic *tātah* in *shloka* 5. The care Duryodhana bestows on plotting this gruesome end of the Pāndavas is seen in his orders to Purochana in *shloka* 16 to set fire to the place "beginning with the gate", so that the only exit is blocked at the very outset.

Shloka 19 provides a good example of the superiority of Prof. Lal's terse version over the verbose prose of others. Here is the Ganguli translation:

"And after the citizens had ceased following the Pāndavas, Vidura, conversant with all the dictates of morality, desirous of awakening the eldest of the Pāndavas (to a sense of his dangers), addressed him in these words."

The transcreation is faithful to Vyāsa in its succinct brevity:

"After they had left,
  Vidura, wise in dharma and truth,
spoke to the eldest Pāndava Yudhishthira
  in order to warn him."

What follows is a fascinating glimpse into the historical milieu of the epic. *Shloka* 20 states that Vidura spoke to Yudhishthira in coded speech incomprehensible to all but the two of them. The Sanskrit term for this in the original text is *pralāpa* (incoherent or delirious speech) and in this particular *shloka* Vyāsa, with very rare gusto, indulges in *anuprāsa* (alliteration-cum-assonance) to the fullest, undoubtedly foxing Ganesha in the process:

prājñah prājñapralāpajñah pralāpajñamidam vachah /
prājñah prājñam pralāpajñah pralāpajñam vachohavravīt //

This is a solitary instance of the use of a code or little known dialect for communicating a secret message verbally with perfect safety, and it once again reveals the empathy between Vidura and Yudhishthira, who are the only two persons to know this tongue and comprehend instantly the impending danger. Therefore, it seems that Vidura has been training Yudhishthira separately in such esoteric matters, just as Drona has been concentrating on Arjuna. It also implies close contact with the *mlechchha* tribes of the north-west frontiers whose speech was termed *pralāpa*. It will be recalled that Yayāti had exiled Turvasu to *mlechchhadesha*, to live among non-Aryans who were regarded as uncivilized barbarians.

Vidura advises the Pāndavas to go underground, literally, and to take this opportunity to gain knowledge of the countryside and the people over whom they are to rule in the days to come. The enforced incognito exile will also force them to learn self-control while sharing the lot of ordinary folk:

"Travelling brings knowledge.
  Keep moving. Let the stars
in the sky guide you. Unite
  the five senses, and escape oppression."—147.27

The last line, of course, can be interpreted to signify advice that unity among the five brothers will alone save them.

Note that it is Kuntī, neither Bhīma nor Arjuna, who anxiously enquires about the import of the mysterious conversation between Vidura and Yudhishthira. In the succeeding sections we shall see how she brings matters to a head to engineer their safe and unsuspected escape. Section 148 irresistibly recalls Alexandre Dumas, as D'artagnan-Yudhishthira explains the situation and the strategy to Porthos-Bhīma! Bhīma's instinctive reaction is to return to Hastināpura, but the more mature and far-sighted Yudhishthira knows that Duryodhana has won over the officials with gifts and that murderous agents would be lurking around every corner. Hence, he feels that the safest course is to bide one's time in disguise and simultaneously gather intimate knowledge of the people and the country by travelling incognito.

Here we also get an extremely rare glimpse of the man behind the unruffled mask of calmness and unquestioning acceptance of Dhritarāshtra's commands:

> "If we perish, it is unlikely
> Pitāmaha Bhīshma will be overly upset.
> Why should he unnecessarily
> antagonise the Kauravas?
> Of course it is possible
> Pitāmaha Bhīshma (and other noble Kauravas)
> will be put on a show of dharma.
> (It will help us little, though)."—148.23-24

The bitterness is unusual and unmistakeable: after all, what use is the wrath of Bhīshma and the other Kurus if the Pāndavas are not alive to reap its benefits? This is something that Kuntī must have sensed, because of which she never complained to Bhīshma about the attempts on Bhīma's life. Yudhishthira knows that the five brothers will have to win their birthright through blood, tears, toil and sweat because their father had preferred to dally in the forests instead of shouldering the arduous task of ruling a kingdom. A somewhat similar rumination by Rāma to Lakshmana is found in the *Rāmāyana* during their first night in the forest where he bitterly criticises his uxorious father.

As a first step, we find the brothers assiduously cultivating the support of the people by visiting all Brahmins, officials and even the charioteers, Vaishyas and Shudras. Purochana, shrewd as he is, initially lodges them elsewhere and, only after ten days of festivities, takes them to the house of lac, which they enter like Guhyakas on Mount Kailasha. Guhyakas are attendants of Kubera, the god of wealth, like Yakshas. The appellative is double-edged in significance: not only are the Pāndavas richly accoutred like these guardians of wealth, but like those cavern dwellers, they will also be living every night inside a tunnel being dug by a sapper sent by Vidura.

In *shloka* 16, once again, Prof. Lal's terse rendering makes an impact wholly lost in Ganguli's verbosity:

"Soaked in ghee,
going up in flames—
First wicked Purochana honours us,
then he burns us."

Ganguli renders it thus:

"This wicked wretch, Purochana . . . stayeth here with the object of burning me to death when he seeth me trustful."

Incidentally, Yudhishthira consistently refers to Duryodhana as Suyodhana, showing the character of the eldest Pāndava who will never address even a wicked person appropriately, but always turns the bad "dur" to the pleasing "su"!

Shloka 150.1 states that the Pāndavas stayed a *parivatsar* in this house of lac. This can be rendered both as "one year" and as "half-a-year", for elsewhere we find references to their having stayed for six months in the *jatugriha*. It is when Yudhishthira sees Purochana totally lulled into a sense of security that he tells his brothers that this is the time to set fire to the house and escape, leaving six bodies in the flames. *Shloka* 4 can be translated in two ways. One is that they will flee, leaving six other dead bodies behind. The other is as rendered by Ganguli: "burning Purochana to death and letting his body lie here, let us, six persons, fly hence unobserved by all."

Now comes a fateful opportunity when a Nishāda woman and her five sons fortuitously appear on the scene and sleep in the house overcome by drink. Prof. Lal comments very perceptively in his Preface: "Who fed the six tribals and made them drunk? Not the Pāndavas. The text says it was Kuntī. Here is a scene to equal the gory murder of Duncan, with Kuntī playing the role of a counterpart of the eager yet hesitant Lady Macbeth." Different recensions, however, seek to slur over the horrendous deed on part of the dharma-observing Pāndavas by describing the Nishāda woman as cruel and an accomplice of Purochana. The steel-will of Kuntī, which we glimpsed in her refusal to let Mādrī have more children and in agreeing not to become a *sati*, is seen once more as she assiduously plies her potential victims with drink till they fall into a drunken stupor. As Prof. Lal brilliantly writes, "Instigating Macbeth-Bhīma was Kuntī, bringerforth of men-children only." *Shloka* 10 tells us that Bhīma set fire to Purochana's room as he slept.

We should note that this is not the first instance of discrimination against the Nishādas that happened earlier with Ekalavya. After the Brahmins had killed the very first king, Vena, they had churned his thigh for a successor and when a short, dark person emerged, they rejected it, and called it "Nishāda". From the very beginning, therefore, the Nishādas were marginalised. Satyavatī's marriage with Shāntanu is an example of "positive discrimination" and she succeeds in founding a Nishāda dynasty through her illegitimate son Vyāsa. As we have mentioned earlier, Satyavatī's granddaughter-in-law Kuntī destroys that dynasty, replacing it with her own through her son Arjuna.

In true Kanikan fashion, Dhritarāshtra sheds copious tears at the news of the Pāndavas' supposed death and orders:

> "May nothing be stinted
> in the funeral ceremonies
> of Kuntī and the Pāndavas." (152.14)

Following *shloka* 20 there are 15 *shlokas* in the Bengal recension describing Bhīshma's lament, in which he speaks of the sterling qualities of Kuntī and the five brothers—particularly Bhīma and Arjuna—at length. Of particular interest is the information that, soon after arriving in the royal household, Kuntī succeeded in winning her husband's heart. Vidura advises Bhīshma secretly not to breakdown and tells him what he has done to save Kuntī and her sons. This corrects the abrupt transition from *shloka* 20 to 21.

It is now that we are introduced to Bhīma in all his superhuman strength:

> "Bhīma of great strength
> and stamina, wolf-waisted Bhīma,
> lifted his mother on his shoulder,

the twins on both his sides,
Picked up Yudhishthira
and Arjuna in both arms,
smashed trees with his chest,
smote the earth with his feet,
and pressed steadily on."—150.21-22

The accent is constantly on the Pāndavas' fear of being discovered and their tiredness owing to lack of sleep and nervous strain. Yudhishthira has to ask Bhīma repeatedly to carry all of them. We hear nothing of Arjuna's so-called world-shaking courage and prowess-at-arms. With the *Brahmashīra* weapon Drona had gifted him, he ought to have been able to hold the Dhārtarāshtras to ransom. They all appear to be without any arms as well, because any missing weapons from their lacquer house could hint at their survival.

The immense difference between this and their frame of mind in the similar incognito exile of the thirteenth year, with Draupadī replacing Kuntī, is an indication of the lack of maturity at this stage when their mother's guidance is critically important. In the later instance, Draupadī adumbrates Kuntī's role vis-ë-vis the brothers.

It is instructive to see how effectively Kuntī inspires and controls her sons. When Bhīma is unable to carry them any further, she resorts to an infallible sentimental ruse:

"Hai! I am Kuntī, mother
of five Pāndavas, and I thirst
for water sitting in their midst!"—153.13

She says this repeatedly. In a trice Bhīma, the wind-god's son, takes all of them up again on various portions of his anatomy, moved by his deep and simple love for his mother to disregard physical exhaustion. It is here that the ten thousand elephants' strength that he gained in the *Nāga*-world comes in most useful. Vyāsa takes care to draw on appropriate similes for keeping before us Bhīma's elephantine strength and wind-born speed:

"And his thighs, moving vigorously,
 raised currents of strong wind
like storms in the month of Jyestha-Āshādha;
 he trampled plants and creepers,
Smoothing a path for himself.
 The kings-of-the-forest,
the fruit-and-flower-laden trees
 bowed to his might.
Like an angry sixty-year-old rutting
 elephant-leader of a herd,
juices streaming down the three parts
 of his body—Bhīma pushed on.
So swift was his pace,
 like that of Tārksya or Maruta,
that the Pāndavas, clinging
 to him, felt giddy."—153.2-5

In *shloka* 7, Kuntī is specifically described as *sukumārīm yashasvinīm* i.e., "illustrious, delicately lovely", one of the rare instances of a non-conventional specific description.

The other instance of Kuntī's firm guidance and far-sighted statesmanship is her approval of Hidimbā's infatuation for Bhīma. He is just about to despatch her like her brother, when Yudhishthira stops him on grounds of the sin of killing women. Kuntī, conscious of the need for allies in their forlorn condition, orders Bhīma:

"I can see no way
 of taking fit revenge
for the wicked deeds
 that Duryodhana has done us.
A grave problem of dharma faces us.
 O mahā-learned vrikodara
you know Hidimbā loves you. . . .
Have a son by her. It is dharma.
 I wish it. He will work
for our welfare. My son,
 I do not want a no

from you. I want your promise
now, in front of both of us."—157.47-49

In those first four lines the Kurukshetra fratricide is presaged as inevitable. Its concealed mainspring is Kuntī.

It is important, however, to appreciate that Kuntī does not take an impulsive decision in this respect. She gives Bhīma this command only after she has had Hidimbā prove her bona-fides. Hidimbā guides them to Shālihotra rishi's hermitage where they recoup their energies. She builds them a hut, forecasts that Vyāsa will soon meet them and free them from their troubles, and assures Kuntī that she will transport them over the roughest terrain out of the forest. It is only after this that Kuntī, having consulted Yudhishthira, commands Bhīma to beget a son by Shālakatankati (Hidimbā's proper name). Incidentally, this entire passage (157.22-32, 38-49) is missing from other translations, thereby depriving the reader of a crucial insight into Kuntī's dominant decision-making in bringing-up her sons. How very right her decision is we realise with the birth of Ghatotkacha ("bald, pot-headed") who inherits his mother's original *rākshasa* "beauty":

"A fierce-eyed, large-mouthed baby
with ears like arrows
and a fear-instilling face,
A roaring voice,
brown lips, sharp teeth."—157.62-63

Deeply attached to the Pāndavas, he is to prove an invaluable ally in the Kurukshetra holocaust by saving Arjuna from Karna's infallible Indra-gifted weapon by sacrificing himself:

"Ghatotkacha was a creation of Indra;
He was the mahā-chariot-hero match
for mahā-ātmaned Karna,
possessor of the shakti-missile."—157.77

We do not usually realise that in this epic we see the offspring of two major gods dueling to the death. A parallel occurs in the *Rāmāyana* where the situation is reversed with Vālī, son of Indra, dying in the duel with his brother Sugrīva, son of Sūrya, at Rāma's hands. In the *Mahābhārata* Arjuna, Indra's son, kills Sūrya's son Karna at Krishna's urging. This is a curious theme that Indologists have yet to investigate for its mythic implications.

Once again, it is Kuntī who instructs her first grandchild:

"You are one of us Kauravas.
  To me you are like Bhīma himself.
You are the eldest son of the Pāndavas.
  Therefore, you should help them."—157-74

Kuntī's expert guidance will be seen again in the Ekachakra episode when, to the consternation of the sons, she deliberately sends Bhīma to the ogre Baka, thereby securely entrenching the Pāndavas in the hearts of the grateful commoners. Kuntī's genius is even more apparent in her contriving the marriage of Draupadī to all five sons—a master-stroke ensuring their permanent unity against all odds.

If Kuntī is the guiding and inspiring spirit of the Pāndavas, it is through Bhīma that she seeks to achieve her ends. We have seen how Vyāsa proceeds to build up his presence step by step from the end of section 150 with the awesome picture of this man-mountain bulldozing his way through the forest, carrying his mother and brothers. Bhīma's deep love for them finds plangent expression in his lament as he watches over them asleep on the bare ground (153.22-41). It is here that he begins those imprecations against Duryodhana which will reach a shattering climax in his blood-curdling vows after the dice game. Bhīma is also the first of the Pāndavas to win a woman's heart, even though it is a rākshasi's. His Porthosian egotism is endearing in its naive□é:

"Look at my arms-
  like an elephant's trunk!
Look at my thighs—
  like two iron clubs!

And my chest—
broad, hard as rock!"—155.9

One is irresistibly reminded of Porthos preening himself before the infatuated eyes of the notary's wife. In harmony with this feature of Bhīma's character it is because Hidimbā has been overcome by his "beauty" that Bhīma will not let the *rākshasa* Hidimb slaughter her. Bhīma's supreme confidence in his competence to protect all of them and his perfect self-control in the face of terrible danger should be noted:

"Can a man like me leave
his sleeping mother and brothers
to be food for a rākshasa
and gratify his own lust?
This is my elder brother, he
is like a guru to me.
He is unmarried. How can I
marry before he does?
do you think I am so afraid
of your brother that I will wake
my peacefully sleeping mother and brothers? . . .
. . . Do what you like.
Best of all, bewitching bodied lady,
send your man-eating brother to me." (154.33-34, 36, 38)

It is precisely this weak point in his character that Arjuna exploits when he finds Bhīma hard pressed by Hidimb and not finishing him off quickly:

"Bhīma, mahā-muscled brother, don't fear!
We had no idea
how tired you were
in this fight with the rākshasa.
Here I am, son of Pritha,
ready to help you. . . .
I'll kill the rākshasa."—156.18-19

Bhīma indignantly retorts,

> "Watch me fight." . . .
> "And don't interfere!"—156.20

Arjuna does not desist from persisting to needle him to augment his fury:

> "Bhīma, hurry. Don't play games
> with him. Finish him off!"—156.23

Bhīma's response is to whirl Hidimb round his head and let loose some bombast, which Arjuna again interrupts with biting sarcasm:

> "If you need help," said Arjuna,
> "shout and let me know.
> I'll finish him off for you.
> Kill him! We must hurry.
> Wolf-waisted Bhīma,
> why not let *me* do the job?
> You are tired—you've done
> your best—you need rest."—156.28-29

Naturally, Bhīma's anger explodes in a final spurt of violence in which he kills Hidimb by breaking him in two as he roars like "a wet drum". This episode is an excellent instance of the Bhīma-Arjuna team-up that we will notice again during the *svayamvara* skirmish over Draupadī and the duels with Jarāsandha, Jayadratha and Duryodhana. It remains, however, the only example of Arjuna verbally needling his elder brother to greater heights of fury. In future this will be done by Draupadī.

This section is a particularly fine instance of the transcreative art because there are exquisite lyrical passages like those describing the romantic retreats of Hidimbā and Bhīma's amorous dalliance:

> " . . . forests and mountain—

caves, where flowering trees
  shed fragrance, and near lakes
lovely with lotus and lily. . . .
In woods filled with breathtaking
  beauty of blossoming branches,
in secluded Himalayan retreats. . . .
In the pellucid waters of
  lotus-smiling inland lakes,
on the golden and pearly
  shores of distant seas."—157.55, 57-58

One is tempted to add, "in faery lands forlorn"!

On the other hand, there is the splendid creation of an ominously eerie milieu as the Pāndavas enter Hidimb's forest at night:

"They came to an eerie forest
with hardly any fruits, roots, and water,
  and filled with cruel beasts.
A fearful twilight fell.
  The noises grew fiercer.
Nothing could be seen.
  A howling wind blew.
Many large and small trees, O rājā
  snapped and fell;
the ground was littered with
  fruits, dry leaves and creepers."—153.8-10

The truest bit of transcreation comes in section 154, where Prof. Lal suddenly shifts to a most unconventional "rakshasan" rhythm for Hidimb's slavering monologue. It is here that one feels as if Vyāsa were writing in English itself; so natural, unforced and appropriate is the transcreation. We can feel the transcreator thoroughly enjoying himself in this grotesque rhythm:

"My favourite
Food !
My mouth

Waters. . . .
My sharp
Eight teeth
Will bite
Delicious
Meat.
I'll crunch
The throat
And veins,
And drink
Hot
Fresh
Bubbly
Blood."—154.8-11

A comparison with the similar encounter in the other epic, the *Rāmāyana,* is interesting. There, too, exiled princes are approached erotically by a *rākshasi*: Sūrpanakhā. In both cases the reaction is to assault her, with the difference that in Bhīma's case his elder brother stops him from attacking a woman, whereas the *maryādā purushottama,* the soul of propriety, Rāma actually incites his younger brother to mutilate her. This is because when Sūrpanakhā, furious at being made fun off, decides to kill Sītā, she is combining the roles of the erotically motivated Hidimbā and her cannibal brother Hidimb. Vyāsa has split this into two personae, having one slain and the other's sexual desires gratified. Worse is the fate of the ogress Ayomukhi whose breasts Lakshmana chops off, besides her nose and ears, because she approaches the brothers amorously.

In section 157, *shlokas* 31-37 are adumbrated in 46-51. In the former passage Yudhishthira lays down the condition that Bhīma must be back with them by nightfall after Hidimbā has enjoyed him during the daytime. The *rākshasas* differ from human beings in indulging in sexual activity even during the day. Yudhishthira prescribes this condition after Kuntī has told him that she has no objection to the alliance. In the latter passage, Kuntī explicitly orders Bhīma to beget a son on Hidimbā and Yudhishthira does not speak at all. There is also no precondition about returning

Bhīma to them before nightfall, for the couple stay away till Ghatotkacha is born. The critical edition omits *shlokas* 22-32 (including Kuntī's no-objection) and 36-51 (including the stipulation that Bhīma will stay with her only till a son is born). However, in the process we lose an insight into Kuntī's shrewd guidance of her sons' fates.

As foretold by Hidimbā in 157.25, they meet Vyāsa who clarifies that, because of their misfortunes, he favours them more than the Dhārtarāshtras. To Kuntī he foretells the empire of the Pāndavas and takes them to the house of a Brahmin in Ekachakra, described as a "delightful town" and asks them to await his next visit here.

The key to the conduct of the Pāndavas during their exile is to be found in 158.19 where Vyāsa advises them, "Success attends the man/who adapts to time and place." The rest of the *Ādi Parva* is basically an elaboration of this. They fruitfully utilise their incognito wanderings in studying the Vedas and other sciences (158.5), though how they managed this without staying in any hermitages of Veda-versed sages passes comprehension. More important, roaming in mendicant-garb, they come into close contact with the common man's sorrows, live the poverty-stricken life of the ordinary family and familiarise themselves with the lay of the land. Thus, the exile turns out to be the best of all training schools for equipping them with all that is expected of an ideal ruler. Their over-riding concern for the common man's sorrows, taught to them by Kuntī in the Ekachakra episode, can be seen again when Arjuna deliberately accepts exile by intruding into Yudhishthira-Draupadī's privacy in order to recover the stolen fire-wood of a Brahmin. Moreover, the Pāndavas' exile remains a storehouse of experience proving extremely valuable in the next thirteen years of exile following the defeat in the dice-game, for now they see the land of Matsyas and Kīchakas, their future haven.

The Bakāsura story offers valuable insight into the norms of an ordinary Brahmin family of those times. By placing the family in a situation where a crucial moral choice has to be made, Vyāsa turns the episode into a means for exploration and revelation of character. We come across a similar situation in the *Vana Parva* in the Dharma-crane's questions to Yudhishthira across the corpses of his brothers.

In this context, Prof. Lal's otherwise admirable Preface raises some controversial points. He writes, "It never occurs to him (the Brahmin) that he has also a daughter, and that she also might need saving." The text, however, does not bear this out. It is quite clear that the Brahmin loves all the members of his family equally. In three and a half *shlokas* of deep anguish over his daughter (159.35-38) he makes the situation quite clear:

> "Some men think a father
> loves his son more,
> others think his daughter.
> I love both equally." (159.37)

The passage, however, is a curious mixture of paternal love and selfishness. In *shlokas* 36 and 38 his reluctance to send his daughter as Baka's dinner stems from anxiety that this will mean his being deprived of

> "the heaven reserved for those
> whose daughters have sons. . . .
> How can I sacrifice my innocent
> little daughter, who continues
> My family line and on whom
> depends my heavenly bliss?" (159.36, 38)

This is of a piece with Yājñavalkya's upanishadic pronouncement that everything—wives, children, friends, parents—is precious only because of the *ātman*, none having any intrinsic value. Today when we stridently criticise American individualism as the root cause of social disintegration, it is perhaps prudent to balance our virulence by looking back at what our own ancient texts propound. At the same time, we need to appreciate how "gender preference" with regard to children was sought to be remedied thousands of years ago by loading the daughter with precious promise of other-worldly benefits for her parents via grandchildren.

When the daughter responds, she is not speaking as this particular Brahmin's offspring alone, but as the voice of all daughters of then and now. That is why Prof. Lal's comment remains valid in the wider temporal context:

"A son is like one's own self,
a wife is like a friend,
a loved-and-loving sakhā
a daughter an irritation, an inconvenience.
Remove the irritation.
Let me do my dharma.
I am the one-to-be-given-a way,
so give me away." (161.11, 15)

"In that quiet shloka", writes Prof. Lal, "are many secret tears wept in closed rooms. That shloka to me reads like a *j'accuse* of a great social wrong and an expose of filial pettiness." At the same time, let it be remembered that the author of this heart-piercing *j'accuse* is a male: Vyāsa.

In the context of Prof. Lal's statement, it is imperative to reiterate that the daughter's statement is more of a generalised comment on the prevailing social norms and not applicable wholly to this specific case. Both the Brahmin and his wife are clearly anguished over the fate that might overtake her. The wife repeatedly cries out that in her husband's absence she will be unable to protect their "innocent daughter" and guide her on the path of dharma (160.14), or save her from the approaches of undeserving men "like Shudras seeking the Vedas" who may even take her by force (160.16-17). On the other hand, the daughter's arguments in favour of being sacrificed do not by any means cluster around that j'accuse verse. She musters an impressive array of traditional beliefs, all centring around this key statement:

"After all, children are sought
because they are saviours.
Let me save you. Cross this sea
of sorrow with me as raft."—161.4

The image she uses is later applied to Draupadī more than once as the saviour of her husbands. Note that the daughter uses the word "santāna", "offspring" and not just "son". She also points out,

"My pitrs hope that
  I should bear them a saviour son;
instead, I will save them
  by saving my father's life."—161.6

The clincher comes in a rather Joan of Arcesque demand:

" . . . give me this chance
  to save my family
by doing something difficult to do.
  Let my death give meaning to my life."—161-13

This unexpected flash of courage and firmness sets her apart from her mother and brings her nearer Kuntī in our minds.

The wife's lament brings home to us the vast gulf existing between the *Kshatriyā* Kuntī and the Brahmin housewife, while recalling the similar weakness of Mādrī:

"You will be able to
  Support and protect the children.
It is not possible for me
  to support and protect them."—160.8

Her outcries form a steady downward curve, displaying the gradually wilting strength of character within a single speech. She begins on a highly philosophical note pointing out that, mortality being inevitable, grief is pointless (160.2); passes on to suggest that she should be the sacrifice because it is the wife's dharma to be dedicated to the husband's welfare and also as it will win her renown:

"To do so will give me
  pleasure now; it will

win me renown in this world,
  and undying joy in the next."—60.5

Shloka 7 starkly highlights the Mitākshara family law that was ruthlessly and calculatedly weighted overwhelmingly in favour of the male. A wife was seen merely as a means of procreation. Till she produced a son, her debt to her husband remained undischarged:

"I have already fulfilled
  a wife's duty—by giving you
a son and daughter. I am free
  of my debt to you."

What follows, however, is a sudden departure from scriptural impersonality to personal anxiety and complete breakdown of self-confidence:

"Like birds scavenging
  for a scrap of meat thrown
on the ground, men seek a woman
  who has lost her husband.
Who knows, O finest of the twice-born?
  If wicked men seek me
constantly, I might stray
  from the straight path."—160.12-13

She goes on to state her inability to guide her daughter on the path of ancestral dharma and teach the son the proper skills. Here is a Brahmin lady who is hardly of the tribe of Gārgī, Maitreyī and Sulabhā who held their own, and more in a male-dominated society. The contrast Kuntī presents is even more immediate in its impact. The wholly self-centred world of the Hindu male is exposed unwittingly in this devoted wife's persuasion:

"Men who know dharma say,
  Wealth, relatives, children, wives,

are loved because they save one
when there's a crisis of dharma."—160.27

The next *shloka* is equally revealing of the prevalent social norms:

"Cherish wealth in a crisis.
Cherish a wife with wealth.
Cherish both wife and wealth
for the sake of your *ātman,*
to protect yourself."

That echoes Yājnavalkya's sentiments.

The climax of this bitter expose of Mitāksharan personal law reaches its high point in *shloka* 31 which typifies the archetypal "married" woman as distinct from the "virgin" typified in Kuntī, Satyavatī, Draupadī and Mādhavī:

"O my noble husband, my respected husband,
through me achieve your aim
Sacrifice me, save yourself,
And look after our children."

This is followed by an intensely personal, deeply moving passage where the wife pathetically tries to console her husband with a pitiful attempt at self-deception:

"Those who laid down dharma
ruled that women should never be harmed.
The raksasas also know dharma.
He won't dare kill me.
He will kill a man, but I do not think
He will harm a woman.
O learned-in-dharma husband,
send me to him."—160.32-33

Then comes the solemn elegiac dignity of *shloka* 34, transcending time and space in plucking at the chords of every human heart with its slow yet profound appeal set in majestic rhythm in a superb transcreation:

"Many happy times
  have I spent with you,
many surpassing sweet days
  have we known together.
Much dharma have we
  Practised together.
You have given me two lovely children.
  Death holds no fears for me."

In this instant, the gulf between this frail Brahmin housewife and the *Kshatriya*-queen Kuntī is bridged, and we bow our heads in respect and admiration to the selfless love that is Woman.

The nameless wife's stature and dignity rises as she makes the supreme self-sacrifice of urging her husband to marry again, though the following *shloka* seems to be an unconscious criticism of the wholly unfair family code. It also reveals the social taboo because of which Pāndu had to make such strenuous efforts to convince Kuntī to approach other men for begetting sons:

"To marry again and again is not
  morally condemnable in a man;
for a woman to take a second husband
  is mahā adharma."—160.37

This is despite the totally insecure condition of a widow, aptly compared in *shloka* 12 to a piece of meat fought over by scavenging birds.

Vyāsa's master touch comes at the end of these laments when the little son, seeing them all weeping, picks up a dry grass blade and lisps, "I'll kill him with this!"

"They heard the brave words
  of the lisping hero,
and they laughed and wept
  simultaneously."—161.23

The question remains, however, as to how authentic this episode is. The code of family life that it presents is not corroborated by what we see elsewhere in the epic. The *Mahābhārata* presents a far more flexible and free social code that precedes, by quite some time, the rigid Mitāksharan mores this story exposes. Be that as it may, this episode remains extremely valuable because here Vyāsa comes out, as nowhere else in the epic, in the garb of a chronicler of the life of the common man, not just as the biographer of the lives of great men. And he is not just a chronicler. In magical touches, such as the infant son's sudden exclamation, he reveals the penetrating eye and creative touch of a great creator of human situations.

In section 162 we find an interesting *shloka* about the requirements of Brahmins:

"Brahmins seek first a good king,
then a wife and wealth,
and use king, wife and wealth
to protect sons and relatives."

This Brahmin did not seek out a good king; hence, he says, "we deserve what we get" (162.10). The wife, therefore, is equated with wealth and is something to be used for gaining personal benefit, which is precisely what Yudhishthira does with Draupadī.

Shloka 162.15, "I have no money/to buy a substitute man" is a crucial verse, revealing the prevalence of the scapegoat custom, and recalling the story of Shunahshepa, celebrated in the *Rig Veda,* the *Aitareya Brāhmana,* the *Rāmāyana* and several *Purānas.* Shunahshepa was sold by his father Richika or Ajigarta for a number of cows to king Harishchandra who required a human sacrifice to propitiate Varuna. As the middle son, both father and mother agreed to sell him, the eldest being the father's favourite and the youngest the mother's darling. It was Vishvāmitra who saved Shunahshepa. This "substitute-man" symbol originates in the annual killing of the god-king as a fertility-cum-magical rite that was supplanted by the sacrifice of the scapegoat or "tanist" by a king who was too clever and powerful to succumb meekly to the priestess-queen. Thereafter, it was simply a matter of time till the "weaker" of the species was relegated to her "proper" position in the social and familial hierarchy.[1]

When Kuntī offers to send one of her sons as a substitute, the Brahmin reacts almost violently, refusing to be responsible for the heinous sin of abandoning a guest. Kuntī convinces the Brahmin that her son is invincible, spinning a credible story to prevent him from gossiping of Bhīma's prowess, and asks Bhīma to do the needful. Now, once again, we see how it is Kuntī who is the guiding and controlling spirit. Yudhishthira is aghast at the step she has taken and he is so shaken that he upbraids her rudely, quite out of character:

> "The man who gives us
> confidence that one day we will rule
> the world's wealth after
> killing the sons of Dhritarāshtra —
> What right had you
> to expose him like this?
> Have you lost your reason?
> Have our sufferings unbalanced you?"—164.10-11

This speech brings out two things about Yudhishthira: he places great store by Bhīma and appears to depend wholly upon him for their future hopes and plans. Arjuna figures nowhere, possibly because Yudhishthira was convinced that Karna was unrivalled as a warrior after the display in the tournament. Secondly, since this is the solitary instance where he speaks so bluntly to Kuntī, it shows that he must have been very deeply disturbed indeed at the prospect of their sole weapon being sent into so dangerous a mission for the sake of someone else. Further, he is quite definite that their cousins must be killed so that he and his brothers may enjoy suzerainty. This is in consonance with his admission in the *Vana Parva* that he agreed to the game of dice out of greed, imagining that he would be able to win Hastināpura. Yudhishthira is, indeed, quite a schemer and hardly the weak pacifist he is made out to be in the popular imagination and even by scholars like Buddhadeb Bose and Alf Hiltebeitel. He might well be said to "run silent, run deep".

Kuntī's reply reveals how closely she observes her sons and takes decisions accordingly. Her first concern has been to repay the kindness of this Brahmin who has sheltered them from the wrath of Dhritarāshtra's sons. Then she reassures her much-disturbed eldest son by pointing out that Bhīma's prowess is superhuman, otherwise he could not have carried all of them in his arms during the flight from Vāranāvata, and mentions how a stone-slab was shattered when the newborn Bhīma fell on it. Finally she hands down a lesson in kingship:

"It's a *rājā*'s duty to protect
even the Shudra if the Shudra
seeks protection."—164.25

She mildly snubs her furious son:

"I'm not foolish; don't think me ignorant;
I'm not being selfish
I know exactly what I am doing.
This is an act of dharma.
Yudhishthira, two benefits
will follow from this act—
one, we'll repay a Brahmin,
two, we'll gain mahā dharma. . . .
a Kshatriya who helps a Brahmin
gets the highest heaven
in his after-life."—164.20-22

Then she plays her trump-card:

"BhagavānVyāsa told me to do this.
That is another reason." (164.26)

Inevitably, Yudhishthira capitulates. He is yet to gain his mother's maturity, her ability to observe closely and use experiences for taking quick decisions to further their own cause within the context of the larger interests of society.

Bhīma's excursion to Baka's lair provides some delightful

horseplay. He calmly goes on eating while the ogre showers blows on him. There being no lovely ogress handy for admiring his prowess, Bhīma makes short work of Baka, breaking him in two as he had done with Hidimb. Thereafter, he threatens Baka's kinsfolk till they promise to abjure cannibalism, and quietly leaves, having dumped the corpse at the city-gates.

With section 167 the Pānchāla phase of the Pāndavas' adventures begins. It is prepared for very carefully. A sage visits the Brahmin with whom the Pāndavas are staying and narrates the births of Dhrishtadyumna and Draupadī (the latter's is described as *ayonija* i.e., not womb-born in *shloka* 8). As the Pāndavas want details, we get a repetition of the account of Drona's birth, his obtaining weapons from Parashurāma, the insult by Drupada and the revenge through the Kuru princes. Amid this, there is a *shloka* after 168.21, stating that the sons of Dhritarāshtra and Karna attacked Drupada first and had to flee, that has not been Englished. Again, two verses after *shloka* 22 have been omitted that refer to Arjuna defeating Drupada just as Indra had worsted the Danavas and stating that the Pānchālas were convinced that Arjuna was the greatest warrior alive.

Drupada constantly seeks to avenge his defeat at Drona's hands by obtaining a redoubtable son. In the process we are provided with an interesting insight into the differences—apparently superficial but actually signifying much more—between sages. Yāja, for instance, is open to bribery and worldly attractions, unlike his brother Upayāja. Upayāja has noticed Yāja picking up a fruit from the ground and eating it, not bothering whether it was unclean. Yāja was so fond of eating that it never bothered him that he was eating leftovers from other people's meals. Upayāja is quite firm in refusing to conduct a ritual that has vengeance as its goal. Yāja, with a weakness for worldly goods, is not bothered and agrees, particularly as the shrewd Drupada flatters him in fulsome terms, "though thinking poorly of him" (169.22). Interestingly enough, Yāja has to enlist Upayāja's help in the matter.

Like Janamejaya's serpent-holocaust ritual performed by priests in black robes, this rite draws on non-*shrauta* (sacred) tradition and is death-dealing like *abhichāra* (black-magic) because of which Upayāja, whom Drupada approaches first, refuses to perform it. In emerging from such a rite, Pānchālī shares a quality with her mother-in-law Kuntī whose boon from Durvāsā is described as *abhichāra samyuktam . . . varam mantragramam*, invocations linked by black magic. In particular, as Hiltebeitel has pointed out, it is linked to Yudhishthira's birth because Pāndu specifically urges Kuntī to summon Dharma with *abhichāra* rites, *upachārabhichārabhyam.*[2] Moreover, like the *krityā* in the *Rig* and *Atharva Vedas*, Pānchālī is a combination of blue complexion rising out of the flaming red altar (*nīlalohita*). The emergence of the twins has an interesting parallel in the *Rāmāyana, Bālakānda* (16.11-12). There the *mahadbhūtam* (mighty spirit) who emerges in Dasharatha's *putreshti yajña* (sacrifice to obtain sons), is dark complexioned, clad in red, *krishnam raktāmbaradhāram* (indicative of the smoke and flames of the sacrificial fire). In the *Mahābhārata*, the twin's births are accompanied by skyey proclamations by an unseen mighty spirit, *mahad bhūtamadrishyam khecharam* and the same word *krishna* (dark) is used to describe and name Draupadī who rises from the sacrificial altar, while Dhrishtadyumna emerges from the fire itself, flame-coloured, armed cap-a-pie.

Draupadī's emergence is a bonus, an unintended superfluity. Drupada performed the rite for obtaining a son who would take revenge on Drona and had not asked for a daughter at all. Her birth is accompanied by a skiey announcement that this

> "Loveliest of ladies,
> this dark-skinned beauty Krishnā
> will be the cause of the destruction
> of the Kshatriyas."—169.48

In this fateful role she is like Helen of Troy. She is sent to fulfil the purpose not of Drupada, but of the gods in due time (*surakāryyamiyam kāley karishyati sumadhyamā*),[3] responding to the earth's anguished plea to lighten her burden of oppressive warlords. Significantly, despite being aware of this announcement—or being conscious of it—the gods-engendered Pāndavas wed her and destroy the Kauravas whose birth is entirely human.

Her marriage to the son of Yama, Yudhishthira, reinforces her ominous links with death. Even her very first appearance is as a mysterious *femme fatale* in the context of a twelve year long sacrifice performed by Yama on the banks of the Gangā, during which death stops in the world. She leads the bemused Indra into a nether world like cave where four other Indras lie imprisoned by Shiva, lord of destruction. It is by propitiating that same deity that Drupada obtains Shikhandi to kill Bhishma and Dhrishtadyumna to slay Drona.

Like Athena and Durga, Draupadī springs full-grown in the bloom of youth from the *yajña vedī*, fire-altar, not requiring the matrix of a human womb, ignoring the absence of Drupada's queen who cannot respond to the priest's summons because her toilet is incomplete. "Pānchālī", as she is first referred to, is a word pregnant with double meaning: "of Pānchāla" and "puppet".[4] Ananta Bhatta provides yet another meaning in his *Champubharatam* (VI.83): *chatushpathamandapastambha sālabhañjikeva sarvajana karaparāmarshabhājanam pānchāladuhitā* ("like the puppet standing in a hall at the crossroads is touched by all").[5] This presages how she lives her entire life, acting out not just her father's vengeful obsession, but also as an instrument of the gods to bring death—which had halted during Yama's sacrifice—back into the world, all the while suffering repeated molestation. As she is the only *kanyā* whose appearance is described in detail, the description is worth noting:

"eye-ravishing Pānchālī,
Large-black-eyed,
Dark-skinned Pānchālī,
Lotus-eyed lady,
Wavy-haired Pānchālī
Hair like dark blue clouds,
Shining coppery carved nails,
Soft eye-lashes,
Swelling breasts
Shapely thighs."—169.44-45

Drona, knowing that Dhrishtadyumna has been born to kill

him, does not hesitate to become his weapons-teacher, because he knows fate is ineluctable and that thereby his glory will be the greater.

In the Bengal recension, we find thirty-six *shlokas* after 169.56 that Prof. Lal has not transcreated, which are essential to the story. In them, Drupada learns of the supposed death of the Pāndavas in Vāranāvata and laments the death of Arjuna, whom he had wished to make his son-in-law. This reveals the Pānchāla king as a shrewd politician out to exploit the rift between the cousins for gaining his own ends. Drupada's guru tells him that from certain signs he is convinced that the Pāndavas are alive and that the way to draw them to Pānchāla is to hold a *svayamvara* for Draupadī. The Brahmin visitor then informs Kuntī of the date of the ceremony, adding that Pānchālī may even choose her second son (Bhīma) if they are lucky. He adds a bit of information useful for all mendicant Brahmins: that Yajñasena (Drupada) feeds Brahmins daily and respects them highly.

The Pāndavas are desolate and ever-perceptive Kuntī quickly understands the cause of their sorrow and deftly prepares the ground for their abrupt departure. She points out to Yudhishthira that they are finding it difficult to get adequate alms; that the same surroundings, though beautiful, are beginning to pall; and that Pānchāla will be a new place to see; moreover, the king is known to be munificent to Brahmins. Her eldest son, however, is the soul of democratic functioning and never commands his brothers. He tells Kuntī, "I do not know if my younger brothers are agreeable". This is definitely a pre-Mitākshara family, for the *kartā* (head) of a Mitākshara family was supposed to get unquestioned obedience from the family members, and would never condescend to consult them about a decision.

Section 171, which has been retained in its entirety in the Critical Edition, has Vyāsa very clearly tell the Pāndavas that they are to marry Draupadī jointly. He narrates the story of her previous birth in which Shiva gave her the boon of five husbands because she had asked him five times. This story of a previous birth lends divine dispensation for a tabooed act. Thus, presence of Shiva looms larger over the epic.

Vyāsa, no less than Krishna later, is largely instrumental in bringing about the ultimate polarisation in the Kaurava family. Dipak Chandra's *Kurukshetrey Dvaipayan* portrays the politics Vyāsa indulges in to establish the Pāndavas. One suspects that Vyāsa was not above cooking up such a story (the sage and his daughter remain nameless shadowy figures) in his inimitable manner, bringing to bear on it all the weight of his unquestioned authority to ensured this much-desired alliance with the Pānchālas. Simultaneously it maintains unity among the five brothers that alone can thwart the evil forces represented by the Dhārtarāshtras. Elaine Aron's novel *Samrāj* has Vyāsa use the smoke-screen of the sacrifice to have his daughter emerge as Krishnā. It surprising that there is so much consternation among the Pāndavas when Kuntī bids them share Draupadī. They seem to have completely forgotten what Vyāsa had told them in Ekachakra while asking them to proceed to Pānchāla. Or, is that passage an interpolation? We will find Vyāsa pulling yet another story out of his hat, one with greater embellishments, to get around Drupada's scruples.

References

1. J.G. Frazer, *The Golden Bough,* Macmillan
2. A Hiltebeitel (2001), p. 188
3. Ibid. pp. 190-91
4. Hiltebeitel (2001) p. 260
5. *Champubharatam,* 1990, p. 405.

15

The Sambhava Parva-VII

Vashishtha and Vishvāmitra

The Chaitraratha section of the *Ādi Parva* is, in a way, a regression to the *Ādivamshāvatarana*, being largely genealogical in content. Here the Pāndavas learn about their ancestress Tapatī, daughter of the Sun-god and Sāvitrī's younger sister. In typically Vyāsan manner, this story, in which Vashishtha plays a major role, becomes the occasion for relating one of the most important episodes in purānik lore: the Vashishtha-Vishvāmitra feud.

From the very beginning of this section Vyāsa's emphasis undergoes a significant shift. So far, Bhīma has constantly occupied centre-stage. It is against him that Duryodhana's plots have been directed; it is he who set fire to the house of lac and bore his exhausted brothers and mother to safety; it is he who rescued them from fearsome cannibals and stood forth as the saviour of an entire town. Arjuna has been noticed only briefly when he needled Bhīma's self-esteem to goad him into despatching Hidimb swiftly. But even this redoubtable archer has been carried in his brother's arms during the initial flight. Now, for the first time, we find that as they reach the river Gangā,

"From here mahā-chariot-hero Dhananjaya
  walked ahead with a torch,
to light the way for them
  and to protect them."—172.3

The last line is significant. Vyāsa is giving Arjuna a new role as protagonist, having abruptly left him in the lurch after building him up during the training under Drona and the vanquishing of Drupada. He does this to prepare us for his winning of Draupadī, otherwise normally we would have expected Bhīma to win the princess. It is, indeed, quite surprising that when the Gandharva king Chitraratha insolently and aggressively announces:

> "I am Angāraparna, the
> gandharva who knows no power
> save his own. I am strong!
> Proud! I am Kubera's friend. . . .
> And when I am here,
> none comes here—no god,
> no human, no corpse-eating beast.
> Who do you think *you* are?"—172. 13, 15

It is Arjuna who retorts and is the sole speaker throughout. We would have expected the impetuous and passionate Bhīma to have exploded in indignation at such insolence. The only other speaker is Yudhishthira who has a couple of lines to his credit, typically by way of pardoning the defeated Gandharva. The rhetorical exchanges between Angāraparna and Arjuna are interesting. Arjuna launches into an elaborate description of the Gangā, its tributaries and its holiness, extending his reply precisely to one *shloka* more than the Gandharva's challenge—a bit of one-upmanship, epic style!

> "This is the holy Gangā falling
> from the golden peaks
> of Himavant
> into the ocean
> where seven streams enter. . . ." (172.18)

The descent of the Ganges is one of those archetypal memories of Hinduism, captured for all time in living rock in the massive Mamallapuram sculpture, and related in the *Rāmāyana,* with Shiva singing her praises in the *Brahmavaivarta Purāna.* In the next *shloka*, while referring to the seven streams, Arjuna describes the river Sarasvatī as *plakshajātām* "rising from the plāksha-tree", which, alas, has disappeared along with this most sacred of Rigvedic rivers. The five other streams are Yamunā, Rathasthā, Sarayū, Gomatī and Gandakī. In *shlokas* 21-22, Krishna Dvaipāyana is referred to as having stated that the twin aspects of Gangā are Alakanandā flowing through the celestial regions and Vaitaranī running through the sphere of the manes.

The combat that ensues is the second duel with arms in the epic. The only such previous confrontation has been the Bhīshma-Shalya fight. Arjuna, we find, has been carrying a shield, with which he blocks Angāraparna's arrows, and retorts with the fire-missile gifted by Drona, after giving, in typical epic-fashion, the genealogy of the weapon. The question remains how these weapons appear, because so far there has been no sign of the brothers carrying any arms. The reader's presumption was that the weapons had been left behind in the gutted house of lac so as not to arouse any suspicion of the Pāndavas' survival. Be that as it may, Arjuna justifies the use of so supernatural a weapon because "gandharvas are said/to be superior to mortals" (172.27). We recall that while giving Arjuna this weapon, Drona had warned him not to use it on a human or anyone of little strength (141.11). When the Gandharva falls, his wife Kumbhīnasī rushes to beg that he be set free, which Yudhishthira grants. In the *Rāmāyana* Kumbhīnasī is the daughter of the titan Sumālī and the Gāndharvī Ketumatī and in some versions she is the mother of Rāvana. Not to be outdone, the Gandharva, though defeated, launches into a similar description of his magical lore, acquired by the acrobatic endurance of standing on one leg for six months. Arjuna is not impressed and rejects the offer of this knowledge of magical vision. He chooses, instead, to accept the gift of a hundred horses for each of the brothers, possibly the first record of Arab horses being presented to Indian princes:

"Gods and gandharvas ride them;
they are divinely-hued,
and thought-swift; they look lean,
but never tire of slacken."—172.49

Arjuna gladly gives his fire-missile in exchange, counting the horses as equally valuable, for they are the strength of *Kshatriyas.*

A curious point is that Arjuna does not bother in the least to preserve their disguise. In 172.37 he flamboyantly announces to the Gandharva that "Yudhishthira, ruler of the Kurus" has spared his life. We do not find either Kuntī or Yudhishthira reprimanding Arjuna for disclosing their identity. Is this also preparation for the final unmasking of the Pāndavas at the *svayamvara*? Of course, it could also be that Gandharvas were not known to interact with humans and therefore there was little danger of the secret reaching Duryodhana.

Arjuna wants to know whether through any inadvertent fault of their own the Pāndavas had provoked this attack by the Gandharva. Angāraparna's reply is that they lacked sacred fire, sacred oblations and a priest. It is not clear why lack of a priest should prompt such an assault, though being without the sacred fire is a serious transgression for those disguised as Brahmins. *Shlokas* 69-70 make it quite clear that the real reason for the unprovoked attack was the Gandharva's vanity: he wanted to show-off before his wife. Chitraratha provides a reason for his defeat:

"Brahmacarya is the best dharma.
And you practise it.
That was why you were able
to defeat me in battle."—172.72

He insists on the necessity of their having a priest, for this will win victory even for a sex-indulging *Kshatriya* over night-rangers:

"It is a rājā's duty, therefore,
to choose an illustrious purohita
who will refine what he possesses,
and acquire what he needs. . . .
Mere bravery is not enough,
nor nobility of birth.
A king without such a Brahmin
never expands his realm."—172. 78, 80

He describes such Brahmin-ministers or counsellors as those conversant with the scriptures, truthful, self-controlled, imparting sound moral advice in sensible, well-spoken words. We are moving towards an era of Brahmin priests-cum-counsellors that will culminate in the all-powerful Chānakya in the Mauryan times.

Very cleverly and unobtrusively, Vyāsa slips in the phrase "scion of Tapatī" twice in Angāraparna's speech, inevitably prompting Arjuna's query. This leads to the love story of Samvarana and Tapatī which has been superbly recreated by Subodh Ghosh in his Bengali masterpiece *Bhārat Premkathā.*[1] Vyāsa's version is typically bare and masculine in its rugged-appeal, but for a single passage where with his characteristic brevity and trenchant force he describes Tapatī:

"Her body shone
  like a straight flame,
her happy spotless beauty
  was like the moon's.
She stood, a black-eyed beauty
  on the hill-top,
statuesque,
  like a golden girl.
The hill, its creepers,
  its bushes, all flamed
with the golden beauty
  of the golden girl."—173.26-28

A second Cleopatra indeed in Chitraratha-Enobarbus' glowing description! And how superior the transcreation is to the Ganguli and van Buitenen translations:

"In splendour of her person she resembled a flame of fire though in benignity and loveliness she resembled a spotless digit of the moon. And standing on the mountain-breast, the black-eyed maiden appeared like a bright statue of gold. The mountain itself with its creepers and plants, because of the beauty and attire of that damsel, seemed to be converted into gold." –Ganguli

"The mountain plateau on which the black-eyed girl was standing seemed with its trees and shrubs and lianas to be bathed in gold." —van Buitenen

Tapatī is also set apart from the conventional full-hipped, heavy breasted and elephant-trunk-thighed Indian beauty by the repeated emphasis on her large black eyes and golden skin. Do we have here a foreign beauty from Iran?

Samvarana, crazed with love for Sūrya's radiant daughter, seeks the help of his priest Vashishtha who obtains Sūrya's concurrence to the union, and brings Tapatī with him.

"The lady of ravishing eyes
descended from the sky
like lightning irradiating
the ten points of the heavens."—175.33

Samvarana's infatuation with Tapatī leads to his neglecting the kingdom, resulting in a twelve year long famine from to lack of rain, till Vashishtha makes him return to his capital. Earlier, in 94.35-47 Vaishampāyana had stated that during Samvarana's reign his kingdom was afflicted with famine and the Pānchālas drove him out of his kingdom into the forest. Here, however, the reason cited is the king's infatuation. The kingdom is won back through Vashishtha's help (94.45-36). Hence the importance of having a priest of prowess. It is, again, poetic justice that the descendants of Samvarana, who was deprived of his kingdom by the Pānchālas, should have them as allies against their Dhārtarāshtra cousins.

Section 176 administers something of a cultural shock: here is Arjuna, a royal prince allegedly well versed in the Vedas and Vedantas, ignorant of so famous a sage as Vashishtha:

"O chief of the gandharvas,
who was this bhagavān rishi
whom you have described
as the purohita of my ancestors?"—176.4

From the silence of the other brothers and Kuntī it is apparent that they are no better off. Shall we infer that their schooling was limited to weapons-training and a superficial acquaintance with vedic rituals, with the Purānas completely left out? Even their vedic knowledge must have been limited to the *Brāhmanas* and *Sūtras* because Vashishtha is the *rishi* of the seventh *mandala* of the *Rig Veda* just as Vishvāmitra is of the third. Anyone studying these *mandalas* would have come to know Vishvāmitra's hatred of Vashishtha (*sūkta* 53). Arjuna's query reveals that the *Rig Veda* was already well in the background with the emphasis on the *Yajur Veda* and the *Sūtras,* i.e. the ritualistic aspects. The *Rig Veda* had already become incomprehensible for the *Mahābhārata* generations who did not have a single *rishi* among them besides Vyāsa. We find references only to priests adept at rituals, not to seers composing *sūktas* embodying their perceptions of *Rita,* the Eternal Truth lying hidden behind the golden lid of evanescent creation.

The ensuing account of the Vashishtha-Vishvāmitra feud, related from the latter's view-point in the *Rāmāyana,* deals with one of the most gripping and tragic episodes in purānik lore that has been brilliantly used by K.M. Munshi in his novel *Bhagavan Parashuram* and by Sri Aurobindo in his Bengali short-story *Kshamār Ādarsha* ("The Ideal of Forgiveness"). Munshi depicts Vishvāmitra as the visionary *Kshatriya*-turned-*rishi* whose goal is to unite the Dravidian and Aryan cultures to mould them into a single civilisation. Vashishtha opposes this fanatically, resulting in the ruinous War of the Ten Kings described in the *Rig Veda.* Vishvāmitra is also the great seer who created the immortal Gāyatrī mantra, recited by Brahmins to this day, and the rescuer of Shunahshepa from being sacrificed in one of the rare instances of human-sacrifice in the *Purānas.* In this incident many have seen the hidden hand of Vashishtha, for Shunahshepa was Vishvāmitra's nephew and Vashishtha, as Harishchandra's priest, advised this human sacrifice to placate Varuna who had afflicted the king with dropsy for having broken his vow.

The conflict, as narrated by Chitraratha, revolves round Vashishtha's wish-fulfilling cow. Vishvāmitra, king of Kanyakubja, chances upon Vashishtha's hermitage, exhausted after a hunt.

The sage entertains the king and his retinue with all types of food and gifts with the help of his miraculous cow. Naturally, Vishvāmitra decides he must have Nandini, and uses force when the sage refuses to part with her. Nor will Vashishtha oppose the king with violence for, as he tells Nandini,

> " . . .I must overlook
> Vishvāmitra though he beats
> you and drags you away". . . .
> But the mahā-muni
> would not give up patience,
> nor would he break his vow,
> though touched by Nandini's suffering.
> He said, "A Kshatriya's strength
> lies in his body, a Brahmin's
> in the spirit of fortitude,
> I will not give up fortitude."—177. 24, 27-28

This sublime non-violence, however, does not mean that he acquiesces in the rape. He clarifies to Nandini that she is free to stay on if she can. The moment she hears this, the cow produces myriads of Pahlava, Dravida, Shaka, Yavana, Kirāta, Kānchi, Shabara, Simhala, Barbara, Paundra, Hūna, Chīna, Kerala, Chibuka, Khasa, Pulinda and other *mlechchha* hordes who thoroughly rout the king's forces. That list provides an insight into who were considered to be non-Aryan in the epic age. Clearly indicated are the peoples of South India (Pallava, Dravida, Kerala, Kānchi, Pulinda, Simhala), East India (Paundra, Khasa), hills (Kirāta, Shabara, Barbara), North-west frontier (Hūna, Chīna, Yavana). Vashishtha foils Vishvāmitra's arrows and missiles with his spiritual powers. This impresses the king so deeply that he renounces his kingdom and takes up ascesis to win the same powers, aspiring to be styled "brahmarshi" He does not attain this level as long as the spirit of envy and rivalry activates him. For, though he says that "Real strength lies in tapasyā" (177.53), he does not hesitate in getting king Kalmāshapāda possessed by a *rākshasa* and then instigating him to slay all the progeny of Vashishtha. Yet this embodiment of

Brahminhood does not hit back:

> "When Vashishtha learnt
> that Vishvāmitra had schemed
> and got his sons killed, he bore his grief
> it as mahā-Meru bears the earth. . . .
> decided to sacrifice his life
> rather than harm Kaushika-Vishvāmitra."—178.43-44

His attempts at suicide are frustrated because two rivers refuse to cooperate (hence named Vipāshā and Shatadru). He gives up the idea when he finds that his daughter-in-law is carrying his grandson, Parāshara (here we link up with Vyāsa's father). When Kalmāshapāda tries to devour her, Vashishtha exorcises the possession. The amazing extent of his nobility is seen now. This king, who has destroyed all Vashishtha's children, begs the sage to give him a son. It is in *shloka* 44 that Vyāsa lays bare the facts about how childless kings managed to have children by having rishis "bless" their queens:

> "During her fertile period,
> the mahā-rishi Vashishtha
> had intercourse with her,
> as enjoined by divine precept."

No wonder Vashishtha was so named, for his name means "sense-subduer." Such perfect self-control is unparalleled in Puranik lore.

This episode is part of what we have seen as a common affliction of royal dynasties: the inability to have children. In both the Solar and the Lunar lineages this remains a knotty problem for which special rituals have to be performed and austerities undergone. Kalmāshapāda becomes a precursor of Pāndu just as Parāshara parallels Janamejaya. Like Pāndu, while roaming in the forest, the cursed king eats up a Brahmin engaged in coitus with his wife. She curses him that should he have intercourse with his wife, he will die. That is why the king has to approach Vashishtha to impregnate his wife.

What about the queen, Madayantī? What was the state of mind of the royal wives who were made to suffer impregnation by unknown persons? Satya Chaitanya has written a superb recreation of this in his short story, "A Woman of Ayodhya, a womb desecrated"[2] just as Buddhadeb Bose did with Ambikā and Ambālikā in his play *Anāmni Anganā*.

The next two *shlokas* describe the first caesarean operation as the queen uses a stone, *ashma*, to deliver her child when it is not born after twelve years: the operation should more appropriately be known, at least in India, as "ashmakan" instead of "caesarean." The parallel with Gāndhārī's delayed delivery is obvious. Curiously, instead of succeeding Kalmāshapāda in Ayodhya, Ashmaka founds a town named "Paudanya". Here, therefore, is yet another break in dynastic succession in the Solar lineage.

While Chitraratha stops his narrative of the Vishvāmitra-Vashishtha conflict at this point, Sri Aurobindo went beyond this in his short story to describe the moment when Vishvāmitra, at last genuinely penitent and free of envy, approaches Vashishtha to beg forgiveness. Now the magnanimous sage hails Vishvāmitra as *brahmarshi,* that recognition which he has been fruitlessly striving to win from the world and for which he has committed so many crimes. It is in achieving true humility that Vishvāmitra achieves the highest level of seerdom.

An interesting hint concerning further causes of the rift between the two sages is given in 178.15, where it is mentioned that they had a quarrel concerning who would be Kalmāshapāda Mitrasaha's priest (this is the king's full name, as mentioned in *shloka* 25 of section 178). If we take the Rigvedic, epic and purānik accounts in their totality, this feud assumes an extremely significant place in the political history of those times. Vashishtha was originally the priest of the Aikshvaku dynasty of Anaranya in the time of king Traiyyāruna whose son was the notorious Trishanku. He was so named for having raped a Brahmin's newly wedded bride, eaten a cow of Vashishtha's and disobeyed his father. He had been banished and lived with Chandalas. Hence, on Traiyyāruna's death, it was Vashishtha who ruled the kingdom as regent, keeping Trishanku out of the throne. At this time a famine also took place, and Vishvāmitra the Kanauj king, attacked

Vashishtha's realm. However, with the help of tribal and non-Aryan armies, Vashishtha succeeded in worsting Vishvāmitra, who fled to the forest. There Trishanku looked after his family during the terrible famine, earning his gratitude. Vishvāmitra helped Trishanku to regain his throne after this famine, alienating Vashishtha totally. When Trishanku wanted to carry out a sacrifice, Vashishtha flatly refused to officiate. At this, Trishanku called in Vishvāmitra who had composed hymns for the *Rig Veda.* Vashishtha, however, organised a very successful boycott of this ceremony, which prompted Vishvāmitra to create new deities. In *sūkta* 9 of the third mandala of the *Rig Veda,* Vishvāmitra refers to 3339 gods in place of the 33 mentioned in the Vedas. These are the new gods. Consequently, Vashishtha gave up his post here, proceeded to Sudāsa, king of North Pānchāla and became his advisor. In the Battle of Ten Kings, Sudāsa won chiefly because of Vashishtha's advice. Vishvāmitra, who was with his opponents, lost. Yet, we find that later in Sudāsa's *yajña* it was Vishvāmitra who officiated. Possibly because of this Vashishtha left him and went to the Paurava king Samvarana, who had been routed from his kingdom by Sudāsa. With Vashishtha's help, Samvarana defeated and killed Sudāsa and won Tapatī as his wife. Hereafter we find Vashishtha in the kingdom of Kalmāshapāda, king of south Koshala, another Ikshvāku prince, who is used by Vishvāmitra to destroy Vashishtha's entire family. It is quite possible that this occurred before Vashishtha went to Samvarana, as that would explain his abandonment of the ungrateful solar dynasty of Ikshvāku in favour of the lunar dynasty of Puru. After this we find Vashishtha once more back at his original post in the Anaranya dynasty as Harishchandra's priest, counselling him to carry out a human sacrifice for appeasing Varuna. Cleverly, he refused to officiate at this horrendous ceremony. As victim, Shunahshepa, Vishvāmitra's nephew, was chosen and it is through Vishvāmitra's intervention that he escaped. The frustrated Vashishtha now shifted to Northern Koshala, ruled by Dasharatha. But even here Vishvāmitra appeared on the scene and stole all the glory by arranging the marriage of Rāma with Sītā. Vashishtha has hardly any role in the *Rāmāyana,* while Vishvāmitra becomes responsible for the momentous destruction of the *Rākshasas* infesting the forests by bringing about the coming of Rāma.

Another interesting point is that Vishvāmitra's sister married the Bhārgava sage Richika and the Bhārgavas were preceptors of the *Asuras.* When Vishvāmitra revolted against the established gods and "created" new deities, new hymns and a new sacrificial mode in Trishanku's sacrifice, this relationship must have been one of the considerations prompting the gods to take part ultimately in the ceremony despite Vashishtha's ban. This has been explored at length in Acharya Chatursen's great Hindi novel *Vayam Rakshāmah.*

Sections 180-188 reiterate a problem dealt with in the *Āstīka* sub-*parva.* Here both Aurva and Parāshara are determined to exterminate an entire race, the *Kshatriyas* and the *Rākshasas* respectively, just as Janamejaya set about destroying the *Nāgas* much later. This theme of genocide becomes a *leit motif* of the *Ādi Parva* along with the theme of lust.

Parāshara, like Ashtāvakra, calls his grandfather "father" and determines to take revenge on his father's murderer on being apprised of the truth. The difference is that where Ashtāvakra was content with defeating Vandin, Parāshara determines to annihilate all creation. In order to dissuade him, Vashishtha narrates the story of Aurva. The Haiheyas slaughter the Bhrigus, including unborn children, seeking to seize their wealth till they are struck blind by the effulgence of Aurva, who springs forth from his mother's thigh, as Chyavana's birth slew Puloman. Aurva determines to destroy all creation, incensed at the quiescence of the gods in the face of this horrendous massacre. Thereupon, his ancestors' manes reel out a bit of astonishing special pleading claiming that they had deliberately invited the calamity, being bored with life and not wanting to commit suicide. The sophistry is quite mind-boggling because suicide is made out by them to be only the taking of one's own life by oneself, and not deliberately motivating another to kill oneself. Aurva's replies are possibly some of the most memorable passages in the *Ādi Parva.* The anguish that throbs in every *shloka* finds an echo in every reader's heart:

"I am not one whose anger is empty
whose curse is fruitless.
My anger unfulfilled will destruct me
as fire does dry wood.
The man who suppresses
righteous anger
for whatever reason,
will find himself frustrated
in the three-fold path
of Dharma, Artha, and Kāma."—182.2-3

He points out that no one stirred a finger to save the victims:

"And terrible anger surged through me
when the scoundrelly Ksatriyas
began their task
of murdering the living and to-be-born.
Who in the three worlds was there
to help all the pregnant mothers
at that fearful time?
Who helped the fathers?"—182.7

He passes on to voice a sentiment echoed by all victims of injustice:

"Oh, if there was only someone
to punish the wicked,
would there be any wickedness left
in the world to punish? . . .
If I, who have power to punish
do not now punish,
what is to prevent other men
from repeating the crime?"—182.9, 14

Shloka 11 is a famous one, immortalised in Tagore's adaptation:

"The man with power to punish
who does not punish

who he knows deserves punishment,
himself becomes guilty."

The climax of this angry young man's indignation is reached in *Shloka* 13:

"Many rājās and nobles
could have saved my ancestors
yet they did not—they chose
riskless luxury instead.
But I—I have righteous anger
on my side!
I have the power to punish!
I don't have to obey you!"—182.12-13

How refreshingly alive the transcreation is compared to the laboured and stilted renderings of previous translators! Aurva casts his wrath into the ocean, as advised by his manes, and this becomes the *vādavāgni,* the mare-headed, water-consuming fire that erupts to cause universal dissolution at the time of *pralaya.*

Hearing this, Parāshara diverts his creation-annihilating anger and focuses it on the *Rākshasas,* organising a great sacrifice. Wisely, Vashishtha does not try to dissuade his grandson from this second vow: he knows the hot-blood of youth and does not presume on his authority too far. The sacrifice is powerfully reminiscent of Janamejaya's which Āstīka managed to stop. The only difference is that in the case of Aurva and Parāshara the *yajamāna* is himself a Brahmin while in the latter it is a king. Parāshara discards the fire on the northern side of the Himalayan forest where it is still aflame. In his case it is a team of five famous seers who succeed in putting an end to the holocaust: Atri, Pulastya, Pulaha, Kratu and Mahākratu. The first four are the mind-born sons of Brahmā while Pulastya is the ancestor of the *Rākshasas* and Ravana's grandfather. The word "Mahākratu" also connotes "great sacrificer", and may not be the name of a seer, as we do not find any sage of this name in the Purānas. The logic trotted out by them is analogous to the peculiar sophistry of Aurva's manes:

"No raksasa, O great rishi,
could have devoured him
if he had not done
what he did.
Vishvāmitra was merely
an agent in the affair,
like rājā Kalmāshapāda.
Shakti is now happy in heaven."—183.16-17

This looks like shrewd thinking to forestall another vow by Parāshara, this time to destroy Vishvāmitra and Kalmāshapāda. In case this is not enough, Pulastya adds that Shakti and all the other sons of Vashishtha are enjoying themselves like gods in heaven, and that *Vashishtha knows this.* It is rather peculiar that Parāshara does not retort that the same logic can apply in his case, and that he is merely an agent in this destruction of the *Rākshasas,* just as Vishvāmitra was just a blameless instrument in the death of his father. Anyway, the plea succeeds, and the sacrifice is stopped.

It is only at this stage that Vashishtha also chips in, presumably corroborating Pulastya's assertion that he is aware of his progeny's celestial bliss, which only emphasises the speciousness of the argument. If Vashishtha had known this all along, why did he not say so to prevent Parāshara from starting this *Rākshasa*-holocaust? Actually, it is Pulastya himself who almost acts as the devil's advocate by saying:

"Grandson of Vashishtha,
You are being used
In this sacrifice as a tool
for the extermination of
these rākshasas."—183.19-20

It is not clear whose tool Parāshara is supposed to have been; presumably Fate's. One suspects that young Parāshara stops the sacrifice more out of respect for these renowned sages who are pleading with him than because he is convinced by what they say. Aurva's case is also similar. After the indignant refusal to give up his vengeful resolve, he ultimately takes the advice of his ancestors.

The theme of this narrative appears to be the virtue of forgiveness. Besides the supreme example of Vashishtha, this is brought home through Shakti's case also. Shakti, like Shringi much after him vis-a-vis Parikshit, has not learnt to master his anger. His rage, bursting forth against Kalmāshapāda, recoils upon himself just as Vishvāmitra's jealousy of Vashishtha consistently boomerangs until he conquers his own pettiness. The true Brahmana is known by this power of total self-control, by possessing immense spiritual prowess but never using it selfishly.

Section 184 provides an interesting parallel to the Pāndu story. Arjuna leads Angāraparna back to section 179 and wants to know if it was proper for Kalmāshapāda to bid his wife have a child by Vashishtha and whether the sage was not violating his code in agreeing to have intercourse with another's wife. Besides the fact that this reveals the extremely shallow education received by the princes (Bhīshma had narrated instances precisely of such *niyoga* custom to Satyavatī and these purānik stories were supposed to be the staple of the *brahmachārī*'s schooling), it also suggests that Arjuna has a sneaking misgiving about his and his brothers' parentage. Knowing that he and his brothers were fathered on Kuntī and Mādrī by persons other than Pāndu, Arjuna is seeking some sort of an assurance that this *niyoga* custom, long outmoded by his time, is sanctioned by dharma. He, of course, has not had the benefit of listening in to Bhīshma's recounting of this ancient practice. One would dearly like to know what was going on in Kuntī's mind when Arjuna posed this query. Here is a situation worthy of Iravati Karve's pen, which, alas, is silent forever.

Angāraparna, whom Arjuna admiringly addresses as "all-knowing", gives a reply that seems to have been moulded deliberately to satisfy the Pāndavas. Like Pāndu, Kalmāshapāda is cursed by a Brahmin's wife for having killed her husband in the act of intercourse. The curse is also identical: to die in the act of intercourse. The only difference is that she graciously indicates the solution as well: he will have a son through

Vashishtha's intervention. Kalmāshapāda, again like Pāndu, forgets this curse in his lust. Madayanti, unlike Mādrī, repulses him, reminding him of the curse. Thereupon the king seeks out Vashishtha, and prays that he father a son on Madayanti, just as Pāndu had made Kuntī solicit three 'gods'. It is significant that at this point Arjuna should say, "Gandharva, you seem to know everything" (185.1).

180.10 refers to Vashishtha as "son of Mitrāvaruna". It is one of the most important of Purānik myths. Vashishtha, unlike Vishvāmitra, is doubly celestial in origin as both Mitra and Varuna had intercourse with Urvashī, as a result of which Vashishtha and Agastya were born.

In section 185 we find the Pāndavas picking Dhaumya, brother of Devala, to be their priest, as advised by the Gandharva. The choice of Dhaumya itself reveals the decline in spiritual stature of Brahmins. This Brahmin is renowned, presumably, as one of the finest specimens of the current culture, but how far below he is of Vashishtha, Vishvāmitra, Gautama, Bhrigu, Chyavana and the rest! Dhaumya is no better than a Brahmin well versed in the scriptures. He is no seer, nor imbued with Chānakya's statecraft. The same can be said of Drupada's *purohita.* In this epic we find a transitional stage when these Brahmin-priests have yet no role to play in policy-making, with the Kshatriyas fully in control of the society, unlike the *rishi*-dominated Vedic period. The time of all-powerful Brahmin counsellors is yet to come, which is to culminate in Kautilya. However, having Dhaumya with them acts undoubtedly as a tremendous moral boost because they feel that they have as good as won Draupadī and obtained their kingdom and lost glory. The admiration appears to be mutual (185.11).

It is interesting to compare this account of the strife between the two great rishis with the one given in the *Ayodhyā kānda* of the *Rāmāyana.* Where the *Mahābhārata* version centres around Vashishtha and is more favourable to him, the *Rāmāyana* version highlights Vishvāmitra's unique achievement for the benefit of Rāma and Lakshmana, who seem as ignorant of his prowess as Arjuna is of Vashishtha's.

References

1. Englished by Pradip Bhattacharya, *Love Stories from the Mahabharata*, Rupa & Indialog, New Delhi 2005
2. www.indianest.com

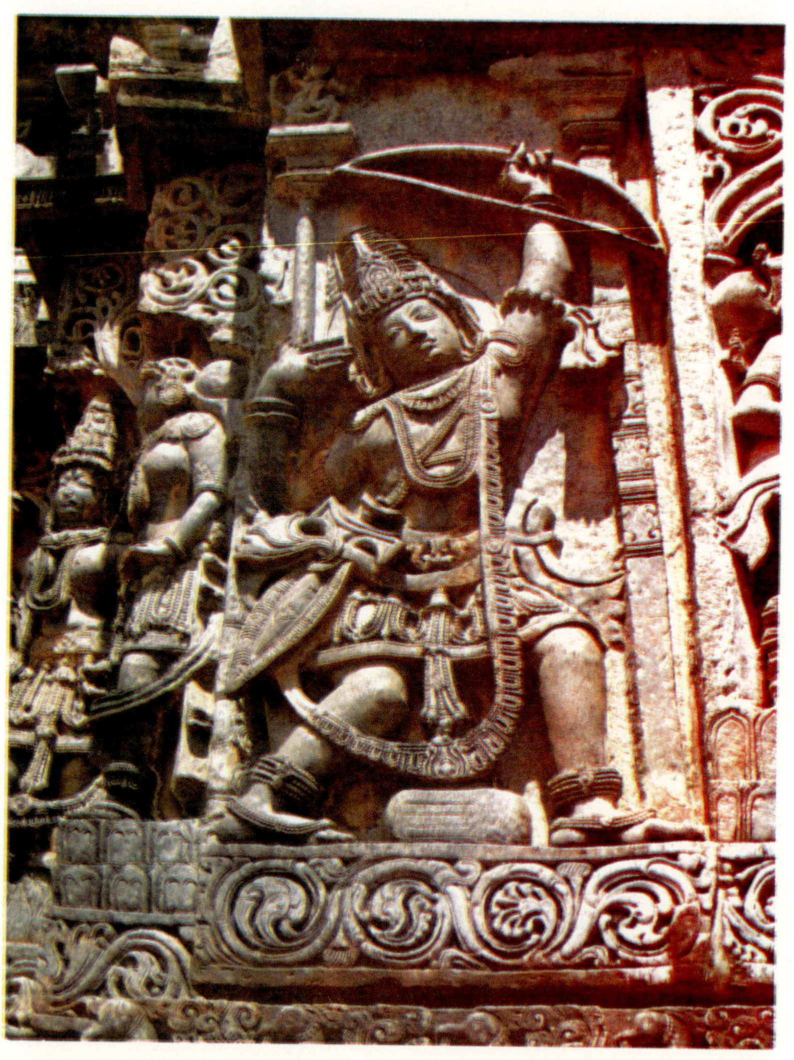

“Arjuna at Draupadi’s svayamvara” photograph from Halebid
by Philip Larson

16

The Sambhava Parva-VIII

Svayamvara and Restoration

With section 186 we are well on the way to the bridegroom-choice ceremony (*svayamvara*) of Draupadī, which is itself a misnomer. For, she is by no means a free agent choosing as her husband the man she likes best, but is just being given away as a prize to the best archer. This is termed *vīrya-shulka*. But of that later. In this particular section, what is interesting is that the Brahmins flocking to the ceremony out of sheer gluttony and sensation-hunger find Bhīma the most promising candidate for winning Draupadī:

> "You are handsome, you are god-like.
>   Who knows, seeing you,
> Krishnā may prefer one of you
>   for herself!
> This brother of yours looks specially
>   handsome and heart-pleasing;
> he is mighty-muscled,
>   and in feats of strength will do well."—186.18-19

Yudhishthira, thereupon, agrees to accompany them to the festival. This, again, supports the contention that Arjuna is not the natural leader among the brothers, and that the Angāraparna episode is Vyāsa's way of deliberately focusing the attention on the third Pāndava by way of preparation for his winning Draupadī. Bhīma, though silent, seems to draw all the attention to himself most naturally. On the other hand, without Krishna, Arjuna is really nowhere.

Apropos the decline in Brahmin spiritual stature, *Shlokas* 6 and 14-17 bluntly and cruelly expose that these Dvāpara Brahmins are rushing to the *svayamvara* purely for entertainment and gain, to gaze open-mouthed at kings and warriors and greedily gather the largesse they distribute. Gone are the days when Kshatriyas would rush to worship Brahmins:

> "They will lavish gifts
> of wealth, cattle, food,
> and countless other luxuries,
> Which we will be happy to receive. . . .
> Actors, praise-chanters, dancers,
> chanters of the Purānas,
> panegyrists, conjurors and wrestlers,
> will come from many lands."—186.14-16

In *shloka* 16 the original is *māgadha.* There is little sense in sensation-seekers looking forward to seeing messengers, though one of the meanings of this word is undoubtedly that. The other meaning, which would be more appropriate here, is "panegyrist of the king" usually associated with *bandin* and *sŭta.* Similarly, the word *vaitālika* in the same *shloka* can signify both "conjuror" and "panegyrist of a king". Finally, *niyodhaka* in the same *shloka* means "wrestler, pugilist".

In section 187 there are a couple of curious statements. It would seem from *shloka* 8 that Drupada is unaware of the supposed death of the Pāndavas in the house of lac, for he is said to secretly wish to marry Draupadī to Arjuna, and to have specially commissioned a bow that none but Arjuna may bend (*shloka* 9). If this was his desire, why did he not approach Bhīshına in the normal manner? If he could not do so because when Draupadī appeared out of the fire the Pāndavas were already "dead", how did Drupada have any inkling that they might be alive?

Next, the conditions Drupada announces, that the man piercing the target will win Draupadī, contradicts the very term *svayamvara*, "self-choice". The whole idea of this ceremony was that the bride would pick her husband out of the assembled Kshatriyas. This freedom of choice (as Damayantī's of Nala and Kuntī's of Pāndu) and the restriction of participation to *Kshatriya* suitors alone, are two essential features of this ceremony that are both violated in Draupadī's case. Not only is she merely a reward in a trial of skill (Dhrishtadyumna bluntly tells her that there is no question of her having any choice in the matter), but neither her father nor her brother intervenes when a Brahmin steps forward to string the bow. This is all the more curious because when Karna comes forward, Draupadī suddenly springs alive and loudly proclaims that she will not marry a *sūta*, even if he hits the target! And this despite Dhrishtadyumna's unequivocal declaration:

"And I give my word—
The noble-born
  handsome and strong
king who succeeds
  today takes to wife
my sister Krishnā."—187.36
"They will aim at the target.
Gracious girl! The hero who hits
  the target you will choose as your husband."—188.25

Karna, of course, is neither "noble-born" nor a king and does not feature in the list of kings Draupadī is given and therefore, strictly speaking, could be rejected despite his success. Draupadī cannot even imagine the horrific fruits this karma of hers will bear in the dice-game, where Karna takes the lead in terming her a whore. Prof. Lal rightly points out in his Preface to fascicule 22,

> "Simply to argue, as the assembled Brahmins do, that Brahmins know more of bowcraft than Kshatriyas, whom they teach, looks like a devious way of making Arjuna a candidate for the archery contest. If Draupadī could be so vehement in rejecting a Sūta suitor, what made her keep silent when a Brahmin stepped forward? Caste-upmanship?"

Following this, however, Prof. Lal indulges in a bit of uncalled-for denigrating of Arjuna, by pointing out that "Arjuna's archery-lustre seems vastly exaggerated". This is not so in Vyāsa, where he and Karna alone are able to bend the bow and only Arjuna can pierce the target. Prof. Lal bases his conclusion presumably on vernacular recensions where Shishupāla, Jarāsandha, Shalya, Duryodhana and Karna all shoot at the target and miss it by various infinitesimal measurements. It is not clear what Prof. Lal means by referring to "the oral tradition" as his authority for this, as the Sanskrit epic itself is an orally transmitted one. It is hardly justifiable to pass opinions concerning a character drawing on facts not occurring in the original text.

Shloka 190.20 is the first reference to the Krishna-Arjuna nexus that is so crucial a relationship in the epic. Arjuna thinks on Krishna before stringing the bow, although there has been no interaction between them so far. This could very well be an interpolation. In 189.9-10 it is Krishna who, despite never having met the Pāndavas, recognises them and points them out to Balarāma. In 191.20-23 he gives us the first physical descriptions of the five brothers. Curiously, of them it is Yudhishthira who alone stands out with some particularised physical features: eyes like lotus-leaves, tall, fair-skinned, gentle-looking, long-nosed, lion-like gait. Arjuna is merely the lion-gaited bow-wielder, while Bhīma is the tree-uprooting hero, and the twins simply "young men/each as handsome as/Kārtikeya". This is quite appropriate, for it is the eldest Pāndava who stands out as an individual, impressing us through sheer individuality of character, not getting lost in the welter of mighty archers and mace-wielders like Arjuna and Bhīma. Yudhishthira is the only complex character among them. Arjuna's only characteristic other than archery is philandering; while Bhīma besides being a Hercules is also Porthos-like in his straightforwardness. Nakula and Sahadeva are just shadows, totally one-dimensional, and little more than names.

At the end of section 190, after *shloka* 33 stating the failure of all suitors and Arjuna's stepping forward, there are two *shlokas* in the *Aryashastra* recension that are relevant and should be included:

"At that Krishna, highest among gods and titans, leader of the Vrishnis, of spacious wisdom, squeezed Rāma's hand in joyful belief that Draupadī was the Pāndavas' now. But others knew not the disguised sons of Pāndu."

Vyāsa's description of Draupadī coming to garland Arjuna is very sensitively transcreated:

"And those who had seen her
  repeatedly, saw her again
as if never seen before:
  without smiling, she seemed to smile;
she radiated feeling; her way of walking
  was a way of speaking."—190.31

The other translations are the poorer for not including this poetically evocative *shloka.*

The rage of the suitors is directed chiefly against Drupada for having deprived them of his daughter after inviting them, and against Draupadī, possibly because of her rejection of Karna, but not against the Brahmin because they feel he did what he did either out of pride or greed. They stress that something must be done so that this does not become a precedent for future *svayamvaras.* When, in opposing them, Bhīma uproots a tree with his bare hands, it is interesting that even Arjuna is awestruck by the feat. The ensuing combat ranges Karna against Arjuna for the first time in battle with the former turning away as he will in every subsequent duel. He "knew a Brahmin's prowess was invincible." This phrase *Brahma-teja* refers to the Brahmin caste's spiritual energy, which was acknowledged as supreme, as Vishvāmitra learned to his cost. Karna's prowess appears vastly exaggerated. In the course of this fight, seeing the disguised Arjuna's prowess, Karna wonders whether he is Bowcraft itself, or Parashurāma, or Indra or Achyuta-Vishnu. In the original (*shloka* 192.17) the word for Indra is *harihaya,* i.e. "the one with bay or golden horses", a curious appellative as Indra's steed Uchchaihshravas is pure white. The epithet harks back to the *Rig Veda* and hints at the identification of Indra with Sūrya, whose chariot is drawn by golden/bay/tawny horses, and with Agni, who is often symbolised as a tawny horse. The comparison with Vishnu-Achyuta (literally "unfallen") suggests the constant refrain running through the epic identifying Arjuna with Nara the archer-sage, and as one of the inseparable pair of Nara-Nārāyana, the latter being another name of Vishnu.

In the fight between Shalya and Bhīma, the former is thrown down but bystanders are amazed to find that Bhīma does not use the opportunity to slay him.

The next four *shlokas* (31-34) require slight re-arranging in order to read properly, for there is no question of Duryodhana being such a redoubtable warrior that only Krishna or Kripa may face him. Van Buitenen has given the remodelled version as follows:

> "For who can battle with Rādhā's son Karna, save for Rāma and Drona and Kripa Saradvata and Krishna, son of Devakī, and the enemy-burning Phalguna? And who can fight back against Duryodhana and Shalya, that most m1ighty king of the Madras, save for heroic Baladeva, and Wolf-Belly the Pāndava?"

Shloka 36 unobtrusively hints at the authority attributed to Krishna, for it is he who intervenes and gently dissuades the kings from further fighting.

In the midst of all this confusion, like the rest of those present in the ceremony, we have also completely forgotten the three other Pāndavas. How is it that they have nothing to say or do in this grossly unbalanced fight of two un-armoured and primitively armed brothers against a fully prepared Kshatriya host? As long back as 190.29, at the first signs of resentment on part of the suitors at Arjuna's success, Yudhishthira and the twin paragons "slipped out of the enclosure", undoubtedly eager to escape the inevitable bloodshed! Draupadī, therefore, is really won by the Arjuna-Bhīma duo. Yudhishthira does not even have a single word to his credit, although one presumes that Arjuna took his permission before stepping forward to try his luck at the test. Nor do we find him whispering any advice or encouragement to his brothers before running away. Possibly he thought that, with so many kings particularly Karna and Duryodhana (of whom he is mortally afraid) offended, their last hour had come and he saved himself and Mādrī's sons (as he will do again in the Dharma-crane episode in the *Vana Parva*) leaving his rash brothers to face the situation. It is a unique instance of desertion in the face of danger that Yudhishthira will not be found repeating in future. It is also not clear where these three brothers go after slipping out of the enclosure. In 192.42-44 Kuntī is anxiously worrying about their delay in returning from their alms-rounds. It is significant that with the introduction of Draupadī, the brothers, for the first time, go off on their own to her ceremony with no indication that they have informed their mother of their destination and taken her permission, as they invariably have so far. Then, in section 193, she takes Draupadī to Yudhishthira who, therefore, is already indoors. Draupadī is brought there by Bhīma and Arjuna alone, not by all five brothers.

Another interesting point missed out by commentators is the staying of the "Brahmin" Pāndavas in a potter's house. This presupposes that the potter was a Vaishya, an acceptable class. Otherwise, it would constitute an inexplicable breach of the social system prevalent in the epic's milieu. It is significant that neither Dhrishtadyumna nor Krishna comment on their choice of residence. It also appears that they are not just sharing the potter's house, but have exclusive use of it, for we never come across this invisible host, unlike the Ekachakra Brahmin.

Section 193.2 is Kuntī's famous pronouncement: "Share and enjoy your alms", uttered "unwittingly" about Draupadī. Yet, is it all that accidental? After all, Vyāsa, while advising them to proceed to Pānchāla, had specifically stated that Draupadī had been blessed by Shiva in her previous birth to have five husbands. Kuntī knows that their primary intention here is to win Draupadī and thereby reassert their right to the kingdom through the alliance with Drupada. She would not have been ignorant of the fact that this was the day for the *svayamvara.* Her farsighted vision had seen the ruination attendant upon any splitting up of the five brothers. What better bond could there be than a common wife? This could, of course, also lead to serious feuds, to prevent which Nārada will come forward with his suggestions later.

The subconscious psychology needs to be studied as well. Kuntī has had sons by Sūrya-Durvāsā, Dharma-Vidura, Vāyu and Indra. In abandoning her first born, she replicates her own abandonment first by her father and then by her foster-father who has no qualms about placing a nubile princess at the exclusive disposal of the eccentric Durvāsā. As she was "persuaded" to lie with four men, so does she create a dramatic scenario where her daughter-in-law has to have five men enjoying her all through life! It is the working-out of deep psychological complexes with a vengeance. Strangely enough, the Pāndavas do not seem to have any recollection of what Vyāsa had told them in Ekachakra about Draupadī becoming their common wife. Kuntī immediately approaches Yudhishthira for resolving the dilemma: for her words must not prove false, yet no sin must be committed. Note that Kuntī never even suggests that Draupadī should not be shared. She is quite clear that her words must not become false. Thus, she is characteristically seizing upon a fortuitous (?) statement of hers and turning it to glorious gain.

Yudhishthira suggests that Arjuna, who pierced the target, should marry Draupadī. Arjuna points out that he is only third in precedence and cannot get married before his elder brothers. No one remembers, conveniently, that Bhīma had been ordered to jump the queue and has had a son by Hidimbā. At this point Vyāsa gives us a typically terse *shloka* carrying vast significance:

"The sons of Pāndu heard
These bhakti-filled, affectionate words
of Jishnu-Arjuna. Then one by one
they glanced at the Pānchāla princess.
Lovely Krishnā looked at them.
They looked at each other.
They sat down.
Each had her in his heart."—193.11-12

It is a tribute to Yudhishthira's perspicacity that he immediately perceives that all of them have simultaneously fallen in love with Draupadī. It is now that he recalls what Vyāsa had told them before they set out for Pānchāla: that this princess was fated to have five husbands. The purpose behind this is made quite clear:

"Afraid that dissension might arise
  between the brothers,
Yudhishthira said: "Auspicious Draupadī
  will marry all of us."—193.16

The Pāndavas are filled with joy at this decision, though not appreciating the reason prompting it, which Kuntī alone understands and concurs in.

Krishna and Balarāma enter at this juncture and salute the brothers who are understandably foxed as to how their secret retreat could be discovered. Yudhishthira's query is met with a flattering reply:

"O rājā! Can fire be kept hidden?
Who but the Pāndavas
  could have performed today's feats?. . . .
  May you flourish,
as fire in a cave leaps up and grows!"—193.24, 26

They leave quickly and discreetly so that they are not spotted, having made it quite clear on which side their sympathies lie. The basis of the alliance is the blood relationship through Kuntī, who is their paternal aunt. It is, therefore, again because of her that the Pāndavas ultimately regain the kingdom after vanquishing their cousins with Krishna's help.

How alert Krishna was is seen in section 194, where Dhrishtadyumna is found tailing Arjuna and Bhīma to the potter's hut. It is here that Bhīma's voracious appetite is mentioned by Kuntī, when she advises Krishnā to lay apart a full half of the entire food for him, pointing him out for her as "the fair youth, elephant-huge". She does not introduce the rest. Thus, by sheer physical presence, it is again Bhīma who is in the limelight for Draupadī and us.

Dhrishtadyumna does a bit of sleuthing, drawing appropriate deductions from the martial conversation of the brothers, which he conveys to his father. Drupada has every hope that it is Arjuna who has won Draupadī and that the Pāndavas are alive. Dhrishtadyumna concentrates purely on Arjuna, quite understandably, because he is ignorant of Kuntī and Yudhishthira's decisions about the polyandrous marriage. The description he gives of Arjuna (195.2) is, however, hopelessly vague: large radiant eyes, wearing black deerskin, god-like! He is a lost case as a detective trying to ferret out the true identity of his mysterious brother-in-law.

In *shloka* 4, however, an extremely interesting bit of information is provided: "Krishnā joyfully followed him,/holding on to his deerskin." According to *Manusmriti,* the Shudra bride is to hold on to the garment of her higher-class husband. Here, Draupadī follows the same rite in the belief that Arjuna is a Brahmin. It is also significant that Draupadī adjusts herself without any problems to a life of complete simplicity, lying on the floor at the feet of five brothers, partaking of whatever food they have procured as alms. The strength of character that this shows will make her a worthy counterpart of Krishna and between the two of them the destruction of the Dhārtarāshtras is assured.

Dhrishtadyumna's report also clarifies that Yudhishthira and the two Madrians were already at home with Kuntī when Bhīma and Arjuna arrived with the bride (195.7). It is, therefore, rather strange that he does not report the decision about the polyandrous marriage. Is he deliberately concealing it in order to spare his father this unpleasant shock? The other interesting point is that the Pānchālas are aware of rumours that the Pāndavas had escaped the fiery death planned for them (195.12), while so far it seemed that only Vidura and Bhīshma were aware of this.

Drupada despatches his priest to confirm his son's presumption that it is the Pāndavas who have won his sister. This priest points out that Pāndu was a close friend of Drupada (195.18), a fact hitherto unknown, and also states that Drupada's intention had been to marry his daughter to Arjuna. The latter information must have raised some emotional turmoil in Yudhishthira, being a direct insult to the eldest Pāndava in being bypassed in favour of a younger brother. Yudhishthira's reply is also unusually harsh, prevaricating and very much of a rebuff. He says, in effect, that since Drupada had made his bed, he might as well be reconciled to lying in it. He also points out that this was no *svayamvara*:

> "Rājā Drupada of Pānchāla did not
> give his daughter away
> by free choice. . . .
> he arranged a test of skill.
> For this reason,
> he has no cause to question
> the kind of husband
> obtained—his class,
> character, lineage, family.
> The requirements of the test
> were satisfied by stringing the bow
> and piercing the target."—195.23-24

Drupada, however, does not give up. In a manner reminiscent of Odysseus spotting Achilles disguised among girls, Drupada arranges a display of articles calculated to appeal to the different classes: fruits, garlands and seats to appeal to Brahmins; ploughing implements for the peasantry; tools used in trades for artisans; sports equipment; weapons. It is a shrewd, unobtrusive and completely successful test. The Pāndavas give themselves away as royal *kshatriyas* by the very ease of manner with which they occupy the best seats in the proper order and concentrate on the weapons alone. Now Yudhishthira acknowledges the truth, hinting at their need for refuge:

> "So be relieved;
> We are indeed Kshatriyas;
> your daughter is a lotus transplanted
> from one lake to another.
> And you, mahārājā, are to us
> like a respected superior,

a haven of shelter."—197.10-11

Drupada's response is immediate and undoubtedly sincere, for is not this the opportunity that he has made his life's goal?

"Rājā Drupada pointedly criticised
lord of men Dhritarāshtra...
assured Yudhishthira
of every assistance in the matter
of recovering his kingdom."—197.15-16

The Pāndavas, too, have at long last achieved the alliance they have been aiming at as the means for regaining their birthright.

There is wry humour in the manner in which Yudhishthira breaks the painful decision regarding Draupadī's marriage to her father. Drupada, naturally, has taken it for granted that Arjuna is to be the husband and he announces this to Yudhishthira, who responds with the enigmatic, "In that case, O king,/I too must marry" (197.20). Nonplussed, but with unfailing kingly courtesy, Drupada responds:

"Certainly," replied Drupada,
"you may marry my daughter
if you please; or marry Krishnā
to any brother of your choice."—197.21

Draupadī's wishes are of no consequence whatsoever. She is but a puppet, as her name "Pānchālī" signifies. The reader feels let down coming to such a situation after having lived so far in the company of a heroine like Kuntī. Moreover, Drupada does not seem to realise that he has thrown overboard the very basis of the so-called *svayamvara*, where only the person passing the test could be Draupadī's husband. By his statement, Drupada has virtually acknowledged that she is no longer his to bestow, but Yudhishthira's, to marry her himself or to bestow her on any of his brothers according to his sweet will. This is precisely how he treats Pānchālī-the-puppet.

Yudhishthira now announces their decision, stating that it is Kuntī's will and also in consonance with their pledge (which we have not heard of so far!) to share everything they get equally in the interests of their unity:

"We have an agreement to
share equally any jewel
we get. We will not break
our agreement in this case."—197.24

He also tells a lie—that Bhīma is yet unmarried. Yudhishthira's statement looks forward to 203.8-9 where Duryodhana suggests that seeds of jealousy be sown among the five brothers and:

"Best of all, stir up Krishnā
against her husbands.
They are five—that should be easy.
Get one or two Pāndavas
to find fault with her—in turn
she will be displeased with them."

Karna's scornful reply goes to the very heart of the matter, particularly Draupadī's silent acceptance of this polyandrous union without a word of protest, quite uncharacteristic of so strong-willed a princess:

"Forget this idea of sowing
discord among them.
How can you estrange people
devoted to a common wife? . . .
Forget this idea of alienating Krishnā
with the help of spies.
She chose them when they were poor—
now they're rich.
And it is well-known that a woman
hankers for many husbands.
Draupadī has five—
Why should she be unhappy?"—204.5-8

Unwittingly Karna has plumbed Draupadī's innermost secret—which perhaps even she is unaware of—reaching back to her *tapasyā* in previous births for getting husbands. The snide remark about the insatiable sexual drive of women is a standard male chauvinist jibe that spawned stories in the eastern and southern vernacular retellings of the epic depicting Draupadī's secret longing for Karna as a sixth husband.[1]

The natural bond of birth that binds the Pāndavas to one another is reinforced five times over by being married to the same woman, who takes care to distribute her favours equally among them.

Drupada, naturally, is quite shocked at Yudhishthira's obnoxious demand. To him it is nothing but a gross violation of the prescribed social code. Yudhishthira's response is in words that are deeply ironic. They will rebound at him from no less a person than Bhīshma in the shameful scene of Draupadī's disrobing in open court:

"Dharma, mahārājā," said Yudhishthira,
  "is subtle—who knows
how it works?—Safer for us to follow
  the examples of the ancient past."—197.28

Interestingly enough, he conveniently omits to quote any such precedents. What follows invites comments such as Prof. Lal's in his Preface to fascicule 23:

"He must have been a bit of a prig; also a mother's pet. How else account for his two reasons for marrying Draupadī—'I know what's right' and 'Mother told me'."

"I have never said an untruth,
  never indulged in adharma.
My mother's will is my will
  because I know she is right."—197.29

This is not, however, just a priggish statement. We have to look at Yudhishthira's words in the total context of the situation.

In the first place, the brothers have been brought up wholly by their mother in extremely hostile surroundings. Yudhishthira knows how much they owe their royal upbringing in the court, their later escape from sure death and the events that followed to their mother's remarkable abilities. He and his brothers, therefore, are spontaneously committed to honour her every wish. Moreover, Yudhishthira is convinced that she is right in insisting that Draupadī be their common wife, the reason being forging of an unbreakable bond among them. Since the proposal is thus doubly enforced, being desired by Kuntī and considered justified by them, it cannot be a violation of Dharma. The third argument is Yudhishthira's personal integrity, which is indeed unquestioned and accepted even by his enemies: he is simply incapable of doing what is not dharma. Here he is simply stating a fact, and it is not a vaunting boast or sign of priggishness. However, he is also conscious of the fact that it is easy to pick holes in his arguments simply because the proposal lacks the sanction of tradition and is unprecedented. That is why he is anxious to get it over with as quickly as possible:

> "Our action is within dharma.
> Have no fears about that.
> It is best, O rājā, not
> to to have any doubts in this matter."—197.30

However, 197.28 carries a hint. When we recall that the sons of Kuntī were all born in the Himalayas of unknown fathers, it lends substance to the proposition that they were brought up in a society where polyandry was an accepted tradition, as indeed it still is in the Jaunsar Bawar region of Uttarakhand and Kinnaur in Himachal Pradesh.[2] This explains why Duryodhana felt that the Pāndavas had less claim to the throne than himself. Both his parents were royal, while the fathers of Kuntī's sons were unknown mountain men.

Note that at no stage does Yudhishthira suggest that if Drupada is not agreeable they will give up Draupadī. The alliance is far too important and rich a prize to forsake. The question that arises is whether they would have finally agreed, in case Drupada remained adamant, to let Arjuna alone marry Draupadī. The inevitable consequence would have been to set centrifugal forces in motion, and the joint establishment of Kuntī and her five sons would have gradually disintegrated. Kuntī's wisdom lies in providing her grown sons with a new and more attractive focus to revolve around instead of herself. Draupadī, indeed, is not only like Kuntī in her strong personality, but is also an able substitute in the field of political alliances. Just as through Kuntī the Pāndavas were allied to the powerful Vrishnis and Yādavas, similarly through Krishna's unique empathy with Draupadī that blood relationship is given the sanction of a bond forged through unity of souls, and the trinity of Yājñasenī, Arjuna and Krishna becomes the hub of their wheel of fortune.

Luckily for the Pāndavas, they are spared the trial of having to choose between their mother's wish and giving up Draupadī by Vyāsa arriving precisely at the time when Dhrishtadyumna and Yudhishthira are thrashing out this problem afresh.

To Drupada's query whether it is lawful for a woman to have many husbands, Vyāsa's initial response is negative and he refers to this practice as out moded and no longer supported either by tradition or the Vedas. He, then, draws out the opinions of Drupada, his son, Kuntī and her eldest son. Drupada merely points out that there are no precedents nor any vedic sanction for polyandry. Dhrishtadyumna poses the more practical moral issue: how can the elder brother justify having intercourse with his younger brother's wife? Notice that he does not posit the opposite, being aware of the ancient, though obsolete, *niyoga* tradition of the younger brother impregnating his elder's widow. He goes a step further to demolish Yudhishthira's reply to Drupada in 197.28, that dharma is subtle: precisely for that reason, he says, how is he to know that the proposal is dharma and not adharma? Yudhishthira's argument is, firstly, that he is temperamentally incapable of committing what is in violation of the dharma:

"I have never said an untruth.
  never indulged in adharma.
What my conscience approves
  can never be adharma."—198.13

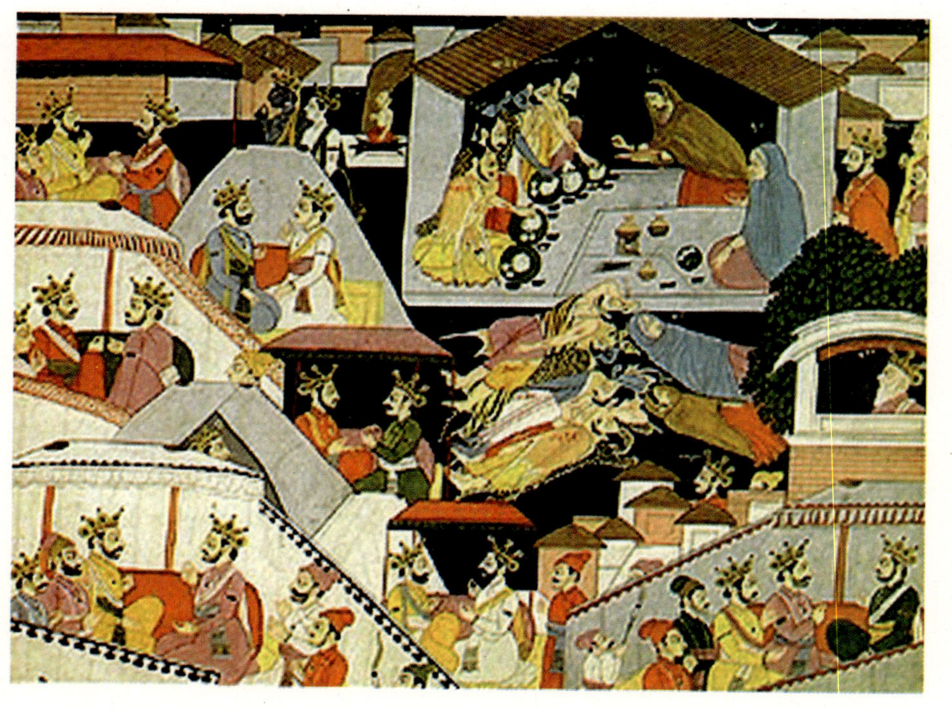

"Kunti, Draupadi, Pandavas" Kangra style miniature c.1800

Secondly, he manages to dig up two purānik precedents: Jatilā and Vārkshī. Of the former, nothing is known beyond the fact that she espoused and served seven sages and belonged to the Gautama clan. She is referred to again in the *Shānti Parva* (38.5), where the women of Hastināpura praise Draupadī, comparing her to Jatilā in the manner in which she has served her five husbands. Of the latter, there is an extended story in the *Vishnu Purāna* (I.15). Kandu, a sage engaged in ascesis, was seduced by the *apsarā* Pramlochā who, while leaving him, exuded the embryo as perspiration that was absorbed by leaves of trees. This was gathered by the wind, given life and form by the moon and called Mārishā. When the ten Prachetās were burning the forests that had overcast the earth, Soma stopped them with a peace-offering of this Vārkshī (tree-born girl) as their common wife. From this union Daksha Prajāpati was born. An eminent precedent, therefore!

Yudhishthira's third point is the importance of obeying one's mother, the greatest among gurus. Here is a unique declaration in this epic, which is predominantly a man's world, of the mother's supremacy. The usual attitude is that of Parashurāma who beheads his mother at his father's behest, for usually it is the father who is the supreme guru. It is here that we find the only exception. Kuntī supports this, pointing out that her words, if fruitless, would brand her a liar, and taint her with untruth.

Vyāsa assures her that this will not happen, and that what she has proposed is, in fact, the eternal law, *sanātana dharma*. This phrase takes us back to sections 104 and 122, the stories of Dīrghatamas and Shvetaketu. There, Vyāsa described the *sanātana dharma* thus:

> "This is the Sanātana Dharma—
> All women of the four castes
>   are free to have relations
> with any man. And the men,
>   well, they are like bulls."—122.14

He takes Drupada apart to disclose to him what this eternal law is and how it originated; but he does nothing of that sort.

Instead he spins two yarns, throws in a bit of hypnotism, and thereby provides the excuses Drupada needs to agree to the eminently desirable alliance. These have been omitted in the Critical Edition.

The first story told by Vyāsa is peculiarly rambling. *Shlokas* 199.1-9 have nothing to do with the actual episode of five Indras being reborn as the Pāndavas. Yet, they articulate extremely important mythic motifs. These nine *shlokas* relate to Yama's performance of an sacrifice in Naimisha forest during which death did not touch the world. The gods, seeing no difference between mortals and themselves in this respect, rushed to Brahmā who assured them that mortals would start dying once the sacrifice was over. It is to reduce the burden of overcrowded earth that the gods plan the battle of Kurukshetra. While returning to the sacrifice of the god of death, Indra finds a lotus floating in the Bhāgīrathī river and seeks out its source. Here we enter the realm of folklore: Indra finds a lovely girl whose tears, falling into the Gangā, turn into golden lotuses. This mysterious *la belle dame sans merci* invites him to follow her if he wants to know who she is and why she is weeping. These questions are never answered. Like the deceiving elf, she leads him to his doom, which he invites by his overweening pride. Insulting Shiva, whom he finds playing dice with his consort, he is imprisoned in a cave with four of his predecessors—Vishvabhuk, Bhūtadhāmā, Shibi, Shānti and Tejasvin—and condemned to be born as a mortal. These Indras still have the gumption to lay down a precondition: that the gods Vāyu, Dharma, Indra and Ashvinikumāras engender them. Here, therefore, we have another account of the divinity of the Pāndavas presented by Vyāsa who is tactful enough to play on Drupada's vanity too. He declares that Shiva assigned the goddess Shrī as their common wife and that she was born miraculously from the *yajña*-fire as Draupadī. Presumably, the reason for becoming the common wife is that Shrī was the *femme fatale* who ensnared each of the haughty Indras. There is a clear analogy with Gangā having to descend to earth because of the Mahābhīsha episode. To this is added the sub-episode of Shiva obtaining Nārāyana's approval to this plan, and Nārāyana himself sending out a white and a black hair into the world: the former becomes Balarāma and the latter Krishna. By saying that Arjuna is Indra, i.e. the last one captured by Shiva, and that Draupadī is Lakshmī, Vyāsa has provided adequate heavenly "background" to the entire affair to circumvent all mundane objections.

In the process, an awkward situation is created. For, Shrī is the consort of Vishnu, who incarnates partially as Krishna. That is the secret of the special bonding between Draupadī and Krishna. However, Draupadī weds Arjuna, a portion of Indra. To resolve this issue, the later *Mārkandeya Purāna* (V.25-26) made Draupadī an incarnation of Indra's wife Shachi instead.

Further, this mini-myth has introduced the motif of the dice-game side-by-side with that of death as a form of sacrifice, which will become major themes.

To capitalise on the impact he has created, Vyāsa gifts Drupada divine sight, with which he sees the Pāndavas as five Indras and is bewildered as well as overjoyed "at the display of *māyā*"—a very revealing word (verse 199.41), and perhaps a hint that it was all a wonderful illusion. Pleased with Drupada's amazement ("O wonder-working paragon of a rishi!"), Vyāsa goes on to buttress the case yet further by retelling the story of Draupadī having asked Shiva for five husbands in a previous birth which he had told the Pāndavas in Ekachakra. In other words, Lakshmī was also a sage's daughter whom no one wanted to marry! This contradiction is not even remarked upon by the stupefied Drupada. His response in 200.4, however, shows that he has not wholly lost common sense. He says, in effect, that as long as no one blames him, Draupadī can have as many husbands as she wants:

"Since Shankara has decided
  that this dharma or adharma
should be so, let it be so! No fault of mine!
  Let them all marry Krishnā."

Either he is not befooled by the "divine sight" etc. and is still doubtful about the morality of such a marriage or the verses regarding the illusory vision are interpolated. What makes him agree is Vyāsa's production of instant purānik precedent, as that will be sufficient authority with which society can be faced when the inevitable flurry of consternation takes place.

Vyasa's account has been embellished in various ways. The Southern recension of the epic states that in an earlier birth as Nālāyanī (also named Indrasenā, daughter of Nala the Nishāda king) she was married to Maudgalya, an irascible sage afflicted with leprosy. She was so utterly devoted to her abusive husband that when a finger of his dropped into their meal, she took it out and calmly ate the rice without revulsion. Pleased by this, Maudgalya offered her a boon, and she asked him to make love to her in five lovely forms. As she was insatiable, Maudgalya got fed up and reverted to ascesis. When she remonstrated and insisted that he continue their love life, he cursed her to be reborn and have five husbands to satisfy her sexual craving. Thereupon, she practised severe penance and pleased Shiva, obtaining the boon of regaining virginity after intercourse with each husband.[3] The Jaina *Nayadhammakahao* picks this up and tells of suitorless Sukumarika, reborn as a celestial courtesan because of her passion, who is again born as Draupadī.[4] According to the *Brahmavaivarta Purāna*,[5] she is the reincarnation of the shadow-Sita who was Vedavatī reborn after molestation at Ravana's hands, and would become the Lakshmi of the fourteen Mahendras in Svarga, of whom five incarnated as the Pandavas. According to this *Purāna* (14.57), after the fire ordeal, the shadow-Sita was advised by Rama and Agni to worship Shiva. While doing so, *kamātura pativyāgra prārthayanti punah punah*, tormented by sexual desire and eager for a husband, she prayed again and again, asking the three-eyed god for a husband five times. Hence, the five husbands of Draupadī.

The multiple wedding now takes place with Dhaumya officiating. It is significant, however, that Dhaumya only conducts the ceremony for Yudhishthira's marriage. Thereafter he leaves the palace (200.12). This indicates his disassociating himself from the polyandrous union.The brothers espouse Draupadī on successive days. Since separate marriages are taking place and the scriptures enjoined that the bride must be a virgin, suddenly we find the divine sage (Nārada) being quoted in 200.14 as declaring that Draupadī regained her virginity every day before each wedding. Drupada loads the empty-handed Pāndavas with great wealth by way of dowry so that they can meet the Dhārtarāshtras on equal footing. The reason for this is stated again:

"Allied now with the Pāndavas . . .
king Drupada feared no one,
  not even the gods."—201.1

In section 201 comes Kuntī's address to her daughter-in-law. The blessings Prithā showers on Draupadī are profoundly ironic, for she knows that this princess will be the cause of the Kurukshetra holocaust and necessarily suffer the consequences of the carnage. Yet she says:

"Most accomplished of women,
  auspicious lady!—
May you have all the world's virtues,
  May a hundred happinesses be yours."—201.11

Draupadī is fated to be one of the most unhappy of women not only because she suffers gross insults and a thirteen year long exile, but because the children she bears never attain anything of their fathers' heroic proportions and are slain untimely in a treacherous attack. We will never see Draupadī as mother, despite her having given birth to five sons. Indeed, there are only fleeting references to their birth and absolutely none to her pregnancy. It is always Draupadī the proud queen, avid to avenge the insults suffered by her womanhood and royalty, who comes before us. She is a splendid specimen of womanhood no doubt, but without the more appealing feminine traits of softness and yielding disposition. There is a hardness in her, as she glitters with a diamond's blinding flashes of splendour, but none of the pearl's soft, ambient glow. She is in the tradition of Devayānī, Shakuntalā and Kuntī rather than of Sharmishthā, Damayantī, Mādrī and Sītā.

At the same time, she stands completely separate from all other women, surpassing them all in her unique ability to establish a harmonious union between five husbands and herself, with Yudhishthira alone having some inkling of where her inmost affections lay. In her relationship with her many husbands she is distinct from both Jatilā and Vārkshī in that Draupadī is very much of an equal partner in the Pāndavas' mission to regain their rights, not a hermit's daughter meekly serving the husband like a dumb slave. Indeed, there are many instances where Draupadī does not hesitate to berate her spouses in no uncertain terms, even accusing them of cowardice and faint-heartedness, which marks her out as a modern woman with a fully developed ego, standing up for her rights and demanding that the so-called stronger sex vindicate her honour. It is Shakuntalā alone who approaches her to some extent.

These aspects of Draupadī, however, will not be seen in the *Ādi Parva,* where she is just a mute puppet being married off without protest to five husbands, except for that solitary spark of life when she refuses to be Karna's prize in the bridegroom-contest.

The other important feature of section 201 is the manifold wealth sent by Krishna for the Pāndavas, including female attendants. The brothers, thus, face the Dhārtarāshtras not as beggars but as princes with elephants, chariots, wealth and the support of both Drupada and the Yādavas. This news, naturally, creates consternation in the Kuru court, while other kings, recalling the Purochana incident, squarely blame Bhīshma, Dhritarāshtra and the Kurus for having tried to harm the Pāndavas.

Among the Dhārtarāshtras there is frenzied consultation and the varied advice make interesting reading. Shakuni feels (222.11-21) that Drupada's power is negligible and this is the right moment for destroying the Pāndavas before the Pānchālas are reinforced by the Vrishnis under Balarāma and the Chedis led by Shishupāla. It is the latter reference that is intriguing. Why should Shishupāla, an ally of the terrible Jarāsandha of Magadha and an inveterate opponent of Krishna, come forward to help the Pāndavas? The only explanation would be the enmity between the Chedis and the Kauravas, because of which the former would avidly seize this opportunity of siding with the Pānchālas to crush Hastināpura. Shakuni's speech, incidentally, is dropped from the critical edition, along with that of Somadatta's son, Bhūrishravā that follows.

Somadatta is the son of Bāhlīka, brother of Shāntanu, and occupies an important place in the Kuru court beside his cousin Bhīshma. A bitter enmity later develops between him and the Yādava or Vrishni prince Shini that is carried on into the next generation and climaxes in the deaths of Somadatta, Shini and Bhurishrava in the great war that is recounted in the *Drona Parva*. Somadatta's son points out that Arjuna and Yudhishthira are deeply entrenched in the hearts of the people and are also much too powerful now with the support of Krishna and Balarāma. This speech offers a rare insight into how others saw Yudhishthira:

"And Yudhishthira knows exactly
when he should use
his own powers, and when seek
the help of allies.
He eschews anger and prefers
gentleness, gifts, secrecy,
and justice as ways
of winning friends for himself.
Yudhishthira has been known
to acquire allies by
lavish gifts of wealth—
transforming even enemies."—202.31-32

More important, he points out that to attack the Pāndavas now in the Pānchāla capital is to invite death, as it is far too well defended. Hence, he advises that peace be maintained and they leave for Hastināpura peacefully. This is what Duryodhana does, in the face of the bald military facts Bhurishravā states.

Vidura, hearing the news, indulges in a rare bit of mockery by greeting Dhritarāshtra with "Luck favours the Kurus". The blind king, ironically called "wisdom-visioned", mistakes this for Duryodhana having won Draupadī and immediately has ornaments ordered for his daughter-in-law. When Vidura breaks the truth, the monarch, masking his true feelings, pretends that he is even more delighted because he loves the Pāndavas even more than his own progeny since they have brought the kingdom the valuable alliance with the Pānchālas. But once he is alone with his sons, they start conspiring to destroy their cousins.

Duryodhana's suggestions rightly elicit Karna's scorn, for they are neither well thought-out nor likely to succeed. His ideas are fourfold, of which the chief is sowing dissension among the Pāndavas or setting Draupadī against them (203.4,8,9,16). The others are: persuading them to stay with the Pānchālas permanently; buying over Drupada and his sons; and assassinating Bhīma, without whom, according to Duryodhana, "Arjuna's not worth one-fourth of Karna." Yet, in the *svayamvara* fight, Bhīma never helped Arjuna in his duel with Karna in any way.

Karna bluntly points out that this policy of "shifty ways" (204.4) has already failed: if Duryodhana could not finish them off when they were living in the same palace, planning to do so through trickery when they are so far away is wishful thinking, particularly when they have powerful allies. Doubly united through a common wife, they cannot be split apart; nor can the upright Drupada be bribed to betray his sons-in-law. Karna, like Shakuni, comes out in favour of a surprise attack, before the Pānchālas and Yādavas are warned, to capture the Pāndavas. Dhritarāshtra, liking this idea, now calls in Bhīshma, Drona and Vidura to finalise the policy, which shows that all of them were aware of the king's true inclinations. It is no longer a hidden intrigue, but a part of state policy that is being debated in council-chamber.

This section also provides an insight into Karna's character as the man-of-action, not the intriguer like Shakuni, and not a hopelessly addled and impractical schemer like Duryodhana:

"The best we can do is—Strike! Strike today,
and uproot them once and for all. . . .
Strength, O lord of the earth, is
  the pride of a Kshatriya.
Strength is the crowning glory
  of the world's heroes. . . .

Conciliation, gifts, bribery, and subversion
will not work.
There is only one way left—
naked strength!"—204.11,18 20

Bhīshma's response revels his commitment to impartiality, viewing both branches of the family as equally entitled to the inheritance. Naturally, he suggests that half the kingdom be handed over to the Pāndavas. He points out to Duryodhana:

"Perhaps by adharma
this kingdom is now yours
but they can equally well argue
it was theirs before it became yours."—205.7

He also buttresses this with a solemn warning to protect their reputation, which may well be tarnished if the Pāndavas are denied their birthright. Indeed, *shloka* 10 is strongly reminiscent of *Othello*:

"Think of your good name
Nothing's more precious than a good name.
Better to die
than lose one's good name."

Shloka 11 reinforces this:

"O Kaurava! Son of Gāndhārī!
A man lives as long as his good name lives
When his good name dies,
he dies."

Bhīshma also points out that, after the house-of-lac episode, it was Dhritarāshtra who was defamed by people, not Purochana. Therefore, the reappearance of the Pāndavas clears the king's reputation and this chance should be taken to further enhance their good name by giving the Pāndavas their due. Drona strongly supports this, with detailed advice on propitiating Drupada.

Karna suddenly interrupts, and virtually insults the two venerable counsellors by questioning their integrity. Yet, his speech is quite disjointed. After boorishly saying that Bhīshma and Drona, though dependent on the king's favours are giving him bad advice, he asserts that Fate alone decides the outcome of an event. He, then, narrates the story of king Ambuvīcha of Rājagriha, so incompetent that his minister Mahākarni seized all power yet failed to usurp the throne because Fate willed otherwise. Karna's advice is not clear at all. He merely says that whether the kingdom will remain Dhritarāshtra's or not depends on fate. Yet, his last words are again a warning to the king to distinguish between treacherous and loyal advice. It is surprising that Drona alone retorts. Bhīshma possibly feels it beneath his dignity to reply to a Sūta's son.

This bristling arrogance of Karna, ever eager to insult his elders and betters, is psychologically a very true delineation of the bastard's mental and emotional make-up, constantly labouring under the stigma of his base or unknown birth and a sense of injured merit. Karna's ire is particularly directed against Bhīshma, possibly because of this grand old Kshatriya's supreme contempt for the charioteer's son. This he takes to such self-defeating ends as to refuse to participate in the war so long as Bhīshma is on the battlefield, an attitude that is Achilles-like in its blind egotism.

As usual, it is Vidura who shows Dhritarāshtra the illogicality of Karna's aspersions on the integrity of Bhīshma and Drona; the advisability of converting the enmity with the Pānchālas into friendship; the impossibility of crushing the Pāndavas, supported as they are by the Yādavas and the Pānchālas and being beloved of the people; and the invincible valour of Arjuna and Bhīma. Vidura, with great daring, points out:

"I warned you once that
   Duryodhana's mischief
would be the cause of
   the annihilation of the kingdom."—207.30

It is in 207.26 that, for the first time, we find that famous phrase, *yatah krishnastato jayah* ("Victory is where Krishna is").

There is a reference to Yādavas as descendants of king Dāshādha which is very rare, the king being nothing beyond a name, though he must have been very famous, otherwise the clan would not have been named after him. The reference to King Gaya as the ideal of dharma and truthfulness in 207.6 is not the *Asura* Gaya, after whom the famous holy spot has been named Gaya-tīrtha but to the royal sage Gaya, son of Amurtarayasa, famed for *yajñas*, about whom we shall hear again in the *Vana* and *Drona Parvas*. Gaya is famed for having conducted a *yajña* of such proportions as will never be surpassed by anyone. The other royal prince Gaya was a brother of Nahusha, but not famed otherwise.

In *shloka* 16, Indra has been referred to as *maghavat*. The word refers to the giving of gifts during *yajñas*, and means "munificent", as Indra was also known as *shatakratu*, "performer of a hundred sacrifices." In 207.20 Vidura points out that the Pāndavas have Balarāma to protect them, Janārdana to counsel them, and also Sātyaki to support them.

Vidura's counselling takes effect, and Dhritarāshtra sends him as his emissary to welcome the Pāndavas home. In the process, however, he refers to the five brothers in an interesting fashion in 208.2:

"I do not deny that Pāndu's sons,
mahā-chariot-heroes,
From the viewpoint of dharma,
are like my own sons."

This looks very much like an unkind reference to the manner in which the Pāndavas were engendered, with Kuntī and Mādrī like common wives to five husbands, the first of whom might very well have been Vidura. In that case this would also be a sly hit at Vidura himself, implying that Dhritarāshtra is well aware why Vidura is so interested in the welfare of the Pāndavas. Again, *Shlokas* 5-6 are playing on the word "good luck":

"This good luck will increase our strength.
Good luck that Purochana is silenced.

O resplendent one,
by good luck is my grief removed."

Significantly, he refers to the *silencing* of Purochana as their good fortune, so that the murderous attempt remains a secret and his apprehensions on this score are set at rest, along with the danger of a sullied reputation.

Drupada, in response to Vidura's message, makes it quite clear that the Pāndavas must decide whether it is in their interest to return to the Kuru kingdom, and that the advice of Krishna will be valuable in taking the decision. Krishna supports Drupada that a return is advisable and Vidura makes plans concerning the departure of Kuntī, her sons and Draupadī.

Shlokas 209.10-16 constitute an extremely important passage describing a conversation between Kuntī and Vidura, as they meet for the first time since the Pāndavas left Hastināpura for Vāranāvata. This passage does not find place in any of the English translations other than Prof. Lal's, and provides crucial material for understanding the undercurrents of relationships that run deep beneath the facade of the supernatural engendering of the Pāndavas. Kuntī, whom we never see in tears except beside Pāndu's corpse, breaks down in tears on seeing Vidura; and in this emotionally vulnerable moment she voices what might be the veritable truth:

She said, "Son of Vicitravīrya,
your sons
by your grace are still living. . . .
So you have cared for your children. . . .
I have looked
after your children through many difficulties.
What should I do now?"—209.11, 13, 14

For the first time Vyāsa describes her as sobbing uncontrollably. Prof. Lal very pertinently asks, "Is Vidura *like* a father to the Pāndavas, or is he *really* a father to them?" The late Iravati Karve argued in favour of the former view with characteristic brilliance in her *Yuganta*. It will be recalled that

Dharma incarnated as Vidura because of Ani-Māndavya's curse, and that the first god Kuntī summoned, at Pāndu's behest, was Dharma. Along with this we have to keep in mind that according to the *niyoga* custom, it was the duty of the junior levirate to impregnate his elder brother's wife. It would, therefore, be only natural for Pāndu to instruct his wife to summon his younger brother Vidura first.

The completely non-*kshatriya* nature of Yudhishthira, so totally different from his brothers, lends support to this argument. How closely he resembles the self-effacing, peaceful, vowed-to-truth character of Vidura! The spontaneous understanding existing between them has been revealed in the scene where Vidura warns Yudhishthira about the house-of-lac before they set out for Vāranāvata. This climaxes towards the end of the epic, as pointed out by Iravati Karve, in the *Āshramavāsika Parva.* There, in 26.25-27, Vidura infuses all his energy into Yudhishthira's body using yogic power as he dies. In 28.15-18, Vyāsa informs Dhritarāshtra that he engendered Vidura, who is none other than the god Dharma, and that he, in turn, (either Vidura or the god Dharma) gave birth to Yudhishthira through yogic powers. Then, in *shloka* 21 Vyāsa says, "He who is Dharma, is Vidura, and Vidura is Pāndava", referring to the identity of Vidura and Yudhishthira. Notice, he does not say, "He who is Dharma is Yudhishthira", but interposes Vidura between them as the engendering link. Now, why should this more or less clear statement of Yudhishthira's parentage come at such a late stage? This seems all the more strange because in this epic we are never left in any doubt about the parentage of people, regardless of the fact of bastardy. Iravati Karve suggests that if it had been known that Yudhishthira was fathered on Kuntī by a *shūdra,* his claim to the throne would have been vitiated vis-à-vis Duryodhana the legitimate son of Dhritarāshtra and Gāndhārī. It will be recalled that Vidura himself is deprived of all rights to the throne—despite the fact that Dhritarāshtra is blind and Pāndu deserts to the forests—because his mother being a maidservant, although Vyāsa is as much his father as of the two princes. Iravati Karve points out, "To prevent anyone's finding out who were the fathers of his children, Pāndu went and lived far away in the Himalayas and apparently the natural fathers of his sons remained unknown and unacknowledged."

The next question that arises is that if Kuntī could approach Vidura once, why did she not do so the next time as well? According to Iravati Karve, the scriptures ordain that "a man should sleep with his brother's wife only when necessity arises to create a son in his brother's name. The prevailing opinion was that this should happen only once, so it is understandable that Vidura did not approach Kuntī again. One thing at least is clear: the *Mahābhārata* which is outspoken about all relationships, has not made a single unambiguous statement about the affection of Vidura and Dharma, or about their relationship." She concludes, "If Dharma is the natural son of Vidura and the legal son of Pāndu, the whole Mahābhārata conflict is no longer between the sons of Dhritarāshtra and Pāndu, but among the sons of all three brothers. The triangular fight does not materialize because Vidura and Pāndu have a common son. Even after his son was crowned he could not become the father of a king. Vidura remained uninvolved, detached. Dharma got all that was his by right, but he got it at such cost that to the end he too remained not only detached but unfulfilled."

Buddhadeb Bose raises the objection that if Vidura were really the natural father, this was bound to have been mentioned in the epic just as the illegitimacy of Karna is. However, this has already been answered by the danger it would have posed to the eldest Pāndava's right to succession.

Again, why does the question of Vidura engendering Yudhishthira by yogic powers arise if he is the physical father? Is Vyāsa merely hinting at a spiritual identity? We are here in the realm of conjecture and arguments can be found for both views. But it would be fascinating to evolve a sub-plot woven round the secret love-affair between Kuntī and *Kshattā* Vidura!

Van Buitenen takes up the Kuntī-Dharma/Vidura union as an example of what he describes as "inept mythification" because of which "the causes that it seeks to elucidate become the murkier". He apparently finds it absurd that god Dharma, who has been incarnated as Vidura, should be invoked to beget Yudhishthira. To van Buitenen the existence of Dharma as Vidura on earth and the continuance of Dharma as a god in celestial regions are mutually exclusive phenomenon. He has not understood the very concept of *amshāvatarana* (partial incarnations) that underpins the epic. To him if Vishnu is incarnated on earth as Krishna, he cannot simultaneously remain in Vaikuntha, although the text clearly states that in all cases partial incarnations are occurring through emanations of the supernatural beings. This is clarified by Vyāsa in his story of the five Indras, which van Buitenen again criticises as full of "foolish associations", where Indra agrees to send out an emanation of his to be born on earth in his stead, as do all the gods and Vishnu at the end of the *Amshāvatarana* (26.48-49, 54). Van Buitenen comments that Pāndu's hesitation in choosing the right god for the *niyoga* rite and finally fastening upon Dharma because none can find fault with an act performed by him, "is extremely silly". His argument is that Pāndu himself was born of a similar rite and that his wife Kuntī has had Karna by Sūrya "before her marriage, and quite unblushingly".

The entire reading seems to be based on misconceptions. It is precisely because Pāndu is overtly conscious of his surrogate-birth that he wants to ensure that there will be no succession problems with his children, since they will be at yet another complete remove from the royal blood of Shāntanu. That is why he seeks to give the act the ultimate sanction of law, by calling upon Dharma himself. This is not an instance of "silliness', but of carefully thought out political wisdom. Again, Pāndu is not aware of Kuntī's pre-marital escapade, nor did Prithā unblushingly bear Karna. The incident was the fruit of a nubile maiden's natural, irrepressible curiosity. Her terror and embarrassment have clearly been recorded in the epic when Sūrya browbeats her into sexual intercourse and bearing his child. Subodh Ghosh has turned it into a splendid study of an unmarried mother's psychology in his short story "Bhaskar O Prithā". The "mythification" is by no mean "inept" or "silly".

What van Buitenen completely fails to grasp is the extra dimension lent to this petty tale of family intrigue and strife over an inconsiderable kingdom in the upper reaches of the Gangā and the Yamunā through the descent of the partial incarnations. It will be recalled that in the *Anukramanikā* itself Vyāsa projects the Kurukshetra war on to an ethical plane, as a battle between Evil and Dharma (*shlokas* 108-109). In the *Amshāvatarana,* Vyāsa expands it further, lending it a cosmic dimension where the Kurukshetra war becomes another 'type' of the archetypal conflict between the gods and the titans, the divine and the anti-divine forces pervading all Creation, that has been typified in the *amritamanthana* myth. As Sukthankar has very perceptively pointed out, "What gives this trivial tale . . . real depth and significance is the projection of the story on to a cosmic background, by its own interpretation of the Bharata war as a mere incident in the ever recurring struggle between the Devas and the Asuras; in other words, as a mere phase in cosmic evolution . . . according to the epic itself, the Mahābhārata War is the expression of a state of tension between two ideal orders of beings, a moral type wherein the gods become incarnate as heroic individuals and an immoral or rather unmoral type which it is the object of the former to destroy. This conflict is an eternal recurrence, a phenomenon assuming in the space-time continuum the most diverse forms and aspects. The *Mahābhārata* thus becomes the type or the archetype of all wars or conflicts of the past, the present or the future."[6]

In the *Vana Parva* this is very clearly brought out where the anti-gods persuade Duryodhana—imprisoned by the Gandharvas and in chagrin determined to commit suicide—not to die, for in that case their cause is a lost one. They also tell Duryodhana that the *Daityas, Dānavas* and *Rākshasas* have incarnated among the *kshatriyas* in order to help the Dhārtarāshtras conquer the Pāndavas who embody the godly forces. That is why the fact that Vyāsa extends the concept of the *amshāvatarana* to include even minor characters becomes so significant. It shows how seriously the poet took this aspect of the *kāvya* he had composed. To quote Sukthankar again, "It should not be imagined that the account of the cosmic character of the *Mahābhārata* is in any sense an 'interpolation'. It may have been an afterthought; but even this afterthought is sufficiently early and deeply ingrained in the texture of the epic. This projection on to a cosmic background raises our epic story at once to a much higher level of thought, giving it for one thing, linguistic and ideological continuity with the Vedic antiquity. It stamps the epic at the same time as the artistic expression of a primordial experience, which, as C.J. Jung puts it, 'derives its existence from the hinterland of man's mind-that suggests the abyss of time separating us from pre-human ages or evokes a superhuman world of contrasting light and darkness.'"[7]

This particular section 209 has as many as 38 *shlokas* that are suspected interpolations, but all of them add to the reader's delight, being related to the description of Yudhishthira's coronation and the Vidura-Kuntī encounter:

"The city was ablaze with curiosity.
As they proceeded, their sight dispelling
all grief and sorrow, those tigers among men
heard, on all sides, peals of joy and welcome
from the ever-loyal citizens."

In another interpolation, we have a vivid picture of Gāndhārī meeting Draupadī as she arrives, and is dramatically ominous:

"Even as she hugged lotus-eyed
Pānchālī, Gāndhārī thought:
"She will be cause of my sons' deaths."—209.43

Thus the fatalistic quality of Draupadī is emphasised and one is reminded of Priam welcoming Helen into Troy.

Another significant development is Bhīma fading into the background. Dhritarāshtra tells Yudhishthira, while advising him to shift to Khāndavaprastha, "Arjuna will protect you" (209.54) which is a far cry from 203.13 where Duryodhana opined that without Bhīma Arjuna is not even worth one-fourth of Karna! This is clearly a deliberate heightening of Arjuna's role by the poet, which receives a tremendous boost in section 216 onwards that Vyāsa devotes wholly to Odysseus-Arjuna's wanderings and amorous victories.

The entire account of Yudhishthira's coronation is considered an interpolation by the editors of the Critical Edition. Besides the richly rewarding description of the ceremony, this portion also provides some more information about Khāndavaprastha. In 209.75-76, Dhritarāshtra tells Yudhishthira and Krishna that it used to be the capital of the Purus at the time of Pururavā, Āyu, Nahusha and Yayāti but thereafter it was razed to the ground by the sages because of the greed of Budha's son. The reference is to the killing of Pururavā by sages, whom he attacked for seizing their golden sacrificial vessels, as the Haiheyas had done with the Bhrigus. In that case, it is not clear how Āyu, Nahusha and Yayāti continued to rule there, unless Dhritarāshtra means to say that the capital was abandoned after Yayāti disinherited all his elder sons in favour of Puru, who might have set up his capital elsewhere. But the reference to its being the capital of the Purus would rule this out as well. The only possible explanation would be that the capital shifted to Hastināpura from Khāndavaprastha after the former was established by Hasti. According to the *Purānas,* however, Pururavā founded the lunar dynasty at Pratishthāna, adjacent to Prayāga, quite a distance from Khāndavaprastha.

It is significant that the Pāndavas are led by Krishna to this place and it is with his guidance that a new capital takes shape, called Indraprastha. It is interesting to study how Krishna gradually looms larger and larger over the Pāndavas' destiny right from the day of the *svayamvara,* and how his presence can be felt more and more in the epic. Thus, in 209.64, Krishna keeps pressing Dhritarāshtra to hasten the coronation after he has announced the decision. Again, it is only with Krishna's consent that the Pāndavas agree to return to Hastināpura. Some interpolator, not appreciating Vyāsa's restraint in never indulging in any display of Krishna's divine attributes, added *shlokas* 81 to 84 where he is made to intercede with Indra to send Vishvakarmā for constructing a palace to match Indra's court itself.

We now get a botanical catalogue which is extremely rare in the epic, for, unlike Vālmīki, Vyāsa does not usually have time for observing nature for her own sake. Prof. Lal presents a curious medley where Sanskrit and English terms are cheek by jowl, creating quite a confused reader-response:

"Groves of mango, hog-plum,
Kadamba, ashoka,
  And sweet-smelling champak,
Punnāga, nāga flowers,
  and bread-fruit trees; sāl trees;
palmyra, tamāla, vakula,
  and the ketaka . . .
  amalakas, lodhras and ankolas;
Rose-apples; trumpet-flower trees;
  kubjakas, atimuktas,
red-oleanders; coral trees. . . ."—209.95, 99, 97, 98

Yudhishthira addresses Krishna as their "household deity", again an obvious interpolation, so out-of-character. Kuntī also speaks in the same manner and makes him promise to keep the Pāndavas in mind. She is made to speak very much like a follower of the medieval Vaishnava *bhakti*-cult, totally out of character. Before leaving, Krishna advises them to pay attention to what Nārada will tell them in the near future, looking forward to section 210.

In section 210, after a long gap, we find Janamejaya surfacing once more, inevitably with a spate of queries, a couple of which appeal to all readers:

"How was their dharma-patni Draupadī
  able to serve them all with equal care?
How is it that they did not fall out
  over their one wife, Krishnā?"—210.2-3

There is an elaborate panegyric on Nārada's encyclopaedic knowledge from *shloka* 10 to 25, which is quite unnecessary and rightly omitted by the Bhandarkar editors, for Vyāsa is pre-eminently business-like in his narration and never indulges in padding. Nārada narrates the fascinating story of how Sunda and Upasunda, *Asuras* of Hiranyakashipu's lineage, slew each other out of jealousy over the *apsarā* Tilottamā. Since they had the boon that they could be slain only by each other, Brahmā had Vishvakarmā create Tilottamā,

"There was no part of her lovely body
that did not,
by superabundance of beauty,
dazzle and delight the eye. . . .
Because every little *tila*, every little part of her
was adazzle with *uttama*,
the finest gems,
Pitāmaha Brahmā named her Tilottamā."—213.16, 18

In order to see her, Shiva grew a head in each of the four directions, while Indra sprouted a thousand large and inflamed eyes all over himself (an instance of mythification to explain away the disfiguring marks of the vulva he had been cursed with by Gautama for seducing Ahalyā). It is, therefore, not at all clear how these two deities alone are said to have maintained their composure unless this refers to their not turning their heads, like the other gods, to follow her circumambulation. Brahmā alone remained with his eyes fixed—but, then, he already had four heads and had no need to sprout any more! Tilottamā approached the *Asuras* draped in a single brief piece of red cloth (we now know the inspiration behind Indian film actresses' dresses), and in the ensuing fight between themselves for possessing her, Sunda and Upasunda killed each other.

Nārada puts this forward as a warning to the Pāndavas, who evolve a rule that Draupadī would live with each of them exclusively for a year by turn. During that period, if their privacy was disturbed by any brother, he would be exiled. Vyāsa has been constantly working towards this since the *svayamvara*. First, he ensured that all the brothers jointly marry Draupadī, so that there would be no disunity among them born of frustrated desire. Then, through Nārada, he ensured that joint-husbanding would not breed dissension, by establishing a system of exclusive-occupation-by-turn.

According to the Critical Edition, the part of *shloka* 30, referring to the one-year period of Draupadī's cohabitation with each brother, is not authentic. In that case, the condition would simply be that none of the brothers should intrude when one of them was secluded with Draupadī. The original phrase is *sahāsīna* (sitting together), which could be interpreted to mean "cohabitation" or "secluded with".

The other controversy is over the duration of the proposed exile for the intruding brother. The Critical Edition's reading is twelve years, while the Southern recensions consistently speak of twelve *months.* It makes little sense to exile a brother during the fledgling condition of their kingdom for as long as twelve years. Possibly, this change of months to years was fostered by the later exile of all the Pāndavas for twelve years and the fact that so much happens to Arjuna, including the marriages with Ulūpī and Chitrāngadā, their sons' births and the abduction of Subhadrā. The further condition of celibacy that is tagged-on is interpreted with admirable sophistry by Ulūpī to enable Arjuna to have a gay time with all the women who solicit him and catch his fancy.

Section 215 once again highlights Arjuna who places public welfare and the reputation of Yudhishthira as a king before his private comfort. He decides to accept exile rather than let a Brahmin's cows be stolen because Draupadī and Yudhishthira are in seclusion in the armoury. Yudhishthira seeks to dissuade him by putting forward a subtle argument:

"No fault attaches if a younger brother
enters a room where an elder brother
and his wife are together;
but an elder brother goes against dharma
if he disturbs the privacy
of a younger brother and his wife."—215.32

Arjuna, however, is no sophist. He wisely insists on observing the rule in word and spirit since to break it would establish a dangerous precedent that might ultimately lead to fatal dissension. What he says has a familiar ring:

"You yourself have taught me",
Arjuna said, "that dharma
is not practised by splitting hairs. . . ."—215.34

The subtle, hair-splitting aspect of dharma will come up again and again in the epic, climaxing in the baffling inactivity of Bhīshma during the public disrobing of Draupadī by Duhshāsana and again to make Drona lay down his arms. Prof. Lal, in his notes to 215.12, raises an interesting query:

" . . . difficult to explain is why Arjuna refuses to accept Yudhishthira's forgiveness and prefers exile. Could it be because, under the terms of the agreement between the brothers, it will take him three years to have physical relations with Draupadī, and the twelve-years' exile at least gives him freedom to embark on a series of fascinating amours?"

That is very probable indeed, with the only objection lying in 284.30 where the rule specifies celibacy. Arjuna raises the same objection when Ulūpī pleads with him to satisfy her desire, but he capitulates with remarkable alacrity when she points out that the vow of continence is only with reference to Draupadī. In this case we do not see Arjuna averse at all to splitting hairs in practising dharma! It offers a fascinating and hitherto unsuspected insight into his character.

References

1. Bhattacharya (2005) p. 101.
2. Recent press reports reveal that the practice is prevalent in Punjab to avoid partitioning of holdings and because of the acute scarcity of nubile girls as a result of indiscriminate female foeticide. "Modern Draupadis", *Times of India*, 7.8.2005 p.8. Also http://videos.sify.com/Tribes-in-India-still-follow-age-old-custom-of-polyandry-ANI-watch-jiqoafhddgf.html
3. Mani (1975), p. 549. He does not provide the reference to the source of this story. Subramaniam (1967), pp. 46-47. A. Purushothaman traces it to Ezhuttacchan's Malayalam version, *Sri Mahabharata Kilippattu* (1500-1600 AD).
4. Sumitra Bai (1991), p.253).
6. *Prakriti khanda,* 14.54-57, *Krishna Janma khanda* 116.22-23.
6. *On the Meaning of the Mahābhārata,* p.62-63.
7. Ibid. pp. 66, 67-68.

17

The Sambhava Parva-IX

Arjuna's Amours and Khāndava in Flames

Section 216 recounts the first of Arjuna's amorous escapades when infatuated Ulūpī abducts the redoubtable hero. The episode brings out some interesting facets of Arjuna's character. After his usual rituals, as he is about to emerge from the river, Arjuna is whisked away by Ulūpī "inflamed with love for him" to the underwater realm of the Nāgas. However, with the same single-minded concentration that he had displayed during Drona's archery test, Arjuna calmly sets about performing the *agnihotra* rituals that the abduction had interrupted. It is only after finishing these rites that he allows himself to react to the incident. The result is that

"the god Agni was greatly pleased,
seeing Dhananjaya-Arjuna
so devoted in his cause."—216.15

This is one of the links between this section and section 225 where Agni approaches Arjuna and Krishna for assistance in consuming the Khāndava forest and gifts them celestial weapons.

Ulūpī is the daughter of the Nāga Kauravya of Airāvata's lineage, whm we recall from the list of snakes reeled out by Sauti in the *Āstīka* sub-*parva*. With true serpentine guile, she gets around Arjuna's objection that he is vowed to celibacy. She interprets the condition prescribed by the Pāndavas to mean that for twelve years the offending brother would deprive himself of cohabitation with Draupadī, and thus be a *brahmachārī* with respect to her alone. Realising that this may not be very convincing sophistry, she urges the "large-eyed hero" that he should look upon her request in the light of his duty to succour the suffering, as she is sorely afflicted by Ananga. Then, she swiftly changes her ground in true womanly fashion to appeal to his heroism and suffer a sacrifice of his dharma if need be:

> "If you help me, your dharma
> will not suffer. O Arjuna,
> even if it should a little,
> Much greater will be your merit
> for saving me."—216.26-27

The appeal again shifts with disconcerting rapidity to blackmail, cheek by jowl with proffered incentives:

> "If you do not take my love,
> I will kill myself.
> O mahā-muscled hero, earn merit
> Of the finest dharma by saving my life."—216.30

Is it to be wondered that Arjuna, "keeping dharma in mind",

> "did all in his power to
> satisfy the daughter of the lord of the Nāgas."—216.33

Arjuna leaves the palace of Kauravya the next morning and gains a boon to conquer all amphibious creatures from "chaste Ulūpī" that comes in extremely handy in the next adventure with the crocodiles. The appellative "*sādhvī*" concerning Ulūpī is very interesting, particularly as it is used for the first time only after Arjuna has gratified her desire for sexual union. This indicates her new status as Arjuna's wife, though no formal rituals were observed, in the Gandharva fashion, hence she is *sādhvī.* The son born to her is named Irāvān who will be killed in the Kurukshetra war like the other sons of the Pāndavas.

The relevance of dharma in Arjuna's capitulation to Ulūpī's

pleas is not a hypocritical or sophistic allusion for justifying fornication. The concept being propounded has its roots in Hindu philosophical thought, which saw Man as embodying the instinct of aggression, as out-going, with Woman as the yielding, inward-going counterpart. The typical expression of this truth was in marriage-by-abduction, which the *Kshatriyas* gloried in and which Arjuna will adopt for Subhadrā. It was, therefore, for the man to solicit and for the woman to give in. For the same reason, the scripture provided that if nature's demands were so powerful as to reverse woman's inward-going and make her approach a man in violation of her natural reticence, taking on, as it were, a certain "manliness" in this aggressive demanding of sexual union, then in such cases it would be gross *adharma,* for the man to refuse. It was Arjuna's duty to respond to such an unusual phenomenon forthwith, particularly as such soliciting was always for begetting a child. To refuse would be to invite the sin of infanticide. Nowhere do we find any condemnation, therefore, of a woman sexually soliciting anyone for this purpose, be it Sharmishthā, Kuntī, Mādrī, Hidimbā or Ulūpī. When such a request is made purely for the purposes of sexual pleasure, i.e. lust, there is no sin in refusing. That is why we find Arjuna refusing to oblige Urvashī in the *Vana Parva,* but acquiescing here in the case of Ulūpī. In the former, woman is violating her dharma by becoming a slave of lust, which is fruitless, barren, self-destroying and, therefore, condemnable. In the latter instance, woman is becoming aggressive in contravention of her normal instincts in response to the deepest call of her nature, viz. to beget children. Unfortunately, in Ulūpī's case it seems to be special pleading because nowhere in the text does she advance this justification (needing a son). The southern recension provides this in a passage in which she is said to be recently widowed, her husband having been killed by Garuda. She and her father desperately need a male issue and that is why she approaches Arjuna.

Arjuna's next adventure is the reverse of the Ulūpī episode. Now it is he who falls in love with Chitrāñgadā, princess of Manipura. This is "Manilura" in the Critical Edition which, curiously, becomes "Manipura" in the *Ashvamedha Parva* for

Arjuna's confrontation with Babhruvāhana. "Manilura" is located in the deep south, nowhere near today's Manipur in the north-east. There are several ballads in Tamil that give Arjuna a couple of amazonian Tamil brides and make Chitrāṅgadā a Pāndya princess, which is why we find significant space suddenly devoted to the heroics of the Pāndya king in the *Drona Parva.* We are not told anything of Chitrāṅgadā's reactions, however.

Tagore metamorphosed this eleven-*shloka* incident into a superb drama of human emotions with profound psychological and philosophical dimensions. His Chitrāṅgadā is infatuated with Arjuna, who rejects her masculine, soldierly garb and plainness. She propitiates the love god to gift her irresistible beauty, which ensnares Arjuna. But this is not love. The passion of lust abates and Arjuna again seeks out that very princess whose plainness he had rejected. Prof. Lal's preface is a good lesson in what can happen if we approach this portion of the epic via Tagore. He writes:

> "Though Arjuna has many amours he has only one love-affair. The infatuated Nāga princess Ulūpī solicits him; he graciously obliges. King Chitravāhana's daughter Chitrāṅgadā—Tagore has a striking play about her—is also obliged when similarly stricken. . . . The only time Arjuna himself takes the initiative in love is with Krishna's sister Subhadrā."

The text, however, does not bear this out at all. 217.16, describing Arjuna's reaction to his first sight of Chitrāṅgadā, says:

> "Wandering in the city
> one day he chanced to see
> Chaitravāhinī-Chitrāṅgadā, lovely-thighed beauty.
> Desire filled him."

It is Arjuna who begs the king to give him his daughter in marriage. Vyāsa does not bring Chitrāṅgadā into the picture to speak a single word. Nor does he give the slightest hint that she is enamoured of him.

It is interesting to see how effective Ulūpī's argument against the vow of celibacy has been. Arjuna seems to erase this wholly from his consciousness. We never find him referring to it hereafter. Obviously, Ulūpī's plea that the vow was with reference to Draupadī alone impressed itself indelibly on Arjuna's mind. We notice in him a singular freedom and lightness, as if a great load has been taken off and he has been freed from restraining bonds. For instance, never again do we find him devoutly engaged in *agnihotra* rituals. Ulūpī seems to have swept away all semblances of his self-imposed *brahmacharya* in the irresistible flood of her eloquent sophistry and ardent passion.

The reference to *putrikā* in 217.24 is a link in the causal chain that culminates in Arjuna being killed by his son by Chitrāñgadā. It is Babhruvāhana alone, of all the Pāndava progeny, who does not participate in the Kurukshetra war, possibly because his right of succession is to the throne of his maternal grandfather under the *putrikā* custom. A similar episode is to be found in the *Rāmāyana* where Bharata is the inheritor of his matrilineal kingdom. That is why he spends so much time away from Ayodhyā with his maternal uncle. This was the condition based on which Dasharatha was given Kaikeyī in marriage. Mantharā and Kaikeyī's plot was to change the *putrikā* agreement into a claim for succeeding to the throne in the paternal line. It is also notable that with Chitrāñgadā Arjuna spends the longest period (three years) among his three amours. And it is she who comes into his life again so very unexpectedly when her son has achieved what all the armies and heroes of the Kauravas had failed to do: kill Arjuna. It is in the same episode that Ulūpī reappears to resurrect her husband. Arjuna advises Chitrāñgadā to join him when Yudhishthira's *rājasūya* ceremony takes place, but she never turns up there. She only comes to the court for the Ashvamedha sacrifice and stays on, living amicably with Ulūpī, Subhadrā and Pānchālī, till the Pāndavas and Draupadī depart on the final journey.

After leaving Chitrāñgadā, thanks to Ulūpī's boon, Arjuna rids five holy spots of the crocodiles infesting the lakes, because of which the *tīrthas* were deserted. The crocodiles, in typical purānik fashion, are *apsarās* cursed by a Brahmin they had tried to seduce.

It is after this that Arjuna and Krishna meet and their unique companionship begins. In 220.5 Vyāsa stresses their being avatars of Nara and Nārāyana, the two primeval rishis. Raivataka mountain, where the Vrishni revels are held, was Balarāma's special domain. To win the hand of Revati, he had won this area from the usurpers of her father's throne. That story forms a fascinating study in the temporal dimension. Revata, father of Revati, is one of the world's earliest kings and of gigantic stature; so is his daughter. They return to earth from Brahmā's realm to find that aeons have gone by and men are like insects before them. Interested readers can look up *Harivamsa* and the *Bhāgavata Purāna* for details of how Balarāma literally cuts Revati down to size. Rajshekhar 'Parashuram' Basu wrote a delightfully humorous retelling of this, "Revati gains a husband."[1]

The curious feature about the Arjuna-Subhadrā affair is that there is, again, not a single hint that Arjuna's emotions are reciprocated by Subhadrā.[2] Indeed, from what Krishna says, it seems that the hero who won Draupadī may not necessarily be Subhadrā's choice in a *svayamvara*:

"Who knows how my sweet sister
  will choose in a svayamvara ?
The best advice I can give is—
  Run off with her."—221.23

Arjuna first gets Yudhishthira's approval to this plan. Notice that no objection regarding his vow is raised, nor are we told of Draupadī's reaction—if at all she was consulted. Actually, the vow seems to have disappeared with Ulūpī. The alliance is a crucial one indeed, for it cements the Nara-Nārāyana bond through more mundane bonds of kinship. The fact that Subhadrā is Kuntī's brother Vasudeva's daughter does not seem to stand in the way of the marriage, although it comes very much within the prohibited degrees enumerated by Manu. Arjuna and Subhadrā are first cousins on the cognate side. The massive dowry that accompanies the bride adds immeasurably to the Pāndavas' strength. In Krishna's speech to the Vrishnis, dissuading them from attempting to rescue Subhadrā, we also get the first instance of the brilliant pleading which is his forte and will be seen again and again when he pleads with the Kauravas, with Karna and finally in the glorious climax of the *Gītā*. Krishna rubs into them that Arjuna is invincible and they must not risk tarnishing their reputation by fighting with him: "no harm compromising", he advises. He also feels that abduction was the right thing because the marriage customs are defective (buying a bride; the uncertainty of *svayamvara*; receiving a bride like an animal) and that Arjuna had resorted to abduction knowing these defects. So here we have a bit of the social critic in Krishna that is so prominently brought out in the *Bhāgavata Purāna* in his abolition of the worship of Indra, his breaking of so many social norms and in the very fact of his being given the supreme place of honour despite not being a king. It is amusing to watch how all the fury of Balarāma's

"Watch me! Today, all by myself,
  I will rid the earth of all Kauravas.
Never, never will I swallow
  Arjuna's insult !"—222.31

is abruptly muted after Krishna has spoken. This also brings out Krishna's complete control over the Vrishnis, only hinted at through such incidents in the epic, but brought out in detail in the *Harivamsa* and the *Bhāgavata Purāna*. Besides all this, Arjuna's abduction parallels Krishna's of Rukminī, thus maintaining the Nara-Nārāyana parallelism. Further, the political importance of the alliance is made quite clear:

"The Yādava ocean of gifts—mingled
  with the Pāndava ocean of wealth—
the whole brimmed over,
  to the dismay of their foes."—223.57

The Draupadī-Arjuna encounter, their first meeting after twelve long years, is a memorable one, for it shows us Draupadī acting coquettishly for the first and last time:

"Kuntī's son, why here?
Go to the daughter of the Sātvatas!
A second knot always weakens the first,
however tightly knotted, doesn't it?"—223.16-17

This is her way of reproaching him for not having observed the vow of celibacy. Arjuna, failing to mollify her, has Subhadrā approach her dressed as a milkmaid. Subhadrā tactfully touches Draupadī's feet and calls herself her maid, which breaks the ice. Surely Draupadī was sorely disappointed that the man who actually won her amongst so many royal suitors had finally come to her with his heart already another's? Saoli Mitra has brought this out most sensitively on stage in her play, *Nāthavati Anāthavat.*

Section 223 gives us the birth of Abhimanyu first, showing the importance it held for the dynasty and then of Draupadī's sons, stating that they were born at intervals of a year. This is contradicted by 223.83, according to which Shrutakarman is born after Arjuna's return from exile. If the exile was for twelve years, this is impossible and Shrutakarman will have been the youngest of them all. On the other hand, if it was a twelve-month exile, Arjuna's turn with Draupadī would have been due on his return. In that case, *shlokas* 23-34 in section 219, where Arjuna sees his son Babhruvāhana and tells Chitrāṅgadā to rejoin him at the time of the *rājasūya yajña,* would be interpolations, as also 217.26-27 according to which Arjuna stays three years with Chitrāṅgadā till she has a son. These are omitted in the Critical Edition. This is also one of the few places (223.81-85) where the reasons for giving the Pāndava progeny their names is given: Prativindhya (like the Vindhya mountains in blocking foes), Sutasoma (as Bhima had performed a thousand *soma yajnas*), Shrutakarmā (being born after diamed Arjuna returned from heroic exploits), Shatānīka (named after an illustrious ancestor) and Shrutasena (born under Krittikā asterism like Kārtikeya/Shrutasena the excellent general).

Section 224, verses 21-26, affords us a rare of prevailing courtly mores during a picnic. Draupadī and Subhadrā are explicitly described as "wine-flushed", while the other ladies are "teetering under the influence of wine", drinking, laughing, dancing, singing and even fighting amongst themselves—hardly a fundamentalist's delight! But, then, the *Mahābhārata* is no place for one who is searching for material to support dogmas. This epic celebrates humanity in all its richness, variety and enjoyment of life, having no place for prudishness. Arjuna and Krishna do not take part in this intoxicated revelry. They quietly slip away to a secluded spot and chat.

Into these sylvan surroundings, heavy with sensuousness and lassitude, steps the discordant and grotesque figure of Agni, summoning the heroes back to the world of strife and pitiless destruction:

> "He looked like a massive Sāla-tree;
> his skin was burnt gold;
> his body seemed to glow
> blue-and-yellow;
> his width was the same size
> as his height.
> His hair was matted;
> he was in rags
> but he shone like the early sun,
> his eyes were like lotus-leaves;
> a reddish blaze radiated from him,
> continuously."—224.31-32

This transcreation does not follow the original faithfully. In line 3, the reference is to "beard" not "body", and the colour is *haripiṅgala* "tawny yellow", not "blue-and-yellow". Lines 4-5 should read, "his height and thickness were well proportioned". In line 11 the blaze or aura is described as *piṅgala,* i.e. "reddish-brown" or "tawny" and not just "reddish". In line 8, the word, 'rags' is one of the meanings of the original *chīravāsa,* but another sense, more appropriate in the case of this Agni disguised as a Brahmin, is "dressed in bark". Van Buitenen curiously renders this as "black-garbed", which neither fits in with the subject, nor is justified by the text. One of the readings of line 10 refers to the *face* as like a lotus-leaf, not the eyes. Agni's request is a peculiar one:

"I am a hungry Brahmin. I eat—and eat!
Vāshaneya-Krishna, Pārtha-Arjuna,
give me something to eat,
for I am hungry."—225.2

Agni states that his indigestion—for this is his ailment—can be cured only by devouring the Khāndava forest which is protected by Indra because his friend Takshaka Nāga, dwells there. Here are sown the seeds of the enmity between Pāndava and Nāga that leads to Takshaka's killing Parikshit, Arjuna's grandson, and culminates in the mighty snake-holocaust of Janamejaya. Then, as now, Takshaka somehow escapes the destruction that envelops all others. In both the incidents, it is Indra who tries to protect Takshaka alone of all the Nāgas. The roots of this peculiar friendship have not been given anywhere in the *Purānas*, except for the solitary clue in the *Āstīka* sub-*parva* where Indra sends down rain to save the *Nāgas* from being burnt up when Garuda flies too near the sun while carrying them on his back. Of course, through the word *nāga*' itself they are very closely linked to Indra, for it stands for "elephant", "clouds" and also "snakes". In the *Nāgas* entwining themselves in the tail of Indra's horse Uchchaihshravas yet another link is forged. The relationship is not to be interpreted in naturalistic terms, but as a myth and a symbol of a piece with the eternal confrontation between water and fire of which Khāndava forest becomes a typical instance.

Thanks to Janamejaya's curiosity, we get to know why Agni is so persistent in his efforts to consume this forest. Readers of the Critical Edition and of van Buitenen's translation are unnecessarily deprived of this relevant and interesting data as it has been omitted as inauthentic. Agni's all-consuming hunger has its source in the *Pauloma* sub-*parva*, where Bhrigu curses him to devour everything, whether clean or unclean. But the dyspepsia is due to King Shvetakī who performed so many sacrifices that even the priests deserted him, fed-up with the smoke. Determined to continue, he propitiated Shiva who asked Durvāsā to help the king complete his hundred-year sacrifice, at the end of which the king finally enters his palace. Here, after *shloka* 58, three *shlokas* have not been transcreated. In Ganguli these run:

"That exalted monarch then entered his own palace, worshipped by exalted Brahmanas conversant with the Vedas, eulogised by chanters of panegyrical hymns and congratulated by the citizens. Such was the history of that best of monarchs, the royal sage Shvetaki, who, when the time came, ascended to heaven, having won great renown on earth and accompanied by the Ritviks and the Sadasyas that had helped him in life. Vaishampāyana continued, at that sacrifice of Shvetaki, Agni had drunk clarified butter for twelve years."

Agni approaches Brahmā with his problem:

"Rājā Shvetakī has over-fed me
  in his yajna.
I do not feel well.
  My radiant strength is waning."

Brahmā's reply reveals a contradiction. In 225.44 Shiva lays down a precondition for helping Shvetakī: he must pour ghee-libations into the fire for twelve years. When he successfully does this, Shiva sends him Durvāsā for concluding the super-*yajña* extending over a hundred years. Yet, Brahmā in 225.63 only refers to twelve, not one hundred and twelve years, of incessant ghee-libations as the cause of Agni's indigestion. The only explanation would be that it was this unrelieved pouring of libations throughout the twelve years of Shvetakī's test that brought about this condition in Agni, and that this was not repeated during the ensuing hundred year *yajña*; or that the hundred year plan was reduced to twelve years. Brahmā's prescription is a very simple one: high animal and vegetable protein diet, free from "ghee". Unfortunately, all the denizens of the forest unite to put out the fire each of the seven times Agni tries to cure himself (225.74). Nowhere in the *Purānas* do we come across so indefatigable a *yajamāna* as Shvetakī who makes even the Brahmins, whose very calling is *yajñas*, refuse to perform any further sacrifices, and ultimately sickens the very sacrificial flame with the fervour of his oblations!

The frustrated and dyspeptic Agni turns once more inevitably to Brahmā and it is in 226.4-5 that Brahmā gives us an explicit avowal of the fact that Krishna and Arjuna are the incarnations of the divine duo, Nārāyana and Nara. It will be recalled that the very first *shloka* of the epic, the invocation, contains obeisances to these two. Prof. Lal writes in his preface to the 25th fascicule:

> "The interlinking of the natural and supernatural states of experience is one way of interpreting the compound; another, the more commonly found in the *tīkās,* is to stress the indissolubility, in Hindu dharma, of the relationship between man and divinity. Nara, the human, and Nārāyana, the divine, are two yet one; Nara is the divine in the human, and Nārāyana the human in the divine. Shorn of erudite philosophical exegesis, it adds up to another variation on the *tat-tvam-asi* theme."

As already mentioned, the Krishna-Arjuna relationship is a unique one. They prefer each other's company to participating in the picnic revelry with the women (224.27-29). Arjuna falls asleep narrating his experiences to Krishna, who eagerly greets him on awakening (220.11-15). Krishna has no hesitation in suggesting that Arjuna abduct his sister, and lends him his own chariot and horses for the purpose, besides persuading the Vrishnis not to take offence at the incident. In the *Udyoga Parva* we come across a unique picture of this relationship as narrated by Sanjaya in section 58. He finds Krishna and Arjuna somewhat inebriated; Krishna lying with his feet on Arjuna's lap, while Arjuna has one foot in Draupadī's lap and the other in Satyabhāmā's! Krishna, it seems, prefers Arjuna to Satyabhāmā and feels no hesitation in having his wife minister to his brother-in-law and soul-companion.

The Khāndava genocidal holocaust raises serious problems. How are we to reconcile the ruthless indiscriminate slaughter of all living creatures, in violation of *Kshatriya* norms of hunting and war, with the character of Arjuna? We recall, then, that one of his names is "Bībhatsu" (dreadful-deed-doer). On the face of it, this seems to be an account of the clearing of a forest for obtaining more cultivable land for the new kingdom of the

Pāndavas. Naturally, all wild animals inhabiting it would have to perish. But, it is quite clear that there are human beings living in it as well. There is the *Dānava* architect Maya, the bird-woman and her children by a Brahmin and, most important, the *Nāgas.* Khāndava is described as situated near the Yamunā. It was from this river that Krishna had banished Kāliya *Nāga* and his entire clan during his youth. Iravati Karve sees this as the colonising campaign of the Aryans, uprooting the forest-dwelling tribes, wholly changing their very habitat and systematically destroying them as a race. Encroaching on fellow-*Kshatriyas*' lands was prohibited. Though they could be conquered and tribute levied, no *Kshatriya* house could be deprived of its kingdom. Expansion was possible only by picking on the forest surrounding the new Pāndava capital, which happened to be a *Nāga* abode under Takshaka. Iravati Karve writes:

> "This plan, it seems, did not go counter to the Kshatriya code. The code applied only to the Aryan Kshatriyas and not to outsiders. . . . The land was usurped after a massacre, a massacre which is praised as a valorous deed. This was because the victims were not Kshatriyas or their Aryan subjects. All the high-sounding morality of the Kshatriya code was limited to their own group. Here again Krishna and Arjuna played the familiar role of the conquering settler. . . . The sole aim was the acquisition of land and the liquidation of the Nāgas. But the cruel objective was defeated. Just as Hitler found it impossible to wipe out a whole people, so did the Pāndavas. All they gained through this cruelty were the curses of hundreds of victims and three generations of enmity." (*Yuganta,* pp. 144, 146)

K.M. Munshi adopts a similar approach in his unfinished epic novel *Krishnāvatāra,* while Dipak Chandra takes it further in his Bengali novel *Agnigarbha Khāndav,* seeing in it a foreshadowing of the Kashmir insurgency.

Takshaka's son Ashvasena is saved by his mother, though she dies in the attempt, and by Indra's intervention. In the *Karna Parva* he launches himself on an arrow that Karna shoots at

Arjuna who kills the serpent. Takshaka himself tries to slay Arjuna during the Kurukshetra war by poising himself on the tip of the arrow Ashvatthāmā shoots, but is foiled by Krishna. He wins sweet revenge by killing Arjuna's grandson Parikshit, but makes a powerful enemy in Uttanka by stealing the earrings he is bringing for his guru's wife. If it had not been for Uttanka, Janamejaya would never have known of Takshaka's involvement in his father's death and the second snake holocaust would not have taken place. Here, at the very end of the *Ādi Parva*, therefore, we once again pick up the thread of the very strong *Nāga* sub-theme that captures every reader at the beginning of the *Mahābhārata*. Yet, it is Irāvān, Arjuna's son by the Nāga princess Ulūpī, who rights so valiantly for the Pāndavas and is the first of their sons to die in the great war. Again, it is the *Nāga* king Āryaka, Kuntī's great-grandfather, who gifts Bhīma superhuman strength. Thus, the *Nāgas* are related to the Pāndavas. We notice, however, that it is the Takshaka clan of *Nāgas* which alone is inimical to the Kurus and that the Pāndavas bring this enmity upon themselves through the unwarranted massacre of the clan in Khāndava.

If, on the one hand, Khāndava-burning shows man's victory over Nature, on the other it recounts a father-son confrontation. Indra fights Arjuna with all the forces at his command and is gratified when his son counters all his attempts to quench the fire. The son is infuriated with his divine father when Indra enables Takshaka's son Ashvasena to escape by blinding Arjuna in a dust storm. Indra's clouds are dissipated by Arjuna's wind-weapon (once again it is either Bhīma or his father Vāyu who is Arjuna's strongest support). 229.29 has Indra lifting his thunderbolt against the two heroes, but nowhere do we find any description of what happens when the infallible *vajra* is flung. Instead, the succeeding *shloka* speaks of the other gods taking up their weapons on seeing Indra seize his thunderbolt; there is no reference to his *flinging* it. Arjuna frustrates Indra's next assault which takes the form of a shower of boulders, culminating in a mountain peak that he shatters into pieces with arrows so that:

"Fragments of the shattered peak
fell through the sky
like the sun, moon and planets
would fall if unloosed."—229.51

Krishna also joins in the carnage as the gods retire:

"Mangled by Krishna's chakra,
the Daityas, dripping
with their own fat and blood,
looked like sunset-streaked clouds."—230.8

The strong resemblance to the slaughter of the *Asuras* after the churning of the ocean (19.23-24) is reinforced by a celestial announcement declaring the heroic duo to be the divine *rishis* Nara and Nārāyana, who had also been responsible for the defeat of the titans in the battle over *amrita.* Indra rejoices on seeing the gods defeated by his son's prowess, and leaves Khāndava to its fiery fate.

The burning of Khāndava is one of the most vivid portions of the epic in visual terms. Vyāsa's description is gruesome and unsparingly so, faithfully catching all the agony and terror of the massive conflagration:

"His seven tongues surrounded
the forest, like the flames
of dissolution at yuga-end,
and he began licking the Khāndava.
O bull-brave Janamejaya!
He screamed and howled
as he circled the forest,
his storm-cloud-roars made
all the creatures tremble."—227.34-35

Vyāsa, however, does not rest content with such a generalised picture. He closes-in for detailed snapshots too, however horrifying:

"Some with burning limbs, some scorched,
some with eyeballs bursting into flame,
some reduced to ashes,
some wildly fleeing...
Some jumped high up,
biting their lower lips,
but dropped instantly back
into the raging fire below.
Some rolled on the ground,
wings twitching, eyes and claws
wrapped in the flames, slowly
roasting to their deaths."—228-5, 7-8

He goes further to dabble in gore, evoking the *vībhatsa rasa*:

"And the flames, fed with flesh,
blood and fat, swirled upwards
in circular smoky wreaths
touching the sky.
Incandescent, copper-eyed Agni,
flame-haired, flaming-tongued,
huge-mouthed god of fire Agni, . . .
Lapped up the ceaseless flow
Of bloody fat.
His face shone with delight,
with the satiety of all desires."—230.36-38

But it is not without its beauty:

"The burning forest, O Bharata,
looked like glittering Meru,
Indra of mountains,
lit up by dazzling sunbeams."—227.36
"Mangled by Krishna's chakra,
the Daityas, dripping
with their own fat and blood,
looked like sunset-streaked clouds."—230.8

There is, however, a third dimension to this conflagration. This is the eternal conflict between fire and water:

"Fire
Clashed
With rain,
Smoke
With cloud,
Fearful
Lightning
Flashed in the forest."—228.22
"So intense was the fire-heat of Jātaveda-Agni
however, that the shafts of rain
evaporated before they had a chance
to touch the forest."—228.20
"Howling winds from turbulent oceans
gathered huge masses
of clouds, and a torrential downpour
hit Khāndava.
Giant thunderclouds spat lightning,
and shattered the sky
with horrendous noise;"—229.14-15

Yet the very weapons with which Krishna and Arjuna drive away Indra's thunderclouds (the former's discus and mace; the latter's bow and chariot) are gifted by Varuna, the water deity! This hints at the basic unity underlying the surface conflict between the elements, without which creation itself could not have taken place. This unity is explicitly referred to in the invocation of the bird-woman Jaritāri and her children to Agni:

"You are the ātman of wind!
You are the body of all vegetation!
Earth and water are your yoni!...
You are the semen of water!
You are the sun sucking
the sap and liquids of the earth.
You return them as rain,

and all things grow.
All plants and green-leaved creepers
are born from you again and again,
O Agni,
the lakes and ponds,
the great ocean itself,
are born from you."—234.7, 16-17

In section 231, verses 23-30 their absentee father Mandapāla hymns Agni too, referring to him in *shloka* 27 as "You are the clouds flashing with lightning" and in *shloka* 29 as "Water depends on you/The universe depends on you'', thus stressing the underlying unity of apparent contraries that makes for creation.

In being identified as the father of all plants, Agni is being linked with Soma. The chariot that Arjuna receives was Soma's chariot in which he fought the *Dānavas*. The identification of two apparently opposing forces points to one of the basic truths of Hindu philosophy: it is the rain-clouds that harbour destructive lightning!

The *Iliad* presents an engrossing parallel to this eternal confrontation between fire and water. As Achilles is about to be swept away in the combined currents of the rivers Scamandros and Simois, Hephaestos steps in to consume the water with fire. The difference between the episodes in the *Iliad* and the *Mahābhārata* is also significant. In the former, the fight is between the deities. While it is in progress, Achilles is not even mentioned. But, in the Khāndava-burning the human involvement is complete and predominant. Indeed, here it is the deity who seeks human help and it is man who worsts the gods. The Khāndava-burning, lasting for fifteen long days (236.14), is, as Buddhadeb Bose points out[3] the apotheosis of human prowess. In his brilliant study of this episode, Basu draws attention to the argument between Draupadī and Yudhishthira in the *Vana Parva,* sections 28 and 29. Yudhishthira points out to the furious Draupadī that if violence were always answered by violence, chaos would be inevitable. After all, he continues, creation itself is the result of the union of two opposing forces: fire in man's semen and water in woman's womb. Similarly, it is through the united efforts of sun and rain that crops grow, trees fructify, plants flower. Man's cooking itself takes place through the union of fire and water.

The reference to Soma having used the ape-pennanted chariot to fight the titans is inexplicable. The famous *devāsura* war revolving round Soma had the titans supporting him against the gods who were fighting to get back the abducted Tārā for Brihaspati. Soma did not fight the titans. The reference could more appropriately have been either to Shiva or to Indra or Vishnu. Here, again, there is a parallel between father and son: Arjuna, like Indra, destroys *Daityas* and *Dānavas* using divine weapons from a celestial chariot.

The gifting of the celestial weapons is itself an extremely crucial episode. It is these weapons and this chariot that cause so much havoc in the great war, though Krishna does not use either the discus with an adamantine centre or the thundering mace Kaumodaki he receives from Varuna. Both these weapons are, of course, Vishnu's as well, thereby establishing implicitly the identity of Krishna and Vishnu. In the description of these weapons, however, there are a few slips in the translation.

In sections 226 and 227 Agni, Krishna and Arjuna are frequently called by their other names. Thus, Agni is referred to as Havyavāhana (226.1, 8), Hutāshana (227.1), Vibhāvasu (226.4), Pāvaka (226.17, 227.24). Krishna is called Mādhava (226.15), Achyuta (227.28), Hrishīkesha (227.30). Arjuna himself is repeatedly called Bībhatsu, which is wholly appropriate (226.10, 229.1) as he is engaged in so horrendous an enterprise.

Only six creatures escape from this holocaust, just as after the huge blood-letting on Kurukshetra just three on the Kaurava side and the five Pāndavas, Sātyaki and Yuyutsu are left alive. The six of Khāndava are: Takshaka's son Ashvasena, the asura-architect Maya who begs for refuge from Arjuna, and the four *shārngaka* birds. It is the last of these that excite considerable human interest despite the crude attempts of interpolators to turn them into actual birds afraid of rats and cats.

The Mandapāla-Jaritāri-Lapitā triangle has been metamorphosed into an exquisite love story by Subodh Ghosh in his *Bhārat Prem Kathā*[4] where he sees it as a conflict between lust and true love that finds fulfilment in offspring. The Mandapāla-Lapitā affair is purely impelled by lust. Mandapāla marries Jaritāri much in the same way as Jaratkāru weds Vāsuki's sister, just to beget sons to succour his ancestral manes. He leaves her for Lapitā once she is pregnant, but gets worried about his family on seeing Agni encompassing the forest in which they dwell. Hence he invokes Agni and persuades him to spare his family. In this invocation, he refers to Agni in his triple and eightfold forms (231.24). In his triple form, Agni is present in the earth, the heavens and the stomach, while his eightfold form is the earth, water, wind, sky, sun, moon, energy and the sacrificer. Van Buitenen glosses this as "the fires of the wife's quarters at the sacrifice, the Soma altar, the main altar, the hut of the Agnidhra priest, the *sadas* area, the rituals (*kratushu)* the *upāsad* rite and the ordinary fire".

The conversation between Jaritā and her four sons oscillates between the sublime and the ridiculous, between the human and the birdly conditions:

> "If we die, you can still have more children;
>   but if you die,
> there will be no one left
>   to redeem our race. . . .
> Do not do anything just because
>   you love us. If you survive
> our father who wants the realms of the gods
>   will be happy." (232.13, 15)

This rendering of *Shloka* 15 needs to be recast to read:

> "Abjure your love for us;
>   it will destroy our race.
> Our father's act,
>   producing us for his desire
> to attain high realms,
>   must not fail."

In a way, this is very akin to the sentiments of the Brahmin and his family as they face the crucial soul-rending moral choice in Ekachakra. But from these lofty heights we plummet:

"We are just lumps of flesh,
without any feathers. If we hide
in the hole, won't the rat
eat us up?" (232.19)

Yet, this too struggles up to somewhat higher plane:

"To be nibbled to death by a rat
is a shameful end.
But even the wise allow
the body's destruction in fire."—232.22

But in the very next *shloka* Vyāsa brings us down with a bump right inside bird psychology as Jaritāri or Jaritā (both forms are used in the narrative) strives to convince her sons that the rat has been carried away by a hawk but they refuse to believe since they have not seen it themselves. This is strongly reminiscent of Chaucer's technique in his *Nun's Priest's Tale* where he shifts from the human to the animal world and back again with bewildering rapidity, presenting the very acme of the mock-heroic. Vyāsa, of course, is not being comic at all, for his birds are facing, typically, a crucial moral choice. Jaritā is caught between the natural instinct to save herself and her love for her children. They, knowing that they cannot escape, show her that self-preservation is the highest dharma in this case, because it will enable her husband to achieve his aim of having progeny. In order to ensure that she leaves them, they deliberately slight her:

"It is not,
mother, that we think what you say
is not true. An agitated person
does not always act responsibly.
After all, what have we done for you?
You don't know who we are.
Why do you take such pains to save us?
Who are we to mean so much to you?"—232.11-12

The implacable ruthlessness of this coldly utilitarian logic seeks to sunder all bonds of affection so that the mother can fly away free. Yet, the children temper the harshness by urging her to seek out her husband to have more sons by him and by pointing out that, should they survive the fire, she can always return to them.

Once Jaritā has left, the four sons break out into a series of invocations to Agni that lifts them completely out of their physical forms into the same sphere as Upamanyu and Uttanka in the *Paushya* sub-*parva*. Indeed, in 234.11, they say, "We are rishis" and Agni recognises these chants as Vedic. Dr. S.N. Pradhan has pointed out[5] that *sūkta* 142 of *mandala* 10 of the *Rig Veda* addressed to Agni is composed by four 'Shārngas' named Jaritri, Drona, Sāriskrita and Stambamitra (the names differ very slightly in the epic version). He suggests that it must have been composed by them while trapped in the burning Khāndava forest. Dr. Pradhan argues that this shows that Vyāsa compiled the Vedas after the destruction of Khāndava forest, incorporating the *sŭkta* of the Shārngakas in the *Rig Veda,* along with compositions by Devāpi and Shāntanu (Mahābhīshaka). Agni spares them and grants them a boon. Immediately there is a sudden, totally unexpected anti-climax as these rishis chanting sublimely come out with the bathetic:

> "O Agni, cats in the forest
> make a habit of eating us.
> O Hutāshana! Destroy all of them."—234.24

Though bathetic, they do end on an eminently practical note, showing that, unlike the sages, they have not lost sight of the facts of everyday life in seeking the Ultimate Truth!

The next scene, however, brings us to the level of human emotions. At the moment of a tearful mother-sons reunion, Mandapāla arrives to be received in stony silence. His hurt is all the greater because, in coming to them, he has had to sacrifice the companionship of Lapitā:

"Who is the first-born ?''
 asked Mandapāla.
"Who next? Who is the third ?
 Who is the youngest?
My sadness speaks to you.
 Why don't you reply?
Oh, I know I deserted you . . .
 but I never found peace elsewhere."—235.22-23

Jaritā's response is exactly like Draupadī's to Arjuna when he returns with Subhadrā:

"Go to sweet-smiling Lapitā
 who is young and lovely.
What you didn't find in me,
 you must have found in her."—235.25

At this point Subodh Ghosh has Mandapāla speak of his realisation of the vast gulf between lust and love and that love finds its fulfilment in the bond that unites two lovers as parents of their children. In the epic, alas, the entire episode takes a completely different turn, much for the worse. Mandapāla breaks into a dull lecture on the proneness of wives to jealousy, hinting that it can invite unpleasant reprisals such as Arundhati's being turned into

 "a smoke-filmed star,
sometimes invisible, sometimes hidden,
 as if she was an evil sign."—235.29

This episode about Arundhati having been jealous of Vashishtha is not found in Hindu mythology. On the other hand, she is celebrated as the paradigm of wifely devotion, being made into a star precisely because of it along with her husband.

Mandapāla admits the cause of his pettishness in *shloka* 31:

"Even as you make fun of me now,
 Lapitā did when I left her."

He also puts forward the usual nauseating justification for his conduct: he had intercourse with Jaritā merely to beget sons, which is what she wanted; with Lapitā because he was attracted to her. According to him, in this he did no wrong and he simply cannot bear being made fun of by both women. His grievance is that when a woman becomes a mother, she cares even less for her husband. Around this sentiment Subodh Ghosh weaves his retelling of this story and has Mandapāla leave Jaritā because he feels neglected once the children arrive. Prof. Lal's comment on the episode in his Preface to fascicule 26 is telling:

> "One could expect great pathos and conflict from such a highly charged dramatic situation. Strangely, Vyāsa allows it to peter off into an inconsequential family rapprochement after Mandapāla launches into a silly Hindu lecture on the waywardness of women, and of wives in particular. Docile Jaritā, good Hindu wife, listens and accepts this not very profound bit of Freudian psychology, and Mandapāla, good Hindu husband, his prodigal conscience salved, emerges, alas, undisputed victor."

Agni, alas, emerges quite a revolting figure, for Vyāsa is ever uncompromising in painting the reality:

> "He drank up whole rivers
> of fat, blood, and marrow ;
> and was pleased, and he relaxed."—236.6

The last few *shlokas* of the section are very important. They record Indra's boon to Arjuna that all the god's divine weapons shall be his, but only after he has propitiated Shiva, which looks forward to the *Kirāta* section of the *Vana Parva,* indicating that Arjuna is not yet fit to hold those weapons. Krishna, characteristically, asks that his friendship with Arjuna be eternal. The Nara-Nārāyana duo's earthly union thus receives divine sanction, which might seem quite redundant but is a way of reinforcing in the mortal sphere a heavenly dispensation.

The Khāndava section ends as it had begun, with Arjuna and

Krishna wandering away to sit on the bank of an entrancing river. But this time they are not alone. The *Dānava* Maya accompanies them and the ensuing conversation will result in the building of the wondrous palace of the Pāndavas that is the cause of their misfortunes in the *Sabhā Parva.*

Yet, what was the use of this holocaust and building of an Indraprastha to rival Indra's court? After the great war, the Pāndavas immediately shift to Hastināpura and we hear not a word of Indraprastha (which was handed over to Krishna's great grandson Vajra) or its much-vaunted palace. What justification could there be for slaughtering so much life for so ephemeral an achievement? It is significant that Krishna and Arjuna are freed of the responsibility for the holocaust by making it appear as the desire of a Brahmin. Iravati Karve writes with typically acute perception:

> "For hardly ten years they had enjoyed the fabulous palace they had obtained by burning a great forest and butchering its inhabitants...No great ruling house is associated with Indraprastha. Except for the burning of Khāndava, no other story in Sanskrit literature is set in it. Indraprastha had no substance, it never took a definite form. Maya-sabhā was not only ill-omened; it was even more insubstantial than the city in which it was built. Born in violence, its dazzling demonic splendour turned out to be a fleeting dream." (*Yuganta,* p. 148)

And so ends the *Ādi Parva* of the *Mahābhārata,* with the Khāndava holocaust preparing us for the even greater sea of blood and gore that is to come. With the *Ādi Parva* we leave behind primeval myths and civilisation in its infancy. Hereafter we will be in the depths of court intrigue and devious politics. The Pāndavas have already lived their best days. What lies for them in the future is blood, agony, sweat and tears. With the *Ādi Parva* the innocence of mankind is also left behind and the drop of poison introduced by Kanika effectively curdles the fortunes of the entire Kuru race. All its mighty heroes and upright men cannot save them from the destruction towards which the Kanikan brains of Duryodhana and Shakuni propel them inexorably.

References

1. *Puranic Tales for Cynical People* (Indialog, 2005) pp. 107-20.
2. In the Southern recension Arjuna woos Subhadra disquised as a hermit whom Balarama houses as a guest and appoints Subhadra to serve him. The parallel with Kuntibhoja-Durvasa-Kunti is clear. The love affairs of Arjuna and Subhadra is elaborately described. There is nothing like this between Arujana and Draupadi.
3. *Mahabharater Katha,* chapter 10
4. P. Bhattacharya (2005)
5. *Chronology of Ancient India* pp. 167-68

18

Looking Back

James Fitzgerald, the translator of the critical text of the *Strī* and *Shānti Parvas* published in 2004, makes an extremely important point about the epic:

> "The Mahābhārata argued for a cultural revolution that was historically successful in several important ways. . . . I have come to see the Mahābhārata not simply as an ancient monument of bygone times. Many themes and motifs in this epic require consideration by the thoughtful people of all kinds today, whether they are particularly interested in India and its history or not."[1]

Looking back at the *Ādi Parva* as a whole, a multitude of salient features—thematic, stylistic and eschatological—swim into view.

Where themes are concerned, there is the recurrent *motif* of Lust with its attendant Quest for Immortality. Initially, they emerge as two separate themes in the Churning-of-the-Ocean and the Kacha-Devayānī episodes, coalescing in the existentially tragic figure of Yayāti. Inheriting the taint of lust from his father Nahusha, Yayāti sums up in himself the entire experience of the self-destructive poison of lust, with its initial violence of sensual orgiastic bliss, seeking in vain to gorge itself to satiation until the body is worn out. Yet, the flames of desire continue to lick the spirit into fresh agonies of torment, forcing Yayāti into the very apotheosis of lust in replacing his worn-out senses by the vibrantly youthful body of his son, only to discover that lust is insatiable. Yayāti's life, indeed, is an interesting study in *hubris* that culminates in a veritable *peripeteia* as he is flung down from heaven in a total reversal of situation, till he who prided himself on being the most generous in the giving of gifts (he even gifted away his daughter to earn unprecedented merit) is forced to accept gifts from his own grandchildren to win back his place in *Svarga.*

Unfortunately, this blood-taint dogs his dynasty as its nemesis, virtually wiping it out. The Pāndavas are only foster-children by unknown surrogates, veritable parvenus aspiring to the ancestral throne, much to the indignation of the Dhārtarāshtras who are the heirs-by-proxy-blood.

Another pattern that emerges is that of the disqualified eldest son. This, again, begins with Yayāti whose elder brother Yati becomes a sage, enabling him to succeed to Nahusha's throne. The pattern is carried on with Yayāti's own progeny, as Puru, the youngest, becomes the dynast. In the next stage, it is Riksha, Ajamīdha's youngest son, who founds the Hastināpura dynasty. His two other brothers, Nīla and Brihadvasu, start the Northern and Southern Pānchāla lines respectively.

The case of Pratīpa's sons is even more interesting. The eldest, Devāpi, seems to have been greatly loved both by his father and the people. Bhīma, in the *Udyoga Parva,* narrates how Pratīpa wept bitterly when the Brahmins challenged Devāpi's right to succeed the king on the ground of his skin-disease. Devāpi, thereupon, took to the forests as a hermit in the order of the vedic sage ārshtisena, and was known thereafter as ārshtisena Devāpi. Bāhlīka, next to Devāpi, also declined the crown, preferring to inherit the kingdom of his maternal uncle (the Shibis). Thus, like Puru, it was the youngest son, Shāntanu, who became king. During a twelve-year drought, attributed to this supersession, Shāntanu requested Devāpi to take-over the throne, but the prince-turned-sage refused and performed a sacrifice that brought down the rains. Strangely enough, the *Vishnu* and the *Bhāgavata Purānas* narrate that Shāntanu's ministers sent Brahmins who deliberately led Devāpi away from the vedic path, so that he was necessarily excluded from the succession as a heretic! This is quite irreconcilable with Devāpi's reputation in all the other *Purānas,* where he seems to be somewhat of an Arthurian hero said to be still alive who will restore the Paurava dynasty in the new *Satya Yuga.*

Devavrata-Bhīshma, Shāntanu's eldest son, again does not succeed to the throne. It is once more the youngest brother, Vichitravīrya, who becomes king. At this stage, the theme of the disqualified eldest is interwoven with an interesting set of parallelisms: Bhīshma and Vyāsa; Satyavatī and Kuntī. Both Bhīshma and Vyāsa are born of Gangā and Satyavatī respectively before the dynastically crucial Shāntanu-Satyavatī marriage. Both are unmarried (Shuka is born to Vyāsa much later, like Drona without a mother) and both are deeply involved in the welfare of the Kurus. One is their protector, the other the surrogate-dynast. Where Bhīshma is the celibate *Kshatriya,* very much of a family man, Vyāsa is the roving *sanyasi* of proven potency, deeply concerned with the family yet peculiarly unattached as an observer, interfering only at crucial stages where Bhīshma remains inexplicably quiescent. Dipak Chandra's Bengali novel *Kurukshetrey Dvaipayana* builds precisely on this relationship which he makes out to be antagonistic.

The other mirror image is that of Satyavatī-Kuntī. Kuntī, like her grandmother-in-law, has a pre-marital son who disappears immediately after birth. Here the Parallelism dovetails into the Pattern, for Karna, the eldest Kaunteya, cannot inherit because of his illegitimacy. In relation to the Pāndavas, he stands much in the same relationship as Bhīshma to the Shāntvanas. The parallel seems to be deliberately stressed in the repeated confrontations between the two, culminating in Karna's refusal to enter the battlefield, like Achilles, so long as Bhīshma is leading the armies. Among the Pāndavas themselves, neither Ghatotkacha, the eldest, nor Prativindhya the first of Draupadī's sons, inherits the empire. Indeed, all eight Pāndava sons are killed (including Ghatotkacha, Irāvān and Abhimanyu) and the dynasty continues only through Parikshit, son of Abhimanyu, born of Arjuna's junior wife Subhadrā. Babhruvāhana, Arjuna's son by Chitrāñgadā and the sons of the brothers by their other wives are nowhere in the picture. They remain mysteriously absent from the battlefield nor do the *Purānas* know of any lineage linked to them.

As a matter of fact, the very lineage of the Kurus is extremely hazy, for the direct line from Puru can only be traced clearly up till Tamsu in the thirteenth generation,. After that, there is an inexplicable confusion and one suddenly chances upon Dushyanta, whose link with this lineage remains extremely fuzzy. On the one hand, according to the *Purānas,* he is said to have been adopted by the Turvasu king Marutta; on the other, according to the epic he is reputedly the son of Ilīna and the grandson of Tamsu. But, state the *Purānas,* this Ilīna is a woman! A similar confusion occurs between Kuru and Pratīpa. Further, with Bharata himself we enter into a major departure from not only the Puru-lineage but from kshatriyahood itself. Bharata seems to have adopted Bharadvāja as his son, and it is this Brāhmin-turned *Kshatriya*—or his son—Bhumanyu who inherits the throne. The *Purānas* name the son Vitatha. Ultimately, when there is a further infusion of mixed Brāhmana blood through Vyāsa's *niyoga* with Ambikā and Ambālikā, we are nowhere near the original Puru-lineage at all. Vyāsa himself is a case of mixed blood, his mother being a fisherwoman. The total break comes, of course, with the Pāndavas, who carry neither Shāntanu's nor Satyavatī's bloodstrain and are Yādava and Madra from their mothers' side.

An allied *motif* seems to be the difficulty in begetting successors. Beginning with Bharata who had to adopt Bharadvāja, it can be seen recurring with Shāntanu who deliberately discards the eminently eligible Devavrata only to have his eldest son by Satyavatī die prematurely, followed by the death of Vichitravīrya, also without any heirs. The engendering of Dhritarāshtra and Pāndu is itself a traumatic affair, both being physically deficient in some way: the one blind and the other afflicted with a skin ailment that seems to be carried over from his granduncle Devāpi. Gāndhārī aborts her foetus out of sheer frustration on hearing of the birth of Kuntī's second child Bhīma. Vyāsa has to appear fortuitously to turn the ball of flesh into a hundred sons and a daughter. Pāndu is cursed to die in intercourse, so the *motif* recurs. It is only with the Pāndavas, free from the ancestral taint of lust doubly reinforced up till Pāndu through Shāntanu and Satyavatī, that we come to untroubled parenthood. Shāntanu himself, it will be recalled, was born to Pratīpa in old age after considerable austerities. Even with the Pāndavas, however, the motif of the problematic succession persists as they lose all their sons and even unborn Parikshit is mortally wounded by Ashvatthāmā and has to be revived by Krishna, just as Gāndhārī's aborted foetus was saved by Krishna-Dvaipāyana-Vyāsa.

From the stylistic view-point, there are such highlights as the all-prose *Paushya* as also the portion of the dynastic account after the Samvarana-Tapatī episode; the story of Yayāti almost wholly in dialogue-form; and the intrusions of Vedic chants in the *Paushya, Pauloma* and *Khāndavadahana* sections, all very significantly addressed to Agni, the mystic fire of the *Rig Veda.*

We have seen the Vyāsan technique of presenting the pith of the matter first, allowing details to be drawn out gradually through answers to questions skilfully interposed at critical stages of the account. An interesting point is that it is not only the professional bards, Sauti *et. al.,* who recite the epic, but also Brahmins such as Lomasha, Mārkandeya and, of course, Vaishampāyana. It is not, as van Buitenen argues, that the baronial-bardic lore was giving way to a tradition of wandering reciters of brahminic lore. After all, Vaishampāyana recited the epic *before* it was picked up by Sauti. There is little evidence of the bardic reciters having ante-dated the Brahmin retellers.

One of the features that irritates a Western reader most is the gratuitous attribution of heavenly or demonic origin to kings and sages that seems, at first sight, to have no relevance at all as it influences the course of events in no way, nor makes any difference as far as the characterisation is concerned. The offending portion is, of course, the *Amshāvatarana* (the partial incarnations). Van Buitenen advises the reader to ignore wholly this "decadent sanctification by mythology of persons standing in no need of saintliness". However, some relevant facts do emerge from this welter of avatarhood that link it up with the entire corpus of Puranik myth.

For instance, the myth of Vishnu incarnating to free his

doorkeepers Jaya and Vijaya, cursed by the seer Sanaka to be born on earth thrice as *Asuras*, is carried on here when Shishupāla is said to be the incarnation of Hiranyakashipu. These doorkeepers were successively born as Hiranyāksha and Hiranyakashipu, Rāvana and Kumbhakarna and, finally, as Shishupāla and Dantavaktra. Vishnu also incarnated as Varāha, Narasimha, Rāma and Krishna to succour them in the swiftest way by killing them in battle.

The entire concept of avatarhood is at the core of Hinduism, conceiving of creation itself as the descent of the Divine into the material world. Each human being is seen as an emanation of the Divine which manifests itself in what may seem to be godly or titanic form, both ultimately stemming from the same Supreme Source. In the *Amshāvatarana,* this concept is taken to its logical extreme, but by no means to a *reductio-ad-absurdum.* To get irritated by this only leads one to such misconceptions as van Buitenen's statement that the momentous vow of Bhīshma "is reduced to the automatic consequence of a curse by a sage, angered over, of all things, a cow." Bhīshma's vow has absolutely nothing to do with Vashishtha's curse, which merely doomed the Vasus to being born on earth; and the vow owes nothing to any sort of pre-existence. To cock a snook at a sage for getting so worked up "over, of all things, a cow" is only to expose one's total ignorance of the symbolic image-structure of the epic through which it duplicates numerous spiritual experiences contained in *Rig Veda.*[2]

The *Mahābhārata,* in the *Ādi Parva,* carries on Vedic mythology to a new stage where Indra has been reduced merely to being king of the gods, worsted by the bird Garuda and the men Krishna and Arjuna, powerless to protect those like Takshaka who seek sanctuary with him, paying the price of arrogance by being imprisoned in a cave by Shiva and made to incarnate on earth. He is no longer the mighty rescuer of the celestial herds stolen by the Panis, riving open Vritra or Vala to release the divine waters, or the shatterer of Dasyu fortresses. Even Vishnu does not play much of a role here, the accent having shifted to a new duo of divine sages: Nara and Nārāyana. Pradhan (1927) maintains that etymologically 'Nārāyana' means 'son of Nara' and that they were a redoubtable father-and-son team of Brahmin warriors who were gradually deified. The latter was ultimately identified with Vishnu from the derivatory meanings of the word 'Nārāyana' (sleeping on the waters') and the fact of his having authored the crucial *Purusha Sūkta* in the *Rig Veda* (X.90) propounding the concept of the One pervading the universe. By identifying Krishna and Arjuna with this duo, the new myth is given more 'body' and appeals more powerfully to the popular imagination.

Pradhan raises an interesting point that 'Nārāyana' means Son of Man (Nara), and that this idea may have travelled to the west through the Essenes or the Therapeutaes, just as among the Buddhists the *Purusha Sūkta* gave birth to the idea of the Avalokiteshvara and among the Hindus to that of the Vishvarūpa in the *Gītā*. As the epic unfolds, it reveals more and more of an infusion of a devotional strain orientated towards Shiva and Krishna, particularly in the discourses of Bhīshma on his bed of arrows. The day of Vedic Indra, Agni and Varuna is past and the purānik Shiva-Vishnu rivalry is implied through the strenuous attempts to make each extol the greatness of the other in the *Anushāsana* and *Shānti Parvas*.

Looking at the epic from the historico-political viewpoint, a clear picture of alliances emerges based on geographical considerations that have been well brought out by van Buitenen. Both Hastināpura, the Kuru capital, and Kāmpilya the Pānchāla capital, are located on the Ganges; the one commanding its upper reaches and the other the lower reaches. Indraprastha, the Pāndava capital on the Yamunā, is opposite Hastināpura, while opposite Kāmpilya is Mathurā, also on the Yamunā. These four capitals, along with Drupada's Northern capital Ahichchhattra, north-west of Kāmpilya, form an oval that constitutes the political hotbed of the epic. It is significant that the Vrishnis promptly arrive on the scene when the Pānchāla-Pāndava alliance is in the offing, since this constitutes a crucial alliance between powers commanding the higher reaches of Yamunā (Mathurā being in control of the lower reaches right up to Chedi ruled by Shishupāla) and the lower reaches of Ganges. By befriending the Pāndavas, the Vrishnis are free from worry about their northern frontiers and can concentrate on extending their hegemony beyond the Ganges-Yamunā confluence into Magadha by killing Jarāsandha with Pāndava help and removing his ally Shishupāla.

Territorially speaking, it is the Vrishnis who benefit most from the Pāndava-Pānchāla alliance. It immediately checks possible Hastināpura expansion at Vrishni expense, while ensuring friendly powers on the North and the East, so that they can expand south-eastwards. Krishna's admirable political acumen can be seen at work here because, in the event of any war, Hastināpura will be facing the joint armies of Indraprastha, Mathurā and Kāmpilya. The necessity of such a conglomeration of forces becomes obvious when we recall how Jarāsandha of Magadha had completely routed the Yādavas of Mathurā with the help of Damaghosa of Chedi (although the latter was himself a Yādava).

The only flaw in this beautifully arranged geometric sketch of a triangular Pāndava-Vrishni-Pānchāla alliance in the oval power-structure posited by van Buitenen, is the fact that the Vrishnis were not located at Mathurā at all but had migrated to Dvarakā on the extreme western coast of India having been driven out of Mathurā by the Magadha-Chedi alliance. Incidentally, in the Kuru raid on Drupada inspired by Drona, it is the North-western capital of Ahichchhattra that is taken away by Drona from the Pānchālas, who had already discarded it in favour of Kāmpilya with the shifting away of the Gangā from Ahichchhattra. It was, therefore, not much of a real territorial expansion by Hastināpura.

Pargiter, in chapter 24 of his *Ancient Indian Historical Tradition*, has essayed a brilliant attempt at recreating history from the *Purānas*, which Dr. S.N. Pradhan has supplemented and set right at many points in his *Chronology of Ancient India*. Subsequently, Dr. P.L Bhārgava has taken up specific issues in *Retrieval of History from the Purānas*. I have tried to provide below some basic information about the locale where these dynasties flourished, so that readers approaching the epic can establish some geographical bearings instead of floating about in a directionless mythical realm.

Pururavā, the founder of the Aila dynasty (so called after his mother īlā, daughter of Manu), had his capital at Pratishthāna, near Prayāga (Allahabad) at the Gangā-Yamunā confluence. He was killed, like the first king Vena, by sages whose golden vessels he tried to seize. Āyu, his eldest son, continued the dynasty at Pratishthāna, while another son Amāvasu founded the Kānyakubja (Kanauj) dynasty that produced Vishvāmitra. Nahusha succeeded Āyu, while his brother Kshatravriddha established himself at Kāshi (Vārānasi) and started a dynasty there whose daughters seem traditionally to have been wedded to kings of Hastināpura. From Yayāti a number of dynasties sprang: from Yadu the Yādavas and the Haiheyas (decimated by Parashurāma and eradicated by Sagara); from Druhyu the Bhojas (whose Kuntibhoja adopted Prithā, daughter of Shūra-Yādava); from Anu the Ānavas in two branches (Shibis in the Punjab and Titikshu's dynasty in Anga, eastern Bihar); and from Puru the Pauravas at Hastināpura, the Pānchālas at Ahichchhattra, the Magadhas at Girivraja (near Gaya) and the adjoining Chedis in Bundelkhand. Turvasu's line, alone, fizzles out tamely. The dynastic lists clearly show that during the time of the Yādava Shashabindu, the Paurava genealogy suddenly becomes confused and there is a considerable gap right up to Dushyanta. This suggests that Shashabindu, who was famed as a conqueror, had possibly conquered the Pauravas. It is his daughter Bindumati who marries Yuvanāshva II of the solar Ikshvāku dynasty and gives birth to the famous Māndhātri who seems to have brought the whole of 'Madhyadesha' under his sway, including the Kānyakubja and Paurava dynasties, pushing back the Druhyus to Gāndhāra (that area being named after the Druhyu king of that name).

Following this, however, it is the Haiheyas who burst forth in tremendous fury from Māhishmatī on the Narmadā, overrun the Kāshī kingdom and constantly terrorise the kingdoms to the north. Their conflict with their family-priests, the Bhārgavas, resulted in these Brahmins allying themselves with the Kānyakubja dynasty (Richika married Satyavatī, daughter of king Gādhi) and ultimately ended in the complete defeat of the Haiheyas at the hands of Parashurāma. Jamadagni, it will be recalled, had strengthened the *Kshatriya* alliance by marrying a princess of the Ikshvākus of Ayodhya. However, the Haiheya power was not crushed. It continued to plague the Ayodhya kingdom till its king Bāhu was forced to flee. He sought refuge with the Bhārgava sage Aurva and it is his son Sagara who finally decimated the Haiheyas and routed invading *mlechchha* hordes. Around the same time the Kāshī dynasty won back its kingdom under Divodāsa II by defeating the Haiheyas. It is his son Pratardana who is one of Yayāti's grandsons and appears in the *Ādi Parva* to donate his merit to his grandfather. It is only after Sagara's death that the Paurava dynasty re-emerges with Dushyanta who had the advantage of having been adopted by the Turvasu monarch Marutta as his heir as well.

The other important dynasty left for mention is that of Videha established by Ikshvāku's son Nimi at Mithilā, just as the eldest son Vikukshi, established the Ayodhya dynasty. All these dynasties—Pauravas, Ānavas, Videhas and Vaishālis (started by Manu's son Nabhānidishta)—gradually surface after Sagara, but the Hastināpura line of Pauravas remains quite undistinguished after Kuru till Pratīpa. Ayodhya enjoys a remarkable efflorescence under Dasharatha and Rāma, only to sink back into obscurity thereafter. The last kings of the two dynasties started by Lava at Shrāvasti and Kusha at Kushasthali were Brihadbala and Shrutāyus respectively. Shrutāyus, king of the Ambashthas, was killed by Arjuna, while Brihadbala of north Koshala was slain by Abhimanyu. However, the dynasty springing from Kusha had another branch which continued at Ayodhya, whose king Dīrghayajña-Uktha was defeated by Bhīma before Yudhishthira's *rājasūya yajña*, and whose famous yoga-knowing monarch Hiranyanābha (from whom Yājñavalkya learnt yoga) was a contemporary of Janamejaya, grandson of Abhimanyu. The only notable pre-Kurukshetra confrontation between the Aila and the Aikshvaku dynasties occurred in the time of Rāma, when Shatrughna defeated Madhu-Yādava's son or descendant Lavana (interestingly termed an *Asura*) and occupied Mathurā. This, however, was an extremely short-lived conquest as Bhīma-Sātvata recovered Mathurā and his son Andhaka reigned there contemporaneously with Kusha and Lava. None of the Pauravas is of any note in this period.

How does the *Ādi Parva* leave us where the story of the Kurukshetra War and the Pāndava-Kaurava conflict are concerned? The seeds of the fratricidal feud are sown during the childhood sports, culminating in the gutting of the lacquer-house. In the meantime, a new figure has been introduced: Karna, who will figure prominently in the coming feud. Again, the Drona-inspired attack on Drupada has laid the basis of a deep hatred of the Kurus in the defeated king that moves him to seek alliance with the Pāndavas as a counterpoise against the Dhārtarāshtras and Drona. The intervening period, occupied by the Hidimbā, Chitraratha and Baka episodes, is the training for the future inheritors of the Kuru kingdom. Simultaneously, these events help to span the time-gap and convey the sense of the long duration of the exile. The marriage with Draupadī and the coming of Krishna provide the Pānchāla-Vrishni-Pāndava triangular set-up to oppose the Kurus at Hastināpura even more effectively with the establishment of a new kingdom at Khāndavaprastha on the Yamunā facing Hastināpura on the Gangā.

The next book of the epic, *Sabhā Parva,* will be concerned with these two capitals and their two Halls of Kings. This time the provocation, the insult to Duryodhana, will come from the magical Pāndava assembly hall, where the Pāndavas behave like the *noveau-riche,* much in the manner of Marlowe's Gaveston the "night-grown mushroom" in Edward II's court. The devastating reply to the thoughtless slight is tortuously prepared and delivered in the Kaurava Sabhā in Hastināpura, repeating the earlier exile-gambit. Only, this time it is not a sugar-coated poison-pill like Vāranāvata, but full thirteen years in exile in the forests. This Yudhishthira secretly welcomes, glad in his heart of hearts to be free from the burden of kingship. We will find him extremely ill at ease in the *Sabhā Parva* and most himself in exile amid the sylvan surroundings of *Vana Parva.*

References

1. J.L. Fitzgerald, *The Mahābhārata* vol. 7, University of Chicago Press, 2004, p. x.
2. Bhattacharya (1984)

Bibliography

Aron, Elaine: *Samraj*, New English Library, London, 1990.

Bai, Sumitra B.N.: "The Jaina Mahabharata" in *Essays on the Mahabharata* ed. A. Sharma, Leiden, E.J. Brill, 1991, p.253.

Balakrishnan, P.K: *And Now Let Me Sleep*, Sahitya Akademi, New Delhi, 2002

Bhaduri, Dr N.P: *Krishna, Kunti, Kaunteya*, Ananda, Kolkata, 1998.

Bhargava, P.L: *Retrieval of History from Puranic Myths*, D.K. Printworld, New Delhi, 1998.

Bhatta, Ananta: *Champubharatam*, ed. Ramchandra Mishra, Chowkhamba Vidhyabhawan, Varanasi, 1990.

Bhattacharjee, A: *Mahabharater Katha*, Aryabharati, Calcutta, 1985

Bhattacharya, P: *The Secret of the Mahābhārata*, Parimal Prakashan, Aurangabad, 1984.

—, *The Mahābhārata TV Film Script: A Long Critique*, Writers Workshop, Calcutta, 1991.

—, *Bankimchandra Chatterjee's Krishna Charitra* translated into English, Classics of the East Series, M.P. Birla Foundation, Calcutta, 1991.

—, *Shivaji Sawant's Mritunjanya—A Long Critique*, Writers Workshop, Calcutta, 1991.

—, "Leadership Insights from the Mahabharata" in *Leadership and Power—Ethical Insights* ed. S.K. Chakraborty and P. Bhattacharya, Oxford University Press, New Delhi, 2001.

—, "Five Holy Virgins, Five Sacred Myths: A Quest for Meaning", *Manushi*, Nos. 141-145, New Delhi, 2004.

—, *Pancha Kanya: the five virgins of India's Epics*, Writers Workshop, Kolkata, 2005.

—, *Love Stories from the Mahabharata,* RUPA, Calcutta, 1998; 2nd ed. Indialog Publications, New Delhi, 2005.

—, Ed. *Revisiting the Panchakanyas*—proceedings of a national seminar (Eastern Zonal Cultural Centre, Kolkata, 2007).

—, Was Draupadi ever disrobed?" and "Mahabharata on the screen" in *Text and Variations of the Mahabharata* ed. K.K. Chakravarti, National Mission for Manuscripts, New Delhi, 2009.

Bhattacharya, P and Sen, S.K: *Prachin Bharatey ebong Mahabharatey Netritva O Kshamatar Byabahar,* Dasgupta and Co., Calcutta, 2002.

—, *Puranic Tales for Cynical People* Indialog, New Delhi, 2005

Bhramar, Ram Kumar: *Arambh, Ankur, Avahan, Adhikar, Agraj, Ahuti, Asadhya, Asim, Anugat, Attharah Din, Anta, Ananta,* Hind Pocket Books, New Delhi, 1984-85.

Biardeau, Madeline: *Hinduism,* OUP, New Delhi, 1989.

Bosch, F.D.K.: *The Golden Germ,* Indo-Iranian Monograph, Vol. 2, Mouton and Co., The Hague, 1960.

Bose, Buddhadeb: *Mahabharater Katha,* M.C. Sarkar and Sons, Calcutta, 1974. English translation by S.Mukherjee, *The Book of Yudhishthir,* Sangam Books, Hyderabad, 1986.

Brockington, M and Schreiner, P: *Composing a Tradition: concepts, techniques and relationships,* Munshiram Manoharlal, New Delhi, 1999.

Campbell Joseph: *Masks of God,* Vol. 4, Souvenir Press, London, 1973.

Chaitanya, Satya: "A Woman of Ayodhya, a womb desecrated", "Brides of the Bharatas", www.indianest.com/writers/satyachaitanya.htm

Chakravarti, Jahnavi Kumar: *Pitrikanya,* DM Library, Calcutta, 1981.

Chandra, Dr. Dipak: *Agnigarbha Khandav,* Dey's Publishing, Calcutta, 2003.

—, *Samragyi Kunti,* Dey's Publishing, Calcutta, 1993.

—, *Tomari Nam Karna,* Dey's Publishing, Calcutta, 1989.

—, *Kurukshetre Dvaipayan,* Dey's Publishing, Calcutta, 1986.

Chattopadhyay, Asim: *Karuna tomaye Kunti,* Modern Column, Calcutta, 1991.

Chattopadhyay, Madhu: *Mahabharatey Janṁakatha*, 2nd ed., Sahityasri, Calcutta, 1991.

Chatursen, Acharya: *Vayam Rakshamah*, 2 vols., Sharada Prakashan, Bhagalpur, 1960.

Chaturvedi, Dr. Chitra: *Tanaya*, Lokbharti Prakashan, Allahabad, 1989.

Cox. G.W.: *The Mythology of Aryan Nations*, 2 vols., Longmans Green, 1870.

Dange, S.A.: *Myths from the Mahabharata*, vol.1, Aryan Books, New Delhi, 1997.

Danielou, Alan: *Hindu Polytheism*, Routledge and Kegan Paul, 1964.

Datta, V.N. and Phadke, N.A.: *"Mahabharata War, A Reality"; "Did the Bharata War Take Place?"*

—, *"The Date of the Bharata War"*—Papers read in a symposium at Vidur Sevasram, Bijnor, 19-21 October, 1975.

Debi, Chitrita: *Aupanishad*, Firma D.K.De, Kolkata, 1398 B.S.

Dharmayug: "On the historicity of the Mahabharata War", Delhi edition, 14.12.75.

Dinkar, Ramdhari Singh: *Rashmi Rathi.*

Dumezil, Georges: *The Destiny of a King*, University of Chicago Press, 1973.

Dutt, R.C.: *The Rāmāyana and the Mahābhārata condensed into English Verse*, Everyman's Library, London, 1910.

Eliade, Mircea: *Myths, Dreams and Mysteries*, Collins, London, 1970.

Ellis-Davidson, H.R.: *Gods and Myths of Northern Europe*, Penguin,1964.

Frazer, Sir J.G.: *The Golden Bough* (abridged), Macmillan, London, 1970.

Frith, Nigel: *The Legend of Krishna*, Sheldon Press, London, 1975.

Ghosh, Subodh: *Bharat Premkatha*, Sri Gouranga Press, Ananda-Hindusthan Prakashani, Calcutta, 1383 B.S.

Ghurye, G.S.: *Vedic India*, Popular Prakashan, Bombay, 1979.

Gilbert, Kenneth: *The Wisdom of the Veda*, Sri Aurobindo Ashram Press, Pondicherry, 1973.

Graves, Robert: *Greek Myths*, Vols. 1-2, Penguin, 1964, 1967.

Greene, D and Lattimore, R: *Greek Tragedies*, Vols. 1-3, Phoenix

Books, Univ. of Chicago Press, 1960.

Griffith, R.T.H.: *Hymns of the Rigveda*, Motilal Banarasidass, 1973.

Gupta S. K. and Ramachandran K.S.: *Mahābhārata—Myth and Reality*, Agam Prakashan, Delhi, 1976.

Gurudutt: *Avataran, Vinashayacha Dushkritam, Sambhavami Yuge Yuge*, Bharatiya Sahitya Sadan, New Delhi, 1967.

Hamilton, Edith: *Mythology*, Mentor Books, New American Library, 1953.

Harding, M. Esther: *Woman's Mysteries*, Rider and Co., 1971.

Harindranath, A: *Mahabharata Resources Page* www.dvaipayan.net

Harivamsa, Aryashastra, Shri Sitaram Vaidik Mahavidyalaya, Calcutta, 1382-83 B.S.

Hariyappa, M.L.: *Rigvedic legends through the Ages*, Deccan College, Poona, 1953.

Hiltebeitel, A: *Rethinking the Mahabharata*, University of Chicago Press, 2001.

Hooke, S.N.: *Middle Eastern Mythology*, Penguin, 1963.

Hopkins, E.W.: *The Great Epic of India*, Punthi Pustak, Calcutta, 1969.

James, E. O: *Myth and Ritual in the Ancient Near East*, Thames and Hudson, 1958.

Jain, K.L: *Chronology of India in Purānas*, Itihas Vidya Prakashan, Delhi, 1990.

Jatavallabhula, D.F.: "The theft of Soma" in Brockington and Schreiner (1999), p.206-7.

Jung, C. J.: *Memories, Dreams and Reflections*, Fontana, 1967.

Jung C.J. and Kerenyi, C: *Introduction to a Science of Mythology*, Routledge, 1951.

Kalkut: *Pritha*, Mondal Book House, Calcutta, 1394 B.S.

Kalyanaraman, A.: *Aryatarangini*, vols. 1-2, Asia Publishing House, Bombay, 1969-70.

Karnad, Girish: *Yayati*, Sarasvati Vihar, New Delhi, 1980.

Karve, Iravati: *Yuganta, the End of an Epoch*, Deshmukh Prakashan, Poona, 1969.

Khandekar, V.S.: *Yayati*, Rajpal and Sons, Delhi, 1977.

Kirk, G.S.: *The Nature of Greek Myths*, Penguin, 1974.

Kohli, Narendra: *Mahasamar*, 8 volumes, Vani Prakashan, New Delhi, 1988-2000.

Kosambi, D.D: *The Culture and Civilization of Ancient India*, Vikas Publishing House, Delhi, 1975.

—, *Myth and Reality*, Popular Prakashan, Bombay, 1962.

Lal, P: *The Golden Womb of the Sun—Rigvedic Songs*, Writers Workshop, Calcutta, 1965.

—, *The Mahābhārata, the Complete Ādi Parva*, Writers Workshop, Calcutta, 2005 (completely revised edition of the text contained in 25 fascicules 1968-70).

—, *The Man of Dharma and the Rasa of Silence*, Writers Workshop, Calcutta, 1975.

— , *An Annotated Mahābhārata Bibliography*, Writers Workshop, Calcutta, 1967.

—, *The Mahābhārata—a Condensation*, Vikas, New Delhi, 1989.

—, *The Rāmāyana of Valmiki*, Tarang paperbacks, Vikas, New Delhi, 1989.

Long C.H.: *Alpha, the Myths of Creation*, Collier Books, New York, 1969.

Macdonell, A.A.: *Vedic Mythology*, Indological Book House, Delhi, 1971.

Mahābhārata, in English prose by K.M. Ganguli, (11 volumes) Bharata Karyalaya Press, Calcutta, 1888-96; reprinted Oriental Press, Calcutta no date.

Mahābhārata: Aryashastra Sanskrit-Bengali recension, Shri Sitaram Vaidik Mahavidyalaya, Calcutta, 1968 ff.

Mahābhārata, in Bengali prose by Kaliprasanna Sinha, Hitavadi Karyalaya, Calcutta, 1310 B.S.

Mahābhārata, in Bengali verse by Kashiram Das, P.C. Majumdar and Bros., Calcutta, 1361 B.S.

Mahābhārata—Saranubad by Rajshekhar Basu, M.C. Sarkar and Sons, Kolkata, 1373 B.S.

Mahābhārata: The Book of the Beginning, translated into English by J.A.B.van Buitenen, University of Chicago Press, 1973.

Mani, Vettam: *Purāna Encyclopaedia,* Motilal Banarasidass, 1975.

Mishra, Dr. D.P.: *Studies in the Proto-history of India,* Orient Longmans, Calcutta, 1971.

Mitra, Shaoli: *Nathabati Anathabat,* M.C. Sirkar, Calcutta, 1397 B.S.

—, *Katha Amrita Saman,* M.C. Sirkar, Calcutta, 1398 B.S.

Monier-Williams, Sir M.: *Sanskrit-English Dictionary*, Clarendon Press, Oxford, 1960.

Mother India, 1952 ff. monthly journal of culture, Sri Aurobindo Ashram, Pondicherry.

Munshi K.M.: *Bhagawan Parashurāma*, Bharatiya Vidya Bhavan, Bombay, 1965.

—, *Krishnāvatara*, Vols. 1-7, Bharatiya Vidya Bhavan, Bombay, 1971.

Munz, Peter: *When the Golden Bough Breaks*, Routledge, 1973.

Nagar Amritlal: *Ekada Naimisharanye*, Lokbharati Prakashan, Allahabad, 1972.

Nibelungenlied, translated by A.T. Hatto, Penguin, 1965.

Ovid: *Metamorphoses*, Penguin, 1964.

Parashuram: *Puranic Tales for Cynical People*, translated by P. Bhattacharya and S.K. Sen, Indialog, New Delhi, 2005.

Pargiter, F.E.: *Ancient Indian Historical Tradition*, Motilal Banarasidass, Delhi, 1972.

Perry J.W.: *Lord of the Four Quarters*, Collier Books, New York, 1970.

Pradhan, Dr. S.N.: *Chronology of Ancient India*, Calcutta University, Calcutta, 1927.

Purāna 1966-1968, Journal published by All India Kashiraj Trust, Varanasi.

Purānas (Mārkandeya, Padma, Vāmana, Vāyu, Vishnu, Brahmavaivarta etc.) Sanskrit-Bengali editions, Nababharat Publishers, Calcutta, various dates.

Purushothaman, A: "Maudgalya-Nalayani Episode from Malayalam Retellings", 2005, www.geocities.com/hairndranth_a/maha/variation/mmv_maudgalya_nalayani.html

Rāmāyana, Aryashastra, 2 vols., Shri Sitaram Vaidik Mahavidyalaya, Calcutta, 1370-71 B.S.

Ramayana—Saranubad in Bengali by Rajshekhar Basu, M.C. Sarkar and Sons, Kolkata, 1336 B.S.

Rai, Ram Kumar: *Mahābhārata Kosha*, Vols. 1-2, Chowkhamba Prakashan, Varanasi, 1964.

Ray, Birendra Kumar: *Mahabharater Charitra*, Malda, 1985.

Robinson, H.S. and Wilson, K: *Myths and Legends of All Nations*,

Bantam Books, New York, 1960.
Rose, H.J.: *Handbook of Greek Mythology*, Methuen, 1964.
Rouse, W.H.D.: *The Iliad*, Mentor Books, New American Library, 1950.
Rouse, W.H.D.: *The Odyssey*, Mentor Books, New American Library, 1950.
Rouse, W.H.D.: *Gods, Heroes and Men of Ancient Greece*, Signet Key Books, New American Library 1957.
Roy J.C.: *Beder Debata O Krishtikal*, Bangiya Sahitya Parishad, Calcutta, 1361 B.S.
Roy J.C.: *Puja Parban*, Vishva Bharati, Calcutta, 1358 B.S.
Roy S.B.: *Prehistoric Lunar Astronomy*, New Delhi, 1976.
Sahni, Bhisham: *Madhavi*, Rajkamal Prakashan, Delhi, 2005, English translation by Ashok Bhalla, Seagull, 2002.
Sanders, N.K.: *The Epic of Gilgamesh*, Penguin, 1964.
Sankalia, Dr. H.D.: *Rāmāyana, Myth or Reality*, People's Publishing House, New Delhi, 1973.
Sankalia, Dr. H.D.: *Aspects of Indian History and Archaeology*, B. R. Publishers, Delhi, 1977.
Saraswati, Swami Pratyagatmananda: *Purāna O VijÒāna*, Sanskrit College, Calcutta, 1969.
Saraswati, Swami Pratyagatmananda: *Veda O Vijñāna*, Sanskrit College, Calcutta 1967.
Sastry, T.V. Kapali: *Rigveda Samhitā*, Vol. 1, M.P. Pandit, Sri Aurobindo Ashram, Pondicherry, 1967.
Sawant, Shivaji: *Mrityunjay: the death of Karna*, translated into English by N.Nopany and P.Lal, Writers Workshop, Calcutta, 1989.
Sen, Dr. Sukumar: *Origin and Development of the Rāma Legend*, Rupa, Calcutta, 1977.
—, *Bharat Kathar Granthimochan*, Ananda, Calcutta, 1981.
Singer, Milton: *Krishna—Myths, Rites, Attitudes*, Honolulu, 1966.
Singhal, Dr. J.P: *The Sphinx Speaks*, Sadgyan Sadan, New Delhi, 1963.
Sri Aurobindo: "Love and Death", *Collected Poems and Plays*, Vol.1 Sri Aurobindo Ashram, 1942.
—, *Vyasa and Valmiki*, Sri Aurobindo Ashram, Pondicherry, 1964.
—, *On the Mahābhārata*, Sri Aurobindo Ashram, Pondicherry,

1981.

—, *The Secret of the Veda,* Centenary Library Edition, Pondicherry, Vol. 10, 1971.

—, *Hymns to the Mystic Fire,* Centenary Library Edition, Pondicherry, Vol. 11, 1971.

—, *Foundations of Indian Culture,* Centenary Library Edition, Pondicherry, Vol. 13, 1971.

Sri Aurobindo and the Mother: *On Avatarhood,* Sri Aurobindo Society, Pondicherry, 1972.

Subramanian, M.V: *The Mahābhārata Story,* Higginbothams, Madras, 1967.

Sukthankar, V.S: *On the Meaning of the Mahābhārata,* Asiatic Society, Bombay, 1967.

—, Epic Studies-6: "The Bhrgus and the Bharata", Annals of the Bhandarkar Oriental Society, 18, 1:1-76.

Tagore, Rabindranath: *Sanchayita,* 10th edition, Vishva Bharati, Calcutta, 1389 B.S.

Tharoor, Shashi: *The Great Indian Novel,* Penguin, 1989.

The New Larousse Encyclopaedia of Mythology, Paul Hamlyn, London, 1968.

Virgil: *Works,* translated by J.W. Mackail, Modern Library, New York, 1950.

Watt, A. W.: *The Two Hands of God,* Collier Books, New York, 1978.

Yoga Vāshishtha Mahā Rāmāyana translated into English by Viharilal Mitra, Vols. 1-4, Bonnerjee and Co., Calcutta, 1891. Reprinted 1999 by Low Price Publications, Delhi and 2000 by Parimal Publications, Delhi.

Zimmer, Heinrich: *Myths and Symbols in Indian Art and Civilization,* Harper Torchbooks, New York, 1962.

IMPORTANT BRAHMIN FAMILIES

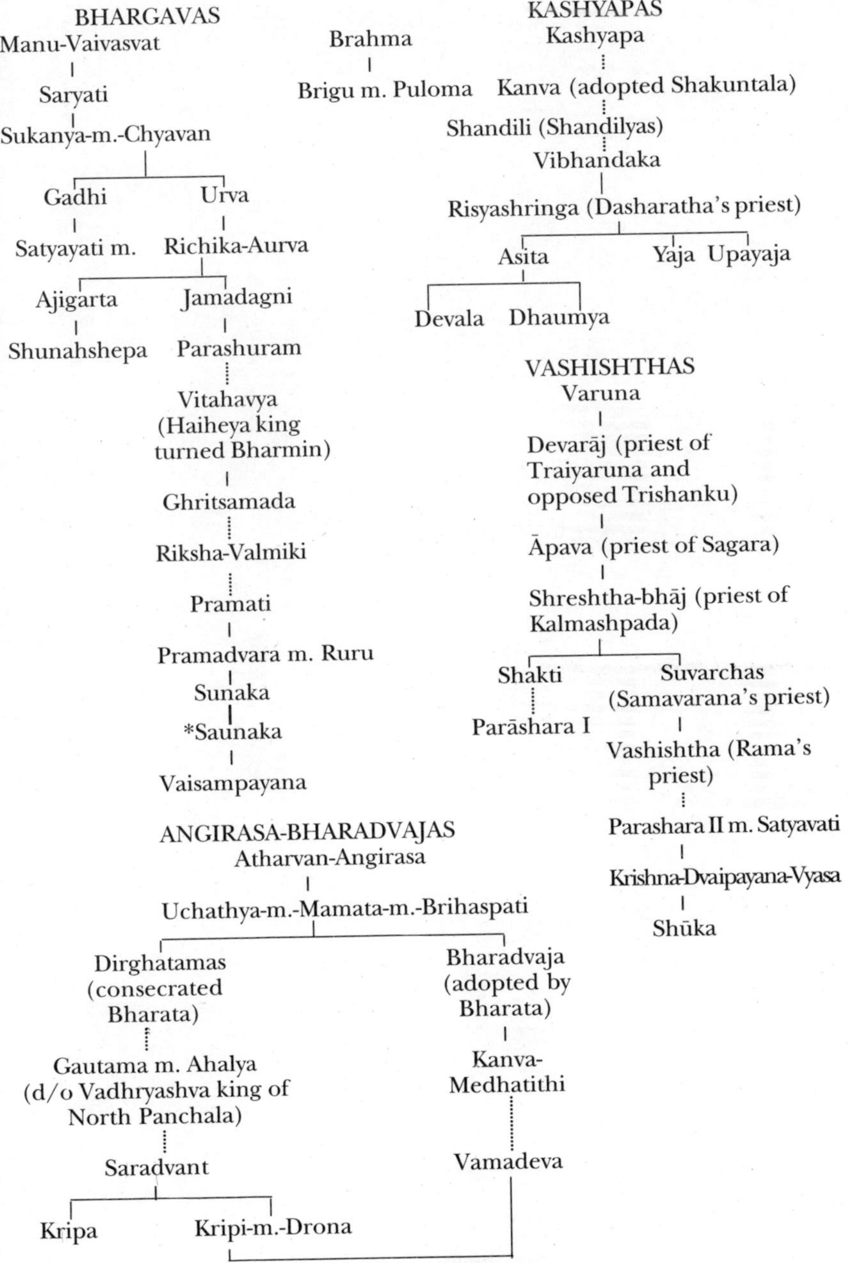

*A descendant of Saunaka, named Indrota Daivapi Saunaka, was possibly a contemporary of Janamejaya, and the person to whom Sauti recited the epic.